Excel

ADVANCED SKILLS

MATHS

YEAR 4

AGES 9–10

ADVANCED MATHEMATICS

Get the Results You Want!

PASCAL PRESS

Allyn Jones

Written for the NSW Curriculum and the Australian Curriculum Version 9.0

Reprinted 2026

ISBN 978 1 74125 657 4

Pascal Press
PO Box 250
Glebe NSW 2037
www.pascalpress.com.au

Publisher: Vivienne Joannou
Project editor: Rosemary Peers
Edited and proofread by Rosemary Peers
Answers checked by Melinda Amaral
Cover and page design by Sonia Woo
Typeset by Julianne Billington
Printed by Vivar Printing/Green Giant Press

The publisher thanks the Royal Australian Mint for granting permission to use Australian currency coin designs in this book.

Contents

Introduction

The aim of the ***Excel*** Advanced Skills: Advanced Mathematics series is to build on and extend students' skills in Mathematics. Each book in the series supports the requirements of the Australian Curriculum (Mathematics) at each year level.

The series consists of six books, one for each year level, from Year 1 to Year 6. The series is supported by other books in the ***Excel*** Mathematics range.

Structure of the book

Section 1

This section consists of twelve double-page units of teaching and learning activities. Each page provides questions on specific topics from the Number, Algebra, Measurement, Space, Statistics or Probability areas of the syllabus.

- **Unit A** provides skills practice.
- **Unit B** provides problem-solving practice of the skills covered in Unit A.

Section 2

This section consists of 30 carefully graded double-page units of teaching and learning activities. Each page provides questions from all areas of the syllabus: Number, Algebra, Measurement, Space, Statistics and Probability.

- **Unit A** provides extensive revision practice in skills-type questions.
- **Unit B** provides extensive practice in problem-solving questions.

Worked Solutions & Answers

Worked solutions are provided for every question to support students' learning. Answers are also provided in bold for quick reference.

How to use this book with the *Excel* Advanced Skills English series

For a complete weekly English and Mathematics program use this book in conjunction with the ***Excel* Advanced Skills English Year 4** book. This way a student will have work set for four days a week—two days for English and two days for Mathematics.

How to assess students' progress

The results of the work undertaken in each unit can be recorded on the marking grids. The marking grids on pages 7, 8 and 9 are easy-to-use diagnostic tools that indicate where students' strengths and weaknesses lie in relation to specific areas of Mathematics. (Please see the example on page 5.) These results can be used to gather extra information about students' progress and their further revision needs.

The *Excel* Basic and Advanced Skills series

If students are experiencing difficulty, require additional practice or need extension in any area of the course, further books are available to support them in the ***Excel*** Basic Skills and Advanced Skills series. (Please see the comprehensive list of ***Excel*** books on page 6.)

The *Excel* step-by-step improvement plan

Step 1

Read the introduction on page 4.

Step 2

The results of the work undertaken in each unit can be recorded on the marking grids.

These are easy-to-use diagnostic tools that indicate both where each student's strengths and weaknesses are in relation to specific areas of Mathematics as well as their ability to work at different levels of difficulty.

These results can be used to gather extra information about each student's progress and their further revision needs.

When marking answers on the grid, simply mark incorrect answers with 'X' in the appropriate box. This will result in a graphical representation of areas needing further work.

Section 1 Marking grid

See the sample Section 1 marking grid below:

Questions	1	2	3	4	5	6
Unit 1A						
Unit 1B		X	X	X	X	
Unit 2A						
Unit 2B						
Unit 3A						
Unit 3B						
Unit 4A						
Unit 4B						

This grid indicates that the student needs extra help and practice with questions in Unit 1B (Whole numbers and place value).

Section 2 Marking grid

See the sample Section 2 marking grid below.

If a student is consistently getting more than one in five questions wrong in any topic, they need help in this area.

An example for the first five units is shown below. If a question has several parts, it should be counted as wrong if one or more mistakes are made.

	Whole numbers and place value	Additive	Subtraction	Multiplication	Division
Questions	1	2	3	4	5
Unit 1A					
Unit 1B					X
Unit 2A					
Unit 2B					X
Unit 3A					
Unit 3B					X
Unit 4A					
Unit 4B					X
Unit 5A					
Unit 5B					X

This grid indicates that the student needs extra help and practice with questions on division.

Step 3

Refer to page 6: *Excel* books to help you get the results you want!

Under each topic there is a comprehensive list of books in our range to help students practise the topic they are having difficulty with.

Each ***Excel*** book has a comprehensive contents page that will identify the appropriate pages in the book to target the specific topic area that is causing problems.

Excel books to help you *get the results you want!*

NUMBER AND ALGEBRA

Whole numbers, place value and patterns

Excel Basic Skills · *Excel* Advanced Skills · *Excel* NAPLAN-style Tests

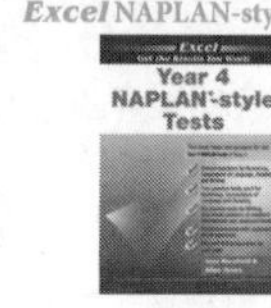

9781741251814 9781741256192 9781741257274 9781741252613 9781741254242 9781741253870 9781741254396

Addition and subtraction

Excel Basic Skills · *Excel* Advanced Skills · *Excel* NAPLAN-style Tests

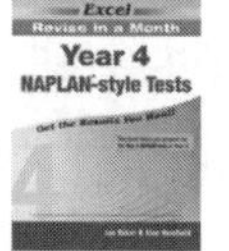

9781864412864 9781741251814 9781741256192 9781741257274 9781741252613 9781741254242 9781741253870 9781741254396

Multiplication and division

Excel Basic Skills · *Excel* Advanced Skills · *Excel* NAPLAN-style Tests

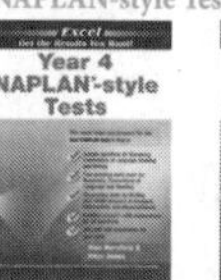

9781864412888 9781740200301 9781741251814 9781741256192 9781741257274 9781741252613 9781741254242 9781741253870 9781741254396

Fractions, decimals and money

Excel Basic Skills · *Excel* Advanced Skills · *Excel* NAPLAN-style Tests

9781741255898 9781864412864 9781741251814 9781741256192 9781741257274 9781741252613 9781741254242 9781741253870 9781741254396

MEASUREMENT AND SPACE

Length, area, volume, capacity, mass and time

Excel Basic Skills · *Excel* Advanced Skills · *Excel* NAPLAN-style Tests

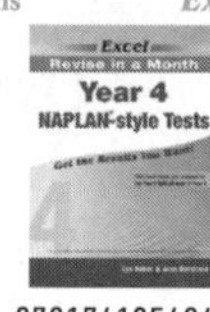

9781741255898 9781864412864 9781741251814 9781741256192 9781741257274 9781741252613 9781741254242 9781741253870 9781741254396

3D shapes and 2D shapes

Excel Basic Skills · *Excel* Advanced Skills · *Excel* NAPLAN-style Tests

9781741251814 9781741256192 9781741257274 9781741252613 9781741254242 9781741253870 9781741254396

Symmetry, transformation, angles and position

Excel Basic Skills · *Excel* Advanced Skills · *Excel* NAPLAN-style Tests

9781741251814 9781741256192 9781741257274 9781741252613 9781741254242 9781741253870 9781741254396

STATISTICS AND PROBABILITY

Chance and data

Excel Basic Skills · *Excel* Advanced Skills · *Excel* NAPLAN-style Tests

9781741251814 9781741256192 9781741257274 9781741252613 9781741254242 9781741253870 9781741254396

Section 1 Marking grid

Number and Algebra
Units 1A & 1B: Whole numbers and place value
Units 2A & 2B: Addition and subtraction
Units 3A & 3B: Multiplication and division
Units 4A & 4B: Fractions and decimals
Units 5A & 5B: Money
Units 6A & 6B: Patterns

Measurement and Space
Units 7A & 7B: Length and area
Units 8A & 8B: Volume, capacity, mass and time
Units 9A & 9B: 3D shapes
Units 10A & 10B: 2D shapes, symmetry and transformations
Units 11A & 11B: Angles and position

Statistics and Probability
Units 12A & 12B: Chance and data

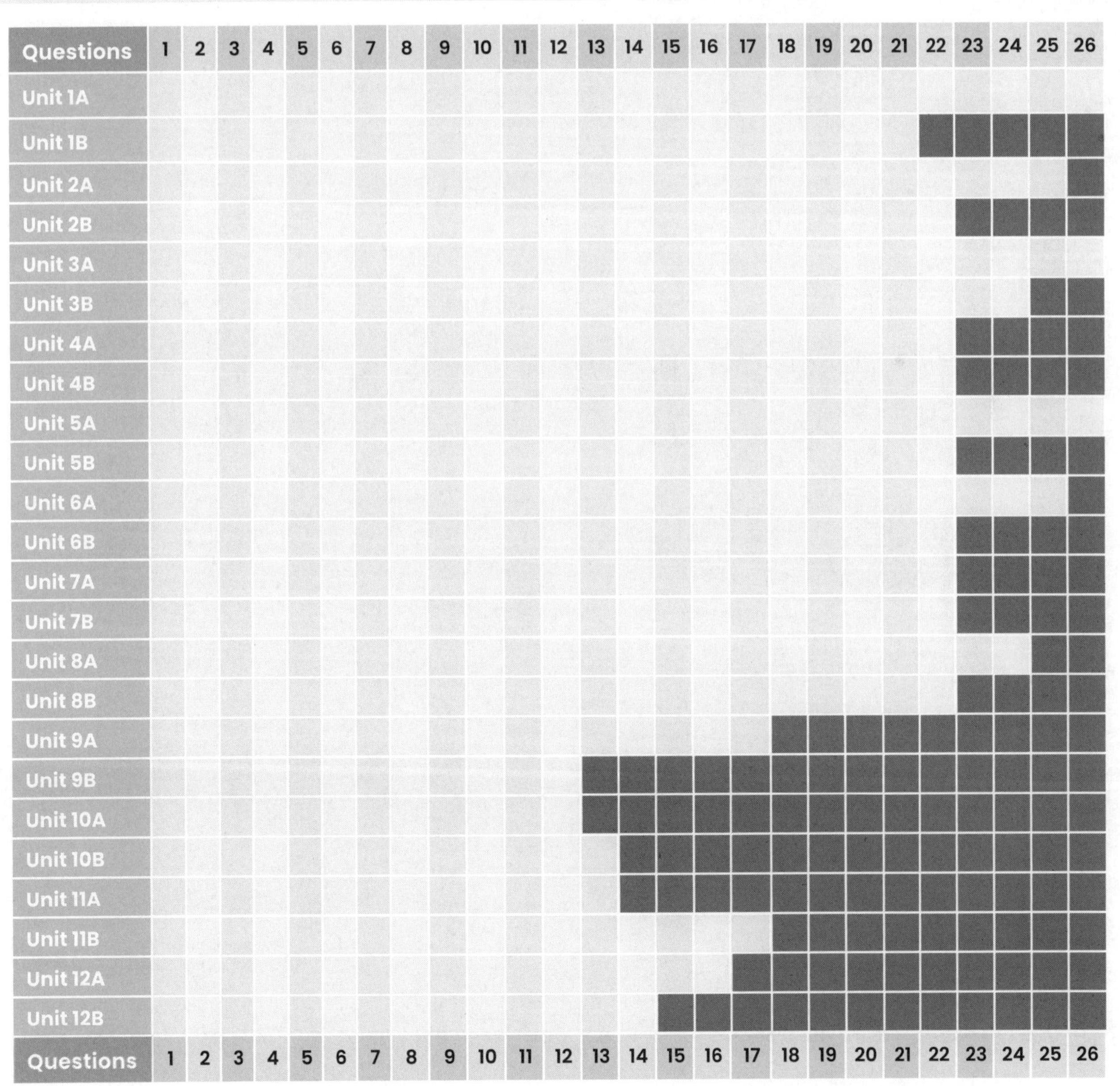

Questions	1	2	3	4	5	6	7	8	9	10	11	12	13	14	15	16	17	18	19	20	21	22	23	24	25	26
Unit 1A																										
Unit 1B																										
Unit 2A																										
Unit 2B																										
Unit 3A																										
Unit 3B																										
Unit 4A																										
Unit 4B																										
Unit 5A																										
Unit 5B																										
Unit 6A																										
Unit 6B																										
Unit 7A																										
Unit 7B																										
Unit 8A																										
Unit 8B																										
Unit 9A																										
Unit 9B																										
Unit 10A																										
Unit 10B																										
Unit 11A																										
Unit 11B																										
Unit 12A																										
Unit 12B																										
Questions	1	2	3	4	5	6	7	8	9	10	11	12	13	14	15	16	17	18	19	20	21	22	23	24	25	26

Section 2 Marking grid

	Number and Algebra									Measurement and Space							Statistics and Probability	
	Whole numbers and place value	Addition	Subtraction	Multiplication	Division	Fractions	Decimals	Money	Patterns	Length and area	Volume and capacity	Mass and time	3D shapes	2D shapes and symmetry	Transformations	Angles and position	Chance	Data
Questions	1	2	3	4	5	6	7	8	9	10	11	12	13	14	15	16	17	18
Unit 1A																		
Unit 1B																		
Unit 2A																		
Unit 2B																		
Unit 3A																		
Unit 3B																		
Unit 4A																		
Unit 4B																		
Unit 5A																		
Unit 5B																		
Unit 6A																		
Unit 6B																		
Unit 7A																		
Unit 7B																		
Unit 8A																		
Unit 8B																		
Unit 9A																		
Unit 9B																		
Unit 10A																		
Unit 10B																		
Unit 11A																		
Unit 11B																		
Unit 12A																		
Unit 12B																		
Unit 13A																		
Unit 13B																		
Unit 14A																		
Unit 14B																		
Unit 15A																		
Unit 15B																		
Questions	1	2	3	4	5	6	7	8	9	10	11	12	13	14	15	16	17	18

Section 2 Marking grid

	Number and algebra									Measurement and space							Statistics and Probability	
	Whole numbers and place value	Mixed operations	Mixed operations	Mixed operations	Mixed operations	Fractions	Decimals	Money	Patterns	Length and area	Volume and capacity	Mass and time	3D shapes	2D shapes and symmetry	Transformations	Angles and position	Chance	Data
Questions	1	2	3	4	5	6	7	8	9	10	11	12	13	14	15	16	17	18
Unit 16A																		
Unit 16B																		
Unit 17A																		
Unit 17B																		
Unit 18A																		
Unit 18B																		
Unit 19A																		
Unit 19B																		
Unit 20A																		
Unit 20B																		
Unit 21A																		
Unit 21B																		
Unit 22A																		
Unit 22B																		
Unit 23A																		
Unit 23B																		
Unit 24A																		
Unit 24B																		
Unit 25A																		
Unit 25B																		
Unit 26A																		
Unit 26B																		
Unit 27A																		
Unit 27B																		
Unit 28A																		
Unit 28B																		
Unit 29A																		
Unit 29B																		
Unit 30A																		
Unit 30B																		
Questions	1	2	3	4	5	6	7	8	9	10	11	12	13	14	15	16	17	18

FOCUS ON WHOLE NUMBERS AND PLACE VALUE

1 Write the number for thirty-five thousand and eight.

2 Use the digits 3, 8, 0, 2, 7 to make the largest possible number.

3 What is the missing number?
_______, 19 700, 19 800, 19 900

4 What is the number 5 more than 9995?

5 What is the missing number?
1781, 1881, 1981, _______

6 Circle the smallest number.

2040 4200 4002 2004

7 Underline the number which is closest to 1500.

1400 1545 150 1440

8 How many of these numbers are less than 2000?

153 203 3999 2001

9 True or false?
14 098 > 1599

10 What is the place value of 3 in the number 73 908?

11 Complete the number sentence.

24 583 = 20 000 + _______ + 500 + 80 + 3

12 What is 9501 rounded to the nearest thousand?

13 Round 18 035 to the nearest ten thousand.

14 Write the number with 2 ten-thousands, 5 thousands, 2 tens and 8 ones.

15 Circle the largest number.

4008 31 000 9999 28 996

16 Write the number 32 090 in words.

____

____

17 Circle the largest number.

thirty-eight thousand

twenty thousand and nine

seventeen thousand, two hundred and thirty-three

18 Use the digits 3, 8, 7 and 5 to make the largest possible even number.

19 Circle the number that is closest to 10 000.

6890 20 000 1001

20 Write the missing numbers.

_______, 1807, 1817, 1827, _______

21 Rewrite these numbers from least to greatest.

65 489 48 999 65 498 49 888

22 Here is a number line.

What is the missing number?

23 What is 13 594 rounded to the nearest 1000?

24 What is the smallest four-digit number?

25 What digit is in the thousands place in the number 65 792?

26 How many whole numbers are between 9990 and 10 000?

FOCUS ON WHOLE NUMBERS AND PLACE VALUE

1 Bella has these five numbered cards.

3 6 7 1 5

She uses the cards to make a four-digit even number. The number is between 4000 and 7000. The digit in the hundreds place is three times the digit in the tens place. What is Bella's number?

2 Liam buys a motorhome which has travelled 59 481 km. How far has the car travelled, to the nearest thousand kilometres?

3 Shirley was born in 1948, Mary in 1939, Martha in 1942 and Geraldine in 1943. Who is the youngest person?

4 Lucy wrote a five-digit number using identical digits. If the sum of her digits is 35, what is Lucy's number?

5 Momo is thinking of a three-digit number. The number is odd. The digit in the hundreds place is three times the digit in the ones place. The digit in the tens place is twice the digit in the hundreds place. What is Momo's number?

6 Nico makes a number using the digits 3, 6 and 5. What is the second-largest possible number he can make?

7 An online video has had 73 659 views. What is this number rounded to the nearest thousand?

8 Lars wrote a four-digit odd number. The largest digit was in the thousands place. The digit in the hundreds place was eight times the digit in the ones place and twice the digit in the tens place. What is Lars's number?

9 What is the difference in the place value of the two 4s in the number 14 734?

10 A large crowd of spectators was at a game. The exact number was rounded to the nearest hundred by the media. Will this number be even or odd?

11 There were 56 849 visitors to the Royal Easter Show on Good Friday. What is this number to the nearest hundred?

12 Gus has these five numbered cards.

5 9 6 3 7

What is the smallest five-digit number Gus can make using the cards?

13 Marty is thinking of an even number between 3000 and 3100. The sum of the digits is 12. Circle the possible number.

3552 4062 3036 3081

14 Skye used the digits 3, 2, 6 and 5 to make the largest possible three-digit number. What is the number one more than Skye's number?

15 Four friends are taking it in turns counting to 100. Olivia calls out 1, Emma, 2, Ava 3 and Sophia 4. Olivia then calls out 5, Emma 6, and so on. Who will call out the number 41?

16 How many hundreds are in the number 7549?

17 Isabella and Charlotte looked at the number 3186. Isabella rounded the number to the nearest hundred. Charlotte rounded the number to the nearest ten. What is the difference in their new numbers?

18 Here are three numbers.

21 871 21 781 21 817

If Amelia arranged the numbers in descending order, what would be the middle number?

19 Write the number which is the total of 40 hundreds and 60 tens.

20 Mia is writing a four-digit number. The digit in the hundreds place is a quarter of the digit in the ones place and half the digit in the thousands place. The sum of the digits is 12. What is her number?

21 Noah added these three numbers: 9010, 5100, 11 290. Circle the number that is the best estimate of Noah's total.

2100 21 000 25 000 35 000

FOCUS ON ADDITION AND SUBTRACTION

1 12 + 17 + 3 + 8 =

2
```
    13
     5
   120
+   28
```

3 60 + 20 + 40 =

4 498 + 2 + 36 =

5 430 + 2000 + 20 =

6 35 + 35 + 25 =

7 What is the sum of 56 and 73?

8 What is the total of 178, 300 and 22?

9 What is the result when 87 is added to 42?

10
```
  1638
+  311
```

11
```
  3226
+ 1432
```

12 100 + 5000 + 23 000 =

13
```
  765
+ 185
```

14
```
  40 373
+ 21 589
```

15 100 − 64 =

16 1000 − 380 =

17 What is added to 53 to give 90?

18
```
  174
−  95
```

19 1000 − 703 =

20 10 000 − 8700 =

21 What is the difference between 500 and 287?

22 110 + ? = 187

23 87 − ? = 68

24
```
  1068
−  457
```

25
```
  3867
−  950
```

FOCUS ON ADDITION AND SUBTRACTION

1. There are 22 students in 4K, 23 students in 4A and 21 students in 3/4N. What is the total number of students in all three classes?

2. William and Ahmed collect basketball cards. William has 168 cards and Ahmed has 211. What is the total number of cards?

3. Lincoln is reading a book. He has already read 76 pages and has another 97 pages remaining. What is the total number of pages in the book?

4. Madison and Pow visited an orchard. Madison picked 59 oranges. Pow picked 21 more oranges than Madison. What was the total number of oranges picked?

5. Mila drove 387 km on Saturday and 298 km on Sunday. What was the total distance?

6. The school library has 64 chairs. Another 38 chairs are removed from classrooms and brought to the library for a parent meeting. How many chairs are now in the library?

7. A box contains red, green and blue counters. There are twice as many red counters in the box as blue. There are 16 green counters and 18 blue counters. What is the total number of counters in the box?

8. Hiro has 78 toy cars. Mitchell has 21 more cars than Hiro. What is the total number of cars?

9. Grace counted the balloons she had bought for her party. There were 12 yellow, 18 green and 20 white balloons. How many balloons did Grace buy?

10. What is the sum of 69 and 55, to the nearest ten?

11. In an election Tahlia received 8652 votes, which was 649 votes less than Wendi. How many votes did Wendi receive?

12. Hunter rode 76 km on Monday, 111 km on Wednesday and 87 km on Saturday. What was the total distance?

13. Theo is 10 years old today. His father is 28 years older than him. Theo's grandfather is 33 years older than his father. What is the total of their ages?

14. There are currently 43 passengers on a bus. At the next stop 16 people get off and 11 people get on. How many passengers are now on the bus?

15. Stathis has 87 golf balls. He gives 23 balls to Aaron and 19 to Vivienne. How many balls does he keep?

16. There are 188 passengers on an aeroplane. If the total seating capacity is 318, how many seats are vacant?

17. When a market opened there were 225 lobsters for sale. By lunchtime only 37 remained. How many lobsters had been sold?

18. A restaurant had 187 orders on Friday night. On Saturday night there were 215 orders. How many more orders were taken on Saturday than Friday?

19. Josephine baked 220 cookies before midday and 150 cookies after midday. In total she sold 360 cookies during the day. How many cookies remain unsold?

20. Here are three numbered cards.

5 7 2

Maeve used the cards to make the largest possible number. Olive used the cards to make the smallest possible number. What is the difference between their numbers?

21. Mikki's video had 189 views. Beatrix's video had 371 views. How many more views did Beatrix's video have compared to Mikki's video?

22. The odometer in Darcy's car shows 65413. The odometer in Cory's car shows 90532. How much further has Cory's car travelled?

FOCUS ON MULTIPLICATION AND DIVISION

1 6 lots of 3 =

2 3 times 9 =

3 $5 \times 30 =$

4 $20 \times 8 =$

5 8 groups of 3 =

6 Circle the multiples of 5.

45 51 20 395

7 Circle the numbers that are **not** multiples of 10.

80 108 2650 5551

8 What is the missing number?

$12 \times 4 = 6 \times$ **?**

9 What is the missing number?

$15 \times 10 =$ **?**

10 Double 90 =

11 Triple 40 =

12 Circle the numbers which are factors of 12.

5 6 8 4 1

13 $17 \times 5 \times 2 =$

14 What is the missing number?

$13 \times 9 = 10 \times 9 +$ **?** $\times 9$

15 $6 \times 0 \times 2 \times 3 =$

16

$$\begin{array}{r} 8 \\ \times \quad 7 \\ \hline \end{array}$$

17 $36 \div 9 =$

18 What is 32 divided by 8?

19 How many 3s are in 27?

20 $5\overline{)45}$

21 $6\overline{)60}$

22 $4\overline{)48}$

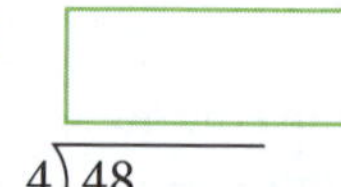

23 What is the remainder in this question?

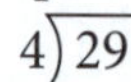

$4\overline{)29}$

24 What is the remainder when 38 is divided by 5?

25 What is the missing number?

$43 = 8 \times 5 +$ **?**

26 What is the missing number?
If $30 \times 7 = 210$,

then $210 \div 7 =$ **?**

FOCUS ON MULTIPLICATION AND DIVISION

1 A box contains 8 coloured pencils. How many pencils are in 5 packets?

2 There are 40 apples in a box. How many apples are in 7 boxes?

3 A horse-drawn carriage can seat up to 6 people. What is the maximum number of passengers in 5 carriages?

4 Abbie swims 6 laps every morning. How many laps will she swim in 14 mornings?

5 Sergio has four times as many marbles as Bryce. If Bryce has 20 marbles, how many has Sergio?

6 A carton contains a dozen eggs. How many eggs are in 10 cartons?

7 A ream of paper contains 500 sheets. How many sheets of paper are in three reams?

8 A lap of the school oval is 600 metres. Sully ran 4 laps. How many metres did Sully run?

9 Each school sent a team of 9 players to the regional netball competition. If 16 schools were competing, what was the total number of players?

10 There are 20 rows of seats in a theatre. Each row has 40 seats. What is the total number of seats?

11 Oranges are to be cut into four pieces. Lawrie has half a dozen oranges. How many pieces can Lawrie cut?

12 A farmer has 30 mangoes. The mangoes are to be placed in boxes of 8. The farmer fills as many boxes as possible.
How many mangoes will be in the partially filled box?

13 Insert either < or > to make this number sentence correct.

$48 \div 4$ **?** $66 \div 6$

14 A book of raffle tickets contains 20 tickets. Bryce sells a total of 120 tickets. How many books did he sell?

15 Ryan emptied 6 boxes of crayons. Each box contained 8 crayons. He gave an equal number of crayons to 12 students and had no crayons left.
How many crayons did each student receive?

16 A group of 50 students are to be placed into teams of 7.
How many teams are possible?

17 A safety light in the harbour flashes 80 times each minute.
How many minutes will it take for the light to flash 320 times?

18 A bookcase has 5 shelves. Dominic has 45 books. He wants to place the same number of books on each shelf. How many books will be placed on the middle shelf?

19 A box can hold 48 chocolates. There are two layers of chocolates. There are three rows of chocolates in each layer. How many chocolates are in each row?

20 Harper arranged some coins in rows. She placed 8 coins in each of 3 rows. She then rearranged the coins into rows of 6. How many rows does she now have?

21 Thirteen students are to be transported by cars. There will be three students in each car.
What is the smallest number of cars required?

22 Ms Bartley gave 36 stickers to nine students. Each student received the same number. What was the total number of stickers given to two of the students?

23 Cassie thinks of a number. There is no remainder when the number is divided by 2 or 3. When divided by 5 there is a remainder of 4.
What is the smallest possible number?

24 Andrea baked 7 batches of cupcakes. There were 6 cupcakes in each batch. She placed 3 dozen cupcakes in boxes.
How many cupcakes remained?

FOCUS ON FRACTIONS AND DECIMALS

1 Shade $\frac{2}{3}$ of the circles.

2 How many quarters of the shape have been shaded?

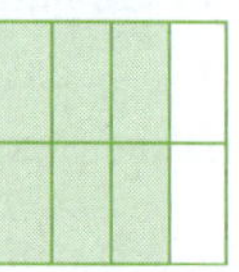

3 What is the missing fraction on the number line?

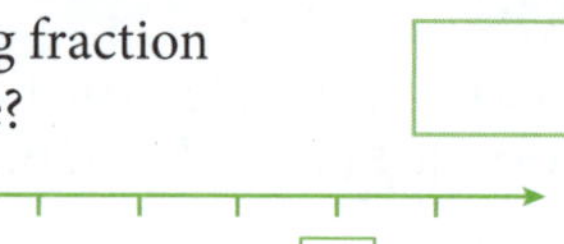

4 True or false? $\frac{3}{6} = \frac{1}{2}$

5 Shade to represent $2\frac{1}{4}$.

6 What mixed numeral is shown?

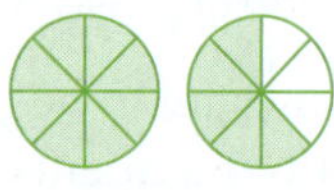

7 How many thirds are in one-and-two-thirds?

8 Write $2\frac{1}{4}$ as an improper fraction.

9 How many decimal places has the number 31.83?

10 What is 39.2 to the nearest whole?

11 Insert either < or > to make a true statement.

3.6 **?** 3.500

12 What is 6 hundredths, written as a decimal?

13 Rewrite $\frac{73}{100}$ as a decimal.

14 What is the place value of the 9 in the number 35.192?

15 Write the number with 2 tens, 3 tenths and 4 hundredths.

16 What is the missing decimal on the number line?

17 Write $40 + 5 + \frac{3}{10} + \frac{7}{100}$ as a decimal.

18 What is the missing number?

6.83 = 6 ones + **?** tenths + 3 hundredths

19 Rewrite $25\frac{37}{100}$ as a decimal.

20 Rewrite 0.03 as a fraction.

21 Arrange these from smallest to largest.

3.7 0.36 3.18 0.83

22 Here is a sequence of numbers.

2.7, 2.8, 2.9, 3

What is the next number?

FOCUS ON FRACTIONS AND DECIMALS

1 The number line is marked in eighths.
Mark the location of $\frac{3}{4}$ on the number line.

0 1

2 There are 12 cards on a table. Tayla turns a quarter of the cards over. How many cards were turned over?

3 Royce bought a packet of six hot-cross buns. His family ate $\frac{2}{3}$ of the buns.
How many buns were eaten?

4 Here are some tennis balls. Jack drew a box around $\frac{3}{4}$ of the balls. How many balls are in the box?

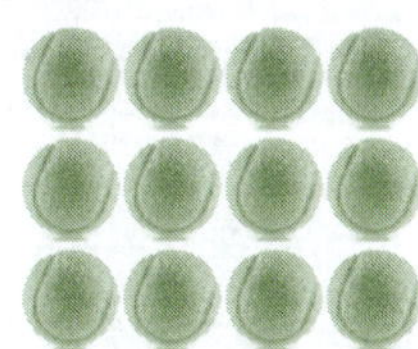

5 How many tenths are in $\frac{3}{5}$?

6 Billy cooks 3 pizzas in his oven. He cuts each pizza into quarters. What is the total number of quarters?

7 Shimona has 12 friends. Half of her friends support the Tigers. How many of her friends do **not** support the Tigers?

8 A shape is made using 20 identical squares. Matt shades $\frac{1}{2}$ of the shape. Kurt now shades $\frac{3}{5}$ of the unshaded squares. How many squares remain unshaded?

9 The shape is made from 6 identical squares.
Reuben shades $\frac{1}{3}$ of the shape. How many more squares should he shade so that $\frac{5}{6}$ of the shape is shaded?

10 What is $2\frac{1}{4}$ rounded to the nearest whole number?

11 Gabi has inflated 24 balloons for her party.
One-third of the balloons are red.
How many red balloons have been inflated?

12 The shape is formed using identical squares.
Four squares are shaded.
Circle the fraction(s) of squares shaded.

$\frac{2}{6}$ $\frac{1}{4}$ $\frac{1}{3}$ $\frac{4}{12}$

13 A tree in the park is 20.49 m tall. What is this height rounded to the nearest metre?

14 Amy wrote the number 12.32. How many times larger is the 2 in the ones place than the 2 in the hundredths place?

15 In the high-jump competition Erin cleared a height of 1.76 m. What is this height, correct to one decimal place?

16 What is half of 3 as a decimal?

17 Round 23.86 to the nearest tenth.

18 What is the missing decimal on the number line?

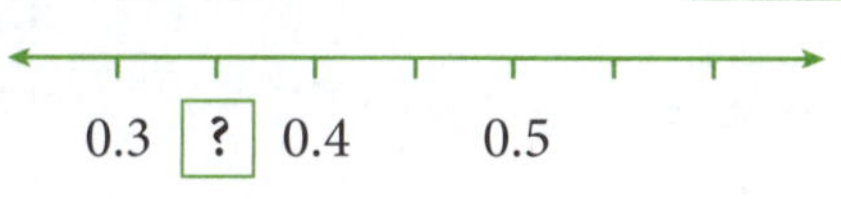

19 Here are the heights of four friends. Georgia is 1.35 m, Hannah 1.32 m, Lenize 1.41 m and Matilda 1.4 m.
Who is the second tallest?

20 Arrange these numbers in ascending order.

$\frac{7}{10}$ 0.08 $\frac{9}{100}$ 0.6

21 Shade 0.5 of the shape.

22 What is the decimal in the middle of *A* and *B*?

FOCUS ON MONEY

1 Here are four prices.

$3.87 $0.99 389c $3

Circle the highest price.

2 Round $19.49 to the nearest dollar.

3 Round 88c to the nearest 10 cents.

4 Circle the best estimate of the total price of buying 4 notebooks at $2.95 each.

$8 $12 $7

5 $5 – $1.60 = ?

6 What is $7000 + $12 000?

7 What is the missing amount?

$3.60 + ? = $5

8 Add $8, 30c, $3, 10c and 5c.

9 How many cents are in $10?

10 Add $10.50, $5.50 and $9.00.

11 Circle the two amounts that round to 80c, to the nearest 5c.

76c 78c 82c 83c

12 What is the missing amount?

$3.60 – ? = $2.90

13 Write three hundred and six dollars and forty cents in symbols.

14 What is the smallest number of coins that add to $1.75?

15 What is $20 minus $8.65?

16 $19 + 150c =

17 What is the missing amount?

$14.95 + ? = $20

18 What is the total of $85 and $25?

19 Sam has $56. Huan has $12 more. How much has Huan?

20 Round 88 cents to the nearest 5c.

21 $8.95 + $4.10 + $17 = ?

Which of these is the best estimate of the total?

$25 $27 $30

22 Gisele has $80, which is $15 more than Liz. How much money has Liz?

23 What is the total value of eight $20 notes?

24 What is the missing amount?

$87 + ? = $100

25 $90 – $20 – $20 – $20 =

26 $180 – $68 =

FOCUS ON MONEY

1 Rahni paid $10 for a loaf of bread priced at $4.15. What amount of change was she given?

2 A carton of custard is priced at $4.20. What is the price of three cartons?

3 Tegan bought a pair of jeans for $89. She used a $100 gift card to pay.
How much money remains on the gift card?

4 Maddy is paid $55 for each hour she tutors. How much will she be paid for 2 hours tutoring?

5 Jesse and Euan are saving for their holiday. Jesse has saved $8675 and Euan has saved $9398. How much more has Euan saved?

6 Corey has eight $50 notes and six $20 notes in his wallet. What is the total amount of money?

7 Harry has $860 in his savings account. He wants to buy a laptop which costs $1350.
How much more money does he need to save?

8 Ruby, Mia and Aaron had a restaurant meal. The total cost was $180. They decided to share the cost of the meal evenly.
How much did Mia pay?

9 A clothes dryer costs $695. A washing machine is twice the price of a clothes dryer.
What is the cost of the washing machine?

10 Milla buys a packet of dog treats for $4.80. How much change will she receive from a $20 note?

11 Erin buys a television for $1190 and a tablet for $870. What is the total cost of the items?

12 Larika buys 2 packets of biscuits. Each packet costs $2.80.
What is the total cost?

13 Tom used cash to buy a kebab and a drink. The kebab cost $7 and the drink $3.50. He received change of $4.50.
How much cash did he use to pay for the two items?

14 Harry and Tamir are comparing the money they earned this month in their casual jobs. Harry earned three times as much money as Tamir. If Tamir earned $400, what was the total amount earned by the two boys?

15 Cooper has eight $2 coins. He uses the coins to buy a beanie for $14.50.
What amount of change will he receive?

16 A roadside stall is selling apples for 55 cents each. Poppy buys 6 apples.
How much change will she receive from a $5 note?

17 Ian bought some bananas at the supermarket which cost a total of $1.82. He paid for the bananas with a $2 coin.
How much change was given?

18 An adult movie ticket costs $18 and children are half price.
What is the cost for 2 adults and 3 children?

19 If 4 pens cost $20, what is the cost of 3 pens?

20 A school needs to buy 60 new chairs. One company offered to sell the chairs for $23 each. A second company priced their chairs at $19 each. How much is saved by buying the chairs from the second company?

21 A bakery sells pies for $6 each. Gretel has a $20 note. She buys as many pies as she can.
What amount of change will she receive?

22 Allie earned $5300 for a month's work. She spent $3100 and saved the rest.
How much more did she spend than save?

FOCUS ON PATTERNS

1 What is the missing number?
6, 10, 14, 18, ________

2 What is the missing number?
85, 75, 65, 55, ________

3 Write the missing numbers in this pattern of numbers.

9	15	21			39

4 What is the missing number?
________, 11, 18, 25, 32

5 What is the missing number?
111, 115, 119, ________, 127

6 Write the missing numbers in this pattern of numbers.

2	4	8	16		

7 What is the missing number?
110, 107, ________, 101, 98

8 Circle the odd numbers.

2136 1112 2461 12 329

9 What is the largest three-digit even number?

10 What is the missing number?

100 − **?** = 65 + 15

11 Write the missing numbers in this pattern of numbers.

110	106	102		94	

12 Here is a pattern of numbers. What is the seventh number in the pattern?

2400, 2350, 2300, 2250 …

13 Here is a pattern of numbers: 1, 3, 9, 27 …
What is the next number in the pattern?

14 A pattern of numbers is written using the rule 'start with 16 and add 3'.
Write the first four numbers.

________, ________, ________, ________

15 Here is a pattern of numbers: 240, 120, 60, 30 …
Write the rule.

Start with 240 and divide by ________________.

16 What is the missing number?

60 ÷ **?** = 5 × 2

17 How many even numbers are **between** 100 and 110?

18 A rule is used to complete the numbers in the bottom row of the table.
What is the missing number?

Top row	1	3	5	7	9
Bottom row	8	24	40	56	**?**

19 What is the seventh number in this pattern?
3, 30, 300, 3000, 30 000, ______, ______

20 What is the third even number after 45?

21 A rule is used to complete the numbers in the table.
What are the two missing numbers?

Top row	12	21		30	12
Bottom row	4	7	5	10	

22 The rule 'add 8' is used to list this pattern.

________ 223, 231, 239, ________

What are the two missing numbers?

23 Here is a pattern of numbers:

205, 195, 185 …

What is the largest two-digit number in the pattern?

24 Write the missing numbers in this pattern of numbers.

128	64			8		2

25 Kade multiplied three odd numbers by three even numbers.
Is his answer even or odd?

FOCUS ON PATTERNS

1 Talitah uses the rule 'start with 38 and subtract 7' to write a list of numbers. Which of these is **not** on Talitah's list?

31 24 16 10

2 Amelia subtracts 12 from **?**. Her answer is 20. What is the missing number?

3 Students are arranged into different-sized groups. There are 4 students in Group 1, 7 students in Group 2, 10 students in Group 3, and so on.
If the pattern continues, how many students are in Group 8?

4 Sienna adds 25 and **?**. Her answer is 48. What is the missing number?

5 ◯ represents a number. If ◯ × 7 = 42, what is the value of ◯?

6 What number plus 30 equals 56?

7 What is the value of ☆ in the number sentence ☆ ÷ 4 = 8.

8 What is the missing number in this number sentence?

42    6

9 □ represents a number. □ + 16 = 5 × 9. What is the value of □?

10 Xavier multiplied his favourite number and 7. Matthew subtracted 12 from 40. Both boys had the same result.
What is Xavier's favourite number?

11 What is the difference between the smallest five-digit odd number and the largest four-digit even number?

12 Which of these symbols, <, = or >, is missing from the number sentence?

12 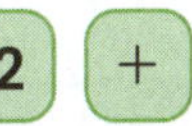 18  48 − 20

13 ⬡ represents a number. 20 – 5 – ⬡ = 6. What is the value of ⬡?

14 Eugenie wrote a number pattern using the rule 'start with 12 and add 8'. What is the difference between the second and the fifth number in the pattern?

15 What number is added to 24 to give the same result as the difference between 60 and 25?

16 Elise wrote numbers using the rule 'start with 3 and add 12'.
What was Elise's fifth number?

17 The third number in a sequence is 22, the fourth number is 28 and the fifth number is 34.
What is the first number in the sequence?

18 Maria is writing a sequence of numbers using the rule 'start with 128 and halve the number'.
What will be the seventh number Maria writes?

19 What is the sixth number in this pattern?

100, 85, 70, 55 …

20 A sequence of numbers is formed by adding 9. The third number in the pattern is 26.
What is the first number?

21 ◯ and △ represent different numbers. It is known that ◯ + 8 = 12 and △ × ◯ = 20.
What is the value of △?

22 Kaylin and Ellie are thinking of their favourite numbers. They multiply their numbers and the answer is odd.
Is Ellie's number even or odd?

FOCUS ON LENGTH AND AREA

1 How many millimetres are in 3 m?

2 What is the missing number?

12 000 mm = **?** m

3 How many centimetres are in 15 m?

4 80 mm = ________ cm

5 A triangle is drawn on a centimetre grid. What is the length of the longest side?

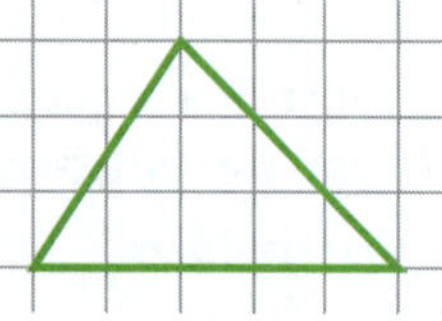

6 Nupur measured the length of a line as 76 mm. What is this length to the nearest centimetre?

7 How many millimetres are in $\frac{1}{4}$ m?

8 A rectangle is drawn on a centimetre grid. What is the perimeter?

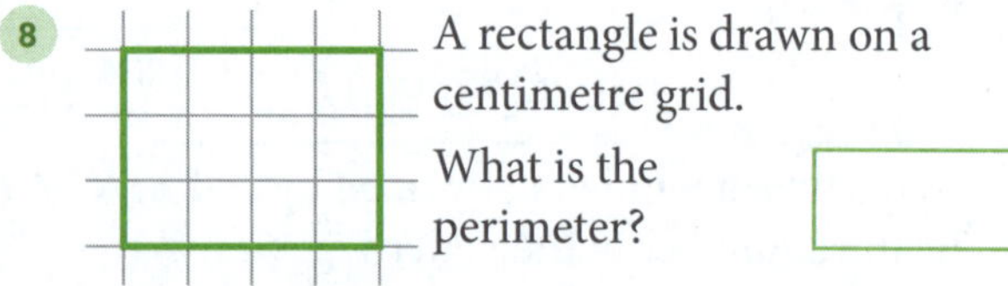

9 The length of a swimming pool is 50 m. Todd swam 600 m. How many laps of the pool did he complete?

10 Add 5 km 285 m to 3 km 605 m.

11 A triangle is drawn on a centimetre grid.

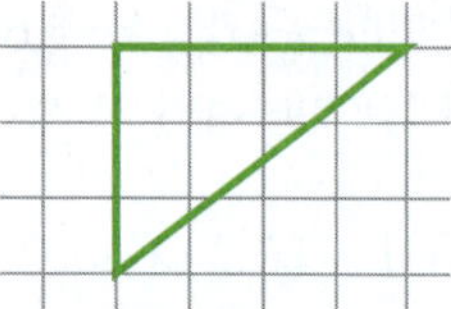

The perimeter is 12 cm. What is the length of the longest side?

12 2.15 m = 2 m ________ cm

13 Rewrite 680 cm in metres.

14 How many kilometres are in the length 6 km 250 m?

15 Circle the shortest length.

4000 mm 300 cm 5 m

16 How many centimetres are in $\frac{47}{100}$ m?

17 A rectangle is drawn on a centimetre grid. What is the area?

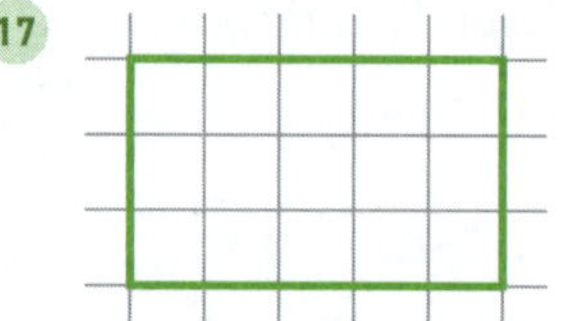

18 Circle the best estimate for the area of a page in this book.

6 cm^2 60 cm^2 600 cm^2

19 What is the area of the rectangle?

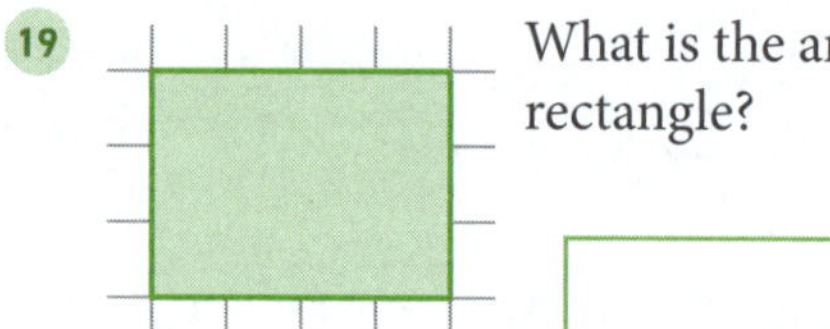

20 A triangle is drawn on a centimetre grid. What is the area?

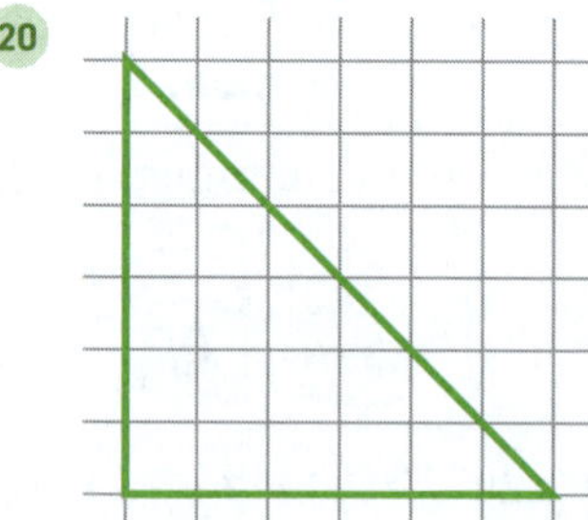

21 Circle the unit you would use to measure the area of the floor in the school hall.

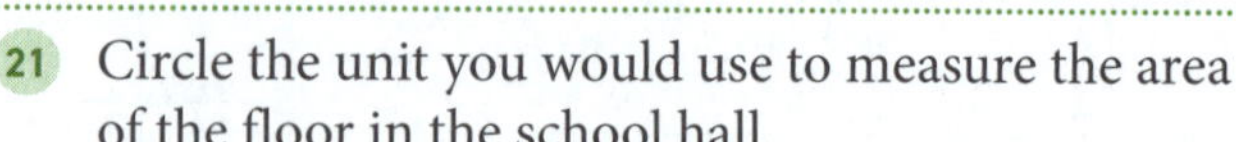

mm^2 cm^2 m^2 km^2

22 Which shape has the largest area?

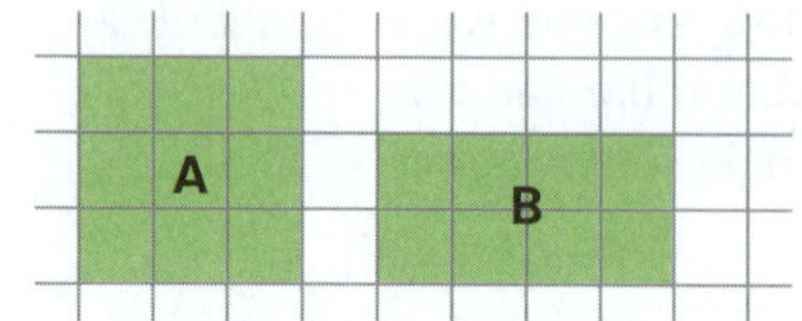

FOCUS ON LENGTH AND AREA

1. Lavinia is 1 m 41 cm tall. Her mother is 36 cm taller than her. What is the height of Lavinia's mother in centimetres?

2. Each side of a square is 11 cm long. What is the perimeter of the square?

3. This morning Millie walked 665 m from her home to a café to pick up a coffee. She then walked back home.
What is the total distance walked?

4. A rectangle is three times longer than it is wide. If it is 24 cm wide, find its length.

5. The length of a running circuit is 3 km 600 m. Tamika ran the circuit twice.
How many kilometres did she run?

6. Sara drew a line 55 mm long. Kaitlyn drew a line twice the length of Sara's line.
What is the length of Kaitlyn's line, in centimetres?

7. What is the total of these three distances, in millimetres?
16 mm 32 cm 2 m

8. A fence 28 m long is to be painted. On Saturday Rory painted 11 m and then on Sunday another 13 m. What length of fence has yet to be painted?

9. A rectangular paddock has a length of 965 m. It is 238 m longer than it is wide.
What is the width of the paddock?

10. A piece of timber is 2 m long. It is cut into three smaller lengths. The shortest length is 45 cm and the longest is 95 cm. What is the length of the other piece?

11. A 5-m length of rope is cut into 10 pieces of the same length. What is the length of each small piece in centimetres?

12. On his second birthday, Owen's mother measures his height as 89 cm. If he expects to double his height when fully grown, what will be Owen's eventual height?

13. A piece of wire is 720 cm long. It is bent to form a regular octagon.
What is the length of each side?

14. Mateo travelled from his home to the beach. He walked 850 m to the bus stop. The bus took him to the stop closest to the beach and he walked the remaining 550 m. If Mateo lives exactly 6 km from the beach, how far did he travel on the bus?

15. A wall is 3200 mm long and 1800 mm high. What is the perimeter of the wall, in metres?

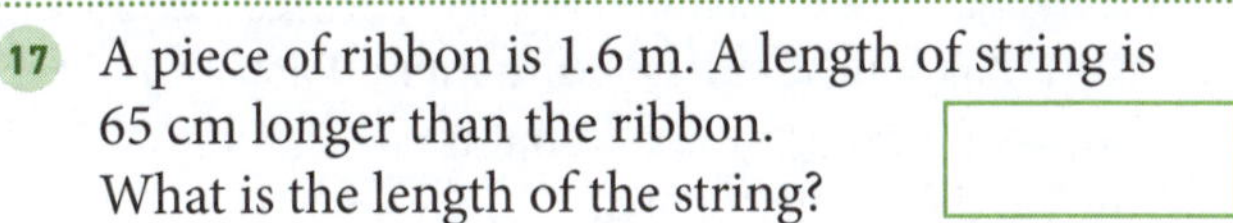

16. Ruth is parked at this road sign. She drives to Dubbo, then to Singleton, passing this sign again. What was the total distance travelled?

17. A piece of ribbon is 1.6 m. A length of string is 65 cm longer than the ribbon.
What is the length of the string?

18. A shape is drawn on a centimetre grid. It covers 18 squares and 10 half-squares.
What is the area of the shape?

19. The shape is drawn on a centimetre grid.

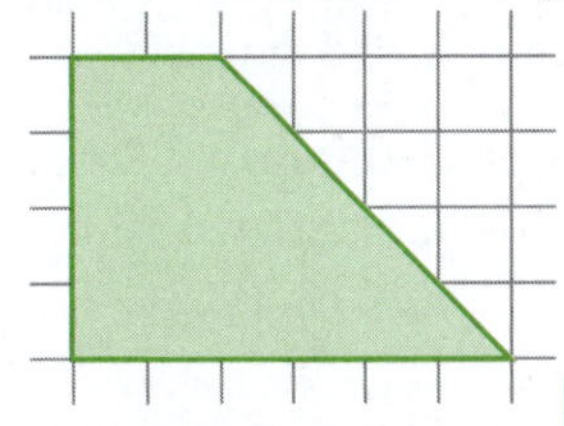

What is the area of the shape?

20. A rectangle is drawn on a centimetre grid.
What is the area of the triangle?

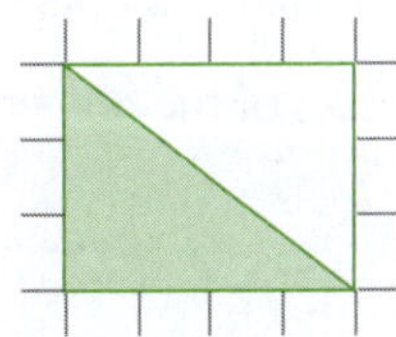

21. A square has a perimeter of 20 cm.
What is the area of the square?

22. A rectangle with a length of 6 cm has an area of 30 cm^2. What is the perimeter of the rectangle?

FOCUS ON VOLUME, CAPACITY, MASS AND TIME

1 How many litres are in 7000 mL?

2 How many millilitres are in half a litre?

3 The capacity of three containers is shown. Circle the largest capacity.

300 mL 2400 mL 2 L

4 Circle the object with a capacity that is closest to 10 mL.

bucket bath spoon

5 What is the missing quantity?
350 mL + ________ = 1 L

6 Rory has four identical containers. Each container holds 500 mL of water. What is the total quantity of water, in litres?

7 9060 mL = ________ L ________ mL

8 How many 2-L containers are needed to fill a 10-L bucket?

9 500 mL is poured from a 2-L bottle of juice. How much remains?

10 6450 g = ________ kg ________ g

11 How many grams is 15 kg?

12 A bag contains 3 kg of rice. What is the mass of the rice in 20 bags?

13 What is the mass of the object, in grams?

14 How many grams are in $3\frac{1}{4}$ kg?

15 Four cylinders have the same mass as one cylinder and a block.

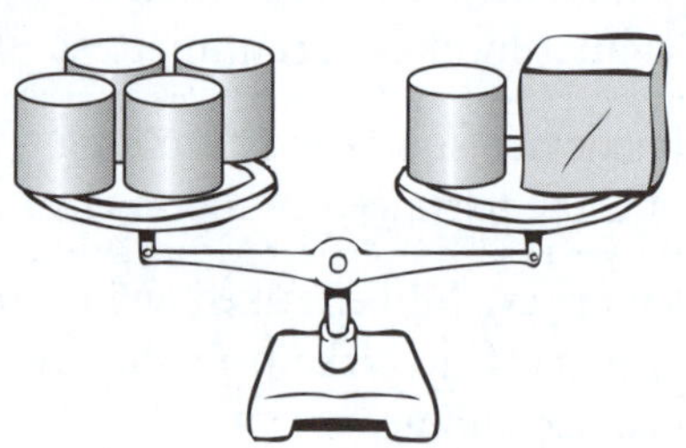

If the block has a mass of 12 kg, what is the mass of each cylinder?

16 What is half an hour before quarter to 11, in digital form?

17 How many minutes are in 5 hours?

18 How many minutes are between 25 to 8 and 25 past 8?

19 ________ h = 3 days

20 What is 4 hours after 10 am?

21 What is the time written in digital form?

22 The time on a digital clock is 4:17. In how many minutes will the clock show 5 o'clock?

23 How many hours are between 3 am and 5 pm on the same day?

24 Draw the time 18 minutes to 4 on the clock face.

FOCUS ON VOLUME, CAPACITY, MASS AND TIME

1 Here is an empty container which holds 1 L when full.
Shade the level of water representing 250 mL.

2 Riley pours 12 buckets of water into an empty container. Each bucket holds 10 L. If the container is now half-full, what is the total capacity of the container?

3 Scott has containers which hold $2\frac{1}{2}$ L, 800 mL and 5 L. What is the total capacity of the containers?

4 Aaron's petrol tank has a capacity of 48 L. At the start of the day the petrol gauge shows half-full. Aaron drives for one hour and uses 10 L. How much petrol is now in the tank?

5 A can of soup contains 420 mL. Chelsea pours three cans into a large saucepan. What quantity of soup is in the saucepan?

6 Sarah has a 2-litre bottle of juice. She pours out 520 mL. What amount of juice remains in the bottle?

7 Here are two jugs which hold some water.
All the water in Jug B is poured into Jug A. How much water is now in Jug A?

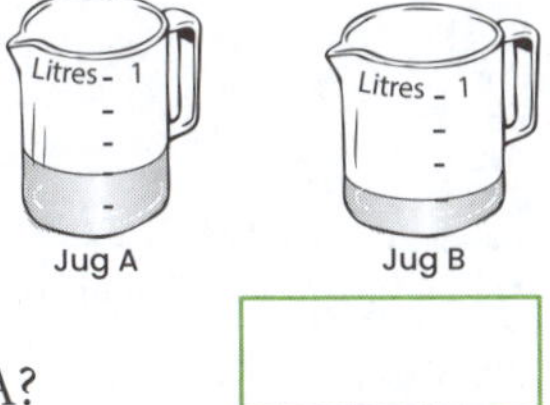

8 A 2-L bottle of soft drink is opened and six glasses are filled. If each glass contains 300 mL, what amount remains in the bottle?

9 A litre of water has a mass of 1 kg. The mass of an empty bucket is 800 g. What is the total mass of the bucket when it contains $7\frac{1}{2}$ L of water?

10 Eloise bought half a kilogram of tomatoes, 280 g of cherries, a 750-g packet of muesli and 3 kg of potatoes. What was the total mass in grams?

11 Buddy made this solid using identical cubes, each with a mass of 5 kg. What is the total mass of the solid?

12 The total mass of three boxes is 100 kg. If two of the boxes each have a mass of 37 kg, what is the mass of the other box?

13 Brooke has a cube, a sphere and a cylinder. The mass of the cylinder is 12 kg. The mass of the sphere is twice the mass of the cube. The cube is 4 kg heavier than the cylinder. What is the total mass of the three objects?

14 When she was born Mackenzie had a mass of 3100 g. At 2 years old her mass had increased by 10 kg. What was her new mass, in kilograms?

15 The pan balance shows identical cylinders and identical spheres.
If a sphere has a mass of 18 kg, what is the mass of a cylinder?

16 Twelve bags of flour have been delivered to a bakery. Each bag has a mass of 25 kg. What is the total mass of flour?

17 A bus is due to arrive at the time shown on the clock. The bus was 20 minutes late. What time did the bus arrive?

18 Jasmyn parks her car in a car park at 8:40 am. The car was parked for 6 hours. At what time did Jasmyn drive out of the car park?

19 A movie commenced at 11:45 am and finished at 1:30 pm. How long was the movie?

20 Chelsea had a 45-minute music lesson this afternoon. The lesson finished at 4 pm. At what time did the lesson commence?

21 It is New Year's Eve and Marie has calculated there are 300 seconds until midnight.
What is the time on a digital clock?

22 Here is a countdown clock set at 5 hours. After 90 seconds, what is shown on the display?

5:00:00

FOCUS ON 3D SHAPES

1. How many flat surfaces has a cylinder?

2. How many curved surfaces has a cone?

3. How many faces has a triangular prism?

4. What 3D shape is formed using this net?

5. How many edges has a hexagonal prism?

6. How many flat surfaces has a cone?

7. Here is a cylinder.

What is the view from the top?

8. Steve used isometric paper to draw this shape.

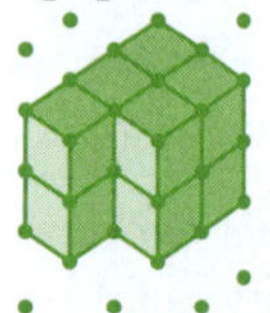

How many cubes are in the shape?

9. How many vertices are on a rectangular prism?

10. Here is a 3D solid.

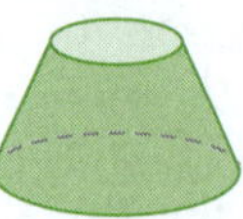

The solid is viewed from the top. Circle the shape which best represents the view.

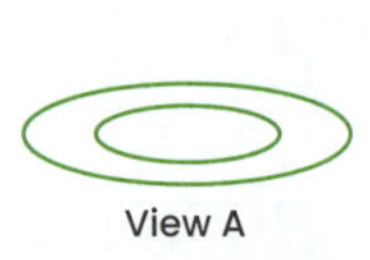

View A

View B

View C

11. Circle the name of the shape with six vertices and five faces.

pentagonal prism triangular prism

square prism

12. Here is a solid made of 11 cubes.

In the space draw the view of the solid from the top.

13. A pyramid has seven faces. Write the name of the shape.

14. A solid has two triangular faces and three rectangular faces. What is the name of the solid?

15. Draw a shape with a curved surface and two flat surfaces.

16. Complete the statement.

An octagonal prism has ________ octagonal faces

and ________ rectangular faces.

17. Draw a pyramid with eight edges, five faces and five vertices.

FOCUS ON 3D SHAPES

1 Ms Thomas pretends to be a shape. She gives these clues:

- I have three dimensions.
- I have one curved surface.
- I have no flat surfaces.

What shape is she pretending to be?

2 Esme views a prism from the top, side and front. Each time she sees a rectangle.

What is the name of the shape?

3 How many more edges has a hexagonal prism than a rectangular prism?

This solid is used to answer questions 4 to 6.

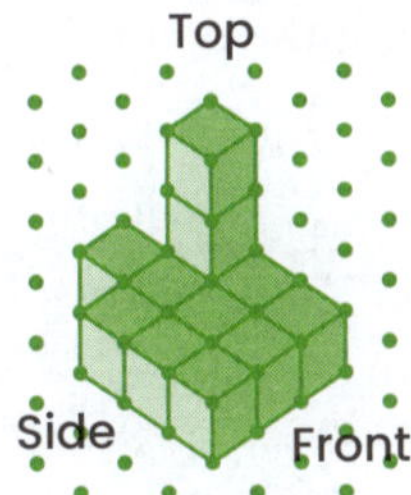

4 Draw the front view.

5 Draw the side view.

6 Draw the top view.

7 Complete the prism.

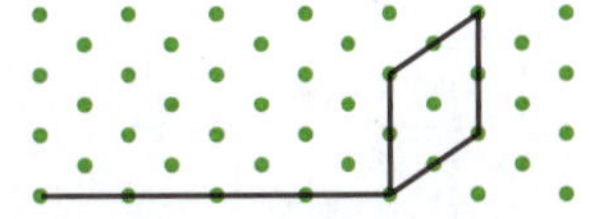

8 What 3D shape has these three views?

Top view

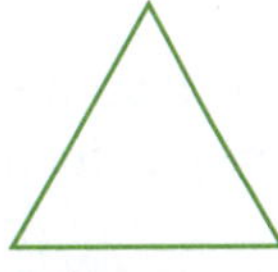
Front view

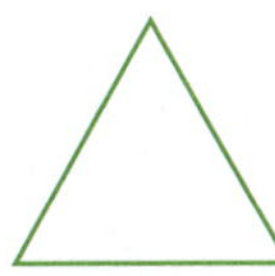
Side view

9 Two identical hexagonal pyramids are made. Maddy glues the base of one pyramid to the base of the other to form a new solid.

How many edges has the new shape?

10 The sum of the lengths of the edges of a rectangular prism is 40 cm. One edge is 3 cm long and another is 2 cm long.

What is the length of the longest edge?

11 How many more faces has a square prism than a square pyramid?

12 Izzy drew the net of a square pyramid. The area of the square is 36 cm^2 and the area of each triangle is 30 cm^2.

What is the total of the areas of the faces of the pyramid?

FOCUS ON 2D SHAPES, SYMMETRY AND TRANSFORMATIONS

1 Draw a straight line on the parallelogram to divide it into a triangle and a quadrilateral.

2 A trapezium is split into two shapes.

Name the shapes.

3 Shade the squares so that the dotted line is a line of symmetry.

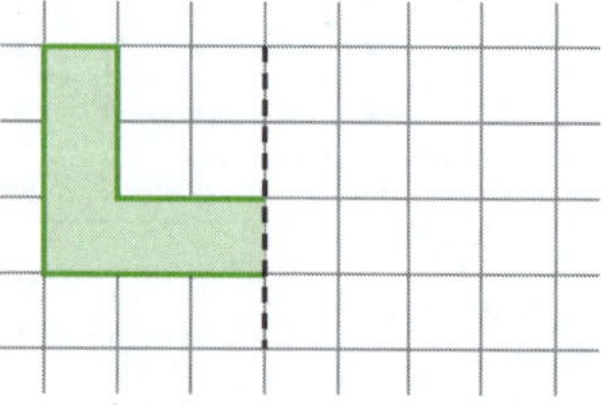

4 Draw the other half of the figure below using the vertical line of symmetry.

5 Complete the diagram if the dotted line is a line of symmetry.

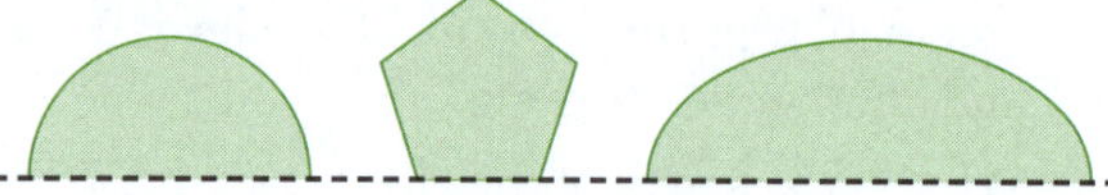

6 Shade the squares so that the dotted line is a line of symmetry.

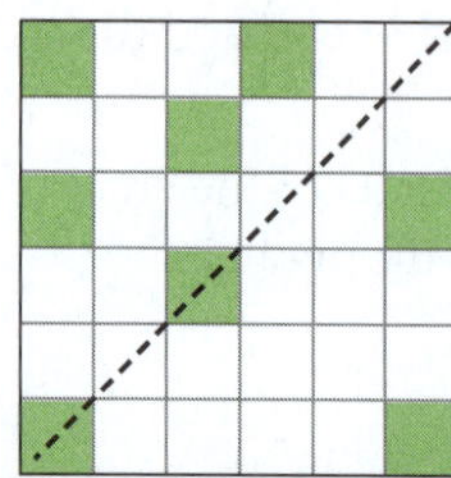

7 Draw the other half of the figure below using the vertical line of symmetry.

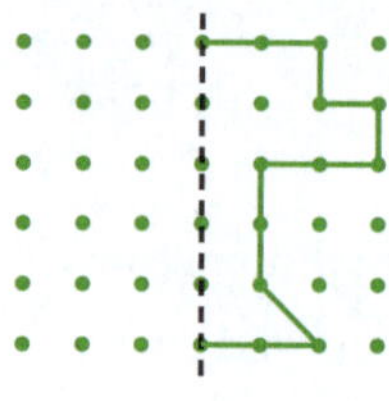

8 Translate the triangle 4 units to the right.

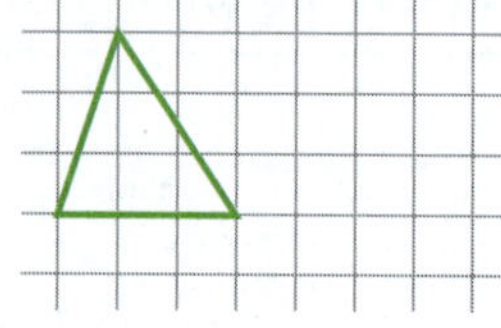

9 Reflect the shape about the dotted line.

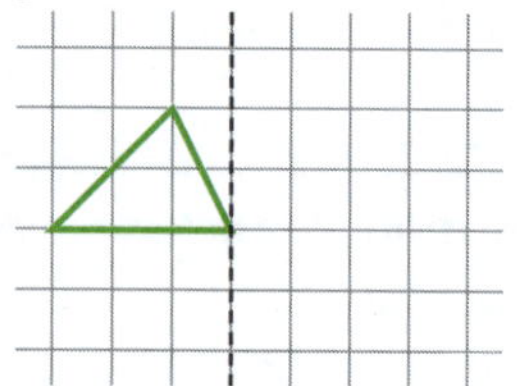

10 Rotate the triangle a quarter turn in a clockwise direction about the point X.

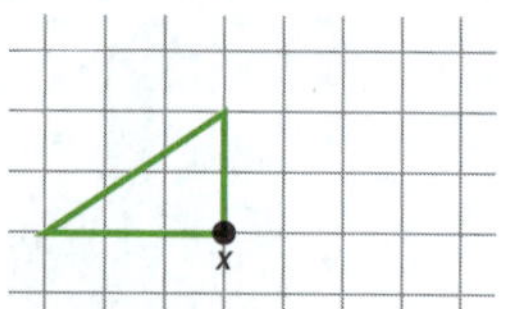

11 Complete the statement.
Shape A is translated ________ units to the ________ to form shape B.

B A

12 Triangle A has been rotated in a clockwise direction about the point X. The image has been named triangle B.

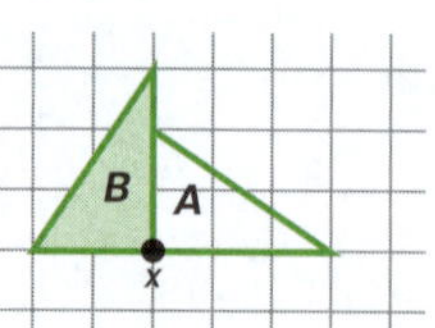

Circle the size of the rotation.

a quarter turn a half turn

a three-quarter turn

FOCUS ON 2D SHAPES, SYMMETRY AND TRANSFORMATIONS

1. Here are two identical trapeziums.
Hannah joins the trapeziums to make a regular shape.
What is the name of her shape?

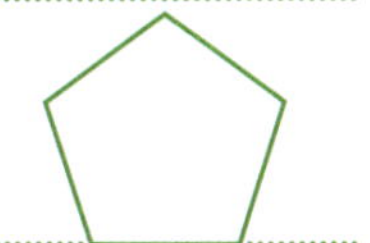

2. Use a straight line to cut the regular pentagon into two quadrilaterals.

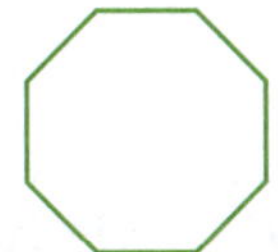

3. Susan uses a straight line to cut the regular octagon into a pentagon and a hexagon.
Show a possible line.

4. Simone has shaded some squares on the grid.
How many more squares should she shade so that the dotted line is a line of symmetry?

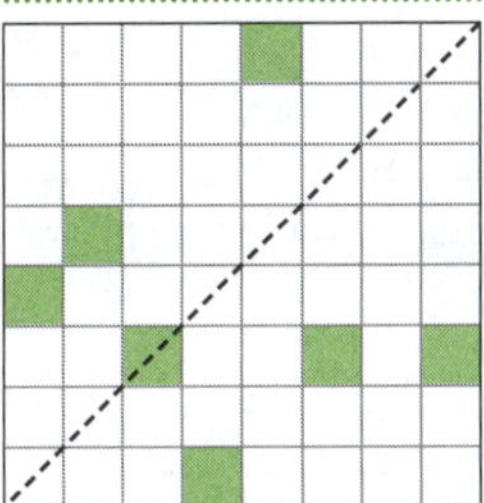

5. Francis has shaded some squares on the grid.
How many more squares should he shade so that the two dotted lines are lines of symmetry?

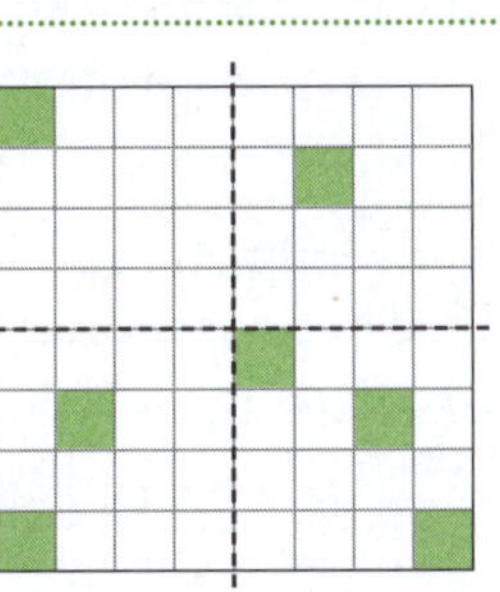

6. Part of a shape is shown. Complete the shape so that the dotted lines represent lines of symmetry.

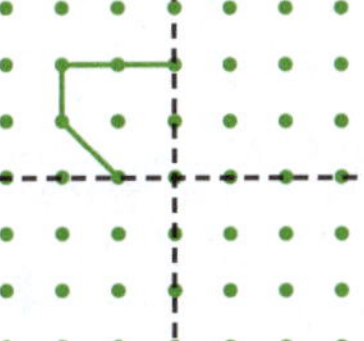

7. Part of a shape is shown. Complete the shape so that the dotted lines represent lines of symmetry.

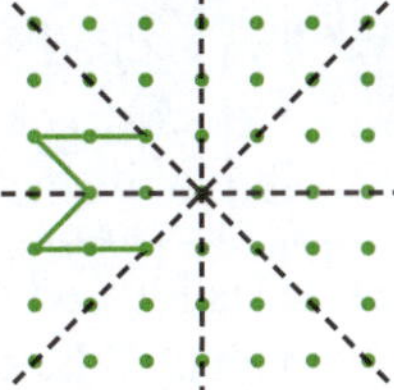

8. A shape is reflected about the dotted line. Draw the image of the shape.

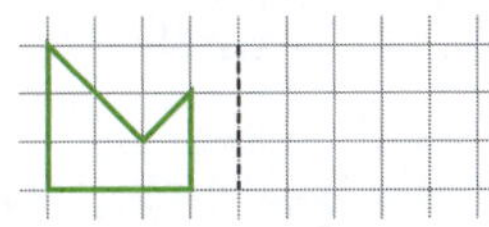

9. Theo rotates this shape a half turn about the point X.
Draw Theo's image.

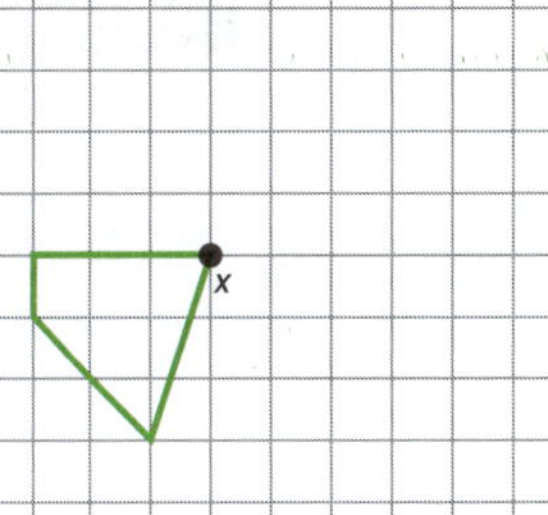

10. The shape is to be rotated a quarter turn in an anticlockwise direction about the point X.
Draw the image of the shape.

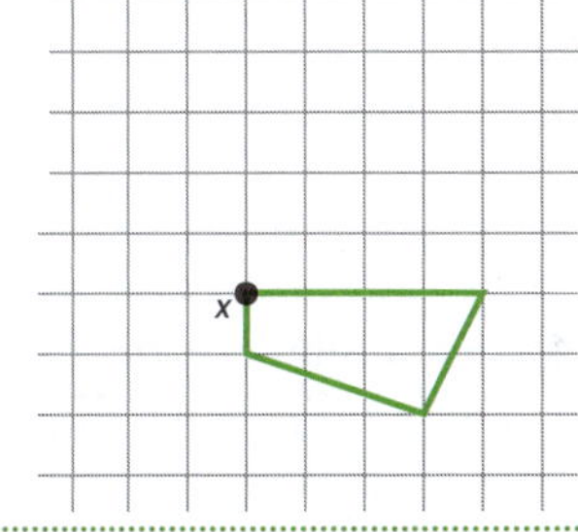

11. Alicia uses two translations to draw the image of a shape. She has shaded the image.

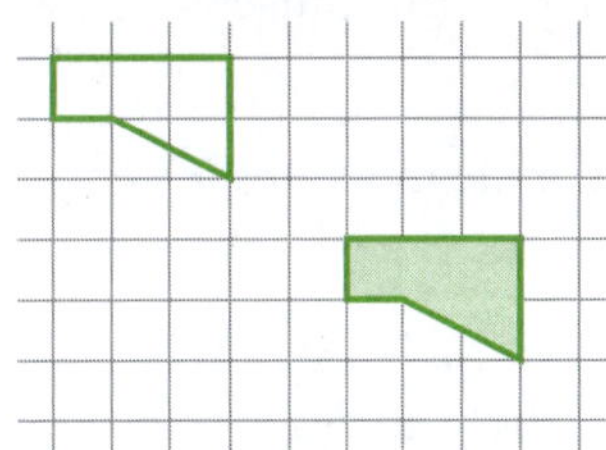

Complete the statement.
Translate ________ units right, then translate ________ units ________.

12. Reflect the shape about the vertical line and then reflect about the horizontal line.

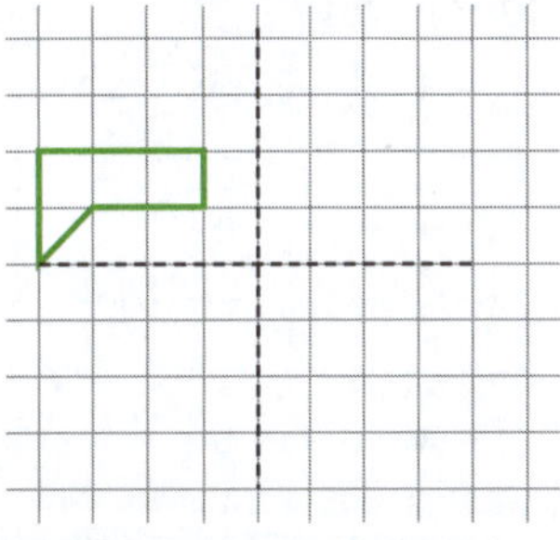

13. Translate the shape to the right 4 units and then reflect about the dotted line.

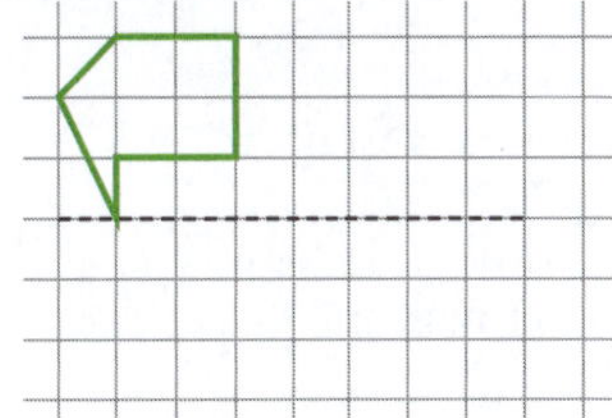

ANGLES AND POSITION

1 Which angle (*A*, *B* or *C*) is the largest?

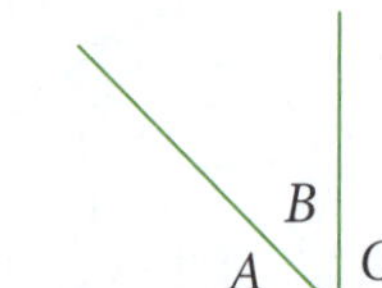

2 Complete the statement.
A reflex angle is more than ________ right angles and less than ________ right angles.

3 Six angles are identified on the shape.

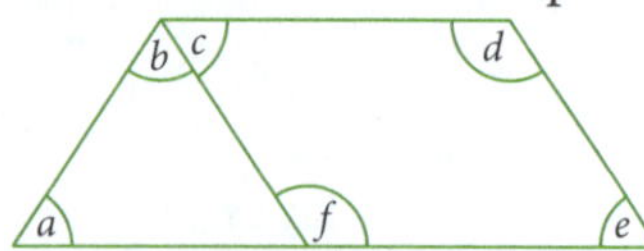

Which angles are obtuse?

4 If a right angle measures 90°, what is the measurement of a straight angle?

5 Which of these angles is reflex?

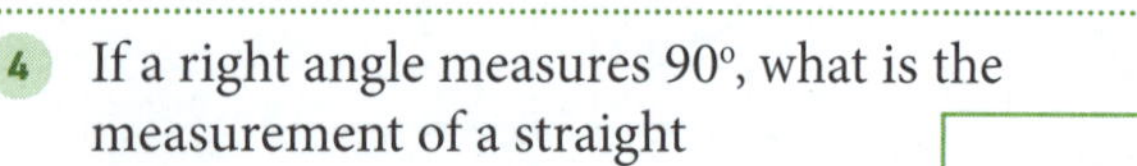

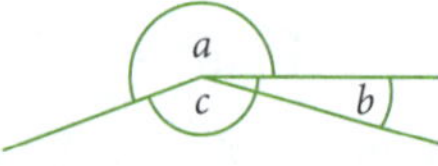

The grid represents a simple map. Towns *A*, *B*, *C*, *D* and *E* are located on the map. The map is used to answer questions 6 and 7.

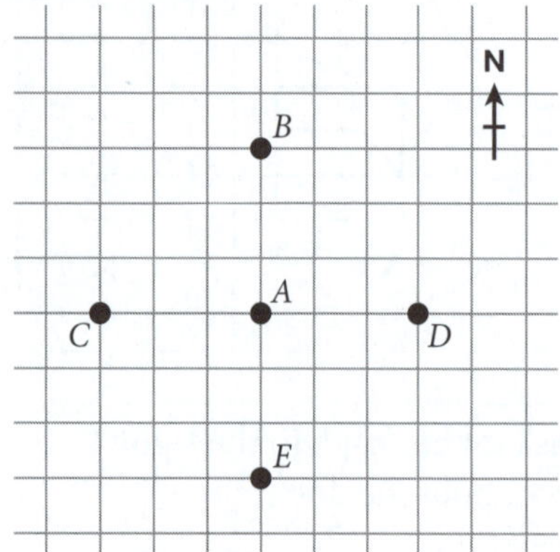

6 Which town is west of *A*?

7 Which two towns are directly south of *B*?

The centimetre grid represents a simple map and is used to answer questions 8 to 11.

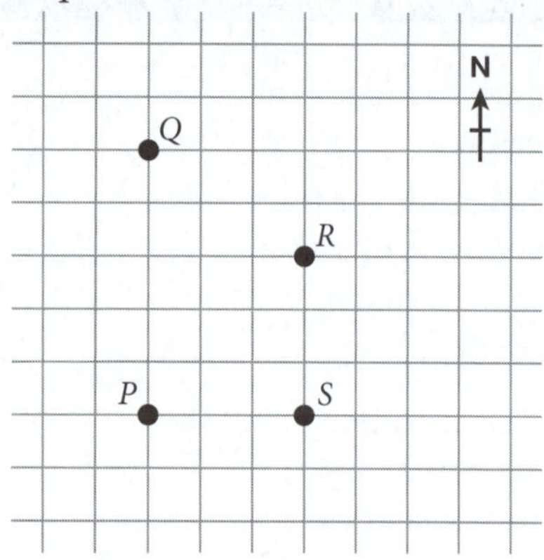

8 Complete the statement.
S is ____________________ of *P*.

9 Circle the correct direction: *R* is ________ of *P*.

south-east north-east

south-west

10 Circle the correct direction: *P* is ________ of *R*.

south-west south-east

north-east

11 How many centimetres are *P* and *Q* apart on the map?

The centimetre grid represents a simple map. The scale used to draw the map is shown. Use the map to answer questions 12 and 13.

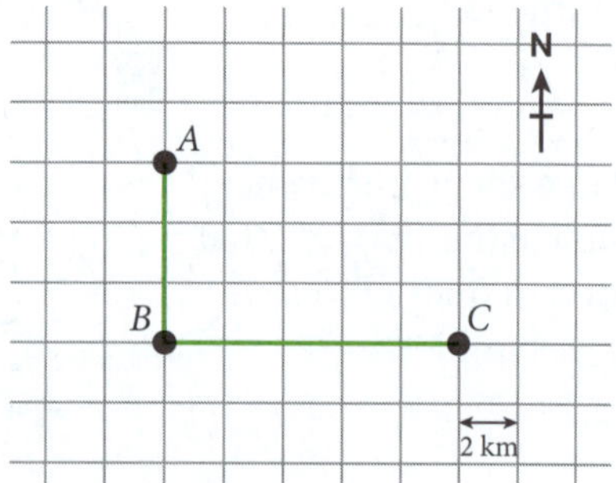

12 Jon walked from *A* to *B* then to *C*. How many kilometres did he walk?

13 *D* is located 4 km south of *B*. *E* is 2 km north of *A*. What is the distance from *D* to *E*?

FOCUS ON ANGLES AND POSITION

1 A clock is showing 9:40. The minute hand moves through a quarter turn.
What is the new time on the clock?

2 The hands of a clock move from 8:00 to 12:00. Circle the name of the angle the hour hand has moved through.

acute right obtuse straight

3 Emily and Katie are standing looking at each other. Emily spins around twice and then faces Katie again. Through how many right angles did Emily rotate?

4 Draw a quadrilateral with two obtuse angles and two acute angles.

5 If a trapezium has two right angles and an obtuse angle, what type is the fourth angle?

6 True or false? An obtuse angle plus an obtuse angle always adds to a reflex angle.

7 True or false? An acute angle plus an acute angle always adds to an obtuse angle.

8 The time showing on an analog clock is 20 past 9. If the minute hand moves through a three-quarter turn, what is the new time, in digital form?

9 Cara is standing south-west of Perveen. What direction is Perveen from Cara?

10 Tamir is looking west. He then makes a three-quarter turn in a clockwise direction.
In what direction is he now looking?

11 Here is the time on a clock when Pedro arrives at the train station. His train arrives after the minute hand has moved through 3 right angles.
At what time does his train arrive, in digital time?

The grid shows a simple map and is used to answer questions 12 and 13.

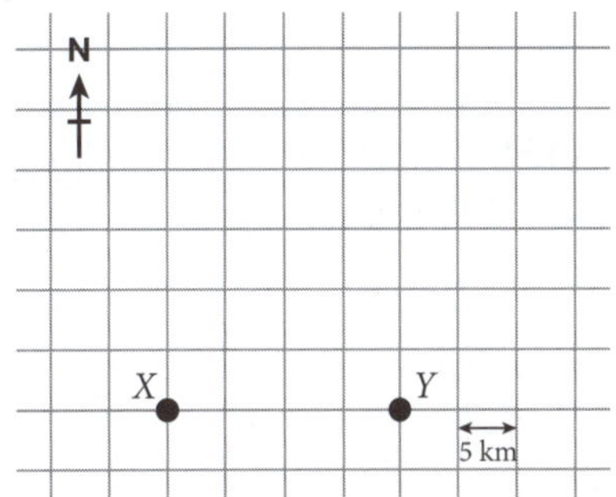

12 What is the distance from town *X* to town *Y*?

13 Town *Z* is located 30 km north of town *Y*. Plot the location of *Z* on the map.

14 Kai left *A* and walked 4 units north to *B* and then 4 units west to *C*. Use the grid to show Kai's journey. What is the direction of *A* from *C*?

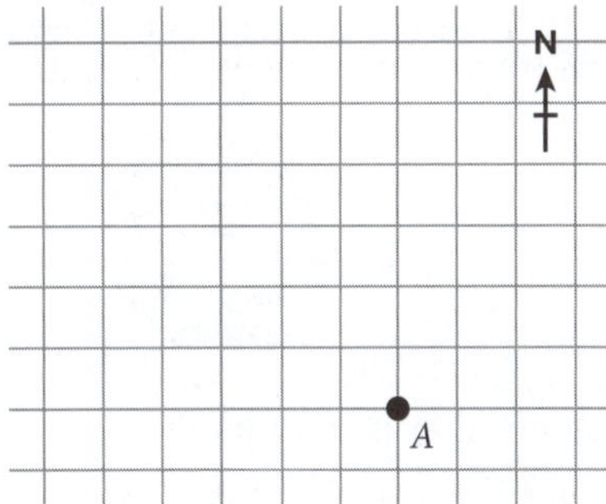

The grid represents a simple map where towns *C* and *D* are 24 km apart. It is used to answer questions 15 to 17.

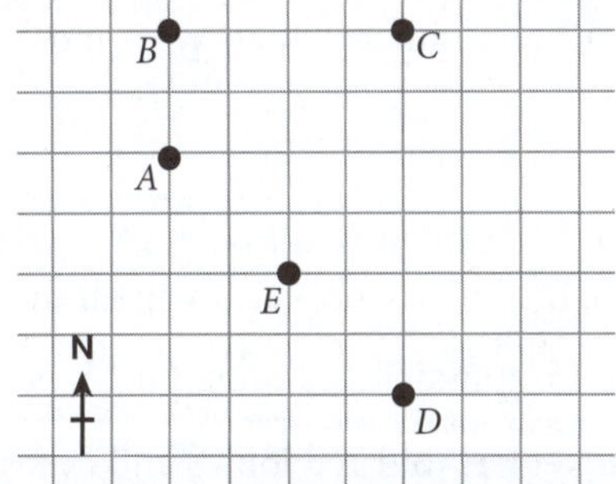

15 Complete the scale used on the map.
1 unit = ________ km

16 What town is the same distance from *A* as it is from *D*?

17 Sam drove directly from town *A*, through *B* and *C* to town *D*. What was the total distance travelled?

FOCUS ON CHANCE AND DATA

1. A bag contains two red, three green and a yellow ball. A ball is chosen without looking.
Which colour is least likely to be selected?

2. A normal dice is rolled. Circle the word that describes the chance of rolling a 7.
unlikely impossible certain

3. A fair coin is tossed. Circle the best description of the chance the result is a tail.
less likely equally likely more likely

4. A raffle has 100 tickets. Sharne buys one ticket. Circle the best description of the chance that her ticket is drawn.
very unlikely impossible very likely

This spinner is used to answer questions 5 and 6.

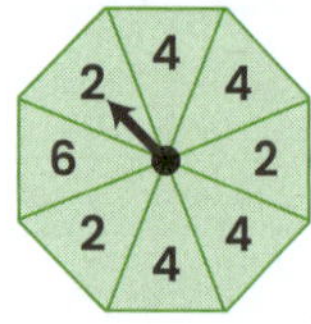

5. Which number is most likely to be spun?

6. Which number is least likely to be spun?

7. Circle the numbers which are impossible to spin.
1 2 3 4

8. A team won their first match of the season. Circle the chance they will win all their games.
impossible possible certain

9. A packet has four red lollies and four blue lollies. True or false?
There is an even chance of choosing a red lolly.

Students were asked what their favourite colour was and the results are shown in a table. This data is used to answer questions 10 to 12.

Favourite colours	
Colour	**Tally**
red	|||
yellow	~~||||~~
purple	~~||||~~ ||||
blue	||||

10. How many students said their favourite colour was yellow?

11. What was the most popular colour?

12. How many students said red or blue?

The graph shows the number of air-conditioners sold by a shop in one week. The graph is used to answer questions 13 and 14.

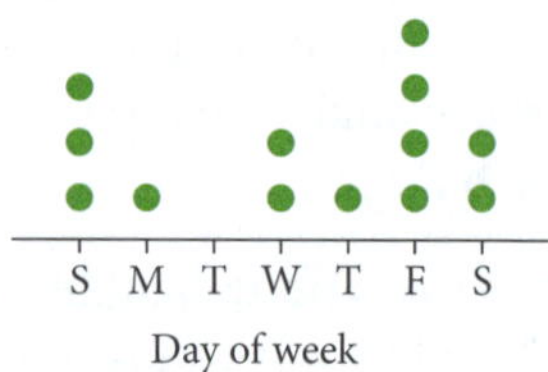

13. How many air-conditioners were sold on Wednesday?

14. On which day were most air-conditioners sold?

Students were asked about their favourite pet. The results are shown in the graph, which is used to answer questions 15 and 16.

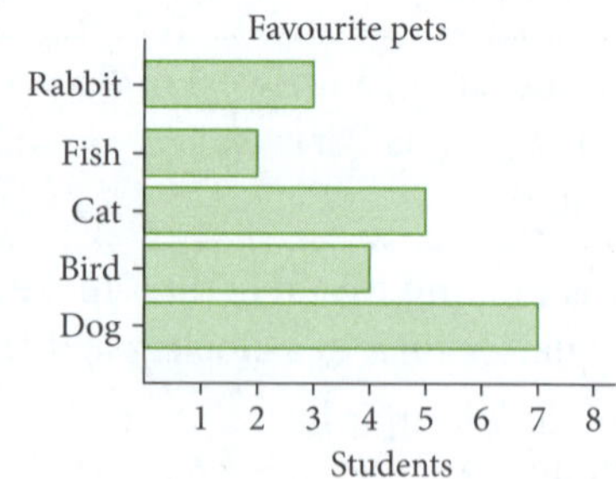

15. How many students said their favourite pet was a cat?

16. How many students said a fish or a bird?

FOCUS ON DATA AND CHANCE

1 The sides of a cube are numbered 2, 4, 5, 6, 7 and 8. The cube is rolled. Circle the best description for the chance of rolling an odd number.

likely even chance unlikely

A group of students were surveyed to find their favourite sports. The graph is used to answer questions 2 to 4.

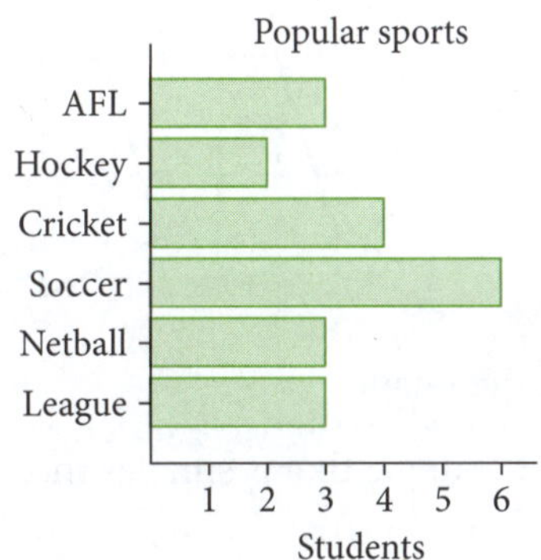

2 What was the most popular sport?

3 How many more students liked cricket than hockey?

4 What was the total number of students surveyed?

The table shows the ages of students who represented the school at the regional swimming carnival. It is used to answer questions 5 and 6.

School representatives	
Age	**Students**
8	5
9	7
10	6
11	8
12	4

5 How many 8-year-old students represented the school?

6 What was the total number of students who represented the school?

The graph shows the number of car sales for Al's Autos and is used to answer questions 7 to 10.

Al's Autos car sales	
Monday	
Tuesday	
Wednesday	
Thursday	
Friday	
Saturday	
Key: = 2 cars	

7 How many cars were sold on Wednesday?

8 How many more cars were sold on Friday than Monday?

9 What was the total number of cars sold on Wednesday and Saturday?

10 On how many days were more than three cars sold?

The graph shows the number of dogs groomed by Pamper Pooch and is used to answer questions 11 to 14.

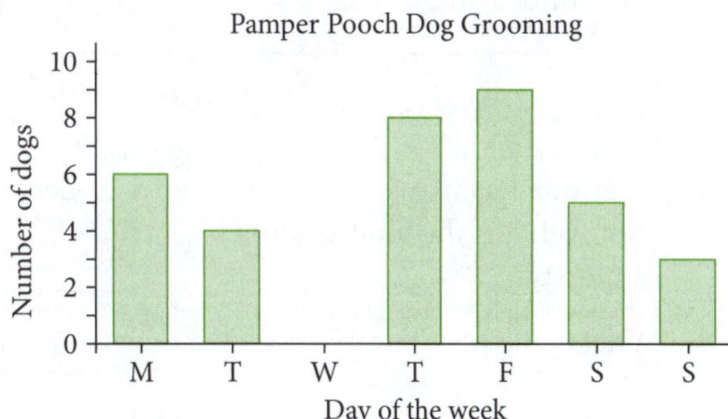

11 Dogs are groomed six days a week. On what day were dogs **not** groomed?

12 How many more dogs were groomed on Friday than Tuesday?

13 On how many days were at least five dogs groomed?

14 The business charges $30 for each dog groom. What was the total amount of money made on Thursday, Friday and Sunday?

NUMBER AND ALGEBRA

1 Express the number 4003 in words.

2 What is the total of 3000, 200, 80 and 7?

3 Lucas is 60 years old. His daughter is 35. What is the difference between their ages?

4 On each of five plates, Ariana arranged six cakes. What was the total number of cakes?

5 Greta has 45 marbles. She arranges them into five rows. How many marbles are in each row?

6 Henry is driving from Sydney to Brisbane. He stops for petrol when he has completed $\frac{1}{4}$ of the trip. What fraction has he yet to travel?

7 Name the decimal plotted on the number line.

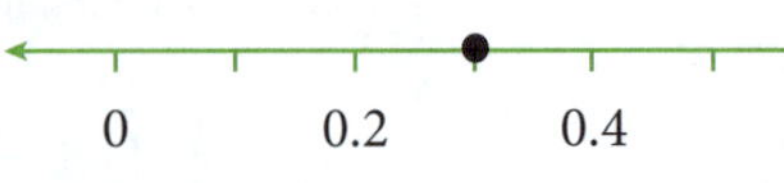

8 Charlotte has two 50-cent coins and a 20-cent coin. What is the total amount of money?

9 What is the next number?

21, 27, 33, 39, ?

MEASUREMENT AND SPACE

10 How many centimetres are in 1 m 23 cm?

11 A bucket has a capacity of 9 L. What is the total amount of water in five buckets?

12 Rice is sold in 10-kg bags. What is the total mass of nine bags?

13 Rob has started to draw a cylinder.

Complete the shape.

14 How many lines of symmetry has a rectangle?

15 The diagram shows a shape and its image after it has been translated 3 units to the right.

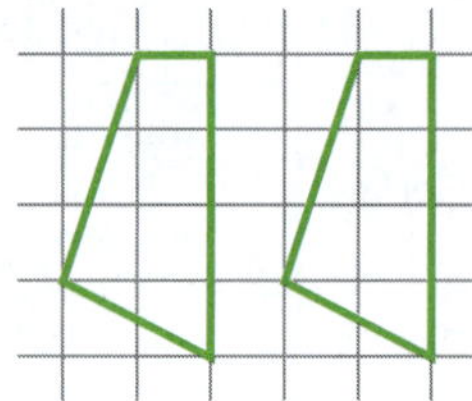

Shade the image.

16 Circle the angle that is smaller than a right angle.

102° 99° 56°

STATISTICS AND PROBABILITY

17 On which colour is the spinner most likely to land?

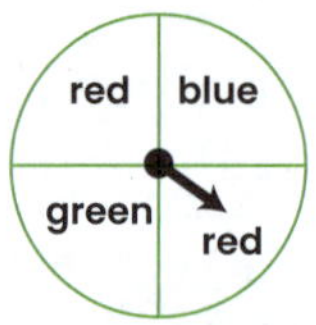

18 A group of students were asked to choose their favourite sport from a list. The table shows the results of the survey.

Sport	Tally
soccer	𝍸 |
netball	||||
cricket	𝍸 ||
rugby league	𝍸
swimming	𝍸 |||

What was the most popular sport?

NUMBER AND ALGEBRA

1 Use digits to rewrite two hundred and nine thousand and five.

2 What is 4000 + 2000 + 30 + 40?

3 The final score in a match is 112–58. What is the difference between the scores?

4 Bella added these numbers.

What was her total?

5 True or false?
$36 \div 3 \div 2 = 36 \div 6$

6 After 30 minutes Mia has completed $\frac{2}{3}$ of her fitness class. What fraction remains?

7 Name the decimal plotted on the number line.

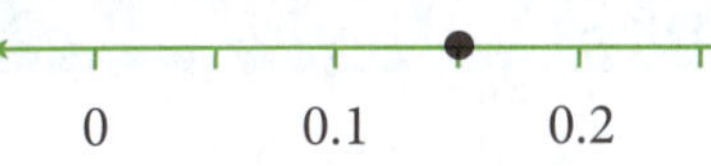

8 Theodore has seven 20-cent coins and a 5-cent coin. What is the total amount of money?

9 What is the missing number?

, 19, 28, 37, 46

MEASUREMENT AND SPACE

10 How many millimetres are in 7 m 36 mm?

11 Andrew fills a 9-L bucket twenty times to water his garden. How much water does he pour on his garden?

12 A bag of seed has a mass of 3 kg 200 g. What is the total mass of four bags?

13 Liselle has started to draw a prism.

Complete the shape.

14 How many lines of symmetry has a parallelogram?

15 The diagram shows a shape and its image after it has been translated 4 units down. Shade the image.

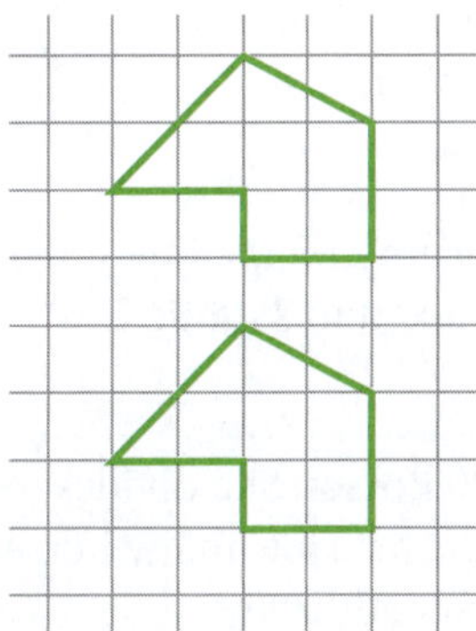

16 Circle the angle that is smaller than a right angle.

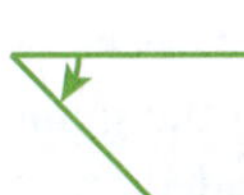

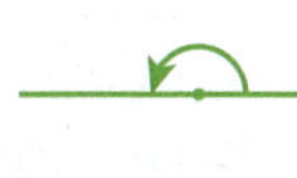

STATISTICS AND PROBABILITY

17 On which number is the spinner most likely to land?

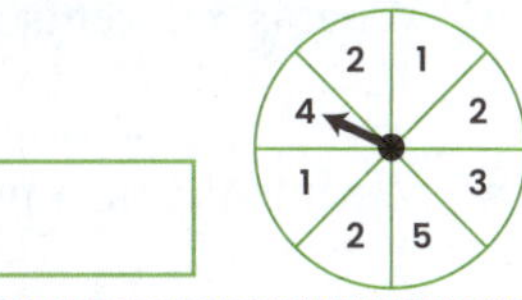

18 A group of students were asked to choose their favourite sport from a list. The table shows the results of the survey.

Sport	Tally
soccer	𝍸 I
netball	IIII
cricket	𝍸 II
rugby league	𝍸
swimming	𝍸 III

How many students were surveyed?

NUMBER AND ALGEBRA

1 Here are three numbers.

9830 9380 9308

Christine rearranged the numbers from lowest to highest. What was her middle number?

2 Wei added 50 and 48. What was her total?

3 The sum of two numbers is 90. If the smaller number is 30, what is the larger number?

4 Every morning Mary-Kate walks 3 km. How far has she walked in 7 days?

5 Jess has 20 horses. She divides them evenly into four paddocks. How many horses are in each paddock?

6 A shape has been divided into five equal parts. Ming shades two parts.
What fraction of the shape has **not** been shaded?

7 Use a decimal to write zero point four three.

8 What is 375 cents in dollars?

9 What is the next number?

35, 30, 25, 20, ?

MEASUREMENT AND SPACE

10 A fence is 30 m long. Levi has painted 18 m of the fence. What length remains to be painted?

11 Anne has three identical glasses. Each glass holds 200 mL. What is the total capacity of the glasses?

12 How much time is between 9 am and 2:00 pm?

13 How many flat surfaces has a cylinder?

14 Draw a dotted line on this shape to split it into two parallelograms.

15 The triangle on the left has been translated to form the triangle on the right.

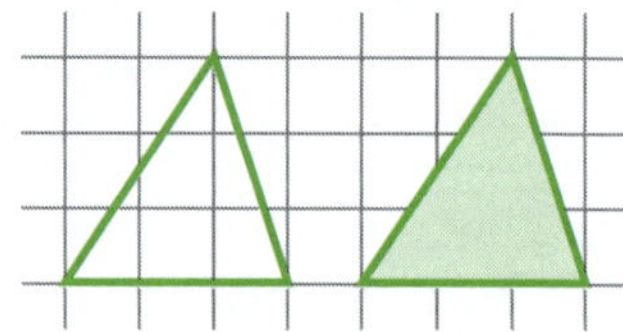

How many units has the triangle been translated?

16 Gianna is standing at a lookout and faces south. She makes a quarter turn in a clockwise direction. Which direction is she now facing?

STATISTICS AND PROBABILITY

17 Circle the least likely outcome.

It will rain tomorrow.

The sun will rise next Wednesday.

18 The colour of vans passing the school in one hour was recorded.

Colour	Number
white	28
black	6
blue	3
yellow	3

How many vans were **not** white?

NUMBER AND ALGEBRA

1 Emily wrote these four numbers. Circle the largest number.

40 702 4720 40 720 40 270

2 Theo has 24 cards in one pile and 16 in another. What is the total number of cards?

3 The sum of two numbers is 764. If the smaller number is 321, what is the larger number?

4 Cam gave six balls to each of nine friends. How many balls did he give away?

5 A teacher has 48 counters and divides them evenly between four students. How many counters will each student receive?

6 A shape has been divided into 12 equal parts. Isabella shades seven parts. What fraction of the shape has **not** been shaded?

7 Use a decimal to write eight point zero nine.

8 What is 2643 cents in dollars?

9 What is the missing number?

?, 86, 80, 74, 68

MEASUREMENT AND SPACE

10 Darcy cuts a length of 43 cm of wire from a 1-m roll. What length remains on the roll?

11 An oil can has a capacity of 500 mL. The can is half full. How much oil is in the can?

12 How much time is between 8:30 pm and midnight?

13 How many flat surfaces has a cone?

14 Draw two dotted lines on this shape to split it into three triangles.

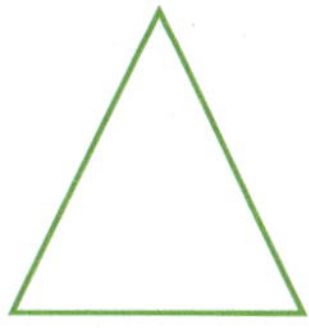

15 The shape on the left has been reflected to form the shape on the right.

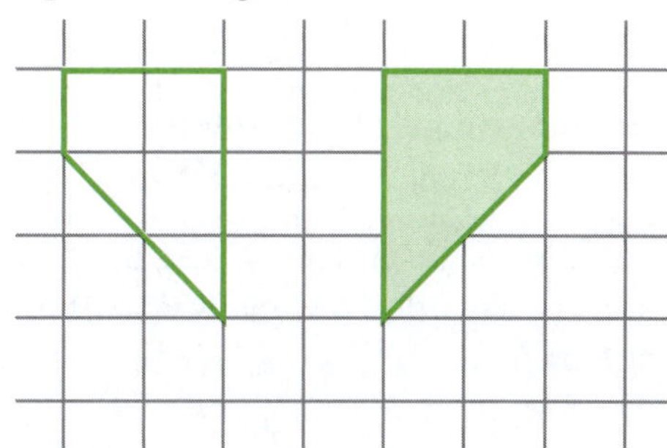

Using a dotted line, draw the line of symmetry.

16 Scarlett is standing at a lookout and faces east. She makes a half turn. Which direction is now behind her?

STATISTICS AND PROBABILITY

17 Circle the equally likely outcome.

rolling a 2 using a fair dice

tossing a head using a fair coin

18 The colour of vans passing the school in one hour was recorded.

Colour	Numbers
white	28
black	6
blue	3
yellow	3

What was the total number of vans that passed the school?

NUMBER AND ALGEBRA

1 Kyah wrote the number 49 378. What digit is in the thousands place?

2 Casey has 12 red balloons, eight white balloons and six pink balloons. What is the total number of balloons?

3 Barnaby thinks of a number. He adds the number to 70 and the answer is 100. What is Barnaby's number?

4 Jean-Luc swims six laps of his backyard pool. Each lap is 8 metres. How far does Jean-Luc swim?

5 Liam has 56 cards. How many groups of 7 can Liam make?

6 Shade $\frac{11}{12}$ of this shape.

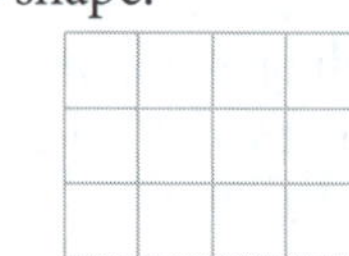

7 On the number line, plot the decimal 0.4.

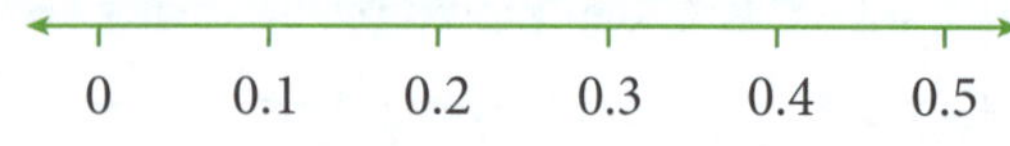

8 What is $5.38 in cents?

9 What is the next number?

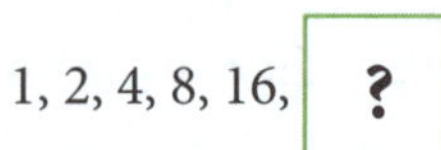

MEASUREMENT AND SPACE

10 Lance rode 24 km on Tuesday and 33 km on Thursday. What was the total distance ridden in the two days?

11 Connor has a 600-mL bottle of water. He drinks 200 mL. How much water remains?

12 How many grams are in 7 kg?

13 Symon draws a cube. How many edges has the shape?

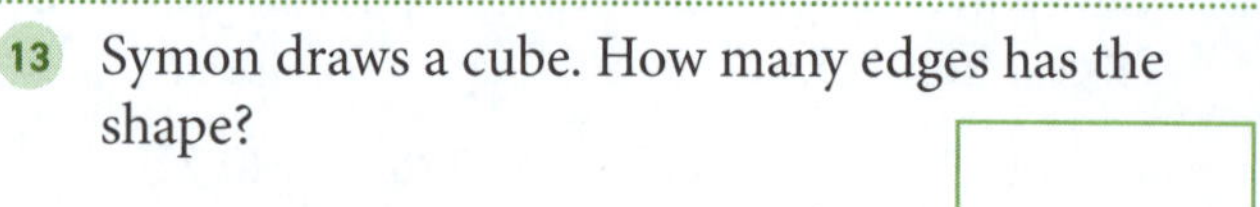

14 Draw a dotted line that splits this rectangle into two equal squares.

15 Thomas translated the shape 3 units to the right.

Draw the image.

16 Circle the shape which has at least one right angle.

hexagon circle rectangle

STATISTICS AND PROBABILITY

17 A box contains four numbered balls. A ball is selected without looking.

Which number is more likely to be selected?

18 The graph shows the number of houses built in a new subdivision.

Month	Houses
May	🏠🏠
June	🏠🏠🏠
July	🏠🏠🏠🏠
August	🏠🏠 and part of 🏠
Key 🏠 = 4 houses	

How many houses were built in August?

NUMBER AND ALGEBRA

1 Harrison formed a five-digit number with 3 in the hundreds place. There was a 5 in the ten-thousands place and a 2 in the ones place. There was an 8 in each of the other places. What was Harrison's number?

2 What is the total of 41, 32 and 26?

3 Whitney thinks of a number. She adds 389 to her number and the result is 1000. What was Whitney's number?

4 Each school desk has four legs. How many legs are on 20 desks?

5 How many times can Jason take 20 away from 140 to give 0?

6 Shade $\frac{2}{3}$ of this shape.

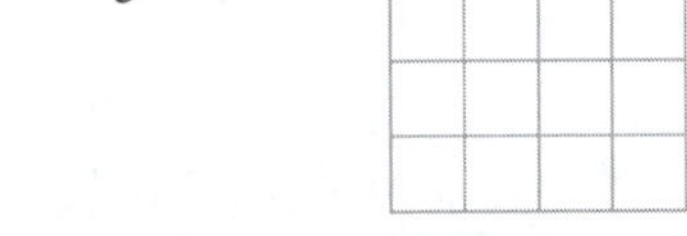

7 On the number line, plot the decimal 0.03.

8 What is $90.40 in cents?

9 What is the next number?

5, 10, 20, 40, 80, ?

MEASUREMENT AND SPACE

10 What is the sum of 12 mm and 7 cm, in millimetres?

11 A 2-L bottle of juice is opened and 800 mL is poured into a jug. What amount remains in the bottle?

12 How many grams are in 5 kg 250 g?

13 Leo draws a 3D shape which has six rectangular faces. In the space draw Leo's shape.

14 Draw a dotted line that splits this rectangle into two rectangles.

15 Greg translated the shape 3 units to the left.

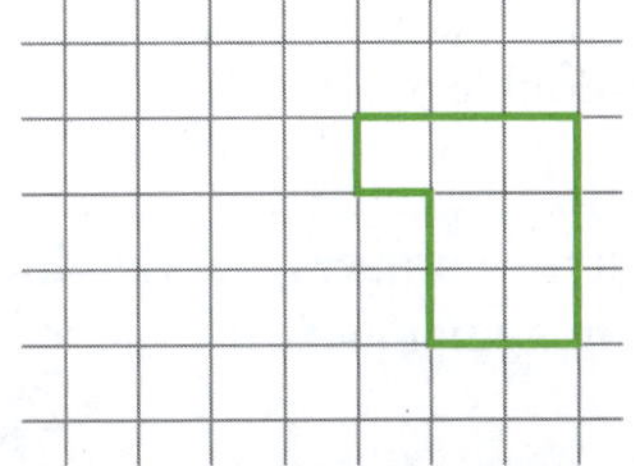

Draw the image.

16 Draw a quadrilateral with exactly two right angles.

STATISTICS AND PROBABILITY

17 A box contains four numbered balls. A ball is selected without looking.

James said it is impossible to select an even number. Is James correct?

18 The graph shows the number of houses built in a new subdivision.

Month	Houses
May	🏠🏠
June	🏠🏠🏠
July	🏠🏠🏠🏠
August	🏠🏠½🏠
Key 🏠 = 4 houses	

How many houses were built in the first three months?

NUMBER AND ALGEBRA

1 Jordan wrote the number 8447. How many times larger is the first 4 than the second 4?

2 In a herd there are 37 Friesian cows and eight Jersey cows. What is the total number of cows in the herd?

3 David has 100 marbles. He gives 45 marbles away. How many marbles does David keep?

4 What is double 60?

5 Circle all the numbers that can divide into 12 with no remainder.

2 4 5 8

6 Here are eight balls. Colour a quarter of the balls.

7 What is the place value of 2 in the number 58.29?

8 Silas bought an apple which cost \$0.65. If he paid \$1, how much change did he receive?

9 Two even numbers are added. Is the result even or odd?

MEASUREMENT AND SPACE

10 Noah used a ruler to measure the length of a pen.

What is the length in centimetres?

11 Andy plans to paint his bedroom. He buys two 500-mL cans and a 4-L can. How much paint does Andy buy?

12 Here are two clocks. Clock A shows the time Laura arrives at a train station. Clock B shows the time her train will arrive. How many minutes will Laura wait until her train arrives?

Clock A Clock B

13 How many curved surfaces has a sphere?

14 Draw a dotted line to split this triangle into a trapezium and a smaller triangle.

15 How many quarter turns make a full turn?

16 The map shows the location of five villages.

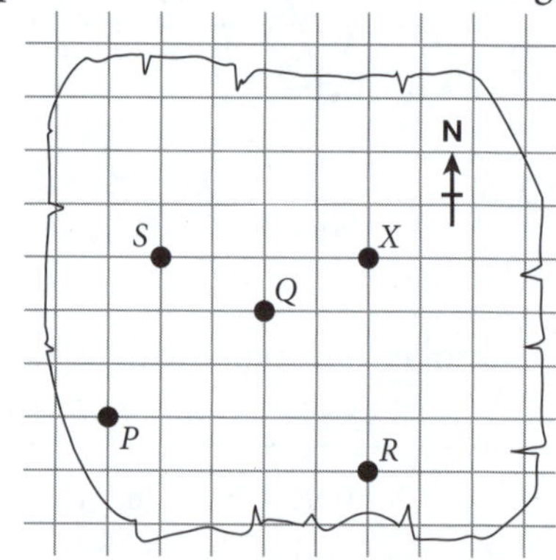

Which village is directly south of *X*?

STATISTICS AND PROBABILITY

17 Which number is most likely to be spun?

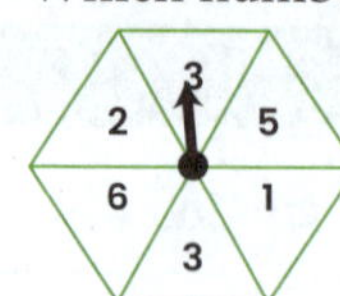

18 The ages of the members of the school band are recorded in the table below.

Age	12	13	14	15	16	17
Number	3	9	11	8	4	3

How many members are under the age of 14?

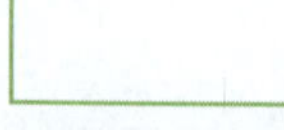

NUMBER AND ALGEBRA

1 Clare wrote the number 940 348. How many times larger is the first 4 than the second 4?

2 In one mob Garry counted 36 kangaroos. Later he counted 44 kangaroos in another mob. What was the total number of kangaroos?

3 Ronald has 1000 sheep in a pen waiting to be shorn. By lunchtime 580 sheep have been shorn. How many sheep remain?

4 On each of five mornings Ross cycled 20 km. What is the total distance cycled?

5 Circle all the numbers that can be divided into 36 with no remainder.

6 8 12 16 18

6 Matthew draws eight circles. He shades $\frac{3}{4}$ of the circles. How many circles are shaded?

7 What is the place value of 5 in the number 10.452?

8 Declan bought a bottle of soft drink which cost $3.20. If he paid $5, how much change did he receive?

9 An odd number less than 100 is added to an even number greater than 50. Is the result even or odd?

MEASUREMENT AND SPACE

10 Abigail used a ruler to measure the length of a crayon and a pencil.

How much longer is the pencil than the crayon?

11 A container holds 5 L of water. Andrew pours $\frac{1}{2}$ L from the container. How many millilitres of water remain in the container?

12 The diagram shows the image of a clock at two different times on a Tuesday morning.

How much time has elapsed between the times on the clocks?

13 How many curved surfaces has a hemisphere?

14 Draw a dotted line to split this rectangle into a trapezium and a triangle.

15 Complete the statement.
A three-quarter turn in a clockwise direction is the same as a ____________ turn in an anticlockwise direction.

16 The map shows the location of five villages. There is no compass drawn on the map. Village *E* is south of *C*.

Complete the statement.

Village *A* is ________ of *D*.

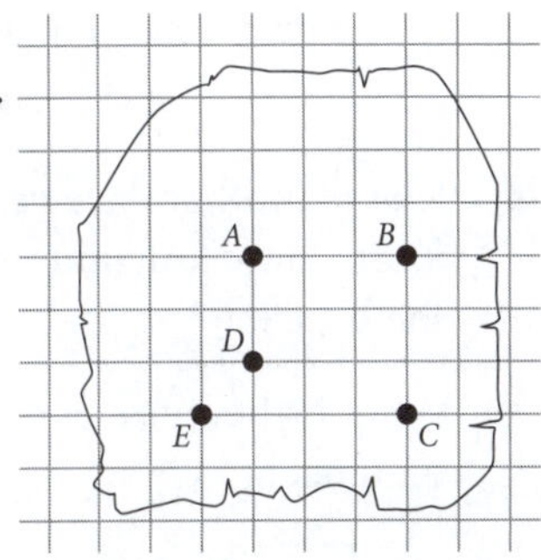

STATISTICS AND PROBABILITY

17 Emma said it is equally likely to spin an even number as it is to spin an odd number. Is she correct?

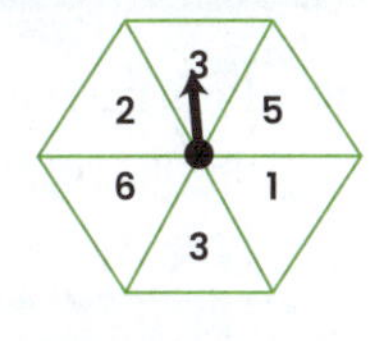

18 The ages of the members of the school band are recorded in the table below.

Age	12	13	14	15	16	17
Number	3	9	11	8	4	3

How many members are between 13 and 16 years old?

NUMBER AND ALGEBRA

1 Here is a number 31 670. Hannah adds 200 to the number. What is the new number?

2 Chelsea has two stacks of cards. One stack has 15 cards and the other has 17. What is the total number of cards?

3 Candice subtracts four hundred from 900. What is her answer?

4 Alyson multiplied eight by four. What is her answer?

5 What is the remainder when 20 is divided by 6?

6 Shade $\frac{1}{6}$ of this shape.

7 Circle the decimal that equals 4.3.

43 4.03 4.300

8 Kiara's mother gave her \$10. She bought a pen for \$5.50. How much money did she have left?

9 What is the missing number in this number sentence?

12 + **?** = 20

MEASUREMENT AND SPACE

10 Lois used a ruler to draw a line 12 cm long. What is the length in millimetres?

11 Some water has been poured into this jug.

How much water is in the jug?

12 Lucy's birthday is 12 days after Esme's birthday.

March

Sunday	Monday	Tuesday	Wednesday	Thursday	Friday	Saturday
					1	2
3	4	5	6	7	8	9
10	11	12	13	14	15	16
17	18	19	20	21	22	23
24	25	26	27	28	29	30
31						

If Lucy was born on 20 March, on what day was Esme born?

13 Here is a 3D shape made of identical cubes.

Draw the front view of the shape.

14 Draw a dotted line to show the line of symmetry of the shape.

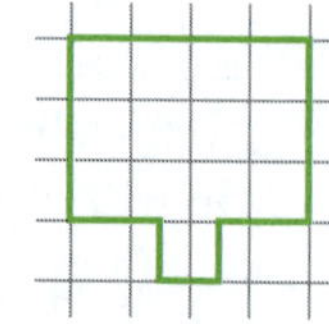

15 Sally reflected the shape about the dotted line.

Draw the image.

16 Here is a regular hexagon. How many angles are larger than a right angle?

STATISTICS AND PROBABILITY

17 A bag has two red balls and four green balls. Which colour is more likely to be selected from the bag?

18 Students were surveyed to find their favourite day in the school week.

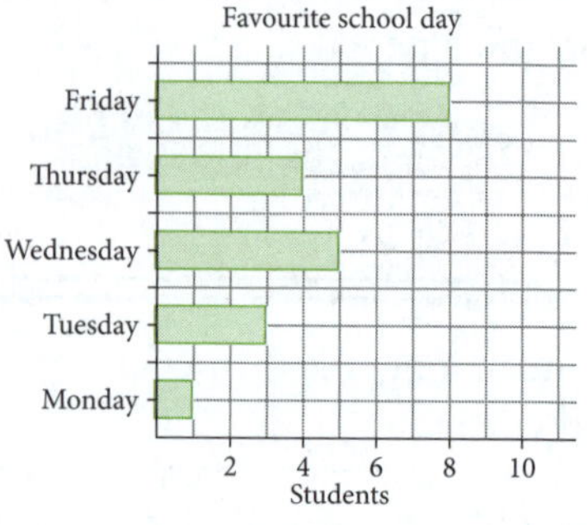

What was the favourite day for most students?

NUMBER AND ALGEBRA

1 To the number 143 739 Rhali adds 5000. What is the new number?

2 Magdalena counted the number of books in her bookcase. There were 12 books on the top shelf, 16 on the second, 14 on the third and 18 on the fourth. How many books were in the bookcase?

3 Aaron subtracts twenty hundreds from 8670. What is his answer?

4 Cans of soft drink are sold in boxes of 12. How many cans are in three boxes?

5 Soren thinks of a number. He divides his number by 5. The answer is 8 with a remainder of 3. What is Soren's number?

6 Shade $\frac{2}{3}$ of this shape.

7 Circle the largest decimal.

3.7 3.07 3.60

8 Remi is given $40 for her birthday. She buys a second-hand game for $29.50. What amount remains?

9 What is the missing number in this number sentence?

74 + **?** = 110

MEASUREMENT AND SPACE

10 Elijah used a ruler to draw a line 270 mm long. What is the length in centimetres?

11 Some water has been poured into this container.

How much more water is needed for it to contain 1 L?

12 Ben's birthday is 11 days after Mabel's birthday.

March

Sunday	Monday	Tuesday	Wednesday	Thursday	Friday	Saturday
					1	2
3	4	5	6	7	8	9
10	11	12	13	14	15	16
17	18	19	20	21	22	23
24	25	26	27	28	29	30
31						

If Mabel was born on 28 March, on what day was Ben born?

13 Here is a 3D shape made of identical cubes.

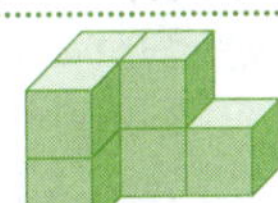

Draw the top view of the shape.

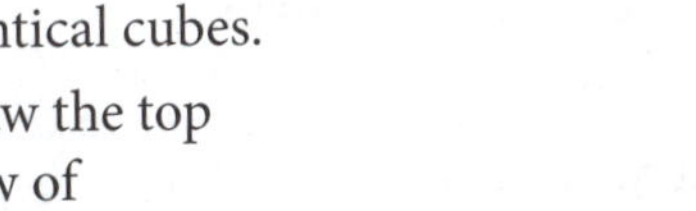

14 Draw a dotted line to show the line of symmetry of the shape.

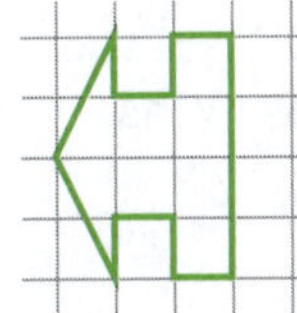

15 Axel reflected the shape about the dotted line.

Draw the image.

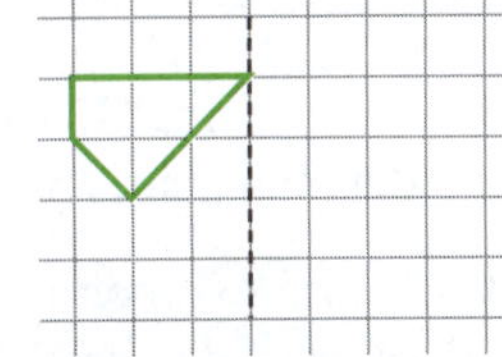

16 Draw a hexagon with three right angles.

STATISTICS AND PROBABILITY

17 A fair coin is tossed at the beginning of a cricket match. In the last four tosses the coin has landed on a head. Oliver says the next toss will certainly be a head. Is he correct?

18 Students were surveyed to find their favourite day in the school week.

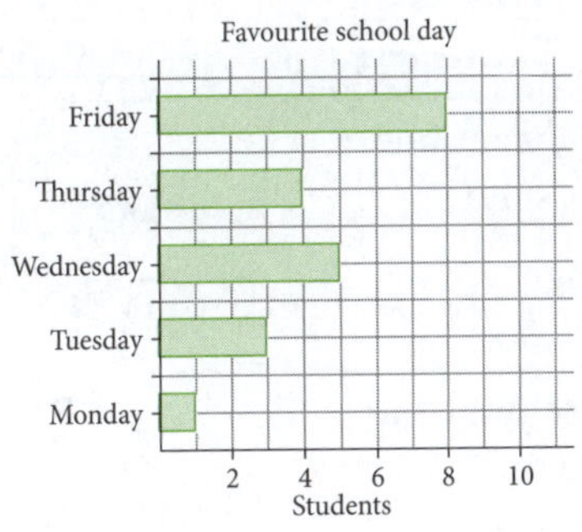

How many students were surveyed?

NUMBER AND ALGEBRA

1 Jared wrote the number twenty-six thousand, two hundred and forty. How many digits are in the number?

2 In a koala colony there were 71 males and 86 females. What was the total population of koalas?

3 After making 96 cupcakes, Mia sold 54. How many cupcakes remain?

4 Hot-cross buns are sold in packets of six. Breda bought seven packets. How many buns did she buy?

5 Dave had 24 mandarins. He gave three mandarins to each of his friends. How many friends received mandarins?

6 What fraction of the shape is shaded?

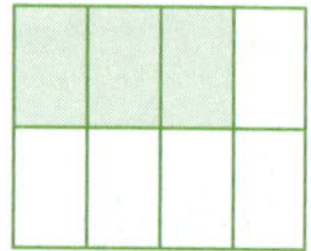

7 Henry wrote 13.672. How many decimal places has Henry's number?

8 A café sells coffees for $5.50. How much did Pedro pay for two coffees?

9 What is the missing number in this number sentence?

42 – ? = 20

MEASUREMENT AND SPACE

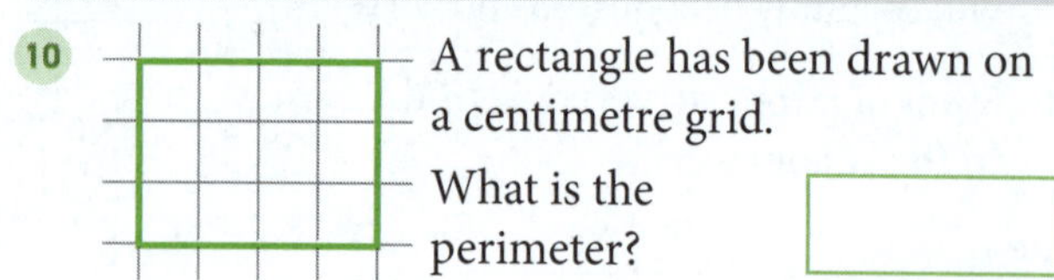

10 A rectangle has been drawn on a centimetre grid. What is the perimeter?

11 How many cubic-centimetre cubes are in this solid?

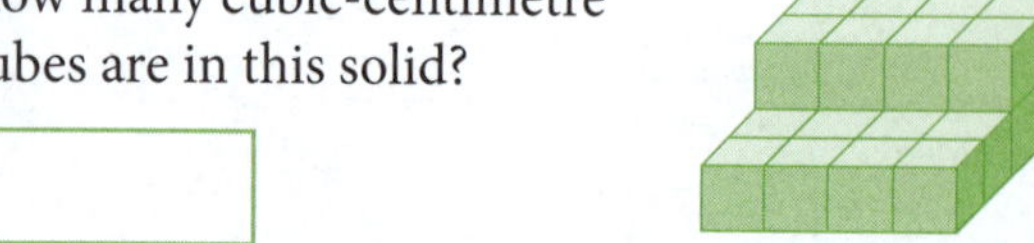

12 On the clock face draw the time twenty-five to eleven.

13 Here is a cylinder. Draw the front view of the shape.

14 Use a dotted line to divide the trapezium into two triangles.

15 The triangle on the right has been translated to form the triangle on the left.

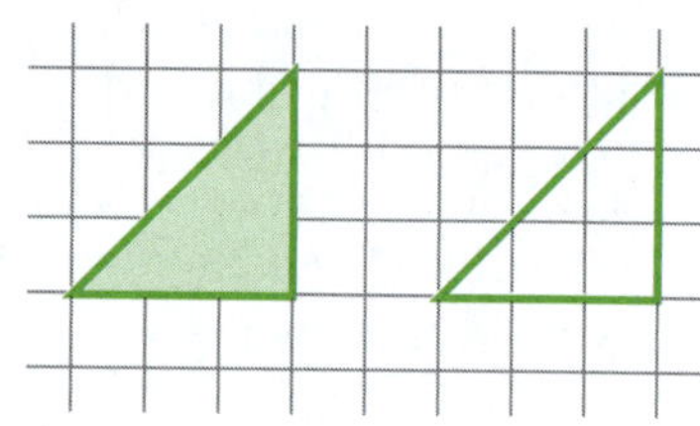

How many units has the triangle been translated?

16 The map shows the location of six towns. Which town is directly east of town *B*?

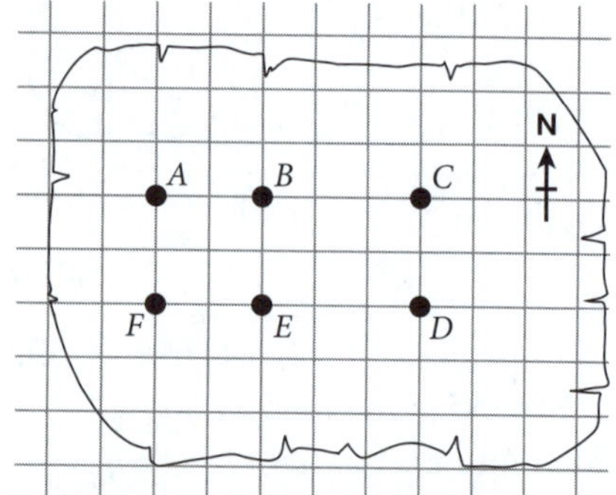

STATISTICS AND PROBABILITY

17 The spinner has three red, two green and a purple section. Some of the sections have been labelled. Use letters to complete the labels.

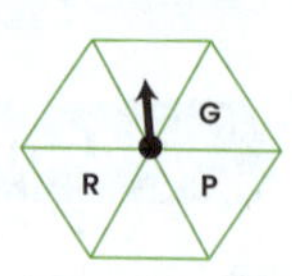

18 The number of pies sold by a bakery before 9 am is recorded.

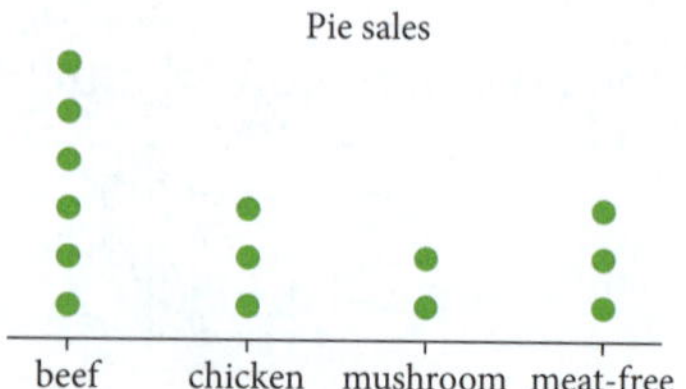

How many meat-free pies were sold?

NUMBER AND ALGEBRA

1 Tristan wrote the number one hundred and eight thousand and forty-one. How many digits are in the number?

2 One morning Hayley counted 16 magpies, 14 cockatoos and 28 ibises flying over her house. What was the total number of birds counted?

3 Greg picks 260 oranges to sell at his roadside stall. After an hour he has sold 75 oranges. How many remain?

4 Mila is to set up eight Christmas trees in a store. Each tree is to have 20 baubles. What is the total number of baubles required?

5 Milo has 48 cards. He divides them into nine groups and has three left over. How many cards are in each group?

6 Circle the fraction of the shape that has been shaded.

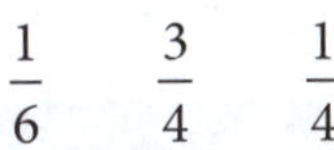

$\frac{1}{6}$ $\frac{3}{4}$ $\frac{1}{4}$

7 Circle the number with the smallest number of decimal places.

3.87 9.231 13.14 536.9

8 Cedric bought three bags of pool salt. If each bag cost $8.50, what was the total cost?

9 What is the missing number in this number sentence?

73 – ? = 58

MEASUREMENT AND SPACE

10 What is the perimeter of the rectangle with dimensions 3 cm and 2 cm?

2 cm

3 cm

11 How many cubic-centimetre cubes are in this solid?

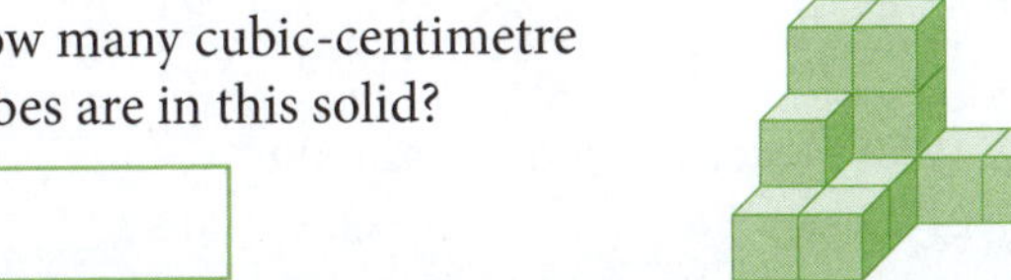

12 On the clock face draw the time which is 20 minutes after 10:45.

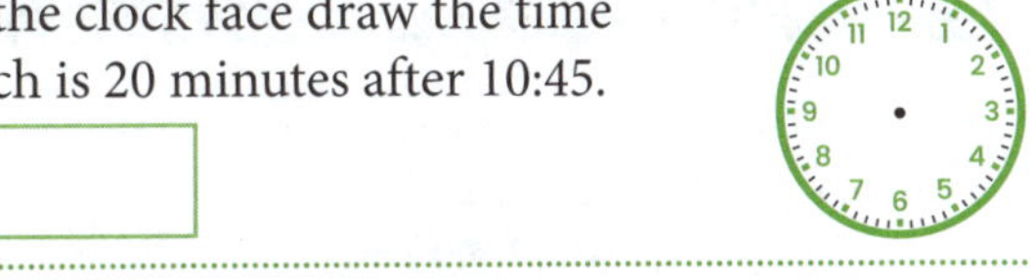

13 Here is a cylinder. Draw the top view of the shape.

14 Use a dotted line to divide the hexagon into two trapeziums.

15 The shape on the left has been translated to form the shape on the right.

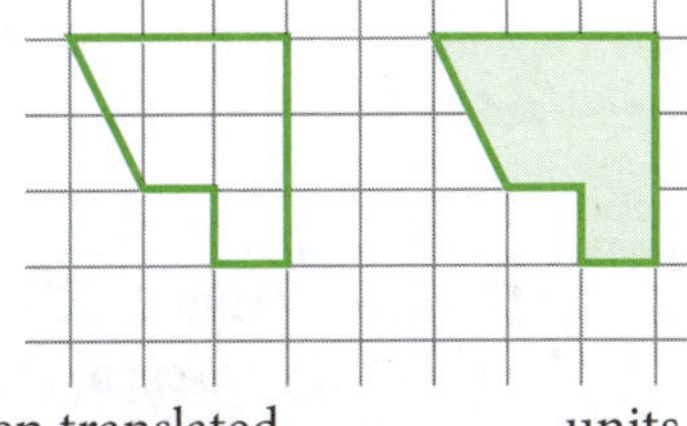

The triangle has been translated __________ units to the __________.

16 The map shows the location of six towns. Which towns are directly west of town *D*?

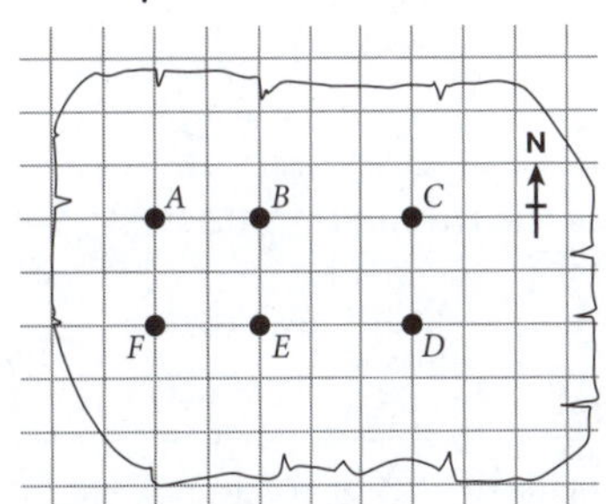

STATISTICS AND PROBABILITY

17 The spinner has an equal number of red and green sections.

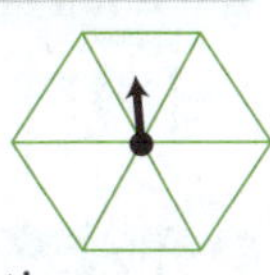

Use the letters *R* and *G* to label the sections.

18 The number of pies sold by a bakery before 9 am is recorded.

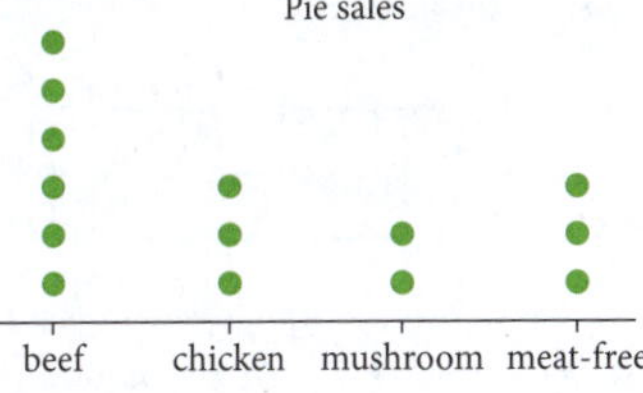

What was the total number of pies sold?

NUMBER AND ALGEBRA

1 Greg owns a property with an area of 4520 hectares. Round the area to the nearest 100 hectares.

2 Sarina added 45 and 55. What was her total?

3 Two hundred and sixty chairs have been placed in the school hall for a student assembly. When all students are seated there are 12 vacant chairs. How many students are seated?

4 Dakota is three times as old as Elle. If Elle is 9 years old, how old is Dakota?

5 Ophelia has 39 plums. She wants to place the plums in bags of seven. How many plums will she have left over?

6 Three identical circles are drawn. Circle the shape with the greatest area shaded.

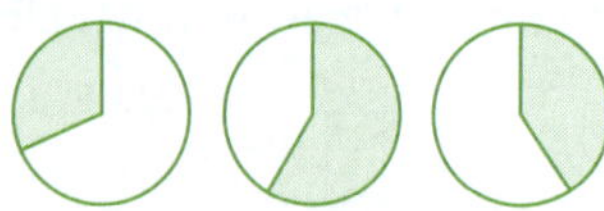

7 What is the missing number?

$0.9 = \frac{\square}{10}$

8 Willa bought a game of Jenga for $27. How much change will she receive from $40?

9 What is the missing number?

, 16, 8, 4, 2, 1

MEASUREMENT AND SPACE

10 A shape has been drawn on a centimetre grid. What is the area of the shape?

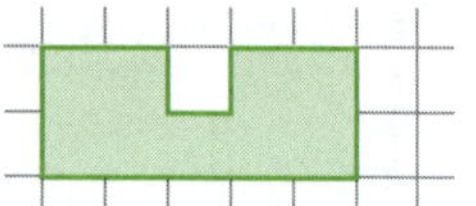

11 A drum contains 12 L of water. A jug will hold 2 L. How many times can the jug be filled with water from the drum?

12 Two years ago the mass of Ava's dog Sally was 15 kg. Sally's mass has since increased by 7 kg. What is the mass of Sally now?

13 What shape are the faces of a cube?

14 Rhea joined these two shapes to form a rectangle.

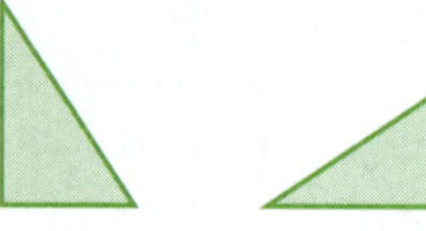

Draw the rectangle.

15 The shape is to be translated 4 units to the right.

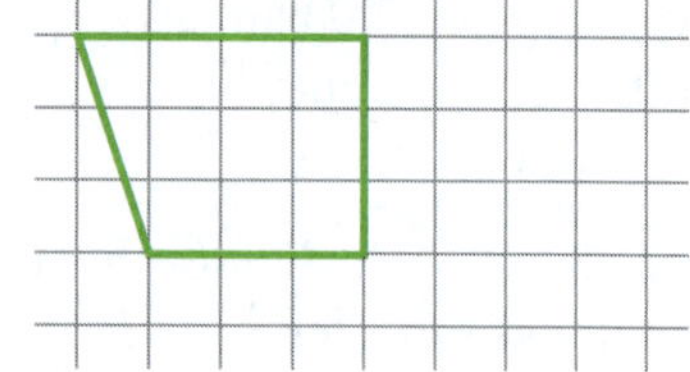

Draw the image.

16 How many half turns make a full turn?

STATISTICS AND PROBABILITY

17 Emery tossed a coin 20 times and recorded the results in a table.

Outcome	Tally
heads	卌 III
tails	卌 卌 II

How many times did the coin land on heads?

18 The savings of four students are shown on the graph.

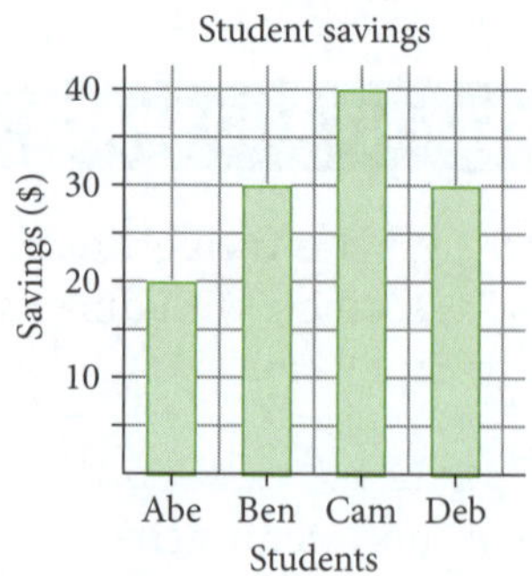

Who saved the smallest amount of money?

NUMBER AND ALGEBRA

1 The number of people who visited a botanical garden last year was approximated as 127 000. Which of these could be the actual number of visitors?

12 690 127 503 127 409 126 499

2 What is the number 578 more than 850?

3 Dane subtracted 3610 from 5720. What is his answer?

4 In a wildlife park there are four times as many kangaroos as there are wombats. If there are 12 wombats, how many kangaroos are there?

5 Ivy has baked 64 small cakes. She places the cakes into boxes of six. How many boxes can she fill?

6 Circle the shape with the greatest fraction shaded.

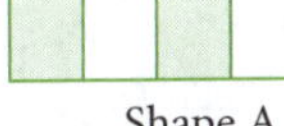

Shape A

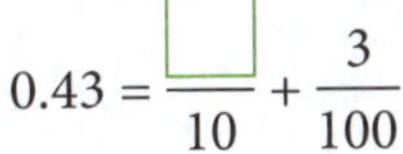

Shape B

7 What is the missing number?

$0.43 = \frac{\square}{10} + \frac{3}{100}$

8 Reuben bought two bags of potatoes. Each bag cost $5.80. What was the total cost?

9 What is the missing number?

? , 1000, 100, 10, 1

MEASUREMENT AND SPACE

10 A shape has been drawn on a centimetre grid.

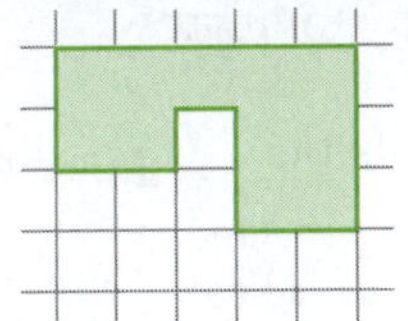

What is the perimeter of the shape?

11 How many cubic-centimetre cubes are in this solid?

12 The mass of a brick is 2 kg 270 g. What is the total mass of two bricks?

13 How many rectangular faces has a hexagonal prism?

14 Simeon joined these two shapes to form a trapezium.

Draw the trapezium.

15 Here is the image of a shape that has been translated 5 units to the right.

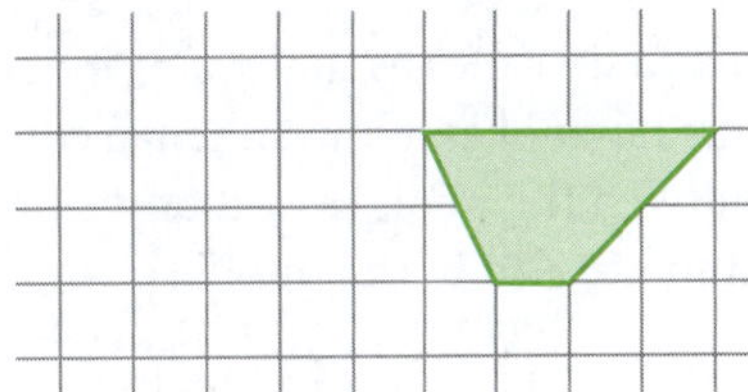

Draw the original shape.

16 How many quarter turns make a half turn?

STATISTICS AND PROBABILITY

17 Henry tossed a coin many times and recorded the results in a table.

Outcome	Tally
heads	卌 卌 ||||
tails	卌 卌 卌 |

How many more times did he record a tail than a head?

18 The savings of four students are shown on the graph.

How much more money was saved by Cam than Abe?

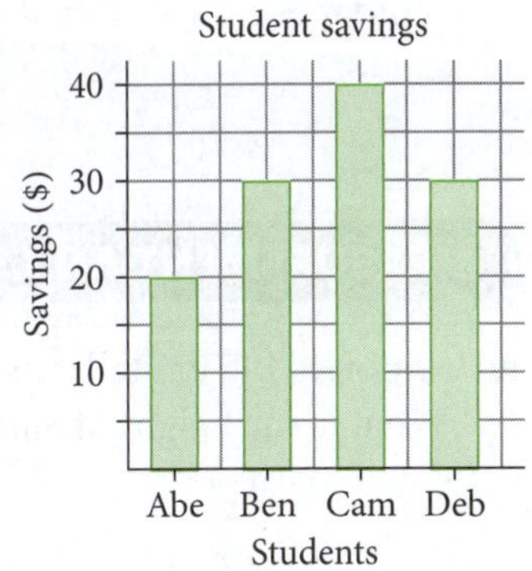

NUMBER AND ALGEBRA

1 Lisa uses these five numbered cards to make numbers.

What is the largest four-digit number she can make?

2 What is the missing digit?

64 + ? 3 = 97

3 Marco grows watermelons and sells them at a roadside stall. If he originally has 45 watermelons and sells 28, how many remain?

4 There are six times as many children in a swimming pool as adults. Shenae counted 11 adults in the pool. How many children are also in the pool?

5 Jackson buys a bag of 24 oranges. He plans to eat three oranges each day. How many days will the oranges last?

6 What fraction has been plotted on the number line?

7 What is $\frac{7}{10}$ written as a decimal?

8 Elio has a total of $60 to give to his three children. Each child receives the same amount. How much will each child receive?

9 What is the missing number in this number sentence?

? − 17 = 30

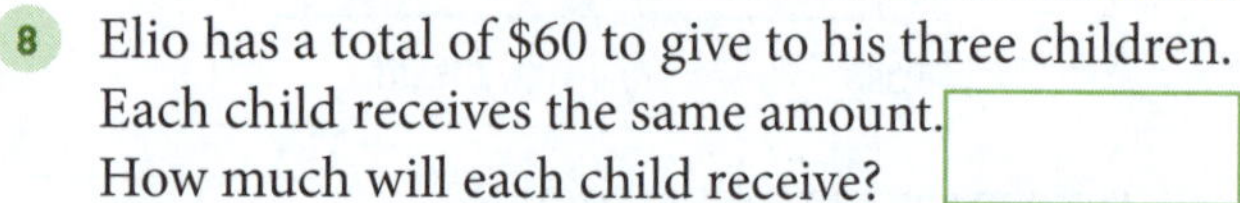

MEASUREMENT AND SPACE

10 Simon is 146 cm tall. His father is 30 cm taller. What is the height of Simon's father?

11 There is 100 mL of cough syrup in a bottle. Cassandra's mother gives her 15 mL of syrup. How much cough syrup remains?

12 Use the blank clock face to show the time 9:17.

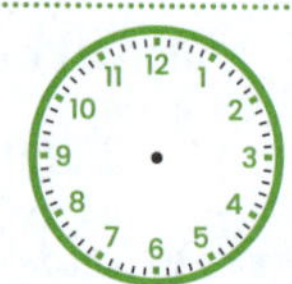

13 Here is a 3D shape made of identical cubes.

Draw the front view of the shape.

14 Daisy has shaded some squares on a grid.

Shade more squares so that the dotted line is a line of symmetry.

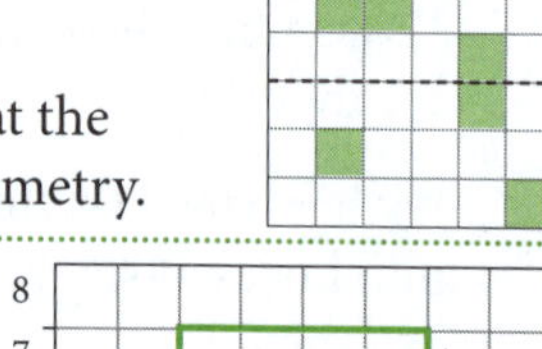

15 The shape is to be translated 3 units down.

Which of these is covered by the image?

E5 C4 C8

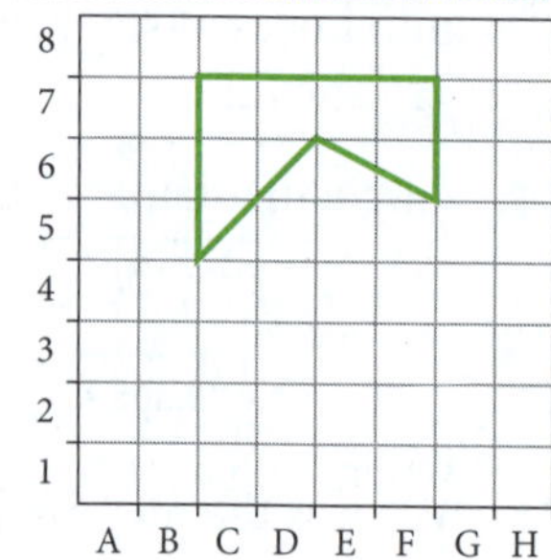

16 The map shows the location of five towns.

Which town is south-west of town *T*?

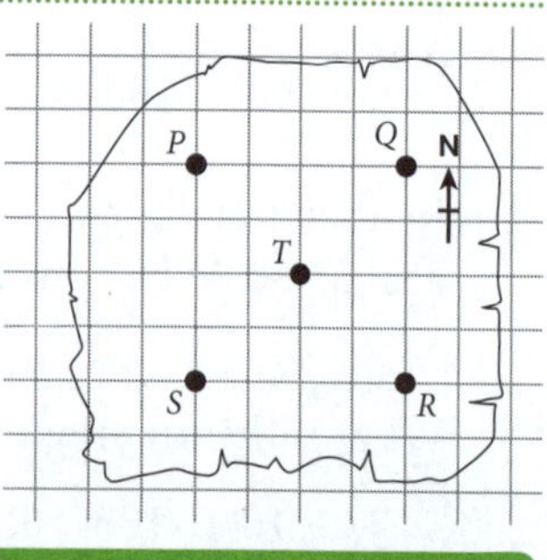

STATISTICS AND PROBABILITY

17 There are 23 students in a class. Which of these words describes the chance that a student has their birthday tomorrow?

impossible possible certain

18 The number of bikes sold in four days is recorded in the table.

On what day were the most bikes sold?

Bike sales	
Day	**Number**
Monday	2
Wednesday	3
Friday	5
Saturday	6

NUMBER AND ALGEBRA

1 Lisa uses these five numbered cards to make numbers.

2 9 7 5 3

What is the number 10 less than the smallest four-digit even number she can make?

2 What is the missing digit?

78 + ? 5 = 123

3 Every morning a farmer milks 436 cows. After an hour there are 98 cows remaining to be milked. How many cows have already been milked?

4 A netball club has 16 teams in the local competition. If there are 10 players on each team, what is the total number of players?

5 What is the remainder when 70 is divided by 6?

6 What mixed numeral has been plotted on the number line?

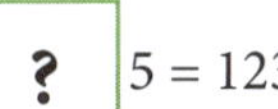

7 Express $8\frac{3}{10}$ as a decimal.

8 The price of a saucepan is $69.95. At a sale the price dropped by $10. What is the new price?

9 What is the missing number in this number sentence?

? − 28 = 45

MEASUREMENT AND SPACE

10 A car odometer shows the distance travelled in kilometres. At the start of a journey Naomi's car had travelled 13 710. When the journey finished it showed 13 916.

How far had Naomi travelled?

11 Sam has a 1-L container of milk in his fridge. He pours 180 mL of milk on his cereal. How much milk remains in the container?

12 Use the blank clock face to show the time 3:48.

13 Here is a 3D shape made of identical cubes.

side view

Draw the side view of the shape.

14 Riley has shaded some squares on a grid.

Shade more squares so that the two dotted lines are lines of symmetry.

15 The shape is to be reflected about the dotted line.

Which of these is covered by the image?

D6 F4 E3

16 The map shows the location of five towns.

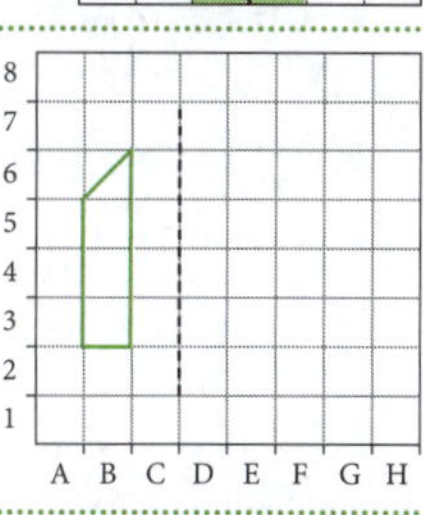

Olivia travelled from *P* to *T*. In which direction did she travel?

STATISTICS AND PROBABILITY

17 Jaime rolls a normal dice. Circle the word that describes the chance that Jaime rolls a number more than 4.

impossible possible certain

18 The number of bikes sold in four days is recorded in the table.

What was the total number of bikes sold?

Bike sales	
Day	**Number**
Monday	2
Wednesday	3
Friday	5
Saturday	6

NUMBER AND ALGEBRA

1 Elise is starting at 996 and counting by twos. What is the fourth number counted?

2 Laila threw three darts at a board. She scored 14, 9 and 26. What was the total of her three darts?

3 A total of 400 people visited an exhibition today. If 260 entered before midday, how many entered after midday?

4 A spider has eight legs. What is the total number of legs on six spiders?

5 Aurora has 24 shells. She uses an equal number of shells to make six necklaces. How many shells are on each necklace?

6 Locate $\frac{3}{5}$ on this number line.

0 1

7 What is $\frac{27}{100}$ written as a decimal?

8 Stamps cost $1.10 each. Orion has six letters that he needs to post. What is the total cost of the stamps?

9 8, 12, 16, ________, 24, 28
What is the missing number in the sequence?

MEASUREMENT AND SPACE

10 A shape has been drawn on a centimetre grid.

What is the area of the shape?

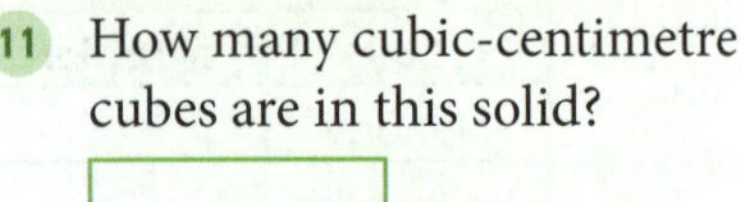

11 How many cubic-centimetre cubes are in this solid?

12 Simone has two bags of rice. Each bag contains 500 g. What is the total mass of rice?

13 How many edges has a rectangular prism?

14 How many diagonals has a rectangle?

15 A shape is being reflected over the dotted line. Part of the image is drawn.

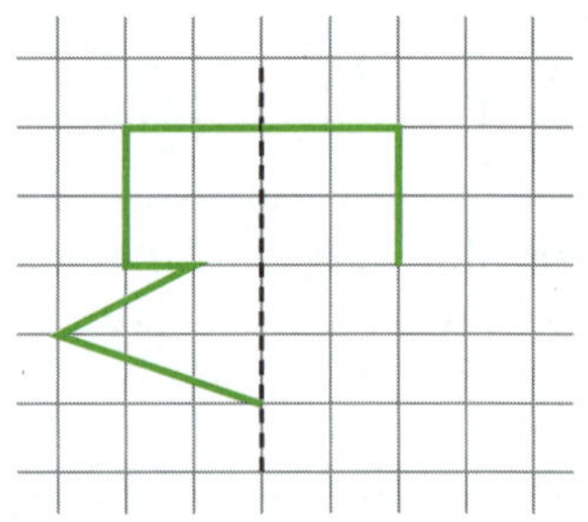

Complete the image.

16 The clock shows 10 o'clock.
What is the time if the minute hand moves a quarter turn?

STATISTICS AND PROBABILITY

17 A box contains numbered balls.

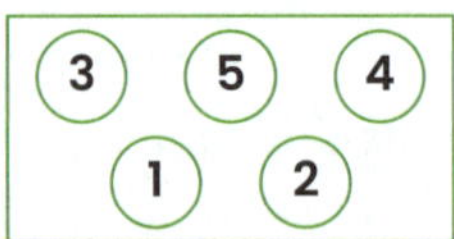

A ball is chosen without looking. Circle the certain result.

The number is even.

The number is less than 6.

18 The graph shows the number of after-school activities that a group of friends participate in each week.
Which person was involved in only one activity?

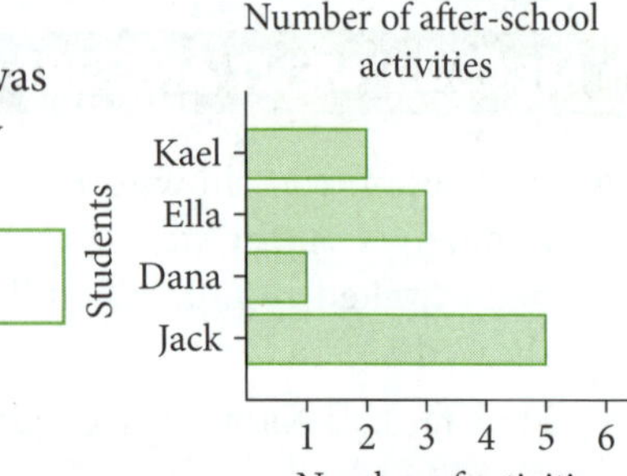

NUMBER AND ALGEBRA

1 How many whole numbers are between the largest even four-digit number and the smallest odd five-digit number?

2 The final score in a basketball game was 59 to 48. What was the total number of points scored in the match?

3 There were 5600 spectators at a match between the Lions and the Tigers. 3700 were supporting the Lions and the remainder were supporting the Tigers. How many spectators were supporting the Tigers?

4 Jessica planted eight rows of beans. In each row there were seven plants. What was the total number of bean plants?

5 Sixty birds are to be relocated into three enclosures. Each enclosure will have an equal number of birds. How many birds will be in each enclosure?

6 Locate $\frac{1}{3}$ on this number line.

0 1

7 What is $3\frac{9}{100}$ written as a decimal?

8 The price of a lawnmower is $380, which is a drop of $50 from the usual price. What is the usual price of the lawnmower?

9 27, 23, 19, ________, 11, 7
What is the missing number in the sequence?

MEASUREMENT AND SPACE

10 A triangle has been drawn on a centimetre grid.
Circle the best estimate for the area of the triangle.

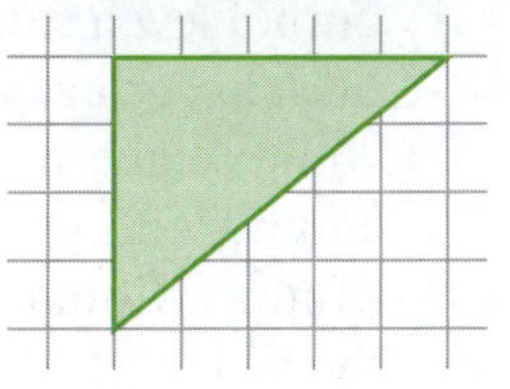

7 cm^2 10 cm^2 13 cm^2

11 A drum contains 12 L of water. A jug that holds 2 L is filled 8 times with water and poured into the drum. How much water is now in the drum?

12 Cassie feeds her dog 110 g of food each day. What mass of dog food is used each week?

13 How many faces does a pentagonal prism have?

14 Draw all the diagonals of this shape.

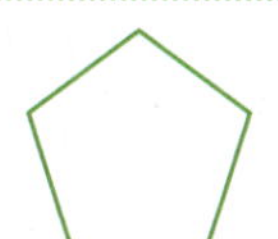

15 A shape is reflected over the dotted line.

Draw the image.

16 A clock is showing the time of 2:00. What is the time if the minute hand moves a quarter turn?

STATISTICS AND PROBABILITY

17 A box contains numbered balls.
A ball is chosen without looking. Circle the less likely result.

The number is even. The number is odd.

18 The graph shows the number of after-school activities for a group of friends each week.
How many friends were involved in more than two activities?

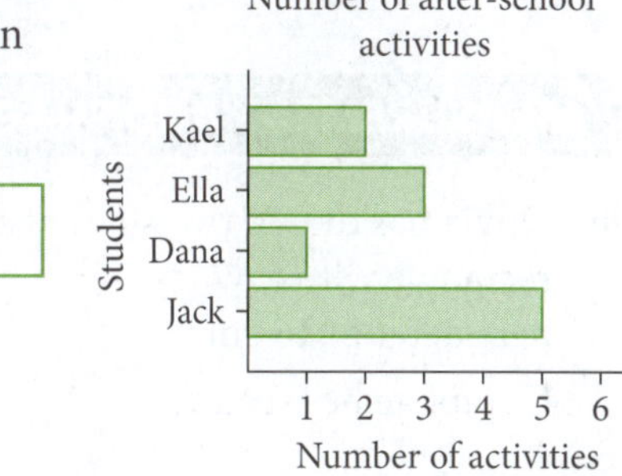

NUMBER AND ALGEBRA

1 Joel used these cards to form the number eight thousand and twenty-nine.

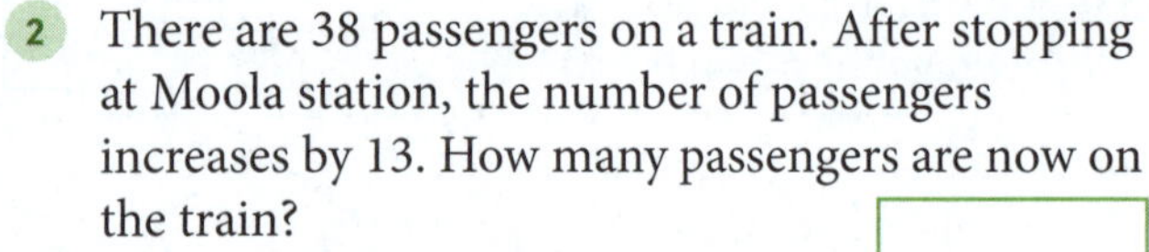

What is the missing number?

2 There are 38 passengers on a train. After stopping at Moola station, the number of passengers increases by 13. How many passengers are now on the train?

3 There are 80 footy cards in a set. Jamie has collected 53 cards. How many more cards are needed to complete the set?

4 Ned has cooked three pizzas and cuts each pizza into six slices. What is the total number of slices?

5 There are 10 books on each shelf of a bookcase. If there is a total of 50 books in the bookcase, how many shelves are in the bookcase?

6 What is the missing number?

$\frac{7}{4} = 1\frac{?}{4}$

7 Circle the number less than 1 which has a 6 in the hundredths place and a 2 in the tenths place.

1.26 0.206 0.26 2.615

8 Magnus bought a calculator for $16.50 and a glue stick for $2.10. What was the total cost?

9 Jay is counting by 5s starting at 10. What is the fourth number he counts?

MEASUREMENT AND SPACE

10 Olivia has drawn two sides of a rectangle with a perimeter of 16 cm.

Complete her rectangle.

11 A solid is formed using three layers of 10 cubes. Each cube has a volume of 1 cm³. What is the volume of the solid?

12 Ottilie arrives at the bus stop at 10:15. She waits 8 minutes for her bus. At what time does her bus arrive?

13 Lochie uses five cubes to make this solid. Draw the side view of the solid.

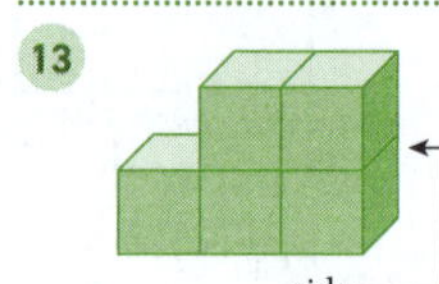

14 Here is a trapezium. How many pairs of parallel sides has the trapezium?

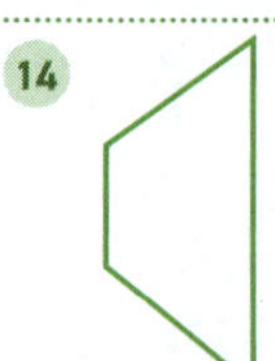

15 The shape is to be translated 3 units up.

Which of these is covered by the image?

D5 B4 C8

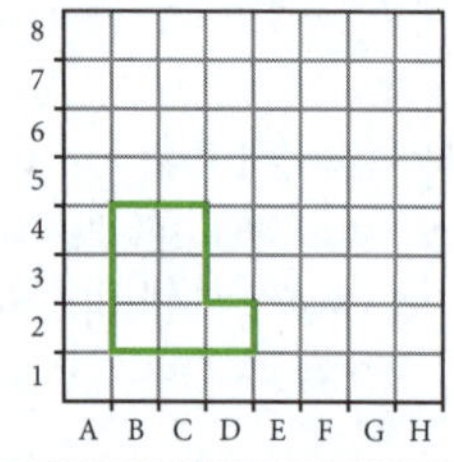

16 The map shows the location of six towns.

What town is directly west of *E*?

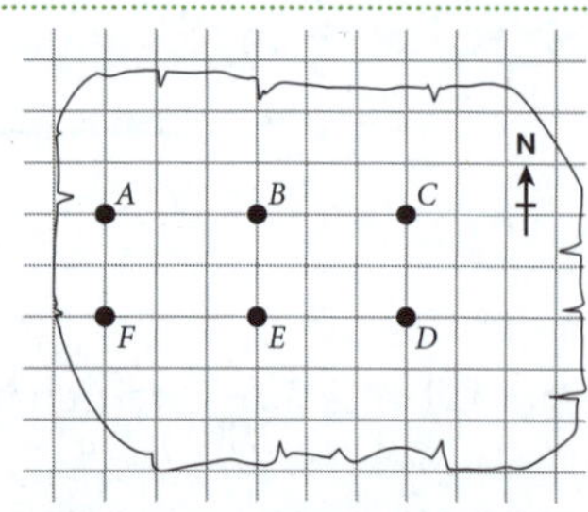

STATISTICS AND PROBABILITY

17 A bag contains jelly beans. There are 12 red jelly beans and 16 black jelly beans in the bag. Without looking, a jelly bean is removed from the bag. What is the more likely colour chosen?

18 Students recorded the season in which they were born. Eleven students were born in spring, seven in winter, eight in autumn and six in summer. Complete the table.

Season of birth	
Season	**Number**
Summer	
Autumn	
Winter	
Spring	

NUMBER AND ALGEBRA

1 Matt makes four-digit numbers using these cards.

How many numbers between 3000 and 7000 can be formed?

2 Last week a total of 118 tickets had been sold for the school musical. This week another 65 tickets were sold. How many tickets have now been sold?

3 Emily buys five dozen eggs. She uses 28 eggs to make some cakes. How many eggs remain?

4 Josh cuts 10 apples into quarters. How many quarters are there?

5 Each table in a restaurant has four chairs. There are 48 people seated and every chair is used. How many tables are in the restaurant?

6 What is the missing number?

$2\frac{1}{3} = \frac{?}{3}$

7 Write a number between 12 and 13 which has a 5 in the hundredths place and a 2 in the tenths place.

8 Jade bought a bag of grapes for $3.68 and loaf of bread for $4.20. What was the total cost?

9 Roman is counting by 5s, starting at 2. Which of these is a number he will count?

28 35 31 37

MEASUREMENT AND SPACE

10 Finley has drawn one side of a rectangle with a perimeter of 18 cm.

Complete the rectangle.

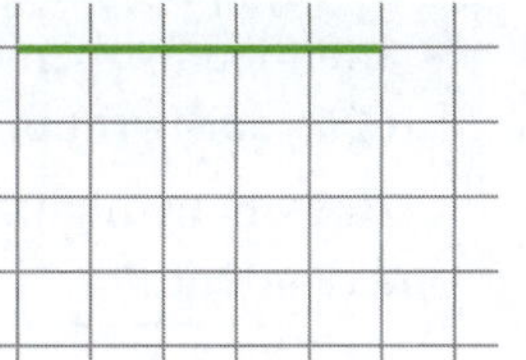

11 A solid is formed using four layers of 12 cubes each. Each cube has a volume of 1 cm^3. What is the volume of the solid?

12 Freya has a dental appointment at 3:10. She arrives 12 minutes early. At what time does Freya arrive?

13 Campbell uses seven cubes to make this solid.

Draw the view of the solid from the left

14 Henry measured the lengths of the sides of a triangle. Two of the sides were each 8 cm. Which of these is **not** a possible length of the third side? Circle the length(s).

6 cm 12 cm 17 cm

15 The shape is to be reflected about the dotted line. Which of these is covered by the image?

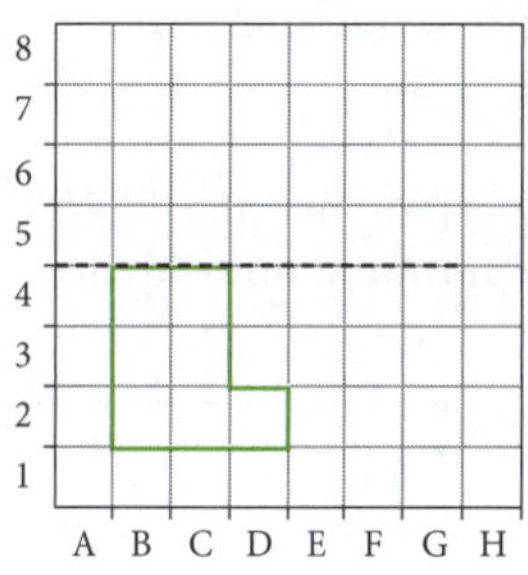

B4 C6 D6

16 The map shows the location of six towns.

Which town is south-east of *B*?

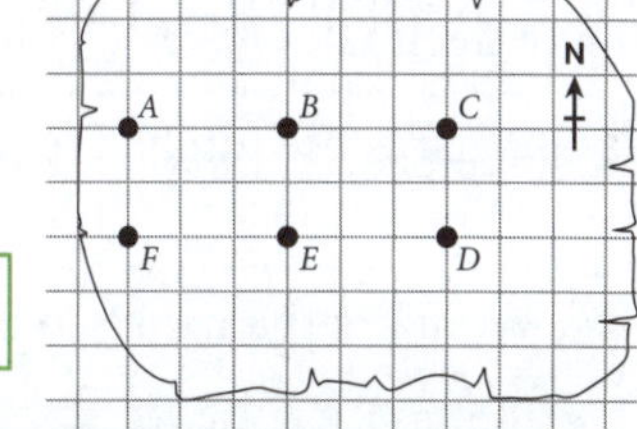

STATISTICS AND PROBABILITY

17 A bag contains 24 jelly beans. There are 14 red jelly beans and the remainder are black. Without looking, a jelly bean is removed from the bag and eaten. What is the more likely colour chosen?

18 Thirty students recorded the season in which they were born. Ten students were born in spring, nine in winter and six in autumn. Write the numbers in the table and work out how many students were born in summer.

Season of birth	
Season	**Number**
Summer	
Autumn	
Winter	
Spring	

NUMBER AND ALGEBRA

1 What is the missing number?

3672 = 3000 + 600 + ? + 2

2 There are 36 adults and 28 children on a ferry. What is the total number of passengers?

3 What number subtracted from 20 leaves 9?

4 Kale is collecting cricket cards. Each packet he buys contains five cards. How many cards are in nine packets?

5 What is the remainder when 31 is divided by 9?

6 Here is a shape made of identical squares. Jayce has already shaded one square.

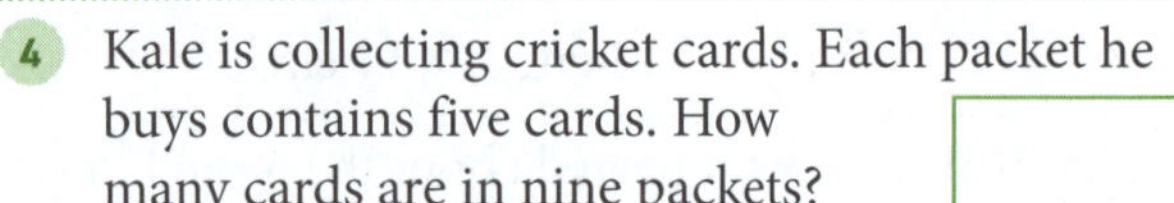

Four-fifths of the shape needs to be shaded. How many more squares will Jayce shade?

7 What is $4 + \frac{3}{10} + \frac{9}{100}$ written as a decimal?

8 What is the total of $43 and $39?

9 What are the next two numbers in this sequence?

34, 38, 42, 46, ________, ________

MEASUREMENT AND SPACE

10 Callum competed in the shot-put. In his first attempt he threw 8 m 15 cm. What is this distance in centimetres?

11 A jug contains 220 mL of water. Sharne adds 1 L of water to the jug. How many millilitres of water is now in the jug?

12 Kai and his brother Loki measured their mass on the bathroom scales. Loki was 6 kg heavier than his brother. If Kai measured 28 kg, what was Loki's mass?

13 Sam built a 3D model with four triangular faces and one rectangular face. What is the name of the shape?

14 How many lines of symmetry has this quadrilateral?

15 Eva rotated the shape a quarter turn clockwise about the point X.

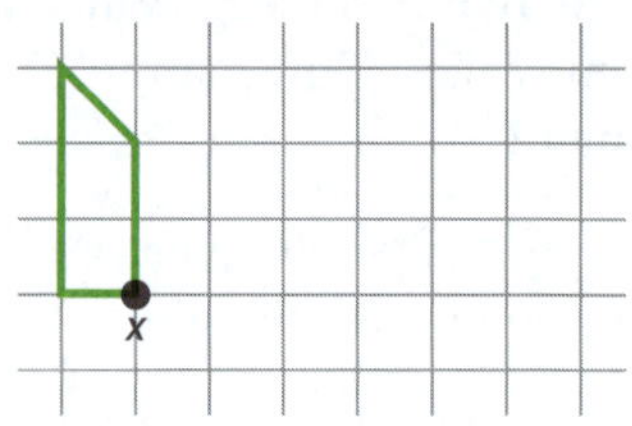

Draw the image.

16 Circle the correct word missing from the statement.

The angle between the minute and hour hand is ________ than a right angle.

smaller larger

STATISTICS AND PROBABILITY

17 Silas cut these shapes out of cardboard.

His friend closed their eyes and pointed to a shape. Circle the chance they pointed to a shape with four sides.

likely unlikely certain impossible

18 The graph shows the number of Friday nights attended by members of a youth group.

How many nights did Ava attend?

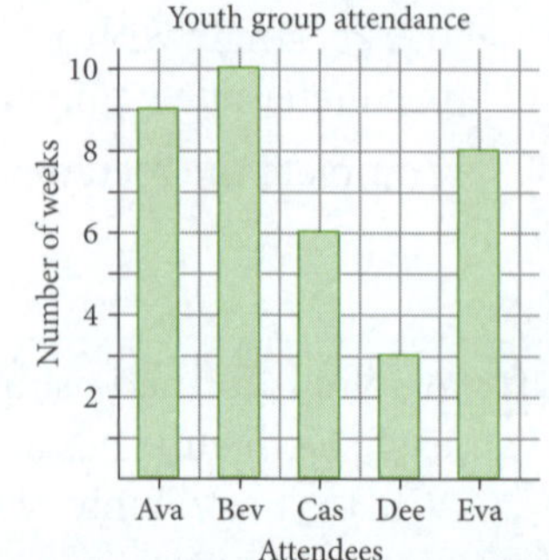

NUMBER AND ALGEBRA

1 What is the missing number?

50 000 + 80 + 2 = ?

2 Bethany cycled 30 km on Monday and Wednesday mornings. She cycled 45 km on Friday and Saturday afternoons. On the other days she rested. How far did she cycle during the week?

3 What number subtracted from 60 leaves 34?

4 How many sides are on nine hexagons?

5 Silas thinks of a number. He divides his number by 7. The answer is 9 with a remainder of 6. What is Silas's number?

6 Here is a shape made of identical squares. Nicole has already shaded one square.

Two-thirds of the shape needs to be shaded. How many more squares will Nicole shade?

7 What is $600 + 4 + \frac{5}{100}$ written as a decimal?

8 What is the total of $32, $40 and $16?

9 What are the next two numbers in this sequence?

94, 87, 80, 73, ______, ______

MEASUREMENT AND SPACE

10 Eli measured the length of his stride as 90 cm. He walked 20 steps. How many metres did Eli walk?

11 A watering can contains 8 L 670 mL of water. Dion pours 3 L 260 mL of water on a tree. What amount of water remains in the watering can?

12 A carton contains 10 cans of beans. The mass of each can is 430 g. What is the total mass of cans in the carton?

13 A pyramid has six triangular faces as well as a base. What is the shape of the base?

14 How many lines of symmetry has this shape?

15 Asher rotated the shape a quarter turn clockwise about the point X.

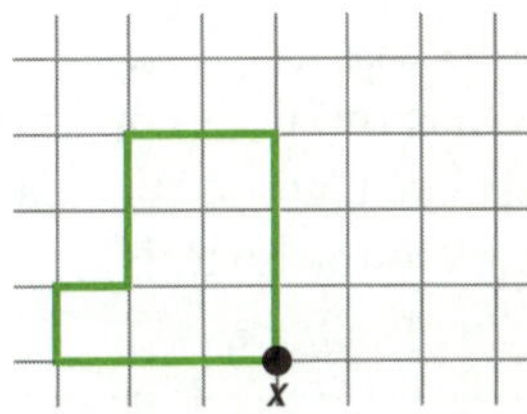

Draw the image.

16 Circle the correct word missing from the statement.

The angle between the minute and hour hand is ______ than a right angle.

smaller larger

STATISTICS AND PROBABILITY

17 At the official opening of a store, every fifth shopper is given a discount voucher. Eva visits the shop. Circle the chance that she is given a voucher.

impossible unlikely

likely certain

18 The graph shows the number of Friday nights attended by members of a youth group. Who attended twice as often as Dee?

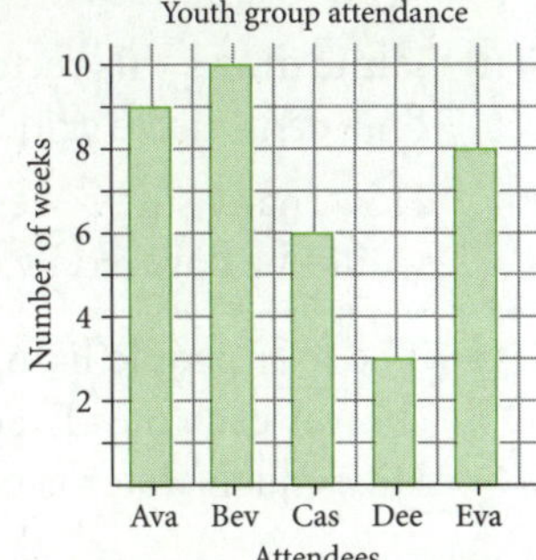

NUMBER AND ALGEBRA

1 A museum exhibition has 2949 visitors. What is the number of visitors, to the nearest thousand?

2 Deni has 12 marbles in one bag, nine marbles in a second bag and 13 marbles in a third bag. How many marbles has Deni in total?

3 Carey needs to sign up 100 sponsors for her fundraising walk. She already has 72 sponsors. How many more sponsors does she need?

4 Mr Jenkins has five boxes on his desk. In each box there are six calculators. What is the total number of calculators in the boxes?

5 A box contains 32 apples. The apples are arranged in four layers. How many apples are in each layer?

6 Here are six avocados. Draw a box around one-third of the avocados.

7 Write the number represented by 8 hundreds, 9 tens, 2 ones and 4 tenths.

8 Helena bought $4.77 worth of salami at a deli. The price was rounded to the nearest five cents. How much was Helena charged?

9 What is the next number in this sequence? 2, 20, 200, ________

MEASUREMENT AND SPACE

10 Jamie draws this rectangle on a centimetre grid.

5 cm

1 cm

How many square centimetres would be covered by the rectangle?

11 The four people living in an apartment have a shower each day. Every shower uses 90 L of water. How much water is used each day?

12 Circle the time that is 5 minutes before 10 to 6.

10 to 11 5 to 6 quarter to 6

13 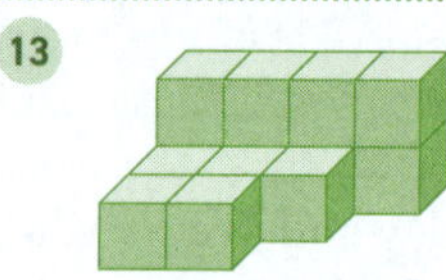

Here is a 3D shape made of identical cubes.

Draw the front view of the shape.

14 Draw a regular quadrilateral.

15 The shape is to be reflected about the dotted line.

Draw the image.

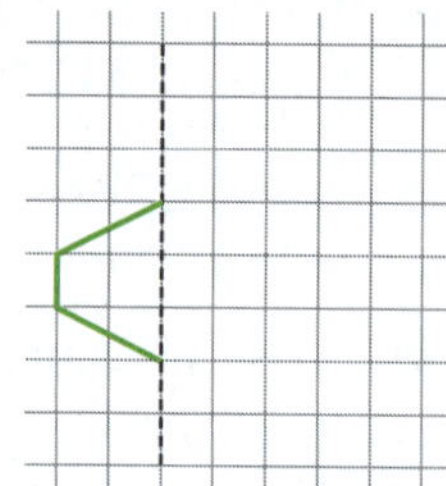

16 The map shows the path used by Xi to walk from *A* to *E*.

In which direction did Xi walk between *B* and *C*?

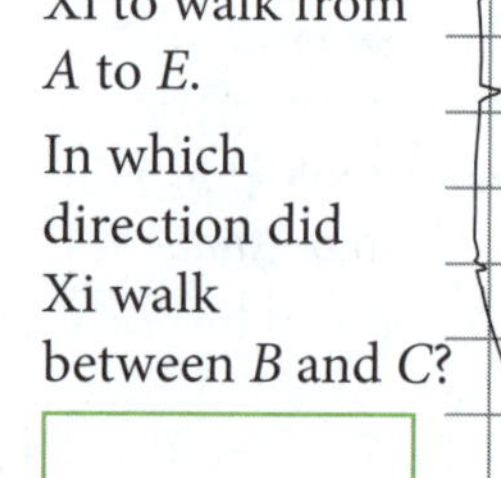

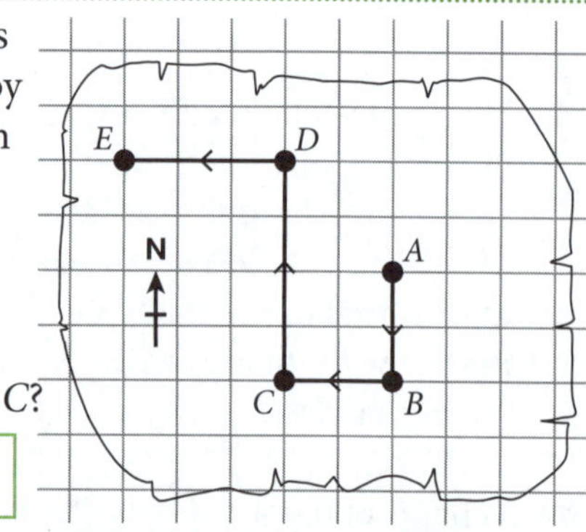

STATISTICS AND PROBABILITY

17 These numbered cards are placed in a bag.

7 3 9 5 1

One card is chosen from the bag without looking. Circle the chance that the card is even.

certain likely unlikely impossible

18 The graph shows the number of pages Olivia read during the week.

On how many days did Olivia read more than 14 pages?

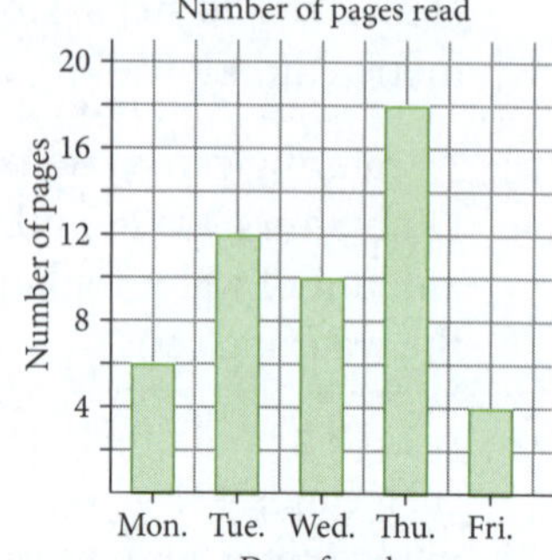

NUMBER AND ALGEBRA

1 The total number of people who watched a video on social media was 895 782. What is this number, to the nearest ten thousand?

2 For the school market day Gisele, Brooke and Sloan baked cupcakes. Gisele baked 36, Brooke 24 and Sloan 16. What was the total number of cupcakes baked?

3 A bookstore had 110 books for sale. If 87 books were sold in the first week, how many are still available?

4 A container holds 40 peaches. How many peaches are in five containers?

5 What is the missing number?

$$4\overline{)80} = \boxed{?}$$

6 Amaya records the number of netball goals she scored in a game.

卌 卌 卌 卌

Her friend Cali scored a quarter of the number of goals scored by Amaya. How many goals did Cali score?

7 Write the number represented by 3 hundreds, 7 ones and 6 hundredths.

8 Dawson buys bananas and blueberries. The bananas cost $2.21 and the blueberries cost $3.50. What is the total cost, rounded to the nearest five cents?

9 What is the next number in this sequence? 3, 24, 45, 66, ______

MEASUREMENT AND SPACE

10 Silas draws a 5 cm by 4 cm rectangle on a centimetre grid. How many square centimetres would be covered by the rectangle?

11 A swimming pool has 37 500 L of water. James uses a hose to add more water to the pool. After two hours there is 39 000 L in the pool. How much water was added?

12 Use the clock face to show the time that is 25 minutes after 10 to 7.

13 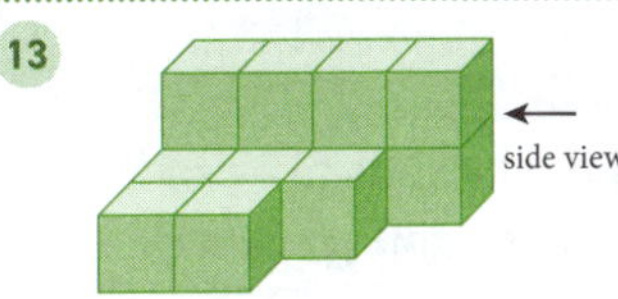

Here is a 3D shape made of identical cubes.

Draw the side view of the shape.

14 Draw an irregular triangle.

15 The shape is to be reflected about the dotted line.

Draw the image.

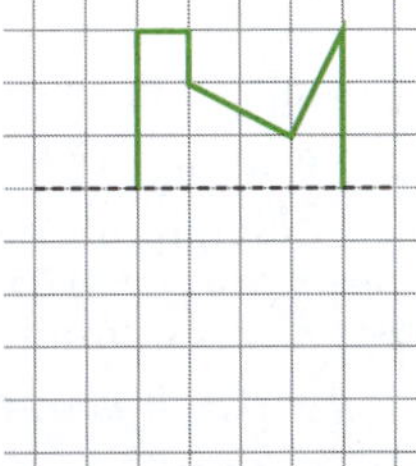

16 Jai drew this map but forgot to show the compass.

He knows that *B* is north of *C*.

What is the direction of *C* from *D*?

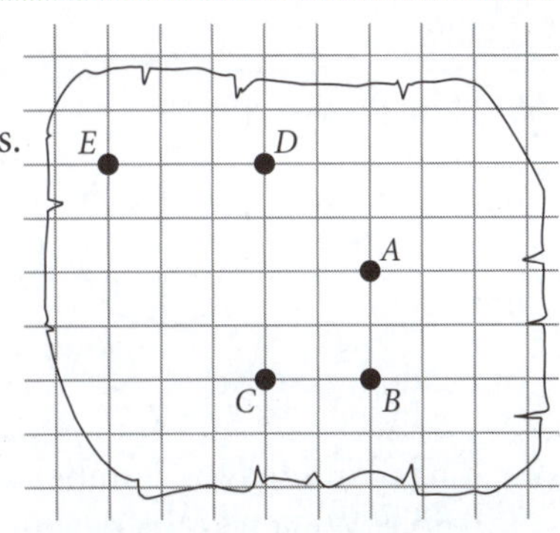

STATISTICS AND PROBABILITY

17 These numbered cards are placed in a bag.

7 3 9 5 1

One card is chosen from the bag without looking. Circle the chance that the card is less than 6.

certain likely unlikely impossible

18 The graph shows the number of pages Emma read during the week.

How many pages were read on the five days?

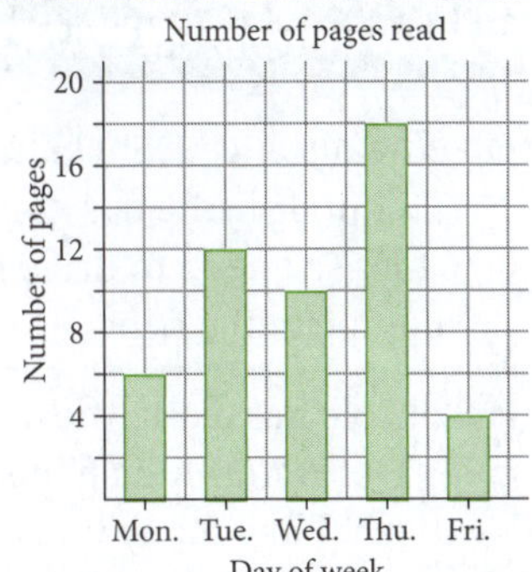

NUMBER AND ALGEBRA

1 Shona wrote the number 7263. She rearranged the digits to make the smallest possible number. What is the new number?

2 George plays a game where he rolls five normal dice and adds the numbers on top of each dice. What is the total if he rolls three 6s and two 1s?

3 A car park has 98 car spaces. By 9 am, 63 cars were parked. How many spaces were still available?

4 Hiro squeezes four oranges to fill a glass. How many oranges will he need to fill eight glasses?

5 A box contains 40 paperclips. Cora arranges the paperclips into eight equal groups. How many paperclips are in each group?

6 Here are two circles.

Shade $1\frac{1}{2}$ circles.

7 Jonas rounded the number 18.6 to the nearest whole. What was the new number?

8 Pallavi bought some craft supplies for $37. What was her change from $50?

9 What is the missing number?

5060, 5070, 5080, 5090, ☐

MEASUREMENT AND SPACE

10 The distance from Gunnedah to Tamworth is 77 km. If Esme has already driven 56 km, how far does she need to drive to complete the trip?

11 Nicole has a dual-flush toilet. A full-flush uses 5 L of water. A half-flush uses 2 L less than a full-flush. How many litres of water are used in a half-flush?

12 Helga opened a 200-g bag of peanuts. She ate 50 g of peanuts. What mass remains in the bag?

13 A 3D shape has one flat surface, one curved surface and does not have an apex. Circle the name of the shape.

cylinder cone hemisphere

14 Avra has started to draw a shape. The dotted line is a line of symmetry.
Complete the shape.

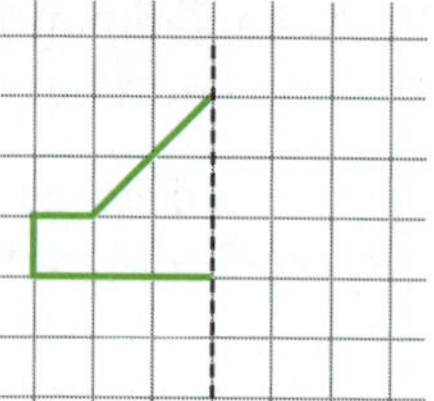

15 Agnes used the dotted line to reflect the triangle.
Draw the image.

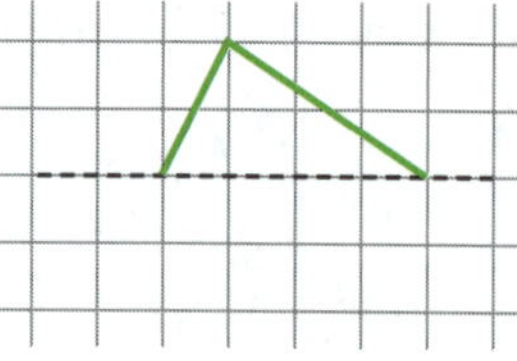

16 Here is a trapezium.
Tick the angles that are larger than a right angle.

STATISTICS AND PROBABILITY

17 A small ball is hidden under one of the cups.

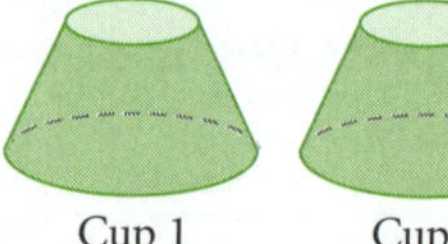

Cup 1 Cup 2 Cup 3

Dylan chooses Cup 3. Circle the chance he has chosen the cup which contains the ball.

certain likely unlikely impossible

18 The number of goals scored by some teammates is recorded.

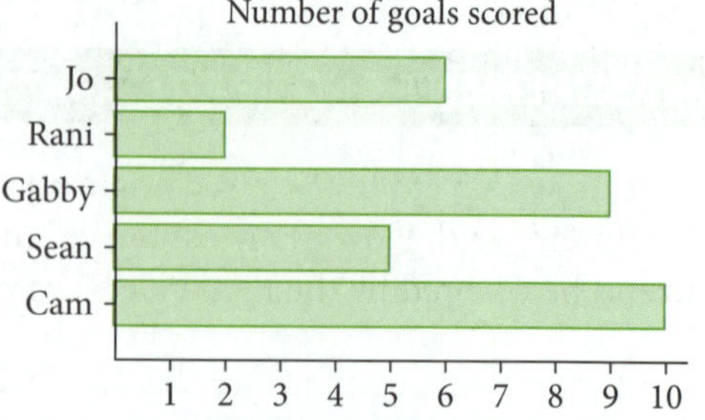

What was the total number of goals scored by Sean and Cam?

NUMBER AND ALGEBRA

1 Kelly wrote the number 189 324. She rearranged the digits to make the greatest possible number less than 800 000. What is the new number?

2 Scottie is 9 years old. His father is 32 years older than Scottie. What is the total of their ages?

3 In an election Tarek received 760 votes and James 340 votes. How many more people voted for Tarek than James?

4 What is the missing number?

$23 \times 6 = 20 \times 6 + \boxed{?} \times 6$

5 A club has purchased 120 new soccer balls. The balls are evenly distributed among 10 teams. How many balls are given to each team?

6 The shape consists of three rows of rectangles.

Shade $1\frac{1}{3}$ rows of rectangles.

7 Valentina rounded a number to be 13.8. Which of these is the possible number before rounding?

13.74 13.7 13.84

8 Elena bought a book for her daughter costing \$15.90. What was her change from \$20?

9 What is the missing number?

1234, 2345, 3456, 4567,

MEASUREMENT AND SPACE

10 Lucas places eight identical pencils end to end. The length of each pencil is 12 cm. What is the total length of the pencils?

11 In every wash Liam's dishwasher uses 15 L of water. If he uses the dishwasher once a day, how much water does he use in a week?

12 A prism balances four identical 80-g cylinders on a set of scales. What is the mass of the prism?

13 Grant has two identical cubes. The face of one cube is glued to a face of the other cube. What is the name of the new shape?

14 Ava has started to draw a picture. The dotted lines are lines of symmetry.

Complete the shape.

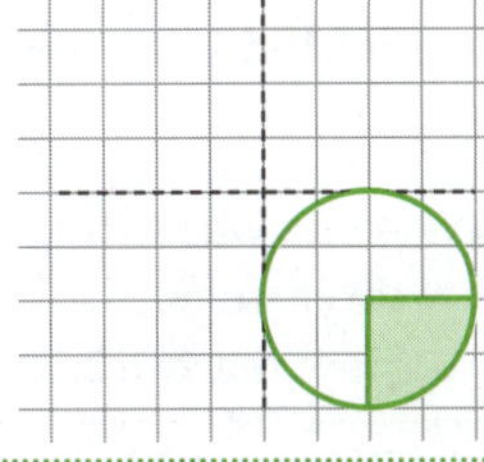

15 Evelyn is translating the shape. She has started to draw the image.

Complete the drawing of the image.

16 The diagram shows a triangle inside a square.

Tick the angles that measure less than a right angle.

STATISTICS AND PROBABILITY

17 Ariana rolled three normal dice and added the top numbers. Circle the chance that the total was 3.

certain likely unlikely impossible

18 The number of goals scored by some teammates is recorded.

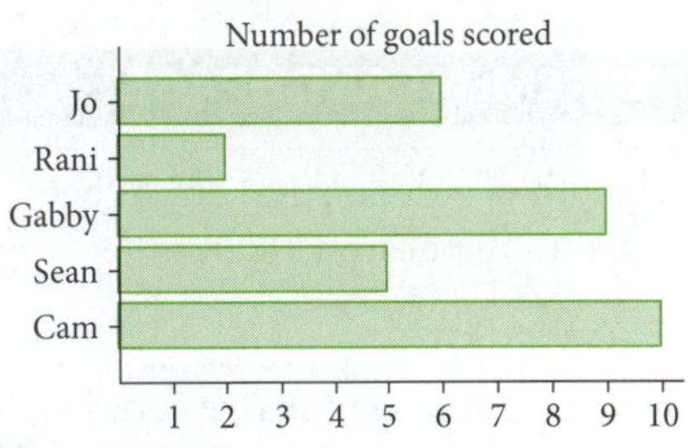

How many players scored more than three goals?

NUMBER AND ALGEBRA

1 On three days it rained. 32 mm fell on the first day, 10 mm on the second and 19 mm on the third. Which of these is the best estimate of the total amount of rainfall?

40 mm   50 mm   60 mm

2 Jayden sold 28 cups of homemade lemonade on Saturday and another 24 cups on Sunday. What was the total number of cups sold?

3 Greta has uploaded 47 videos to social media, which is 16 more than Beth. How many videos has Beth uploaded?

4 Anna was sitting in a park. She saw a man walking three dogs. She counted all the legs. How many legs did she count?

5 Six cakes fill a box. How many boxes are filled using 42 cakes?

6 Here is a number line.

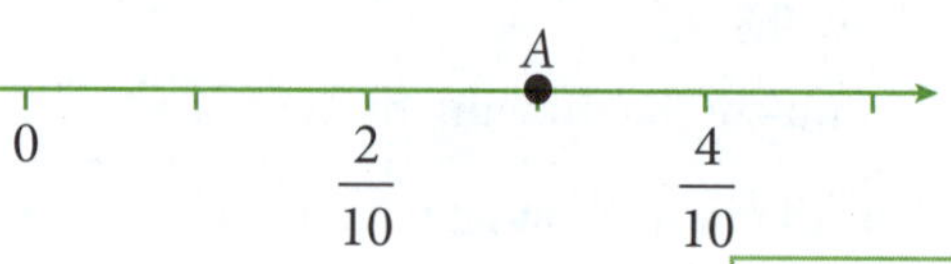

What number is located at *A*?

7 Circle the smallest decimal.

2.1   1.87   0.998

8 Matilda buys a puzzle which costs $11.90 and a magazine for $6. What is the total cost?

9 What is the missing number?

$\frac{1}{10}, \frac{3}{10}, \frac{5}{10}, \frac{7}{10}$, ?

MEASUREMENT AND SPACE

10 The length of a desk is 162 cm. What is this length rounded to the nearest 10 cm?

11 How many cubic-centimetre cubes are in this solid?

12 What is the missing number?

70 minutes = 1 h ? min

13 Here is a pyramid. Draw the front view of the shape.

14 Ling measures the length of each side of a rhombus. She adds the lengths and her total is 20 cm. What is the length of each side of the rhombus?

15 The shape is to be translated 4 units left.

Draw the image.

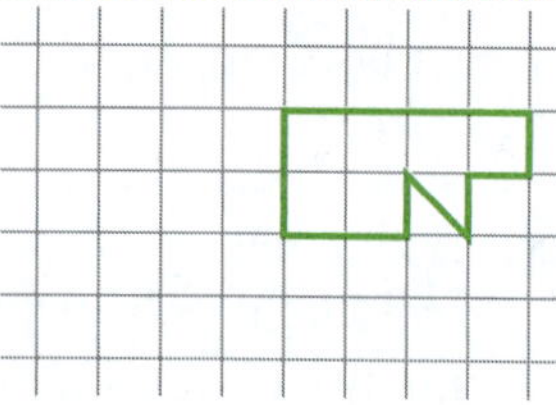

16 The map uses a scale where 1 unit represents 5 km.

What is the distance from *B* to *C*?

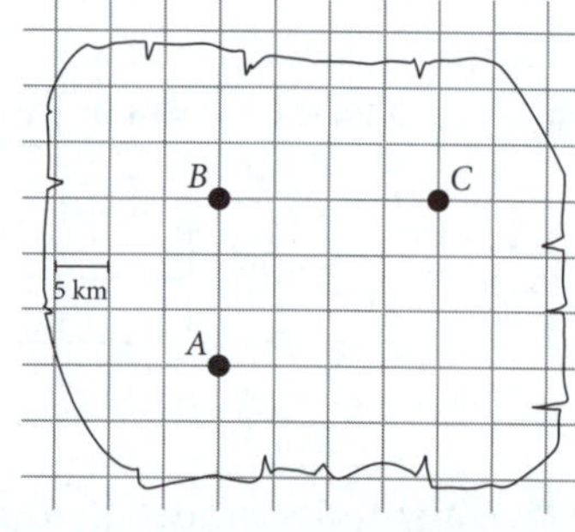

STATISTICS AND PROBABILITY

17 The arrow on this spinner is spun.

True or false?

There is no chance that the arrow lands on blue.

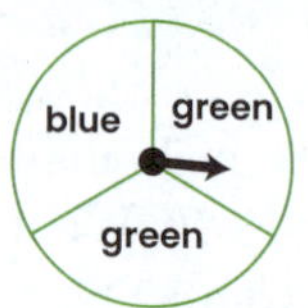

18 The number of hours students spent watching television yesterday is recorded in the graph.

How many students did **not** watch any television?

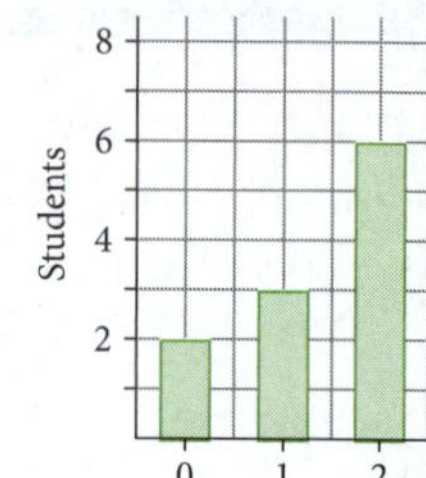

NUMBER AND ALGEBRA

1 A band played two shows across a weekend. There were 23 890 people at the concert on Saturday and 19 711 on Sunday. Which of these is the best estimate of the total number of people?

40 000 45 000 50 000

2 Mona played in four games in a netball gala day. She scored nine goals in one game, 15 in another and 10 goals in each of the other games. How many goals did she score in total?

3 Jesse is 15 years older than Xavier and Xavier is 20 years older than Huan. If Jesse is 45 years old, how old is Huan?

4 A ream of paper contains 500 sheets. How many sheets are in three reams?

5 How many 15s are in 1500?

6 Ashton counted the cars in a car park. Half of the cars were white. If there were 20 white cars, how many cars in the car park were **not** white?

7 Circle the largest decimal.

3.09 2.987 3.1

8 Lola had a gift card loaded with $80. After she bought a gift for her mother there was only $26 value left on the card. What was the cost of the gift?

9 What is the missing number?

$\frac{1}{8}, \frac{3}{8}, \frac{5}{8}, \frac{7}{8},$ ☐

MEASUREMENT AND SPACE

10 The length of one of Eliza's shoes is 24 cm. What is the combined length of the pair of shoes, in centimetres?

11 How many cubic-centimetre cubes are in this solid?

12 What are the missing numbers?

150 minutes = ☐ h ☐ min

13 Here is a pyramid. Draw the top view of the shape.

14 Alexander has drawn a kite. One side is 10 cm and another side is 4 cm shorter. What is the sum of the lengths of the kite?

15 The shape is to be reflected about the dotted line. Draw the image.

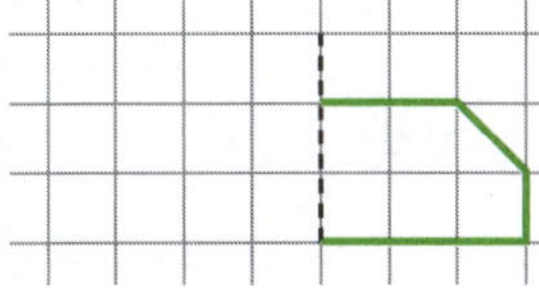

16 The map shows the homes of three friends Meg, Ava and Vic. Ava lives 300 metres north of Vic. How far does Meg live from Vic?

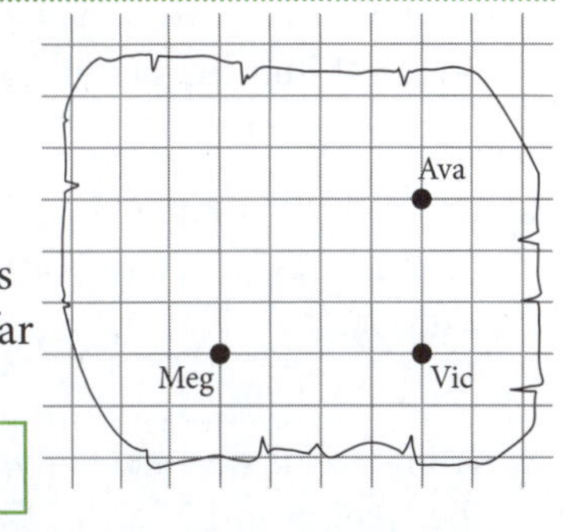

STATISTICS AND PROBABILITY

17 The arrow on this spinner is spun. True or false?

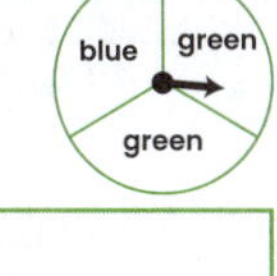

It is more likely that the arrow will land on green than blue.

18 The number of hours students spent watching television yesterday is recorded in the graph. How many students watched at least 3 hours of television?

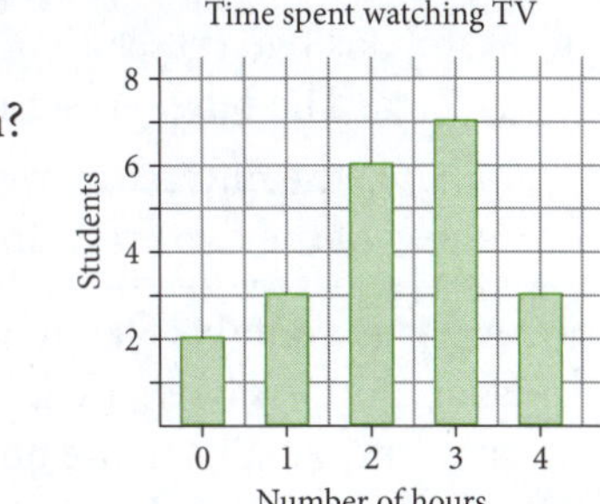

NUMBER AND ALGEBRA

1 Remy is thinking of a number between 61 and 87 where the digits add to 16.
What is the number?

2 The temperature at 5 am was 8°. By 10 am it had risen 16° and by 2 pm it had risen another 5°.
What was the temperature at 2 pm?

3 Beverly scores 26 points in her team's total score of 48. How many points were scored by the other players?

4 Tom has a bag of marbles. He gives six marbles to each of his four friends and keeps 12 marbles. How many marbles were in the bag at the start?

5 There are 20 toys in a box. An equal number of toys are to be given to eight children. What is the greatest number of toys each child can be given?

6 Caiden bought two dozen eggs. She uses half a dozen eggs each day. For how many days will the eggs last?

7 What is the decimal halfway between 6 and 7?

8 Lara bought some groceries which cost $16.88. What is this amount rounded to the nearest 5 cents?

9 What is the missing number?

0.36, 0.39, 0.42, 0.45, ?

MEASUREMENT AND SPACE

10 Kabil has two erasers. The length of one eraser is 3 cm. The other eraser is 26 mm.
What is the difference in the length of the two erasers?

11 A bottle contains 800 mL of shampoo. Half of the shampoo has been used. What amount remains in the bottle?

12 Three identical blocks have a total mass of 24 kg. What is the mass of each block?

13 Circle the shape with eight edges.

octagonal prism square pyramid

hexagonal pyramid

14 Draw the other half to make the picture symmetrical.

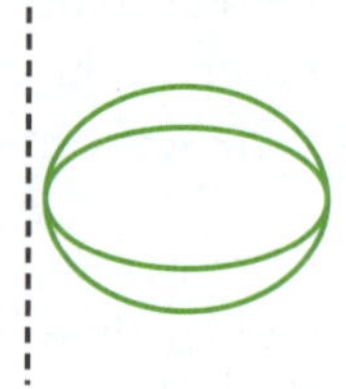

15 The triangle is translated 3 units to the right.
Draw the image.

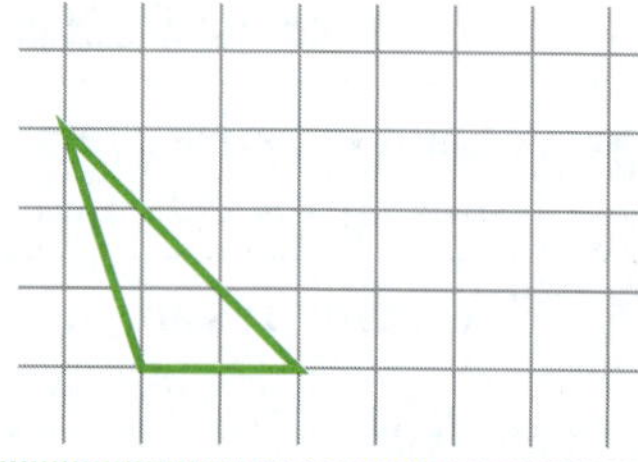

16 An obtuse angle is larger than a right angle, but less than a straight angle.
Circle the obtuse angle.

STATISTICS AND PROBABILITY

17 A bag contains a red ball, a purple ball and a black ball. Two balls are drawn out at the same time. Naomi listed two out of the three possible pairs.

red, purple purple, black

What is the other possible pair?

18 Jemima used a table to record the weather each day in April.

Weather in April		
	Rainy	**Dry**
Warm	2	6
Cool	9	13

How many cool, rainy days were in April?

NUMBER AND ALGEBRA

1 Remy is thinking of a number between 240 and 265 where the digits add to 16. What is the number?

2 A playroom has a pit containing 285 plastic balls. Another 115 balls are added to the pit. How many balls are now in the pit?

3 There are 48 blueberries in a container. Andrew ate 20 blueberries for recess and another 20 for lunch. How many blueberries remain?

4 A bag contains 25 sweets. How many sweets are in three bags?

5 A grid of 60 squares is formed. There are 10 rows of squares. How many squares are in each row?

6 Roman has 3 rows of 4 cards. He turns over the cards in one row. What fraction of the cards are turned over?

7 What is the decimal halfway between 6.8 and 6.84?

8 Mitchell bought some bacon which cost $6.15 and olives costing $3.80. What is the total cost?

9 What is the missing number?

0.87, 0.91, 0.95. 0.99, ?

MEASUREMENT AND SPACE

10 Stella is 98 cm tall. How much more does she need to grow to be 1.4 m tall?

11 One water bottle holds 500 mL. How much water will four bottles hold?

12 Six bags of rice have a total mass of 18 kg. What is the total mass of two bags?

13 Circle the two 3D shapes with the same number of edges.

hexagonal pyramid

pentagonal prism

cube

14 Draw the other half to make the picture symmetrical.

15 The kite is translated 3 units to the right.
Draw the image.

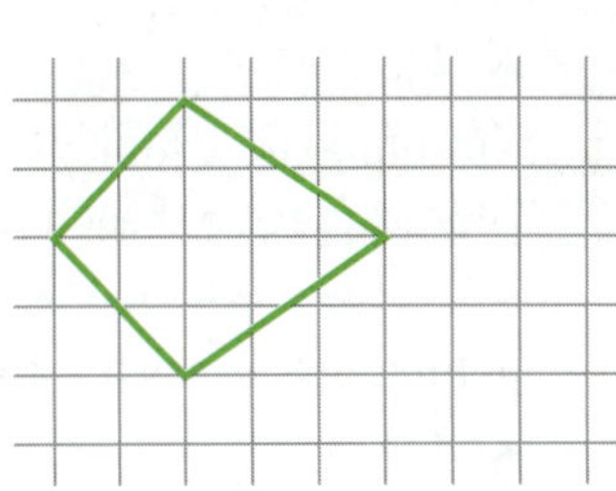

16 Here is a quadrilateral.
How many obtuse angles can be seen?

STATISTICS AND PROBABILITY

17 Ayla has four T-shirts and two pairs of shorts. The T-shirts are white, yellow, blue and red. Her shorts are blue and black. How many different outfits of T-shirt and shorts are possible?

18 Jemima used a table to record the weather each day in April.

Weather in April		
	Rainy	**Dry**
Warm	2	6
Cool	9	13

According to Jemima how many more days were dry than rainy?

NAPLAN-STYLE TEST 1

1 Gabby baked some cupcakes.

She gave one-third of the cupcakes away. How many did she keep?

A 3 B 4 C 8 D 9

2 Erin buys a dog toy for $12.35.
She pays for the toy with this note. 
How much change will Erin receive?

A $8.75 B $8.65 C $7.75 D $7.65

3 Mia placed a counter on E2 on the grid.
She then moved the counter up 5 spaces, to the left 3 spaces and then down 4 spaces.
Where is Mia's counter now?

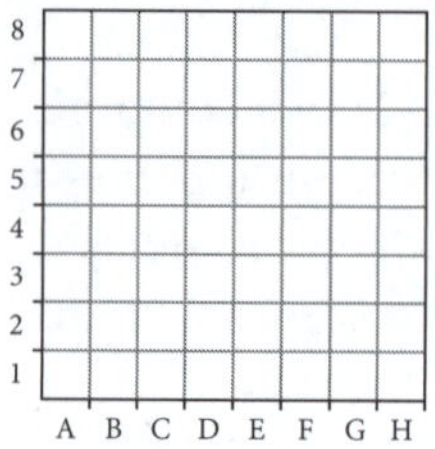

A H3 B B7
C B2 D B3

4 What is the difference between the smallest odd three-digit number and the largest even two-digit number?

A 1 B 2 C 3 D 4

5 Monique drew four shaded figures on a grid.
Monique cut out each figure and arranged them from greatest area to least area.
Which of these is the correct order?

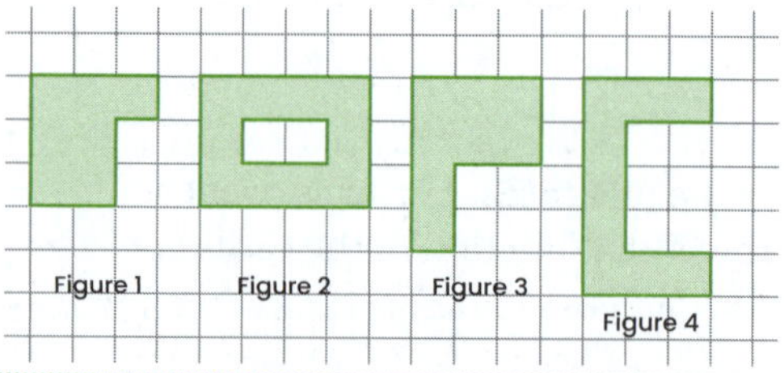

A 1, 2, 3, 4 B 2, 4, 3, 1
C 4, 2, 3, 1 D 2, 4, 1, 3

Figure 1 Figure 2 Figure 3 Figure 4

6 A light on a lighthouse flashes every 8 seconds. A light on a second lighthouse flashes every 12 seconds.
At 9 pm both lights flash together.
How many seconds later will the lights flash together again? ______ seconds

7 Bianca and her mother compared their ages. When Bianca was 6 her mother was 34.
How old will Bianca be when her mother is 50?

A 16 B 22 C 24 D 26

8 Donna walks half a kilometre to school every morning.
At the end of each day, she walks the same distance home.
What is the total distance walked from Monday to Friday?

A 2 kilometres B $2\frac{1}{2}$ kilometres C 4 kilometres D 5 kilometres

9 Here is a sequence of numbers. ________, 17, 25, 33, 41, 49
What is the missing number in the sequence?

A 5 B 6 C 7 D 8 E 9

10 A fraction of the circle has been shaded.
Which rectangle has the same fraction shaded?

A 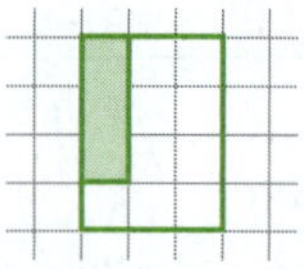 B C D

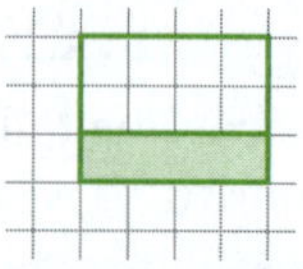

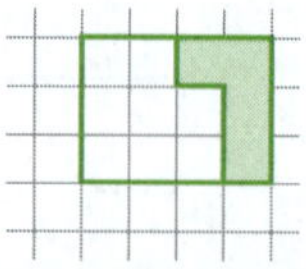

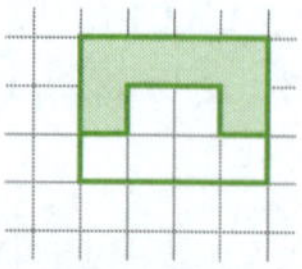

11 Some water is poured into a jug.
Which of these is the best estimate of the amount of water in the jug?

A 360 mL **B** 480 mL **C** 675 mL **D** 810 mL

12 Here are some road signs. Which sign has exactly one line of symmetry?

A **B** **C** **D**

13 Lucas spins the arrow on the spinner and it lands on 4.
He spins the arrow a second time.

Which of these numbers could he get on the second spin?

Select **all** the possible answers.

A 1 **B** 3 **C** 6 **D** 8 **E** 12

14 Last year there were 2390 spectators at the local football grand-final match.
This year 874 more attended than last year. What was the attendance this year?

15 Tickets to a fundraising dinner cost $60.
One-quarter of the money from ticket sales is given to a bushfire appeal.

If 200 tickets were sold, how much money was donated to the appeal?

A $1200 **B** $3000 **C** $4500 **D** $5000

16 The pan balance shows identical cylinders and a prism.
What is the total mass of the four cylinders?

A 20 kg **B** 30 kg **C** 40 kg **D** 80 kg

17 One night Owen recorded the time he went to bed on an analog clock.
The digital clock shows the time he got out of bed the next morning.

Which of these shows the length of time Owen was in bed?

A 2 hours 20 minutes **B** 10 hours 20 minutes **C** 9 hours 20 minutes **D** 10 hours 40 minutes

18 Heidi is reading a book containing 60 pages. So far she has read 40 pages.
Which of these represents the fraction of the book she has yet to read?

A $\frac{1}{20}$ **B** $\frac{1}{4}$ **C** $\frac{1}{3}$ **D** $\frac{1}{5}$ **E** $\frac{2}{3}$

19 Selma is writing a list of numbers that follow all these rules:

- between 22 and 77
- a multiple of 5
- has digits that add to at least 6

Select **all** the numbers Selma can add to her list.

A 24 **B** 30 **C** 45 **D** 51 **E** 63 **F** 70

20 As shoppers arrived at a shopping-centre car park, they were surveyed to find the time it took to drive from their home to the centre. The results of the survey are shown in the table below.

How many shoppers spend more than a quarter of an hour to drive from their home to the shopping centre?

Time spent travelling (minutes)	Number of shoppers
less than 10	4
11 to 15	16
16 to 20	19
21 to 25	17
26 to 30	13
more than 30	6
Total	**75**

NUMBER AND ALGEBRA

1 What number am I? The sum of my digits is 13. I am an odd number between 70 and 90.

2 Penelope uses eight eggs to make a pavlova. How many eggs will she use to make seven pavlovas?

3 The sum of two numbers is 340. If the larger number is 180, what is the smaller number?

4 A bike-hire business had 110 customers last week and 93 this week. What was the total number of customers?

5 How many groups of five hats can Natasha form using 32 hats?

6 Eliana shaded $\frac{7}{10}$ of this shape.

What fraction remains unshaded?

7 Rewrite these decimals in ascending order.

3.2 3.3 3.04

8 What is the total of $1.95 and $0.85?

9 What is the missing number in this number sentence?

12 + ? + 8 = 31

MEASUREMENT AND SPACE

10 A piece of string is 1 metre long. Felix cut the string into two equal lengths. How long is each piece in centimetres?

11 A hot-water urn has a capacity of 16 L. Marge half fills the urn. How much water is in the urn?

12 How many seconds are in 2 minutes?

13 William drew a 3D shape with an apex and two surfaces. How many surfaces were curved?

14 Use a dotted line to show the line of symmetry on this trapezium.

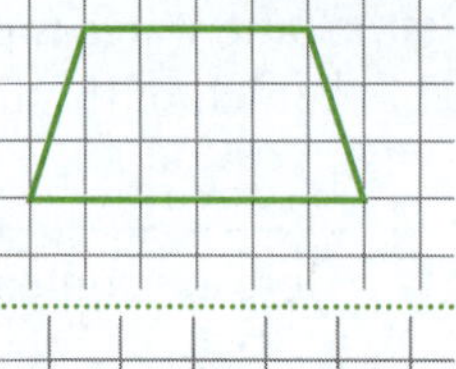

15 Chris rotates the shape a quarter turn in a clockwise direction.

Draw the image.

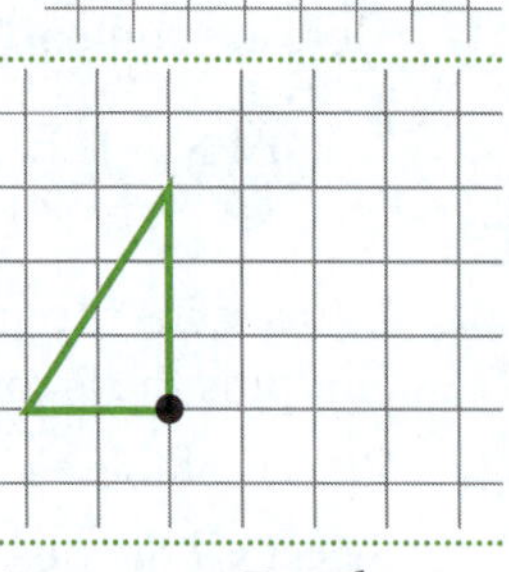

16 From *A*, Andrew walks 3 units west to *B* and 4 units south to *C*. Draw his path on the map.

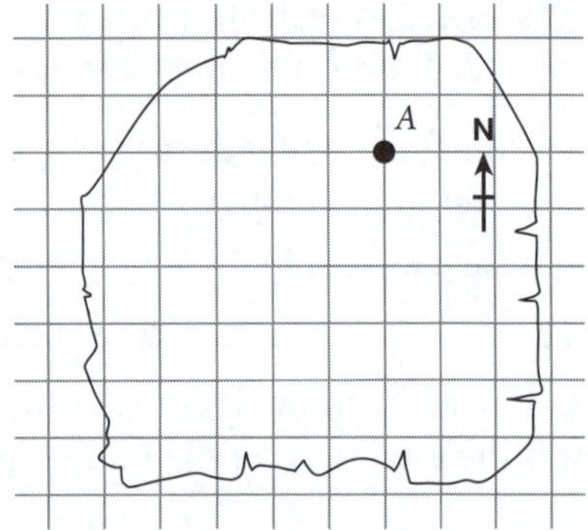

STATISTICS AND PROBABILITY

17 Balls coloured red (R), blue (B) and yellow (Y) are placed in a bag.

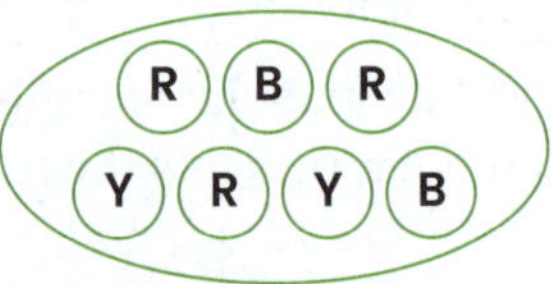

A ball is chosen without looking. Which colour is most likely to be chosen?

18 The results of a survey of students' favourite fruit is shown in the graph.

How many students said their favourite fruit was mango?

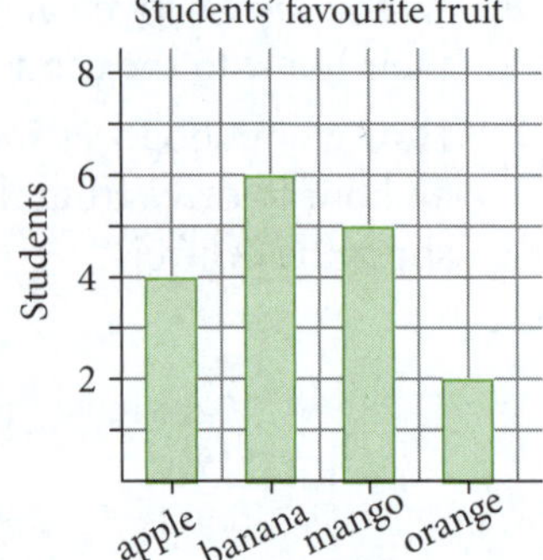

NUMBER AND ALGEBRA

1 What number am I?
I am a three-digit number more than 500.
The digit in the hundreds place is twice the digit in the tens place, which is twice the digit in the ones place.

2 There are 8 weeks remaining in this school term. There is a holiday on a Monday. How many more school days remain?

3 The sum of two numbers is 14 389. If the smaller number is 5680, what is the larger number?

4 Two planes landed at an airport before 6 am. The first plane had 276 passengers and the second 298. What was the total number of passengers?

5 154 potatoes are to be placed into bags of 10 for sale. How many bags can be filled?

6 Layla shaded $\frac{3}{5}$ of this shape. Tess then shaded two more squares.

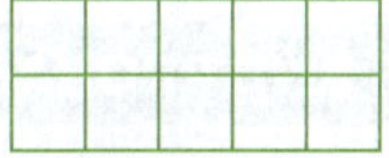

What fraction remains unshaded?

7 What is the decimal halfway between 5 and 5.48?

8 Seamus delivers pizzas and often receives tips. Over three nights he received tips of $21.50, $7.90 and $13.50. What is the total amount of tips received?

9 What is the missing number in this number sentence?

25 + 15 + **?** + 12 = 60

MEASUREMENT AND SPACE

10 A bedroom is $3\frac{1}{4}$ m in length. What is this length in millimetres?

11 A water jug has a capacity of 1700 mL. Owen half fills the urn. How much water is in the urn?

12 How many seconds are there in $4\frac{1}{2}$ minutes?

13 Ava drew a 3D shape with an apex and five faces which are triangular or rectangular. How many faces are triangular?

14 How many lines of symmetry has this kite?

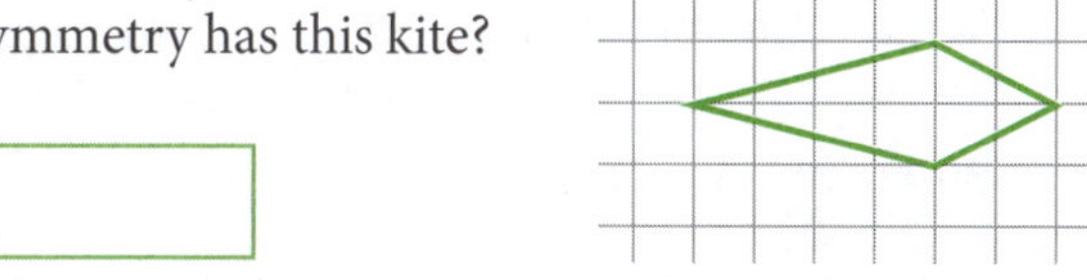

15 Charles rotates the shape a quarter turn in a clockwise direction.
Draw the image.

16 From *A*, Anna walks 4 units south to *B* and 4 units west to *C*. She then starts to walk back to *A*.
In which direction is she now walking?

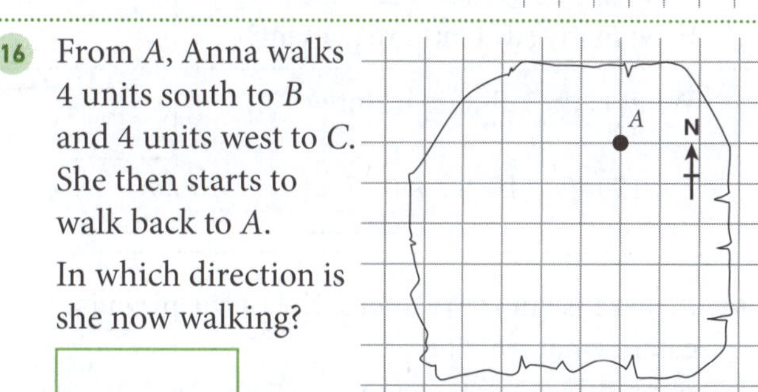

STATISTICS AND PROBABILITY

17 Samuel rolled a normal dice 18 times and the results are recorded in a table.
The number of times Samuel rolled a 5 is not shown. What will be the missing number?

Result	Number of times
1	III
2	II
3	IIII
4	~~IIII~~
5	?
6	III

18 The results of a survey of students' favourite fruit is shown in the graph.
How many students were surveyed?

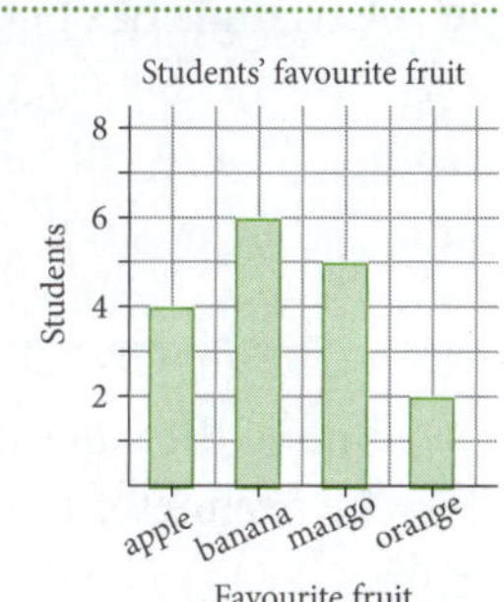

NUMBER AND ALGEBRA

1 The height of a tree is about 80 m, rounded to the nearest 10 m. Which of these could be the actual height of the tree?

68 m 74 m 83 m 90 m

2 Kim wrote this division question. What is the missing number?

30 = 7 × ? + 2

3 Andrew has 160 stamps in one folder and another 316 stamps in another. What is the total number of stamps?

4 A school has 335 students enrolled. On one day there are 24 students absent. How many students are present?

5 What is the missing number?

7 × 19 = 7 × 10 + 7 × ?

6 A pizza is cut into 8 slices. If $\frac{5}{8}$ of the pizza is eaten, what fraction remains?

7 What is the missing number?

$0.37 = \frac{?}{100}$

8 An orange costs 70 cents. Beatrix paid $2 when she bought two oranges. How much change did she receive?

9 What is the missing number?

5 squared = ?

MEASUREMENT AND SPACE

10 A triangle has been drawn on a centimetre grid.

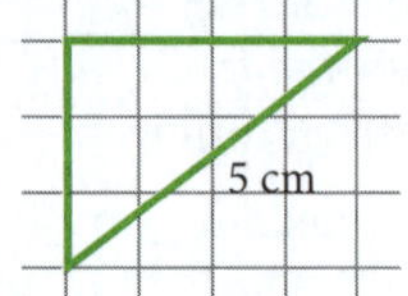

One of the sides is 5 cm. What is the perimeter of the triangle?

11 Water is poured into a jug. How much water is now in the jug?

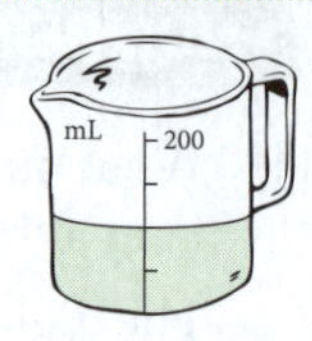

12 A scoop of mixed nuts has a mass of 432 g. What is this mass to the nearest 100 g?

13 Theodore has started to draw a cone.

Complete his drawing.

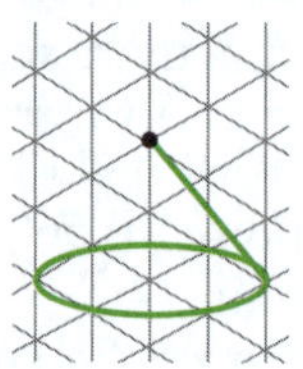

14 Combine these two shapes to form a rectangle.

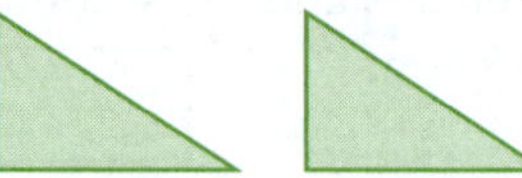

15 An analog clock shows the time of half past 3. If the minute hand moves through a quarter turn, what is the new time?

16 What is the highest possible number of right angles in a triangle?

STATISTICS AND PROBABILITY

17 Anna wrote each of the letters of her name on four cards. She turned them over, mixed them up and pointed to one of the cards. Which of these describes the chance she points to an A?

less likely even chance more likely

18 A group of high-school students were asked to estimate the number of minutes they took to shower each day.

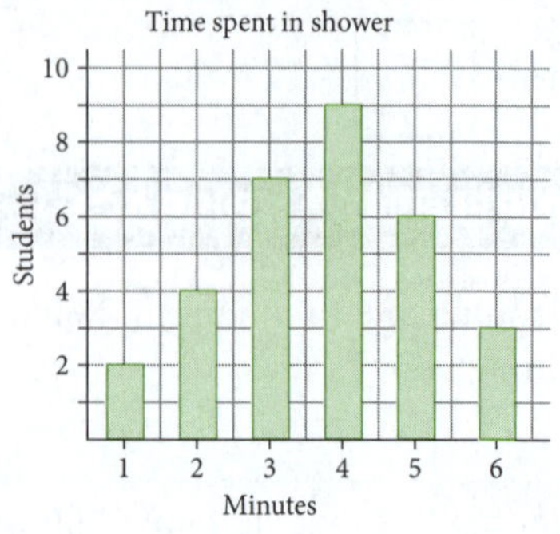

How many students showered for 6 minutes?

NUMBER AND ALGEBRA

1 The population of a city is about 23 000, rounded to the nearest thousand. Which of these could be the actual population?

2301 22 499 23 501 23 499

2 Alice wrote this division question where A and B are standing for positive numbers less than 10.

$68 = A \times 7 + B$

What are the values of A and B?

3 Last cricket season Andrew scored 476 runs. This season he scored 383 runs. What was the total number of runs scored?

4 There are 3400 seats in a grandstand. The seats are either red or blue. If there are 1850 red seats, how many blue seats are in the grandstand?

5 A tray contains 15 mangoes. How many mangoes are in four trays?

6 Maverick is one-quarter the age of Tom. If Maverick is 9 years old, how old is Tom?

7 What is the missing number?

$0.4 = \frac{?}{100}$

8 Harvey bought a pen for \$3.20 and an eraser for 80 cents. What change will he receive from \$5?

9 What is the missing number?

MEASUREMENT AND SPACE

10 A shape has been drawn on a centimetre grid.

What is the perimeter of the shape?

11 How much water is in the jug?

12 A bucket of sand has a mass of 8653 g. What is this mass to the nearest kilogram?

13 Grace has started to draw a pyramid.

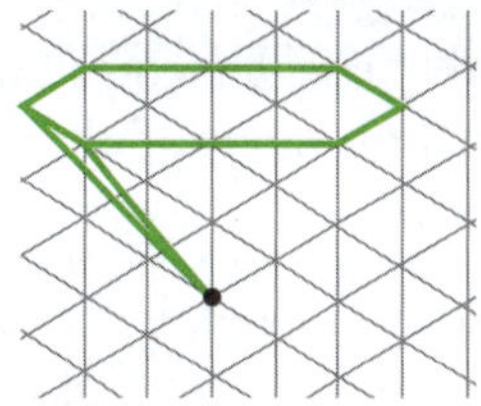

Complete her drawing.

14 Combine these three shapes to form a parallelogram.

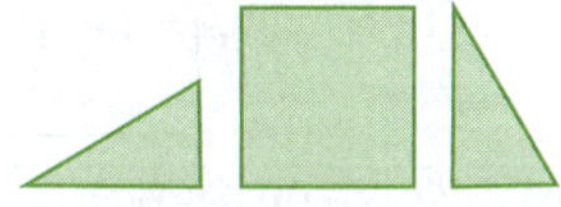

15 An analog clock shows the time of 10 past 6. If the minute hand moves through a three-quarter turn, what is the new time?

16 Connor made this statement: 'I have drawn a quadrilateral which has three angles that are larger than a right angle'. Is this possible?

STATISTICS AND PROBABILITY

17 Robby wrote each of the letters of his name on five cards. He turned them over, mixed them up and pointed to one of the cards. Circle the chance he points to a B.

less likely even chance more likely

18 A group of high-school students were asked to estimate the number of minutes they took to shower each day.

How many students showered for less than 4 minutes a day?

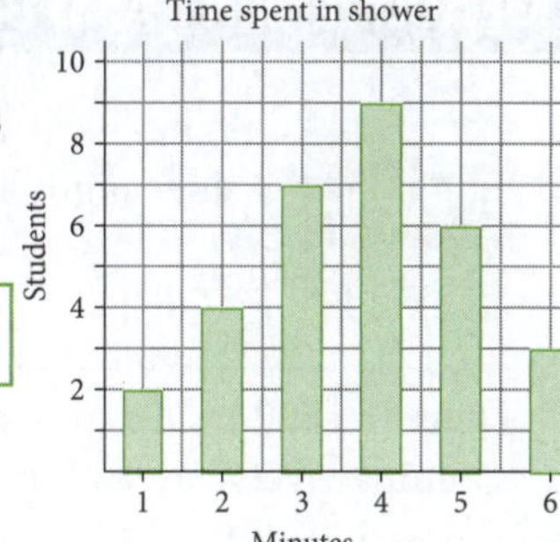

NUMBER AND ALGEBRA

1 Sean uses increasing consecutive digits to write a five-digit number. What is the largest possible number?

2 There are 46 passengers on a bus. If there were 18 children, how many adults were on the bus?

3 Alison divides 24 by each of these numbers.

6 2 5 9

Circle the numbers that do **not** have a remainder.

4 There are 39 students in Year 4, 36 students in Year 5 and 43 students in Year 6. What is the total number of students?

5 A roller-coaster at a theme park has 15 rows of three seats. How many people can ride the roller-coaster at the same time?

6 

Circle the fraction of circles that are shaded.

$\frac{1}{2}$ $\frac{1}{4}$ $\frac{2}{5}$ $\frac{3}{5}$

7 Isabella used her calculator to check $1 \div 10 = 0.1$. What is her answer for $4 \div 10$?

8 Rewrite 5308 cents in dollars and round the amount to the nearest 5 cents.

9 Jasper wrote this sequence of numbers.
12, 25, 38, 51, 64 …

Complete Jasper's rule:
Start with 12 and add ______.

MEASUREMENT AND SPACE

10 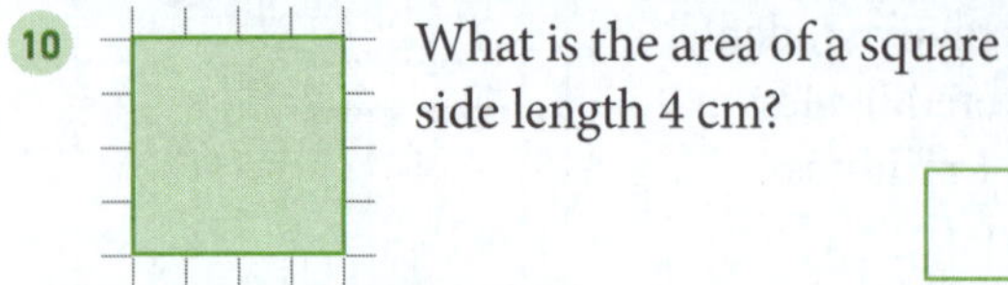

What is the area of a square with side length 4 cm?

11 There is 1500 mL of milk remaining in a container. What is this amount in litres?

12 Rebecca buys two bags of dog food. Each bag has a mass of 3 kg. After a week she has used 2 kg. How much remains?

13 Callie drew a prism. The base of the prism was a shape with 8 equal sides. How many faces has the prism?

14 Using dotted lines, draw the lines of symmetry on this shape.

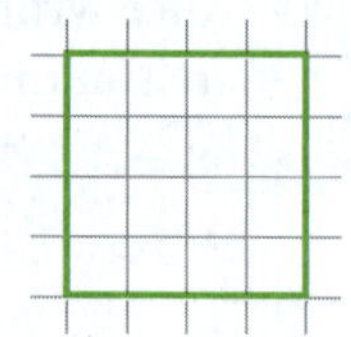

15 The shape is to be translated 3 units to the right.

Which of these is **not** covered by the image?

E4 G6 E5

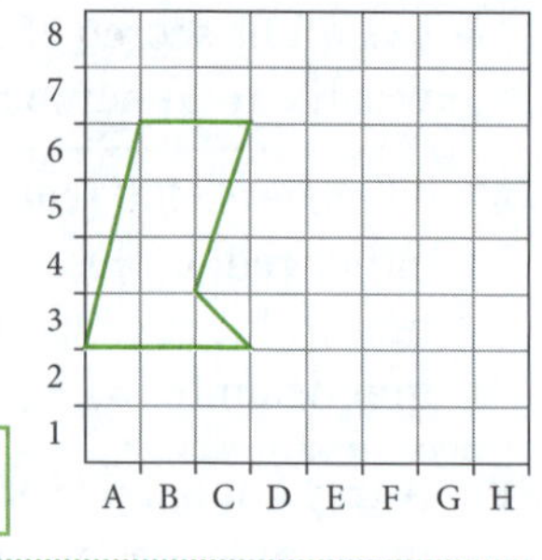

16 The map shows the path Emilia used to walk from *P* to *S*.

In which direction was Emilia walking between *R* and *S*?

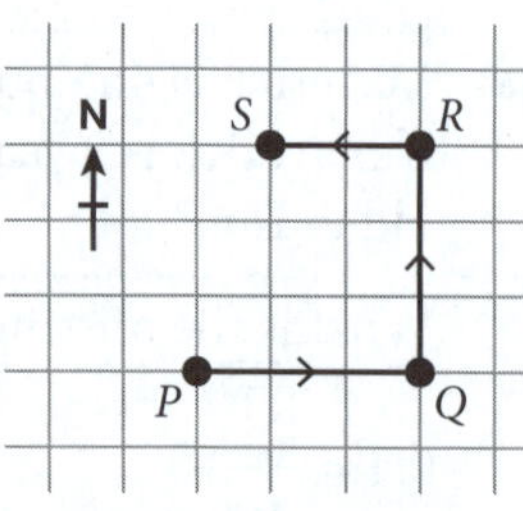

STATISTICS AND PROBABILITY

17 Here are two spinners which have sections coloured red (R) and yellow (Y).

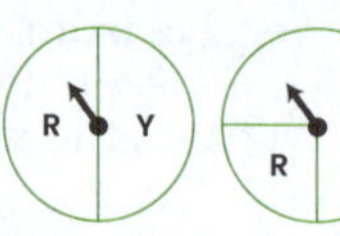

Circle the spinner that has an equal chance of spinning a red or a yellow.

18 The books read by students in four reading groups are shown on the graph.

Group	Books
Wombats	
Kangaroos	
Platypuses	
Koalas	
Key = 4 books	

How many books were read by the Kangaroos?

NUMBER AND ALGEBRA

1 Courtney uses the digits 1, 3, 5, 7, and 9 to write a number larger than 25 000. What is the smallest possible number she can write?

2 A cruise ship had 2964 passengers. If there were 1786 adults on the cruise, how many children were there?

3 Josh divides 25 by each of these numbers.

8 5 3 2

Circle the numbers that have a remainder of 1.

4 On Monday, hens at a poultry farm produced 675 eggs. On Tuesday another 593 eggs were produced. What was the total number of eggs produced?

5 Kellan was stacking coins. He made six stacks of 10 coins and four stacks of eight coins. What was the total number of coins?

6 Rylee has shaded some shapes.
She wants to shade $\frac{3}{4}$ of the shapes.
How many more shapes need to be shaded?

7 Kiel used his calculator to check 54 ÷ 100 = 0.54. What is his answer for 9 ÷ 100?

8 Florence receives a $30 gift card for her birthday. She uses the card to buy a $12 movie ticket and spends $6 on refreshments. How much value remains on the card?

9 Ava wrote this sequence of numbers.
256, 64, 16, 4 …
Complete Ava's rule: Start with 256 and divide by ________.

MEASUREMENT AND SPACE

10 What is the area of a square with side length 8 cm?

11 During an afternoon Mackenzie drank 750 mL of water. What is this amount in litres?

12 Keiran and Horatio caught a fish each. The mass of Keiran's fish was 860 g. Horatio's fish was 50 g heavier. What was the mass of Horatio's fish?

13 A prism has 15 edges. Some of its faces are rectangles. What is the shape of the other faces?

14 Sketch a rhombus and draw dotted lines to show any lines of symmetry.

15 The shape has been translated 3 units to the right.
Which of these is covered by the original shape?
D8 B3 A6

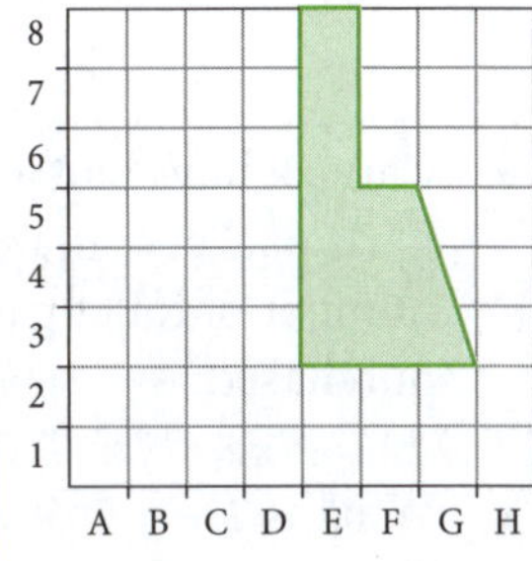

16 The map shows the path Emilia used to walk from *P* to *S*.
After stopping at *S*, she plans to walk the same path back to *P*. In which direction will Emilia walk from *R* to *Q*?

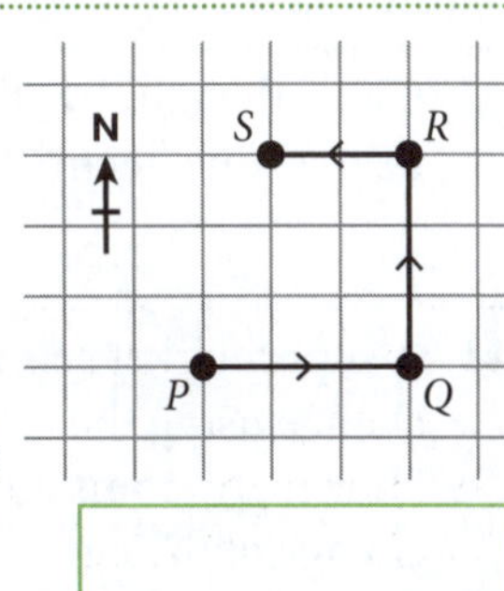

STATISTICS AND PROBABILITY

17 A coin is tossed eight times. How many heads would you expect?

18 The books read by students in four reading groups are shown on the graph.

Group	Books
Wombats	📖 (1½)
Kangaroos	📖📖 (2½)
Platypuses	📖📖📖 (3)
Koalas	📖 (1)
Key 📖 = 4 books	

What was the total number of books read by the four groups?

NUMBER AND ALGEBRA

1 Jessika purchased a car. The odometer on the car showed 67502. What is this distance rounded to the nearest thousand?

2 A school has 276 students born in Australia and 122 born overseas. What is the total enrolment in the school?

3 What is the remainder when 47 is divided by 9?

4 Anna is reading a book containing 120 pages. She has 45 pages to read to finish the book. How many pages has Anna already read?

5 Carrick buys half a dozen packets of toilet paper. Each packet contains 20 rolls. What is the total number of toilet paper rolls purchased?

6 What is $2 + \frac{3}{4}$ written as a mixed numeral?

7 Circle the number that is 5.87 rounded to the nearest one decimal place.

6 5.8 5.9

8 A supermarket self-service checkout dispenses change using the least possible number of coins. How many coins are given for change of $2.35?

9 What is the missing number in this sequence of numbers?

1.6, 1.9, 2.2, 2.5, ?

MEASUREMENT AND SPACE

10 A square has side length 6 cm. What is the perimeter of the square?

11 How many more cubic-centimetre cubes are needed for this shape to have a volume of 12 cm^3?

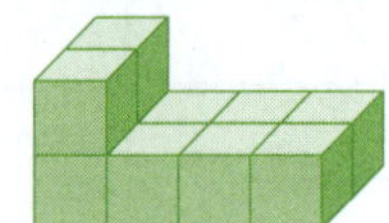

12 A shop opens at 8 am and closes at 5 pm. How many hours is the shop open?

13 Mia has started to draw a cube. Complete her drawing.

14 How many of these rectangles are needed to cover a square with sides of 6 cm?

6 cm

2 cm

15 The shape on the left has been translated.

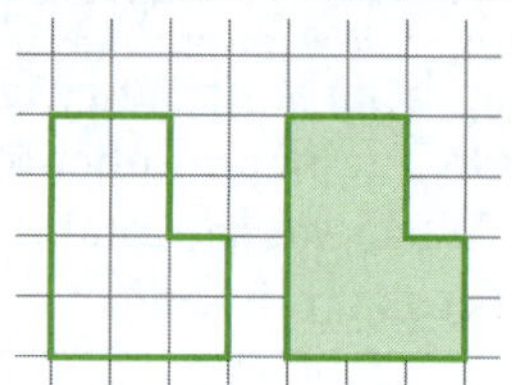

Complete the statement.

The shape has been translated ____ units to

the ______________.

16 The diagram shows a diagonal drawn on a rectangle.

How many angles smaller than a right angle can be seen?

STATISTICS AND PROBABILITY

17 Paolo's favourite ice-cream flavours are strawberry, chocolate and caramel. He can choose scoops of two different flavours in a cone. How many different combinations are possible?

18 The graph shows the number of student votes for their favourite pet.

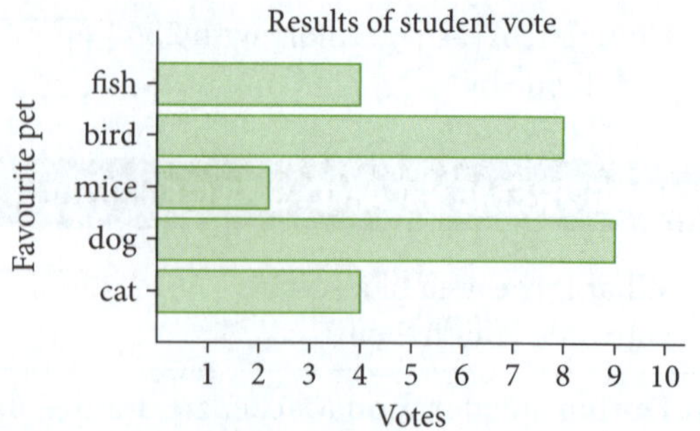

How many students voted for a bird or a dog?

NUMBER AND ALGEBRA

1 Eliza rounds the number 129 478 to the nearest 100. Nicola uses Eliza's new number and rounds it to the nearest thousand. What is Nicola's new number?

2 For a movie screening, a cinema has 176 occupied seats and 124 unoccupied seats. What is the total capacity of the cinema?

3 Laurence is arranging 87 bottles into groups of 9. How many are left over?

4 A raffle has 500 tickets. There have been 280 tickets sold. How many more tickets are yet to be sold?

5 At a concert the first five rows have eight seats each and the next five rows have 10 seats. How many seats are in the first 10 rows?

6 What is $3 + \frac{1}{3}$ written as an improper fraction?

7 What is 14.462 rounded to the nearest tenth?

8 A supermarket self-service checkout dispenses change using the least possible number of coins. How many coins are given for change from $5 if Gracie buys a carton of cream for $2.15?

9 The fifth number in a sequence is 12.6. The sixth number is 12.9 and the seventh number is 13.2. What is the fourth number?

MEASUREMENT AND SPACE

10 Here are the dimensions of three rectangles. Circle any rectangle with a perimeter of 12 cm.

4 cm by 3 cm   2 cm by 4 cm   5 cm by 1 cm

11 Dustin bought a 500-mL bottle of olive oil and a 750-mL bottle of vegetable oil. What was the total quantity of oil?

12 Tamir trains for 40 minutes each morning. What is the total number of hours he trains in three mornings?

13 Leo has started to draw a rectangular prism.

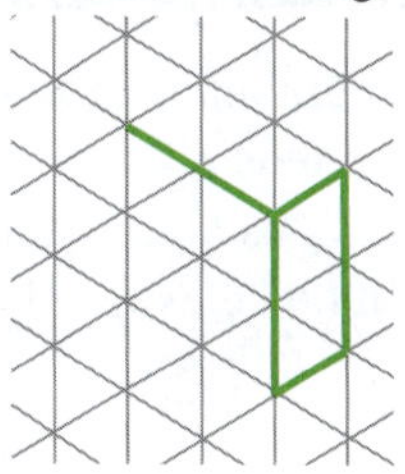

Complete his drawing.

14 How many of these squares are needed to cover a larger square with sides of 4 cm?

2 cm

15 The diagram shows a rectangle which has been translated. The square will have the same translation.

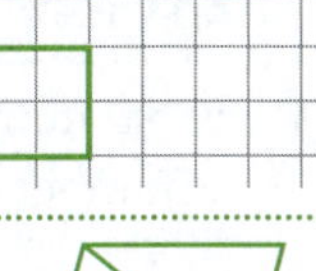

Draw the image of the square.

16 The diagram shows a diagonal drawn on a parallelogram.

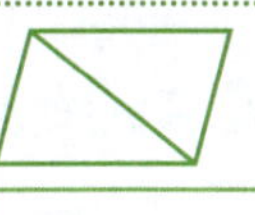

How many angles that are smaller than a right angle can be seen?

STATISTICS AND PROBABILITY

17 The spinner has red (R) and blue (B) sections.

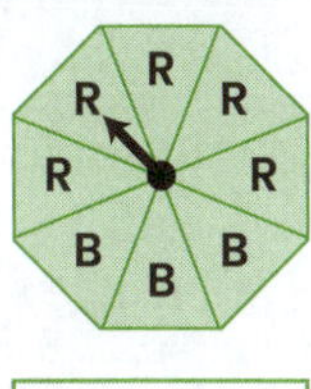

The arrow is spun and it stops on blue. On a second spin it stops on red. On which colour is the arrow likely to stop on a third spin?

18 The graph shows the number of student votes for their favourite pet.

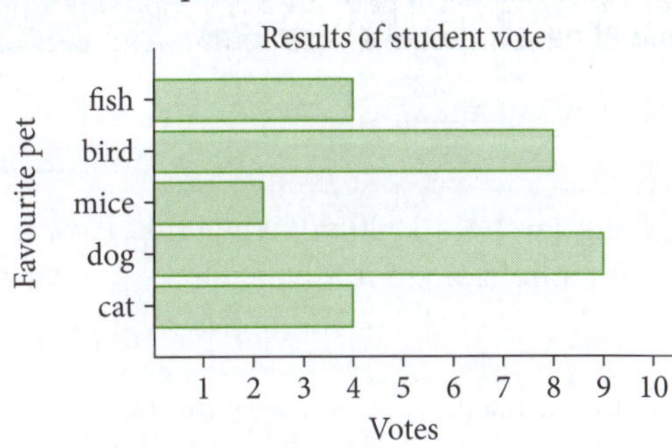

How many pets had at least three votes?

NUMBER AND ALGEBRA

1 Pete wrote a number with odd digits in the thousands and tens place and even digits in the hundreds and ones place. Which of these could be Pete's number?

6478   5952   7459   1296

2 A hardware store sells packets containing 20 screws. If Matt bought eight packets, how many screws did he buy?

3 A teacher has 24 pencils in one jar, 18 in a second and 21 in a third. How many pencils are in the three jars?

4 There are 103 apartments in a new building. If 75 apartments are already sold, how many are yet to sell?

5 What number multiplied by 6 gives a number 3 more than 45?

6 Perveen spent $\frac{3}{10}$ of her pocket money. What fraction remains?

7 What part of this shape has been shaded, written as a decimal?

8 Elias buys a toy for $16.95. He pays for the toy with a $20 note. How much change will he receive?

9 Use either < or > to make a true number sentence.

8×5 **?** 6×7

MEASUREMENT AND SPACE

10 2 m 50 cm = ________ m

11 A jug can hold 1600 mL when full. How much does it hold when it is half full?

12 Andrew used scales to measure the mass of a duck egg and a chicken egg. The chicken egg was 6 g lighter than the duck egg.

If the duck egg had a mass of 64 g, what was the mass of the chicken egg?

13 Draw the side view of a cone.

14 How many more squares need to be shaded so that the dotted line is a line of symmetry?

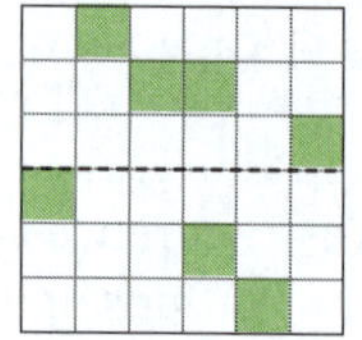

15 The parallelogram is translated 3 units right and then 2 units down.

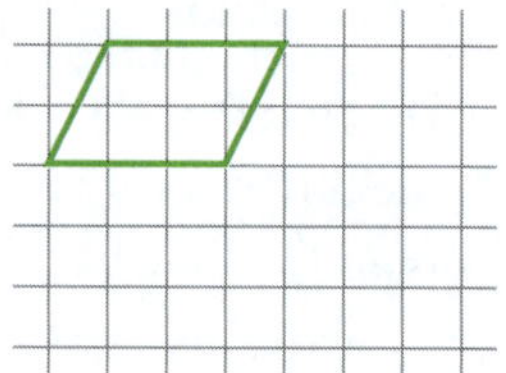

Draw the image.

16 The map shows the location of five mountains.

E is [ ] of *B*.

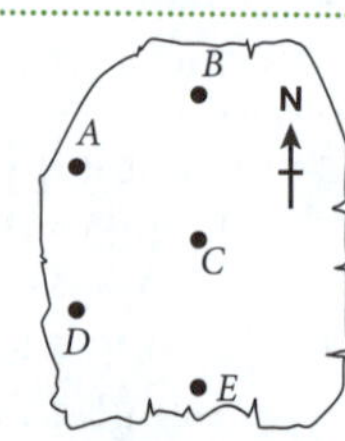

STATISTICS AND PROBABILITY

17 A box contains three cards. The cards are yellow (Y), green (G) and purple (P).

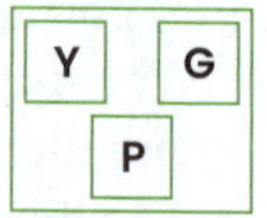

Ivy replaces the yellow card with another purple card. She now selects a card from the box without looking. Which coloured card is she more likely to choose?

18 The number of dogs using a dog park each hour on a Saturday morning is recorded in the table below.

How many dogs were in the park at 10 am?

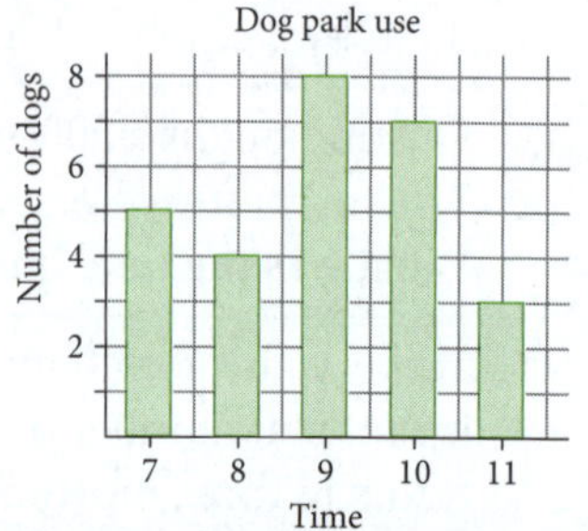

NUMBER AND ALGEBRA

1 What number is 300 less than a four-digit number with identical digits that add to 12?

2 In a section of her wardrobe Emma has three shelves of shoes. On each shelf there are six pairs of shoes. How many shoes are in the wardrobe?

3 Misako read nine books last year. Sophia read four more books than Misako and five fewer books than Ava. What was the total number of books read by the three girls?

4 Cameron and Huan are playing a game. Cameron has scored 23 452 points, which is exactly 5000 points more than Huan. How many points has Huan scored?

5 Alice is thinking of a multiple of 5. When it is divided by 6 there is a remainder of 2. What is the smallest possible number?

6 Here are two squares divided into quarters.

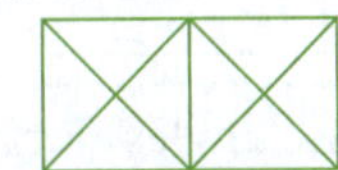

Alana shades $1\frac{3}{4}$ squares. What fraction of a square remains unshaded?

7 Shade 0.7 of the shape.

8 Stathis has $10 to spend on food bought at the canteen. He spent $4.30 at recess and $5.20 at lunch. How much money does he have left?

9 Use either <, = or > to make a true number sentence.

763 – 568  ? 120 + 75

MEASUREMENT AND SPACE

10 5 m 80 mm = ________ m

11 A can contains 375 mL of mineral water. How many millilitres are in two cans?

12 A carton contains a dozen eggs. Each egg has a mass of 70 g. What is the total mass of eggs in the carton?

13 Draw the top view of a cone.

14 How many more squares need to be shaded so that the dotted lines are lines of symmetry?

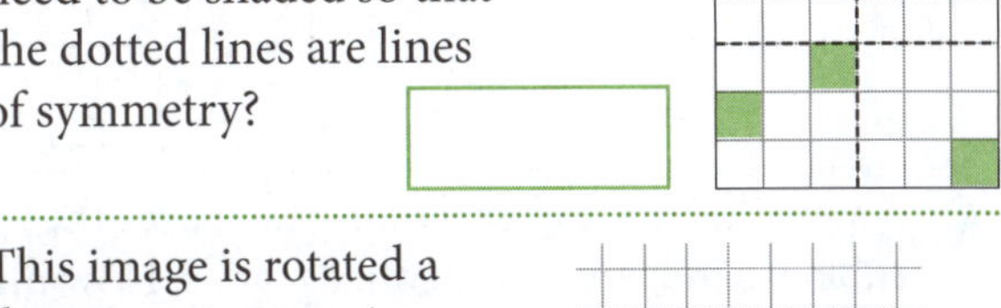

15 This image is rotated a three-quarter turn in an anticlockwise direction.

Draw the image.

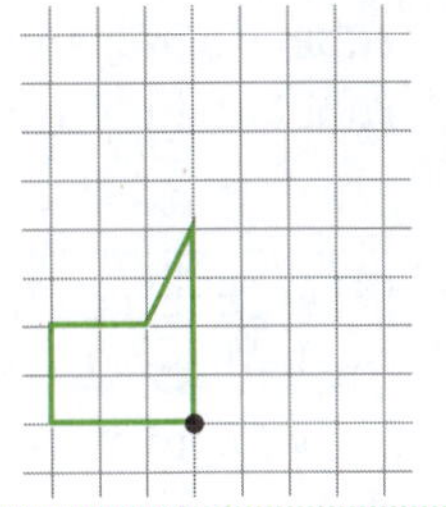

16 The map shows the location of five mountains.

A is south-east of *B*. What direction is *C* from *D*?

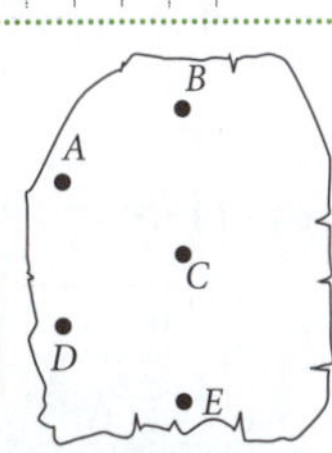

STATISTICS AND PROBABILITY

17 A box contains five coloured discs. The discs are blue (B), yellow (Y) and purple (P).

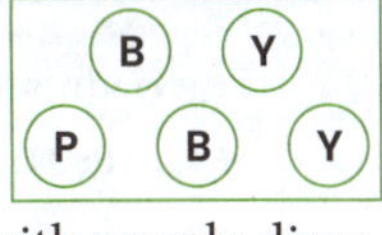

Ezekiel replaces the yellow discs with purple discs. Which coloured disc is he less likely to choose?

18 The numbers of dogs using a dog park each hour on a Saturday morning are recorded in the table below.

According to the graph, what was the most popular time to use the park?

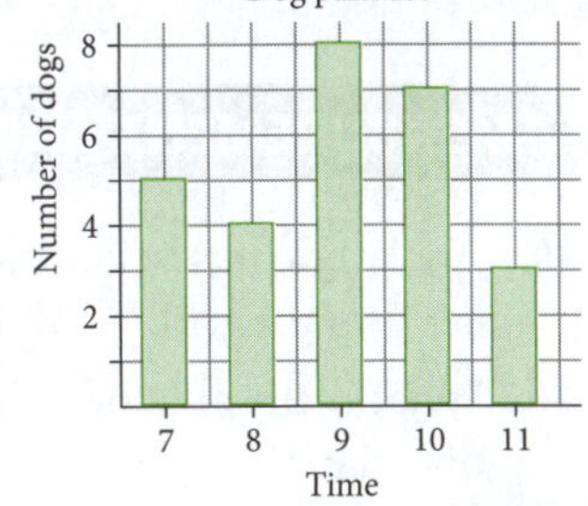

NUMBER AND ALGEBRA

1 Here is a four-digit number with the hundreds digit missing.

6 ? 58

If the digits add to 26, what is the four-digit number?

2 The principal formed groups of 10 students. There was a total of 15 groups. How many students had been arranged into groups?

3 James's grandmother is 67 years old. How old will she be if she lives another 25 years?

4 Amelia has 80 rubber bands. She places the rubber bands into four equal groups. How many rubber bands are in each group?

5 Selena checked her phone messages. In one week she had sent 19 text messages and received 46. How many more text messages did she receive than send?

6 Here is a shape formed using 12 identical squares.

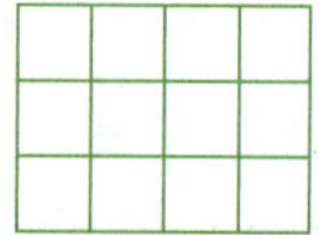

Lexie shaded half of the squares. How many squares are **not** shaded?

7 True or false?
0.4 is less than $\frac{1}{2}$.

8 Andrew bought a packet of cards for \$5 and a yo-yo for \$6.50. How much did he spend?

9 Ming multiplied three odd numbers. Is her answer even or odd?

MEASUREMENT AND SPACE

10 A triangle has been drawn on a centimetre grid.

What is the area of the triangle?

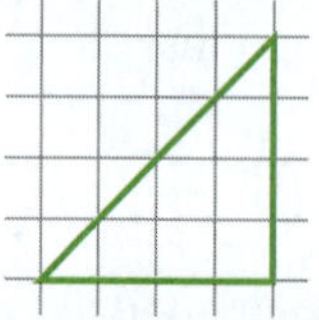

11 A glass holds 200 mL. Tim fills the glass with milk and drinks all but 40 mL. How much milk did Tim drink?

12 How many minutes are there between quarter past 10 and 20 to 11?

13 Henry has started to draw a cylinder.

Complete his drawing.

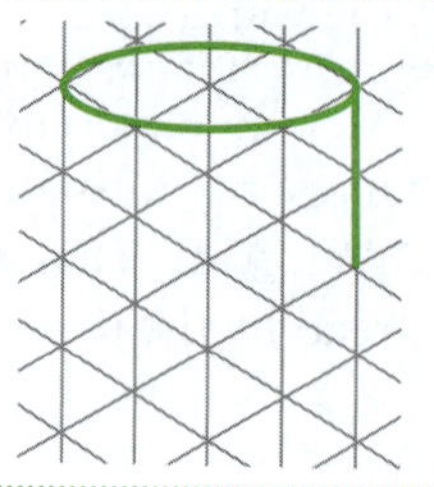

14 Here is a triangle with two sides equal in length. Draw the line(s) of symmetry.

15 The shape is to be rotated a quarter turn in a clockwise direction about X. Which of these will be covered by the image?

E5 D6 G5

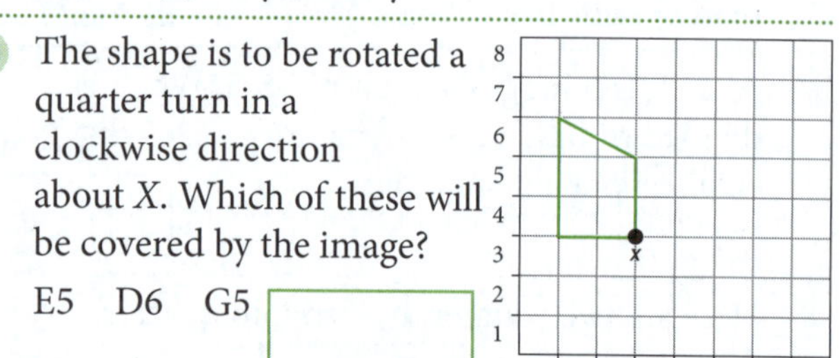

16 Name the obtuse angles in this diagram.

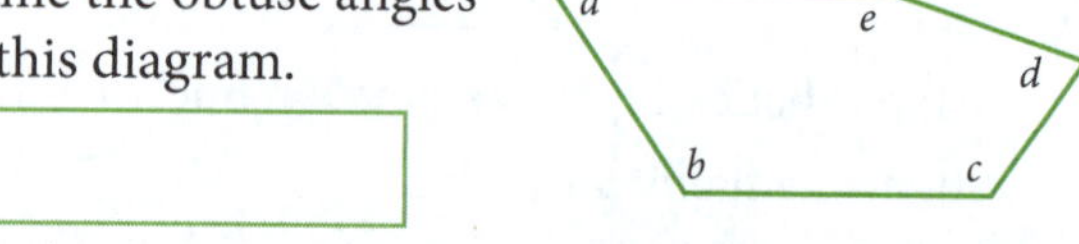

STATISTICS AND PROBABILITY

17 In a bowl there are four apples, five oranges and three peaches. Chloe picks a piece of fruit without looking. Which is the most likely fruit she picks?

18 The points earned by four different sport houses are recorded in the graph.

How many points were earned by the Red house?

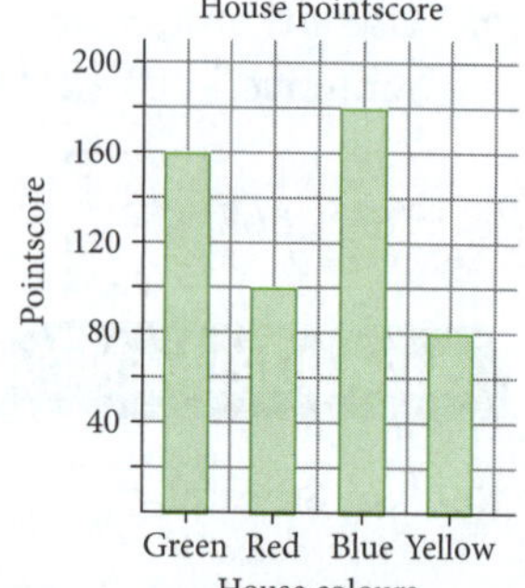

NUMBER AND ALGEBRA

1 The digits in a four-digit number add to 22. The digit in the hundreds place is 9 and is 4 more than the digit in the ones place and 2 more than the digit in the thousands place. What is the number?

2 Every night Ryan reads 12 pages of his book. How many pages does he read in a week?

3 Olek recorded the number of push-ups he completed. On both Monday and Tuesday he completed 32 push-ups. On both Wednesday and Thursday he completed 35 push-ups. What was the total number of push-ups over the four days?

4 A game takes 40 minutes to play. How many games can be played in two hours?

5 Sharreka counted a total of 34 birds sitting in two trees. In the first tree there were 19 birds. How many more birds were in the first tree than in the second?

6 Here is a shape formed using 12 identical squares. Ellie shaded $\frac{1}{4}$ of the shape. Josie shaded $\frac{1}{2}$ of the shape. Circle the fraction of the shape that has **not** been shaded. $\frac{1}{4}$ $\frac{1}{2}$ $\frac{1}{3}$

7 Rob walks $\frac{1}{2}$ km each morning. What is the total distance he walks in five mornings, written as a decimal?

8 Eliana has $20 and buys a coffee for $5.50 and a cookie for $3.20. How much does she have remaining?

9 An even number of odd numbers is added to an odd number of even numbers. Is the answer even or odd?

MEASUREMENT AND SPACE

10 A shape has been drawn on a centimetre grid. What is the area of the shape?

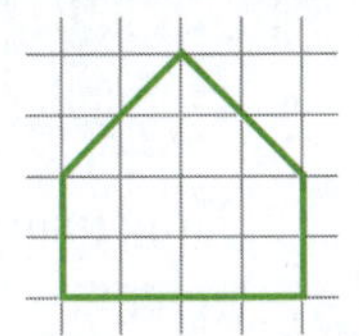

11 Jeremy buys a 500-mL bottle of tomato sauce. He pours half of the sauce into a container. What amount of sauce remains in the bottle?

12 Helena starts work at twenty to nine. She works for 8 hours. What time does Helena finish work, written in digital time?

13 Ella has started to draw a triangular prism. Complete her drawing.

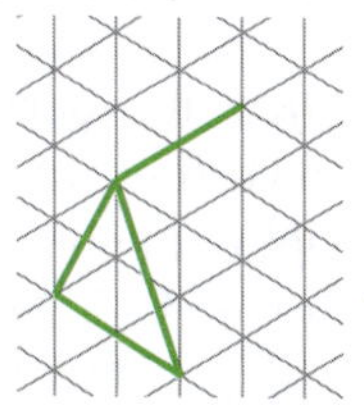

14 Declan drew a shape with four equal sides and four equal angles. How many lines of symmetry has the shape?

15 The shape is to be translated 4 units right and 3 units up. Which of these will be covered by the image?

D6 E5 F6

16 How many right angles form a straight angle?

STATISTICS AND PROBABILITY

17 The dots on the outside of a normal dice are changed. The numbers are now 3, 3, 4, 4, 4 and 5. The dice is rolled. Which number is most likely to be uppermost on the dice?

18 The points earned by four different sport houses are recorded in the graph. What was the total points earned by the top two houses?

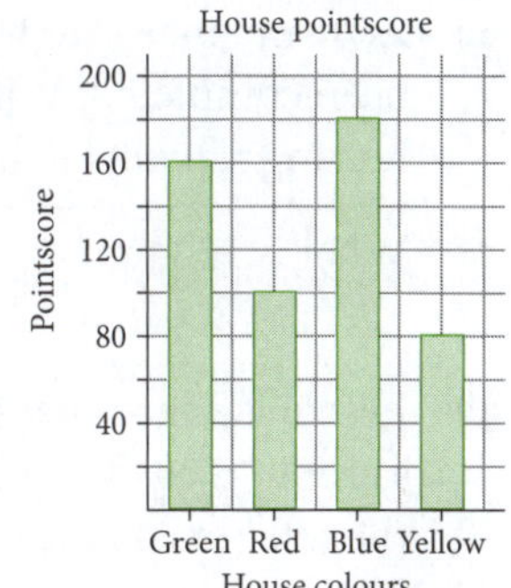

NUMBER AND ALGEBRA

1 Paddy was born in 1946, Poppy in 1968 and Penny in 1959. Who is the youngest?

2 The populations of two small towns are 387 and 510. What is the total of the two populations to the nearest hundred?

3 On a chessboard there are eight rows of squares. In each row there are four black squares and four white squares. How many squares are on the board?

4 Benjamin is given a bottle of tablets to get well. He needs to take three tablets every day. There are 36 tablets in the bottle. For how many days will Benjamin be taking the tablets?

5 An aeroplane has a seating capacity of 289. If 154 seats are taken, how many seats are still available?

6 Divide this circle into quarters and shade $\frac{3}{4}$ of the circle.

7 What is the missing number?

30 hundredths is the same as ? tenths.

8 What is the total of \$4.60 and \$2.70?

9 What is the missing number in this sequence of numbers?

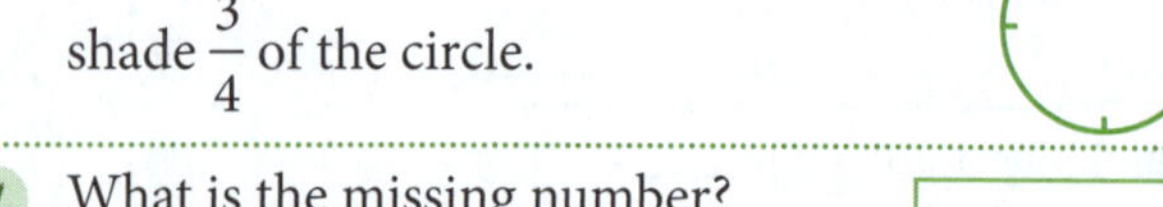

MEASUREMENT AND SPACE

10 A 70-m fence is to be built. After a week, 28 m has been completed. What length of fencing remains to be built?

11 What is 1234 mL in litres?

12 John used three bags of sand to fill his children's sandpit. If each bag had a mass of 15 kg, what was the total mass of sand?

13 Here is a solid made from four small cubes. The solid is dipped in red paint. How many cubes have four faces painted red?

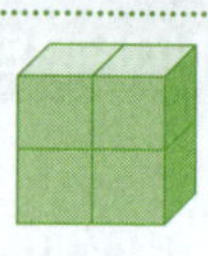

14 Complete the arrow using the dotted line of symmetry.

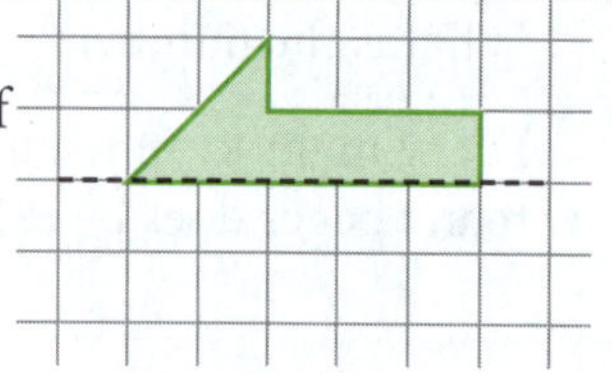

15 Joshua has reflected a shape about the dotted line.

Draw the original shape.

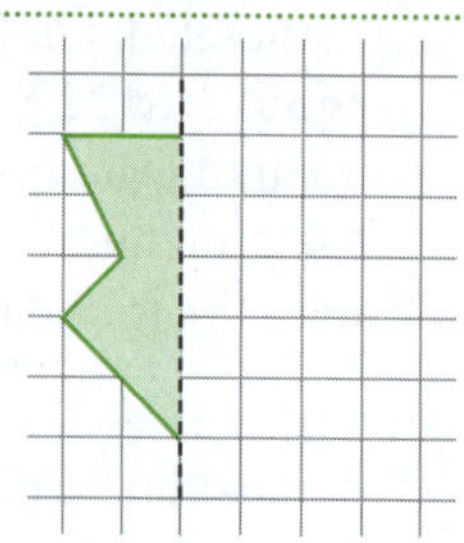

16 The map shows the location of five towns.

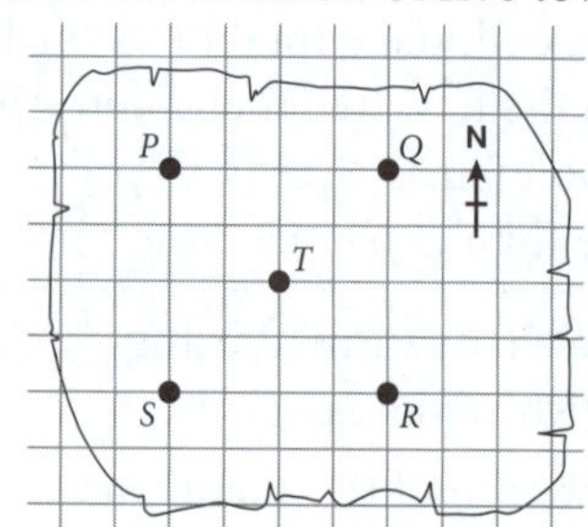

Isabella drives from R to Q. She turns left. In which direction is she now driving?

STATISTICS AND PROBABILITY

17 Circle the spinner with which it is less likely to spin red.

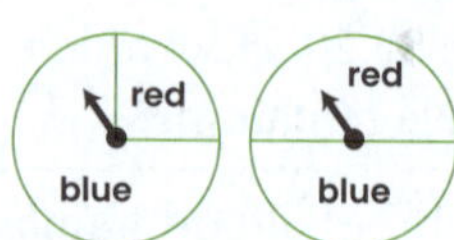

18 The table records the number of tickets sold to adults, children and seniors for a concert.

Category	Tickets
Adults	70
Children	100
Seniors	20

How many more child tickets were sold than senior tickets?

NUMBER AND ALGEBRA

1 Here are five numbers.

7856 7586 7865 7685 7658

The numbers are arranged in order. What is the middle number?

2 The populations in two cities are 46 391 and 86 839. What is the total of the two populations to the nearest thousand?

3 There are eight bags of balls. Each bag contains six red balls and three blue balls. How many more red balls are in the bags altogether than blue balls?

4 Nova has 84 balloons. There is an equal number of red, blue, yellow and pink balloons. How many of the balloons are pink?

5 A grandstand has 3000 seats. If there are 1628 spectators, how many seats are still empty?

6 Divide this hexagon into sixths and shade $\frac{2}{3}$ of the hexagon.

7 What is the missing number?
48 tenths is the same as 4 ones and ? tenths.

8 What is the total of $11.80, $29.50 and $21.85?

9 What is the missing number in this sequence of numbers?

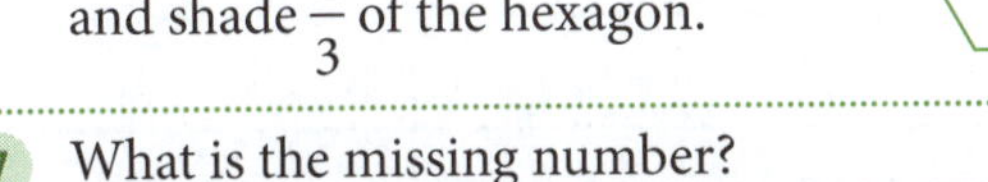

MEASUREMENT AND SPACE

10 A painting measuring 40 cm by 26 cm is to be framed. What length of frame will be used?

11 Evelyn uses four cups of water to fill a jug. She uses three jugs to fill a container.

How many cups can be filled using two containers of water?

12 On average, each person generates 10 kg of waste each week. There are four people living in a household. What is the total amount of waste generated by the household in a fortnight?

13 Here is a solid made from eight small cubes. The solid is dipped in red paint. How many cubes have three faces painted red?

14 Complete the arrow using the dotted line of symmetry.

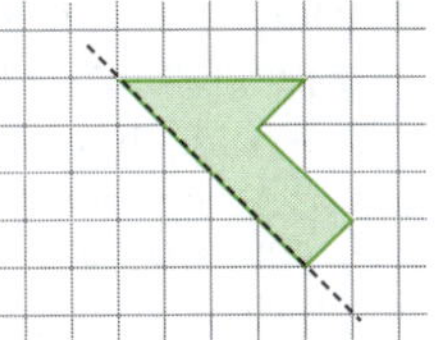

15 Shayna translates the shape 3 units to the left.
Draw the image.

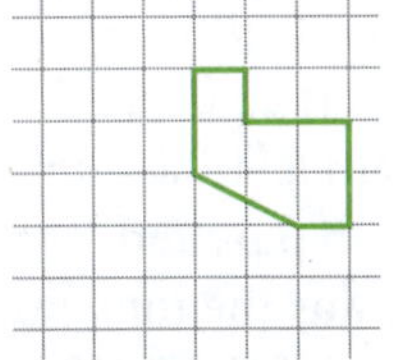

16 The map shows the location of five towns.

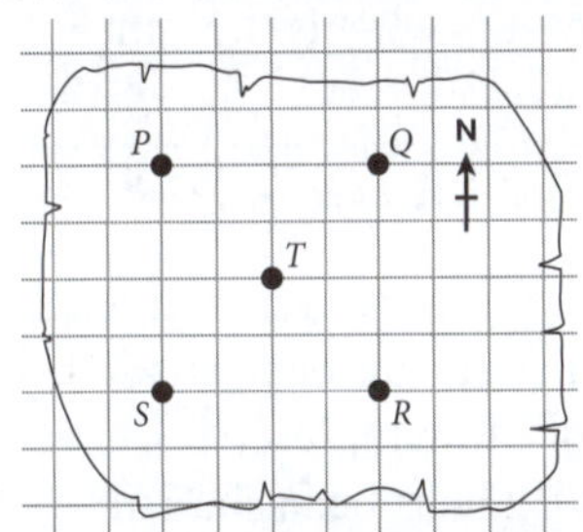

Emily left S and drove to R and then to T. In which direction will she travel if she now drives to Q?

STATISTICS AND PROBABILITY

17 Circle the spinner with which it is least likely to spin blue.

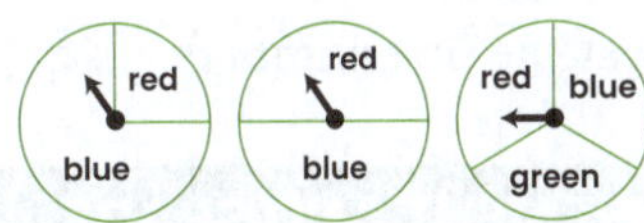

18 The table records the number of tickets sold to adults, children and seniors for a concert.

Category	Tickets
Adults	70
Children	100
Seniors	20

The venue has a capacity of 200 seats. How many seats were still available for sale?

NUMBER AND ALGEBRA

1 Emily writes the number 32 687. She swaps the digit in the thousands place with the digit in the tens place. She also increases the digit in the hundreds place by 3. What is her new number?

2 Mateo has 39 balls. He divides the balls into three equal groups. How many balls are in each group?

3 Over two days Michael had ridden a total of 110 km. If he rode 65 km on the first day, how far did he ride on the second?

4 In a lap-a-thon, Luke completed 18 laps, Samuel 15 laps and Wyatt 11 laps. What was the total number of laps?

5 Janami is four times the age of Advaith. If Advaith is 8 years old, what is the sum of their ages?

6 How many fifths are in 2?

7 Part of a circle has been shaded. Which of these represents the part that has been shaded?

0.2 0.5 0.1

8 Elizabeth receives $8.50 allowance each week from her parents. How much is she paid in a fortnight?

9 Ethan wrote a sequence of numbers using the rule 'add 5'. The third number was 24 and the fourth number was 29. What was the first number?

MEASUREMENT AND SPACE

10 A length of string is 24 cm. It is used to form a triangle with three equal sides. What is the length of each side of the triangle?

11 The solid is made of cm^3 cubes. What is the volume of the solid?

12 Tony can cycle 6 km in 1 hour. At this speed, how far can he cycle in 3 hours?

13 Isla placed a cone on top of a cylinder. Draw the view from the front.

14 Levi drew a regular shape and cut it into two identical shapes. Here is one of the shapes. What shape did Levi originally draw?

15 The shape is to be translated 4 units down. Which of these is covered by the image?
E8 D4 D5

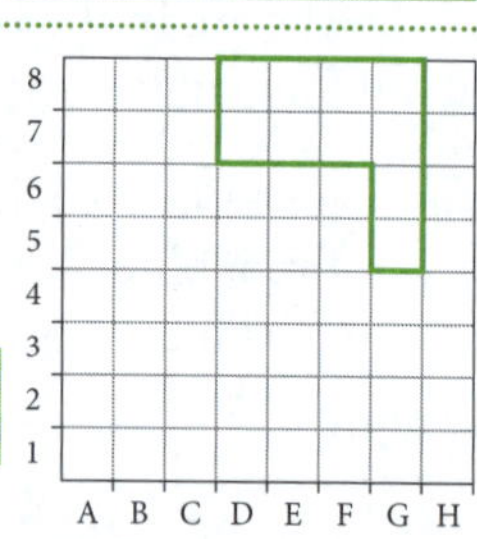

16 Josie looked at the hands of the clock. The hands formed a straight angle. Which of these times could be showing on the clock?
9 o'clock half past 1 six o'clock

STATISTICS AND PROBABILITY

17 The table shows the number of different coloured balls in a box. A ball is chosen without looking. Which colour is most likely to be chosen?

Colour	Number
green	5
brown	3
yellow	6
orange	7

18 The picture graph shows the number of dogs washed by Poodle Plush.

Number of dog washes	
Monday	
Wednesday	
Friday	
Saturday	
Key = ? dogs	

There were eight dogs washed on Monday.

Complete the key: = dogs.

NUMBER AND ALGEBRA

1. Rhys writes the number which is 5 less than 100 000. He then subtracts 4 from the thousands digit, subtracts 3 from the digit in the tens place and adds 2 to the digit in the ones place. What is his new number?

2. Willow brought two punnets of strawberries to school. Each punnet contained 12 strawberries. She shared them equally between herself and three friends. How many strawberries did Willow eat?

3. Elle and Jen walked a total of 17 938 steps. If Elle walked 9653, how many steps did Jen walk?

4. Between midnight and noon, 4967 vehicles used a toll road. Later that day another 6539 vehicles used the road. What was the total number of vehicles?

5. A school hired a bus to transport 50 students to the zoo. Parents also transported students in four cars. Three students travelled in each car. How many students went to the zoo?

6. Circle the fractions that are larger than $\frac{1}{2}$.

   $\frac{5}{8}$ $\frac{4}{10}$ $\frac{7}{12}$ $\frac{26}{50}$

7. Here are three circles. Which of these represents the part that has been shaded?

   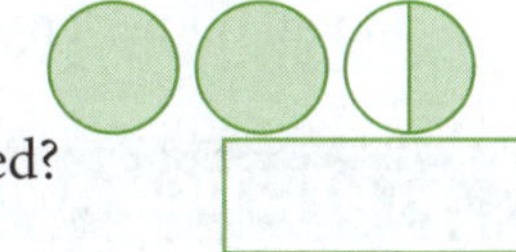

   2.1 2.5 0.25

8. Arlo has $100 to spend. He buys a game for $79.95. How much money has he remaining?

9. Sage wrote a sequence of numbers using the rule 'subtract 7'. The fifth number was 62 and the sixth number was 55. What was the first number?

MEASUREMENT AND SPACE

10. A length of string is 24 cm. It is cut into two equal pieces. One piece is used to form a square. What is the area of the square?

11. The solid is made of cubic-centimetre cubes. What is the volume of the solid?

    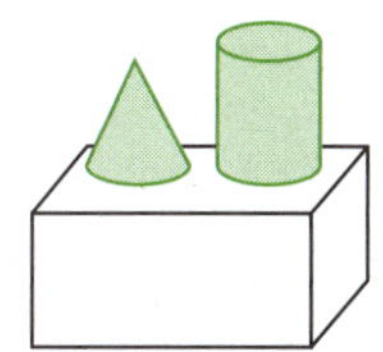

12. Angus drove 80 km in one hour. If he maintained this speed, how far would he travel in 90 minutes?

13. Jasmine placed a cone and a cylinder on top of a rectangular prism. Draw the view from the front.

    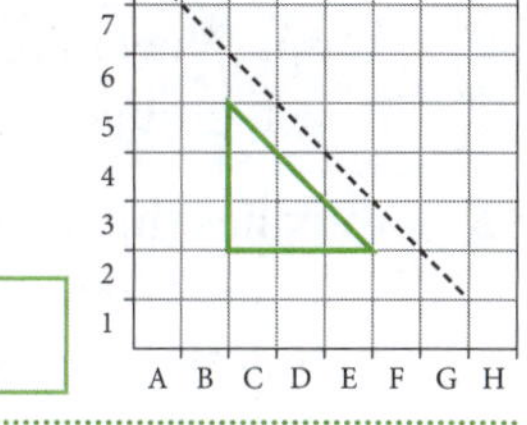

14. Aurora drew the same number of triangles as pentagons. She counted 32 sides on the shapes. How many pentagons were drawn?

15. The shape is to be reflected about the dotted line. Which of these is covered by the image?

    D7 F6 G5

16. How many right angles form a revolution?

STATISTICS AND PROBABILITY

17. A bag contains five pink balls and four purple balls. Two pink balls are removed from the bag. Another ball is chosen without looking. Which colour is more likely to be chosen?

18. The picture graph shows the number of dogs washed by Poodle Plush.

Number of Dog Washes	
Monday	
Wednesday	
Friday	
Saturday	
Key = ? dogs	

The key is missing. If seven dogs were washed on Friday, how many dogs were washed over the four days?

NUMBER AND ALGEBRA

1 There are 3862 stamps in a collection. Luisa rounds the number to the nearest thousand and Teagan rounds the number to the nearest hundred. What is the difference between their two numbers?

2 There were 48 passengers on a bus. At its next stop 27 people got off and 16 got on. How many passengers are now on the bus?

3 What is the missing digit?

```
    4 5
+   ? 7
  -----
  1 3 2
```

4 There are 22 students in Year 4 and 23 students in Year 5. The students are placed into nine equal groups. How many students are in each group?

5 Andy has three water tanks in his backyard. Each tank holds 4000 L when full. What is the total amount of water when the tanks are full?

6 How many halves are in $1\frac{1}{2}$?

7 What is $20 + 7 + \frac{3}{10} + \frac{9}{100}$ written as a decimal?

8 Clara bought an ice cream and received change of $2.30. If she gave the shop assistant $5, how much did the ice cream cost?

9 What is the missing number in this number sentence?

$4 \times 5 = 28 - ?$

MEASUREMENT AND SPACE

10 The length of this rectangle is three times its width. If the length is 6 cm, what is the width?

6 cm

11 Rob has poured some water into a jug. How much water is in the jug?

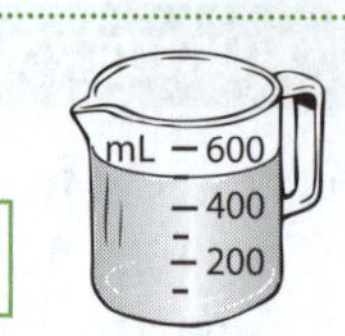

12 A healthy adult should consume a maximum of 50 g of sugar each day. Jason calculated he had consumed 25 g more than he should. How many grams of sugar did Jason consume?

13 Leo cut a sphere into hemispheres. How many hemispheres were made?

14 Minh multiplied the number of lines of symmetry on a square and a rectangle.
What was Minh's answer?

15 The shape is rotated a quarter turn in a clockwise direction about *X*.

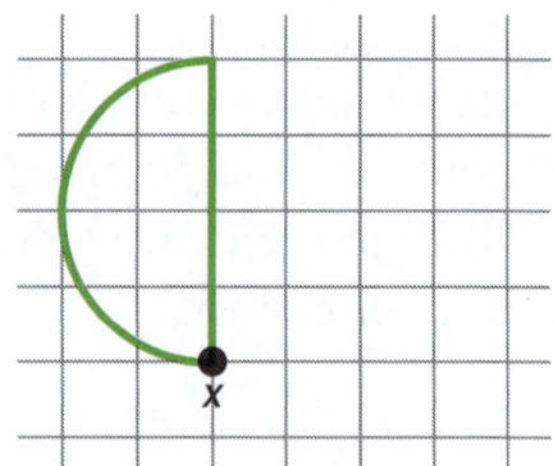

Draw the image.

16 In the space draw a quadrilateral with an acute angle, two right angles and an obtuse angle.

STATISTICS AND PROBABILITY

17 Circle the spinner on which it is impossible to spin yellow.

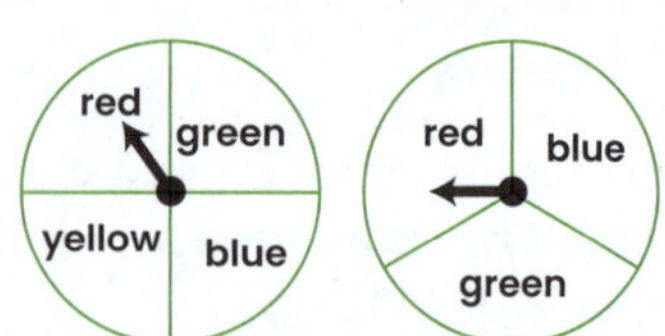

18 The results of a survey to find last night's bedtime of students are recorded below.

How many students were in bed before 9:00?

Time	Number
before 8:30	6
between 8:30 and 9:00	12
between 9:00 and 9:30	9
after 9:30	2

NUMBER AND ALGEBRA

1 There are 126 479 books in a library. Karly rounds the number to the nearest thousand and Jenna rounds the number to the nearest hundred. Which girl's rounding gives the higher number?

2 Levi is 8 years older than Henry. If Levi is 35 years old, what is the sum of their ages?

3 What is the missing digit?

$$\begin{array}{r} 2\ {}^{1}3\ 8 \\ +\ \boxed{?}\ 5\ 9 \\ \hline 6\ 9\ 7 \\ \hline \end{array}$$

4 There are five times as many adults as children on a ferry. If there are 150 adults, how many children are on the ferry?

5 A fruit-shop owner has 10 buckets of apples to sell. Each bucket contains eight apples. At the end of the day three buckets remain. How many apples have been sold?

6 How many tenths are in $1\frac{1}{5}$?

7 Circle the larger number.

$\frac{3}{100}$ 0.2

8 Fiona bought three boxes of cereal at $4.15 each. How much change did she receive from $20?

9 What is the missing number in this number sentence?

$48 \div 6 = 11 - 6 + \boxed{?}$

MEASUREMENT AND SPACE

10 The length of this rectangle is twice its width. If the length is 8 cm, what is the area?

8 cm

11 Water has been poured into two jugs. Tim pours all the water from Jug A into Jug B.

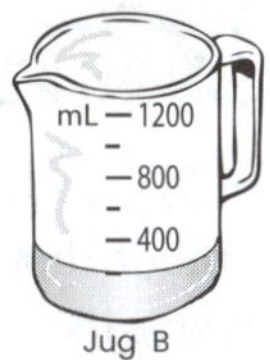

How much water is now in Jug B?

12 A bag contains 1 kg of flour. Charlotte uses 240 g of the flour. What amount remains in the bag?

13 Anna made a model of a triangular pyramid. How many triangular faces has the pyramid?

14 An angle in a parallelogram measures 60°. What is the measurement of the angle opposite?

15 The shape is rotated a quarter turn in a clockwise direction about X. Draw the image.

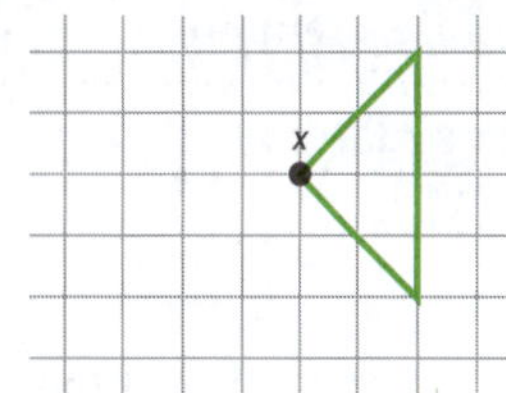

16 Draw a pentagon with two obtuse angles, two right angles and an acute angle.

STATISTICS AND PROBABILITY

17 Circle the spinner on which it is more likely to spin red.

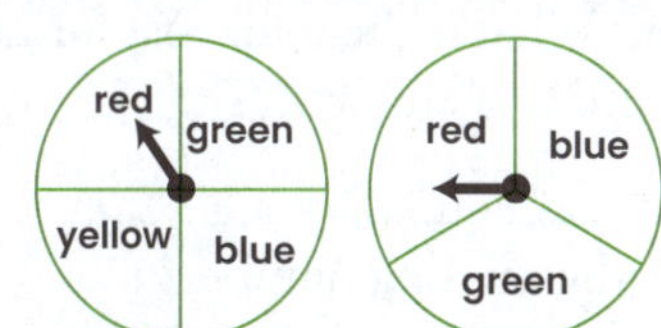

18 The results of a survey to find last night's bedtime of students are recorded below.

Time	Number
before 8:30	6
between 8:30 and 9:00	12
between 9:00 and 9:30	9
after 9:30	2

How many students went to bed after 8:30?

NUMBER AND ALGEBRA

1 Here are five digits: 3, 7, 4, 8, 5. What is the largest even number that can be formed using the digits?

2 Sofia draws a row of octagons. She looks at the octagons and counts 88 sides. How many octagons have been drawn?

3 What is the missing number?

$9 \times 24 = 9 \times 20 + 9 \times$?

4 Jiao and Elsa both collect coins. Jiao has collected 430 and Elsa has 380. What is the total number of coins?

5 A bike shop has 116 bikes in stock. During a sale 75 bikes were sold.
How many bikes remain?

6 Here are six squares.

Kinsley shades one-third of the squares. How many squares are shaded?

7 Locate $\frac{7}{10}$ on the number line.

0 0.2 0.4 0.6 0.8 1

8 Zoo admission costs $35 for adults and $15 for children. What is the total cost for tickets for a parent and two children?

9 What is the missing number?

$3\frac{2}{5}, 3\frac{3}{5}, 3\frac{4}{5}, 4,$?

MEASUREMENT AND SPACE

10 A length of wire is 2 m. The wire is cut into two pieces. If the longer piece is 1 m 45 cm long, what is the length of the shorter piece?

11 A can holds 420 mL of soup. What is the total capacity of two cans?

12 Natalia's tram arrived at 10 minutes to 8. She got off the tram at 4 minutes past 8. How long was the journey?

13 Emma drew a sphere, a cylinder and a pyramid. Which shape has a triangular face?

14 Declan wants to draw a triangle with exactly one line of symmetry.
Complete the triangle.

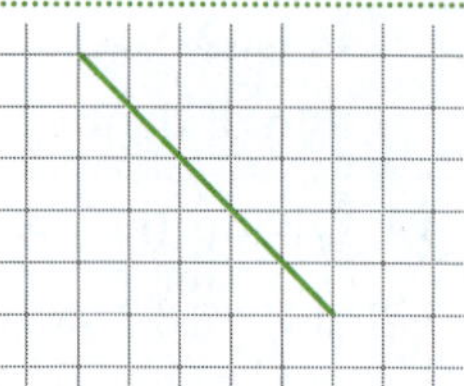

15 The shape is reflected about the dotted line.

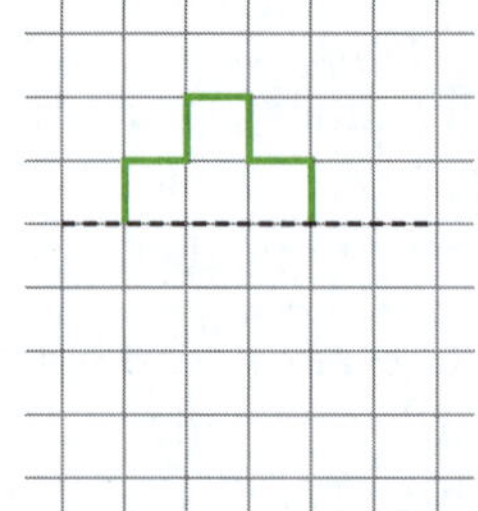

Draw the image.

16 Tick the obtuse angles inside this shape.

STATISTICS AND PROBABILITY

17 A spinner has red, green, yellow and blue sections.
Which colour is the arrow least likely to spin?

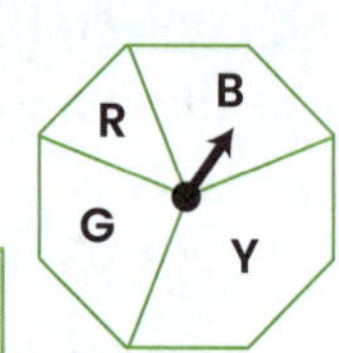

18 The votes for three candidates are recorded in the table.

	Olivia	Harper	Charlotte
Year 3	6	13	8
Year 4	4	12	11
Year 5	8	5	9

How many students in Year 4 voted for Charlotte?

NUMBER AND ALGEBRA

1 Taj used the digits 6, 8, 3, 2 and 7 to make the smallest possible odd number larger than 5000. What is Taj's number?

2 There are 10 biscuits in a packet. Charlotte buys four packets and takes them to a morning tea. There are 20 people at the morning tea and each person eats the same number of biscuits. If all the biscuits are eaten, how many biscuits will each person eat?

3 What is the missing number?

$30 \times 19 = 30 \times \boxed{?} - 30 \times 1$

4 What is the total of the three consecutive even numbers starting at 200?

5 Abbie has made 96 candles. She sells 23 candles on Saturday and 38 candles on Sunday. How many candles remain?

6 Wyatt has eight squares. He shades $\frac{3}{4}$ of the squares. How many squares are shaded?

7 Locate $\frac{36}{100}$ on the number line.

0.3 0.4 0.5

8 An adult ticket to the circus costs $40 and children are half price. What is the total cost for tickets for two parents and three children?

9 What is the missing number?

$2\frac{2}{5}, 2, 1\frac{3}{5}, 1\frac{1}{5}, \boxed{?}$

MEASUREMENT AND SPACE

10 Caleb drew a rectangle on a centimetre grid. The rectangle was 20 cm long and 9 cm wide. What is the area of the rectangle?

11 Jack's lawnmower has a capacity of 9 L of fuel. After mowing, it is only one-third full. How much fuel will he need to fill the tank?

12 Shae practised her spelling for 480 seconds. For how many minutes did she practise?

13 Leigh draws a cube. Each edge is 5 cm. What is the area of the bottom face?

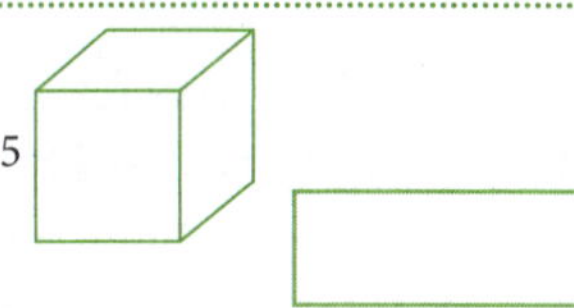

14 Violet draws one side of a triangle with three lines of symmetry.

Complete the triangle.

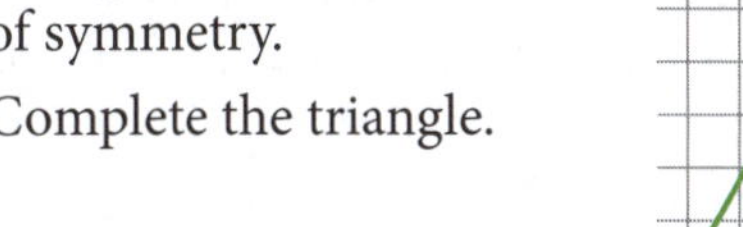

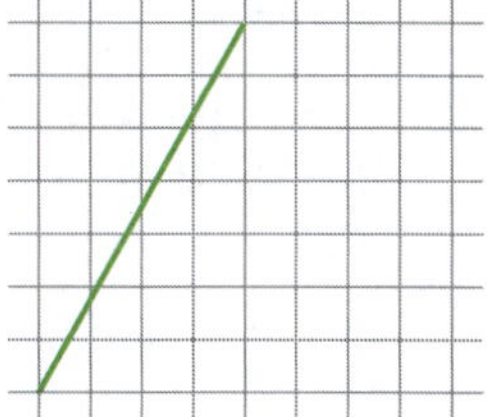

15 The shape is reflected about the dotted line.

Draw the image.

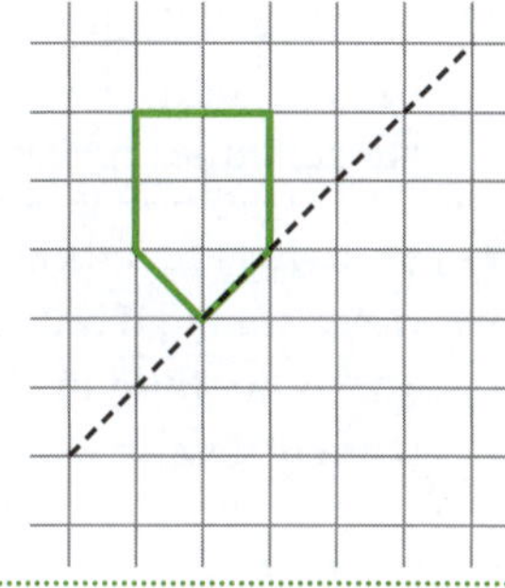

16 A reflex angle is larger than a straight angle but smaller than a revolution. Tick the angles inside this shape that are reflex.

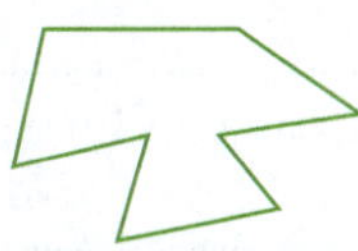

STATISTICS AND PROBABILITY

17 A spinner has red, green, yellow and blue sections. On the first and second spin it points to blue.

What colour is it most likely to point to on the third spin?

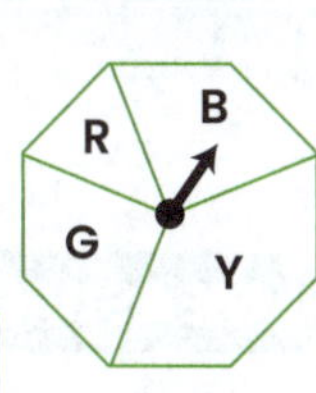

18 The votes for three candidates are recorded in the table.

	Olivia	Harper	Charlotte
Year 3	6	13	8
Year 4	4	12	11
Year 5	8	5	9

How many more votes did Harper receive than Olivia?

NUMBER AND ALGEBRA

1 Fatima has a four-digit PIN to withdraw cash. The digits are in descending order starting with 5. What is her PIN?

2 Peyton has already read 376 pages of her book. There are another 288 pages remaining. What is the total number of pages in the book?

3 In a mathematics competition there are 25 questions. Every correct answer is awarded 4 marks. If Harper answered five questions incorrectly, what is her score?

4 Igor has collected 210 stickers. He gives 53 stickers to his friends. How many stickers does he keep?

5 Students are sitting in three lines. In each line there are eight students. All the students stand up and now stand in six equal groups. How many students are in each group?

6 There are 21 children in a swim class. One-third of the children do not have a sibling. How many children do **not** have a sibling?

7 Write 13 tenths as a decimal.

8 For the school's Winter Appeal, Asher raised \$112 and Hugo \$76. What was the total raised by the two boys?

9 What is double 28?

MEASUREMENT AND SPACE

10 A regular hexagon has a perimeter of 30 cm. What is the length of each side?

11 Ava's fish pond has a capacity of 9000 L. If it currently holds 8300 L, how much more water is needed to fill the pond?

12 An empty container has a mass of 65 g. The container is filled with 120 g of sugar. What is the mass of the container when it is filled with sugar?

13 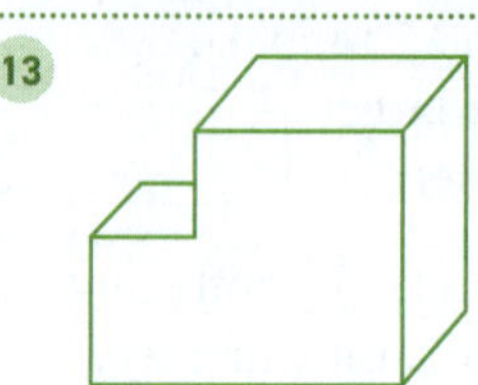

Here is a 3D shape. Laurence picks up the shape and looks at it from all sides.

How many faces has the shape?

14 By drawing two dotted lines, divide this parallelogram into a rectangle and two triangles.

15 The diagram shows the image of a shape that has been translated 4 units to the right.

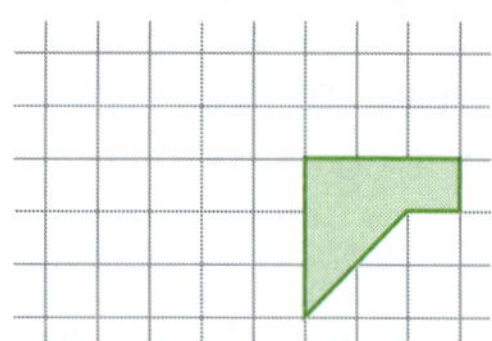

Draw the original shape.

16 The map shows the location of *A* and B.

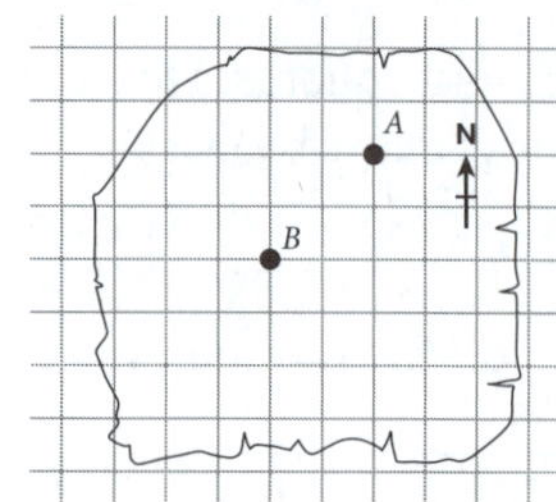

C is directly east of *B* and directly south of *A*. Show the location of *C* on the map.

STATISTICS AND PROBABILITY

17 The faces of a cube are coloured purple or green. The chance that it will land on each colour is equally likely. How many faces are green?

18 Students were surveyed to find the number of siblings they have.

The results are shown in the graph.

How many students had one sibling?

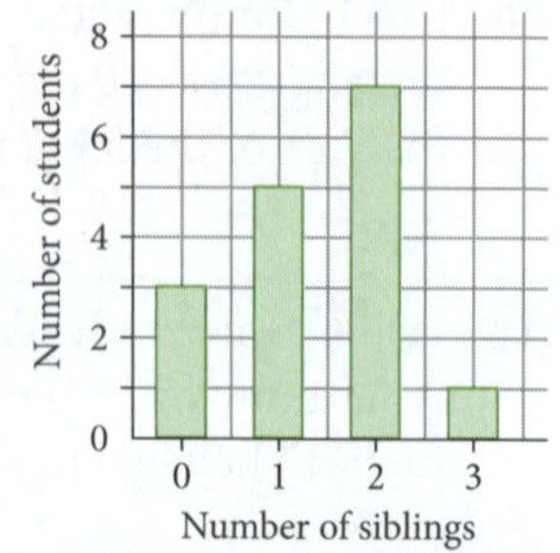

NUMBER AND ALGEBRA

1 Benji needed to change his four-digit PIN. He remembered his PIN as four thousand, six hundred and fifty-three. Benji subtracted 2 from each of the digits in the PIN. What is his new PIN?

2 In an election there were 3563 votes for Ms Green and 2892 votes for Mr Brown. What was the total number of votes for the two candidates?

3 People at an outdoor concert are seated in rows of 50 chairs. If there are 100 rows, what is the total number of chairs?

4 A high school has 1123 students. Today there are 1097 students present. How many students are absent?

5 Eleanor arranged her doll collection into four groups of six dolls. She then placed them into rows of 12 dolls. How many rows has Eleanor?

6 Isaac is collecting sporting cards. There is a total of 36 cards in the set and Isaac has already collected $\frac{3}{4}$ of the set. How many cards has he yet to collect?

7 Write 254 hundredths as a decimal.

8 Freya has saved $78 more than Esme. If Esme has saved $63, what is the total amount saved by the two girls?

9 Two weeks ago Lauren walked 8 km. The following week she doubled the distance and then this week she doubled the distance again. How far did Lauren walk this week?

MEASUREMENT AND SPACE

10 Agnetha has drawn a rectangle measuring 4 cm by 2 cm. She divides the rectangle into two equal triangles. What is the area of the shaded triangle?

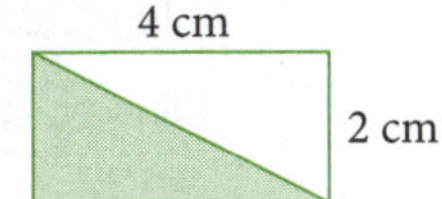

11 Sara bought a 1250-mL bottle of soft drink. What is the capacity of the bottle in litres?

12 Abir used some weights to measure the mass of a package. He used a 2-kg weight, two 500-g weights and a 50-g weight. What was the mass of the package, in grams?

13 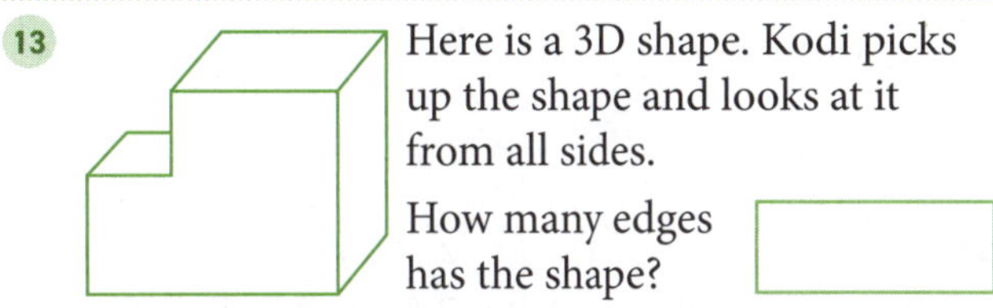
Here is a 3D shape. Kodi picks up the shape and looks at it from all sides.

How many edges has the shape?

14 By drawing four dotted lines, divide this octagon into a square, 4 rectangles and 4 triangles.

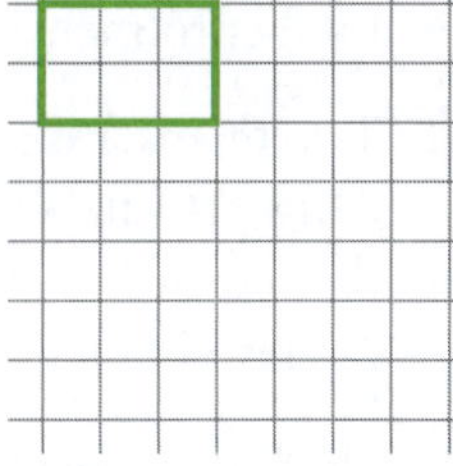

15 The rectangle is translated 3 units to the right and then 3 units down.

Draw the image.

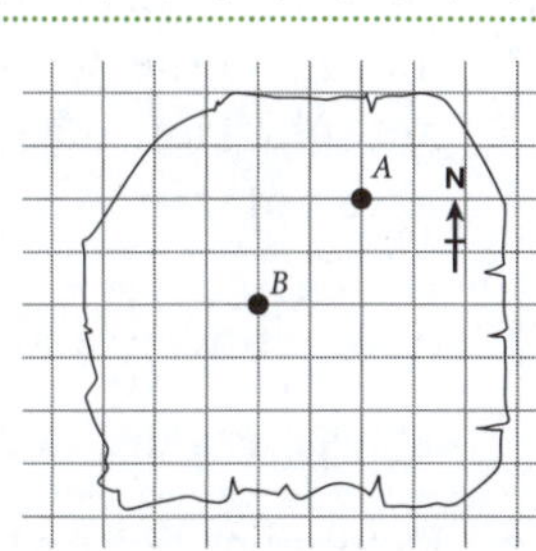

16 The map shows the location of *A* and *B*.

C is directly south-east of *B*. Also *C* and *A* are the same distance from *B*. Show the location of *C* on the map.

STATISTICS AND PROBABILITY

17 The faces of a cube are coloured red, blue or green. What is the chance that the cube lands on purple?

18 Students were surveyed to find the number of siblings they have. The results are shown in the graph.

How many students had at least one sibling?

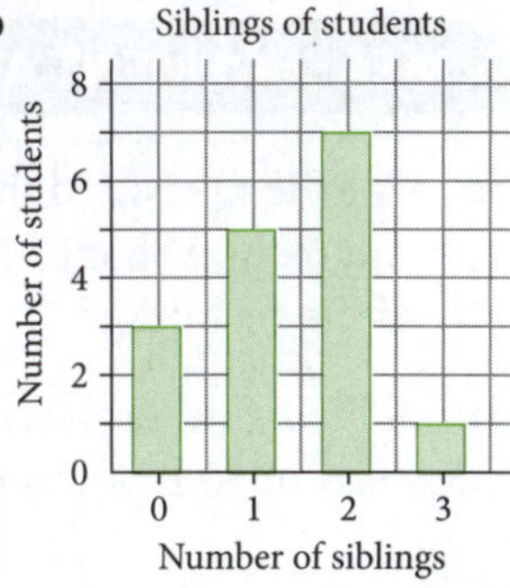

NUMBER AND ALGEBRA

1 Ben wrote the number eighty-five thousand, two hundred and seventy-three. What is Ben's number rounded to the nearest thousand?

2 What is the missing digit?

```
  8 7 8
- 3 ? 5
  -----
  5 1 3
```

3 Brayden placed four chocolates in each of eight bags. He then removed a chocolate from each bag. What is the total number of chocolates in the bags?

4 There are two primary schools in a town. One school has an enrolment of 376 and the other school has 288. What is the total enrolment?

5 Two teams are competing against each other in a tug-of-war. Ava counts 32 legs on the people in the tug-of-war. How many people are on each team?

6 Jaxon baked 24 cakes for the school cake stall. By the end of the day one-quarter of his cakes were not sold. How many of his cakes were **not** sold?

7 Add $\frac{3}{10}$ and $\frac{4}{10}$ and write the answer as a decimal.

8 Delphi has twice as much money as Lulu. Maeve has $20 more than Lulu. If Lulu has $30, how much more money has Delphi than Maeve?

9 Kai started with 2 and wrote down the first 40 even numbers. What was his last number?

MEASUREMENT AND SPACE

10 Charlie measured the sides of a rectangle as 10 cm and 6 cm. What is the perimeter of the rectangle?

11 A litre of water has a mass of 1 kg. What is the mass of 10 L of water?

12 Phil has a bag of 20 identical marbles. The total mass of marbles is 120 g. What is the mass of each marble?

13 Here is a solid made from eight small cubes. The solid is dipped in red paint.

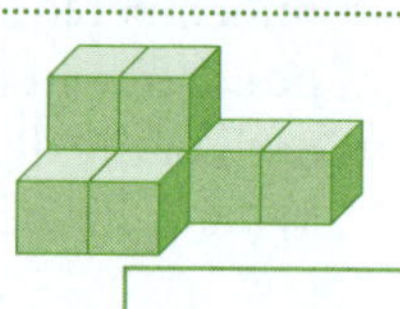

How many cubes have five faces painted red?

14 Here is a hexagon. How many diagonals can be drawn on the shape?

15 The shape is rotated a quarter turn in a clockwise direction.

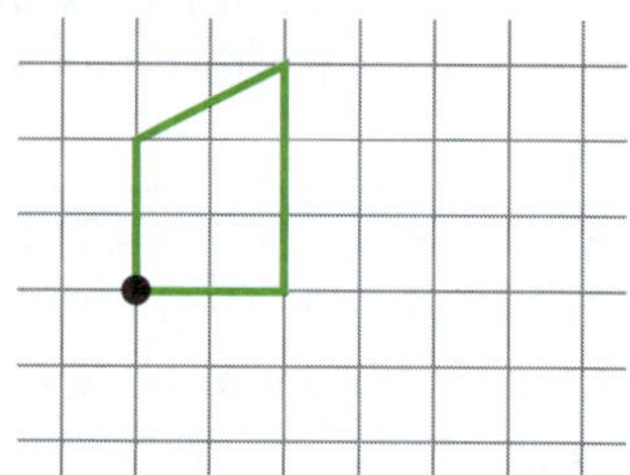

Draw the image.

16 The diagram shows a triangle drawn inside a square. Six angles have been named.

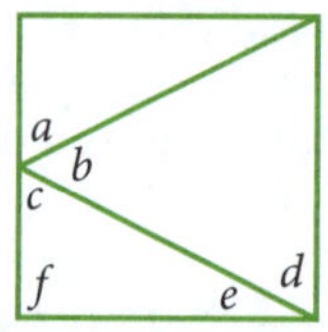

Which angle is a right angle?

STATISTICS AND PROBABILITY

17 A jar contains 30 red jelly beans and 20 black jelly beans. Sam chooses a jelly bean without looking. What colour is more likely to be selected?

18 A group of people were asked for their favourite food from four options. The results are shown in the graph.

How many people voted for Japanese food?

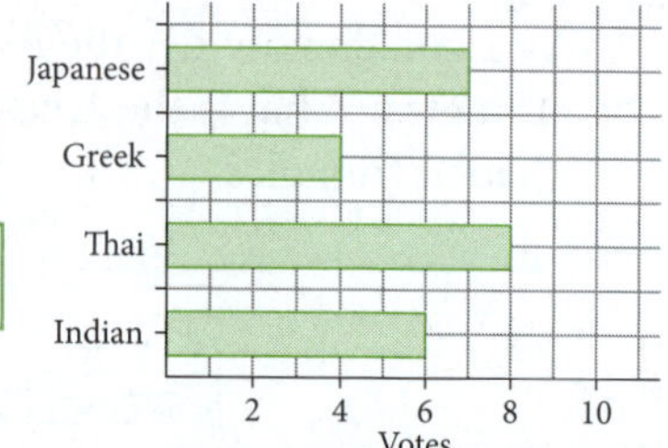

NUMBER AND ALGEBRA

1 Indiah writes a four-digit number. There is a 7 in the thousands place and a 6 in the tens place. The other two digits are eights. She then rounded the number to the nearest hundred. What is the new number?

2 What is the missing digit?

$$\begin{array}{r} 2\,4\,5\,7 \\ -\quad 2\,?\,4 \\ \hline 2\,1\,7\,3 \end{array}$$

3 Sam has a dozen hens. Every hen lays five eggs each week. How many eggs are laid in two weeks?

4 The attendance at two games on Friday night were recorded as 9207 and 7431. What was the total attendance?

5 A teacher gave the same number of blocks to each of her 22 students. If she gave out 66 blocks, how many blocks did each student receive?

6 There are 25 students in Cameron's class. Cameron is planning to invite half the students to his party. How many students will be invited?

7 In the number 0.66 the value of the 6 in the tenths place is ________ times the value of the 6 in the hundredths place.

What is the missing number?

10 100 1000

8 Daphne made 10 scarfs to sell at a market for \$20 each. By the end of the day she had earned \$120 for the sale of the scarfs. How many scarfs were **not** sold?

9 Quinn added the first 30 odd numbers. Was the total even or odd?

MEASUREMENT AND SPACE

10 Alice measured the sides of a rectangle as 3 cm and 12 mm. What is the perimeter of the rectangle in millimetres?

11 A litre of water has a mass of 1 kg. What is the mass of 250 mL of water?

12 Andrea fills a bag with 340 g of peanuts, 260 g of cashews and 100 g of walnuts. What is the total mass of nuts?

13 Here is a solid made from eight small cubes. The solid is dipped in red paint. How many cubes have only two faces painted red?

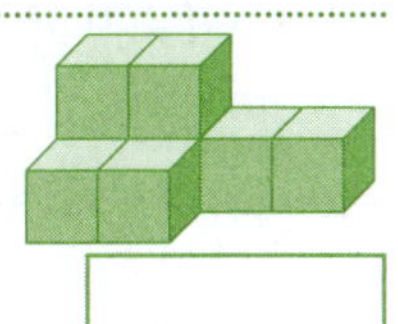

14 The table shows the number of diagonals for different shapes.

Shape	Number of diagonals
triangle	0
rectangle	2
pentagon	5
hexagon	9
heptagon	14

How many diagonals has an octagon?

15 The shape is reflected about the dotted line and then translated 2 units left.

Draw the image.

16 The diagram shows a triangle drawn inside a square. Six angles have been named. How many of the named angles are acute?

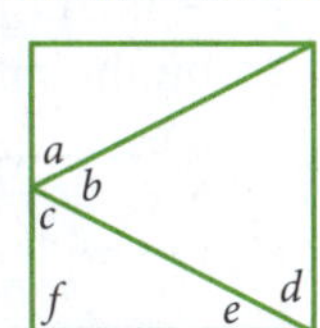

STATISTICS AND PROBABILITY

17 Chris makes a spinner with red (R) and blue (B) sections. The colour of one section is missing. What is the missing colour if it is **less likely** that blue will be spun?

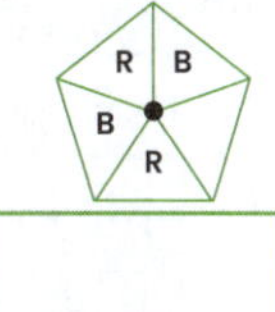

18 A group of people were asked for their favourite food from four options.

The results are shown in the graph but the scale used for the number of votes has been left off. If 12 voted for Indian food, how many more voted for Thai than Greek?

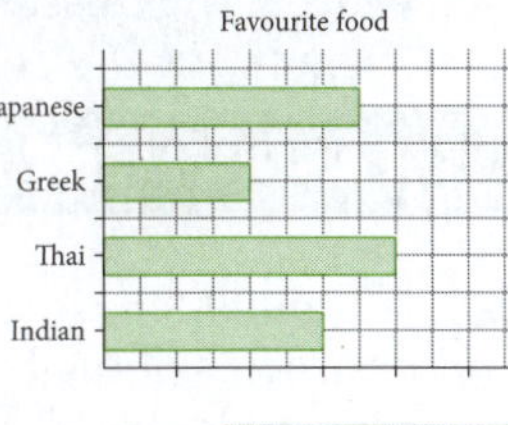

NUMBER AND ALGEBRA

1 Sam thought of a four-digit number. He then swapped the digits in the thousands and ones places. His new number was 4982. What was his original number?

2 What is the difference between the numbers 278 and 136?

3 On a cruise ship there are 1750 adults and 400 children. What is the total number of passengers on the ship?

4 In a soccer competition a win is worth 3 points and a draw worth 1 point. During a season, Eloise's team won eight games and had four draws. What is the team's total point-score?

5 As $8 \times 4 = 32$, circle the correct mathematical sentences.

$32 \div 4 = 8$ $\quad$ $8 \div 4 = 32$ $\quad$ $32 \div 8 = 4$

6 There are 21 books on the class reading list. Bella has already read $\frac{1}{3}$ of the books. How many of the books has she read?

7 Which is the missing number on the number line?

2 ? 3

8 How many dollars are in 9750 cents?

9 The numbers in the bottom row of the table have been found using the rule 'double the number in the top row and add 4'.

Top row	3	5	7	9
Bottom row	10	14	18	?

What is the missing number?

MEASUREMENT AND SPACE

10 A triangle has two sides with length 8 cm. If the perimeter of the triangle is 20 cm, what is the length of the third side?

11 The petrol tank in Mateo's car holds 50 L. The tank is full at the beginning of a trip and Mateo uses 29 L over a journey. What amount remains?

12 Dion arrived at the bus stop at 9:35. He waited 18 minutes for his bus to arrive. At what time did the bus arrive?

13 Alison rolled a pair of normal dice. What is the total number of faces on the dice?

14 How many more squares need to be shaded so that the dotted line is a line of symmetry?

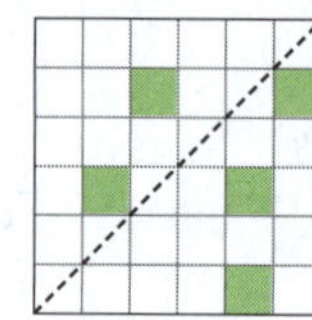

15 The shape is reflected about the dotted line.

Draw the image.

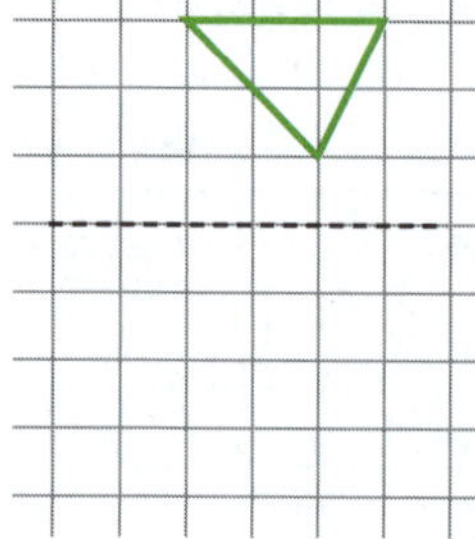

16 The compass is missing from a map showing the location of four towns.

If *A* is north of *B*, what is the direction of *D* from *B*?

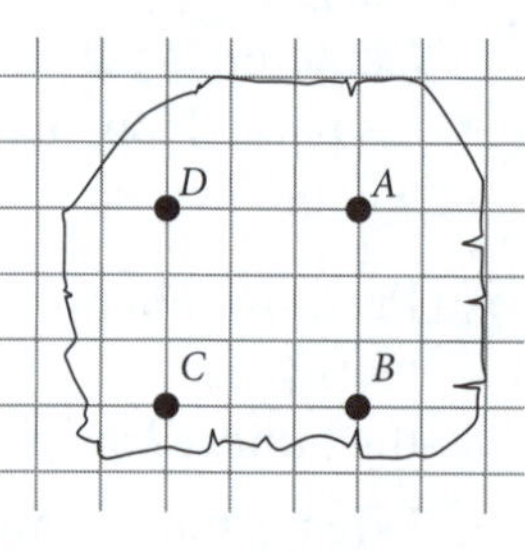

STATISTICS AND PROBABILITY

17 Here is a box containing red and blue balls. A red ball is more likely to be chosen than a blue ball. Label the balls using the letters R or B.

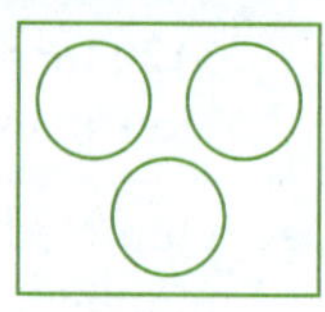

18 The graph shows the hair colour of students in Year 4.

How many more students have blonde hair than red hair?

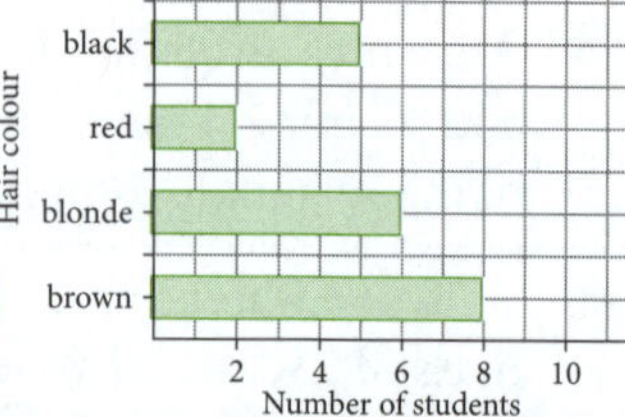

NUMBER AND ALGEBRA

1 James used the four digits larger than 5 to make the largest possible four-digit number that is odd. What is the number?

2 Two towns have populations of 13 896 and 4753. What is the difference between the two populations, to the nearest hundred?

3 A recycling factory processed 7560 bottles on Monday, 3786 on Tuesday and 5603 on Wednesday. What was the total number in the three days?

4 An apartment building has four floors. Each floor has nine apartments. Each apartment has two bedrooms. What is the total number of bedrooms in the building?

5 As ▲ × ● = ■, circle the correct mathematical sentences.

● ÷ ■ = ▲   ■ ÷ ▲ = ●

6 12 students were asked about the way they travel to school. Half of the students catch the bus. Half of the remaining students walk. How many students do **not** catch the bus or walk?

7 Which is the missing number on the number line?

3 4 ?

8 On a driving holiday, Jordie stopped three times to buy petrol. He spent \$96.28, \$56.30 and \$87.02. What was the total cost?

9 The numbers in the bottom row have been found using the rule 'triple the number in the top row and subtract 7'. Complete:

Top row	4	7	8	*B*
Bottom row	5	*A*	17	29

A =

B =

MEASUREMENT AND SPACE

10 The perimeter of a square is 40 cm. What is the area of the square?

11 At the start of a journey a car has 32 L of petrol in its tank. During the journey the driver bought another 28 L. At the end of the journey there was 10 L remaining. How much petrol was used?

12 The flight from Sydney to Perth takes 5 h. From Sydney to Darwin the flight takes 4 h 35 min. What is the difference between the two times?

13 On the centimetre grid paper draw a sketch of a rectangular prism with faces which have areas of 6 cm^2, 8 cm^2 and 12 cm^2.

14 How many more squares need to be shaded so that the dotted lines are lines of symmetry?

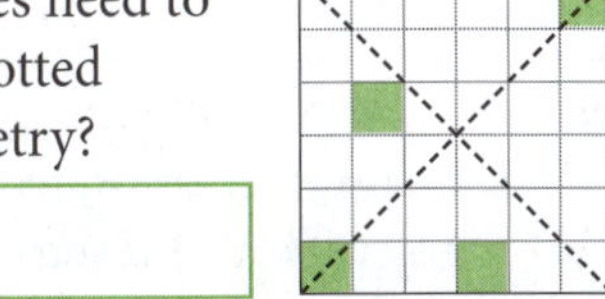

15 The shape is rotated a quarter turn about *X* in a clockwise direction and then translated 2 units left.

Draw the image.

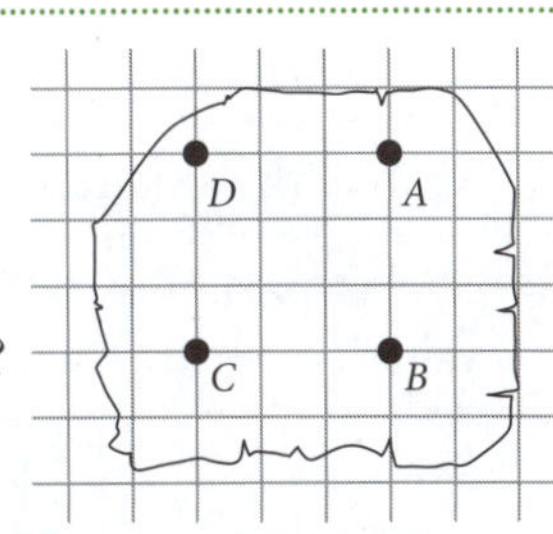

16 The compass is missing from a map showing the location of four towns.

If *C* is north of *B*, what is the direction of *B* from *A*?

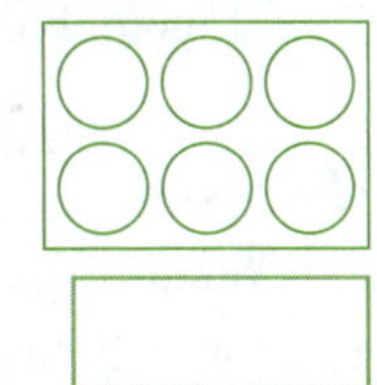

STATISTICS AND PROBABILITY

17 The diagram shows six balls in a box. The balls are either red or blue. Choosing a red ball without looking has the same chance as choosing a blue ball. Label the balls using the letters R or B.

18 The graph shows the hair colour of students in Year 4.

There are 29 students in Year 4. How many students were **not** surveyed?

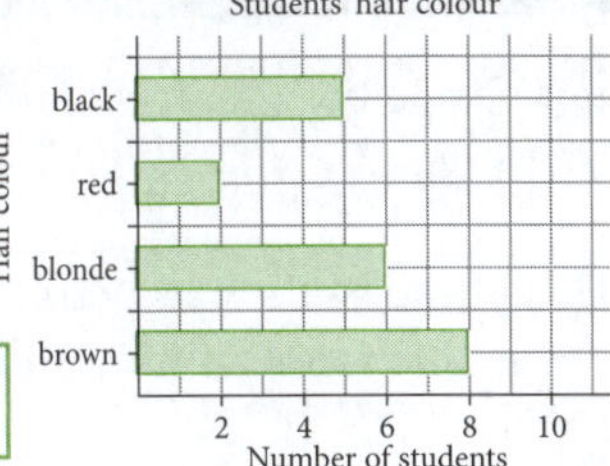

NUMBER AND ALGEBRA

1 Here is a four-digit number with a missing digit.

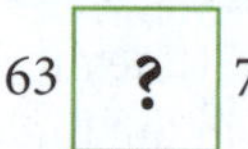

The sum of the four digits is 21.
What is the four-digit number?

2 Boris divides his age by 4. He gets an answer of 5 with a remainder of 2. How old is Boris?

3 At the school's swimming carnival Mawson house finished with 790 points. It was 105 points behind Hunter. How many points had Hunter house scored?

4 A supermarket sells bags of carrots. Milla buys six bags. If there were 12 carrots in each bag, how many carrots did she buy?

5 Harlow has 48 golf balls. He gives 13 balls to Tobias and nine balls to Milo. How many balls does Harlow keep?

6 Miranda wrote these fractions.

$\frac{1}{3}$ $\frac{1}{8}$ $\frac{1}{4}$ $\frac{1}{5}$

Circle the smallest fraction.

7 What part of this shape has been shaded, written as a decimal?

8 Hazel has been given $50 to spend on her holidays. After a week she has $28 remaining. How much money has she spent?

9 Here is a sequence of numbers: 12, 19, 26, 33 … What is the sixth number in the sequence?

MEASUREMENT AND SPACE

10 Circle the greatest length.

1001 mm 1 m 102 cm

11 There is 4.5 L of petrol remaining in a tank. What is this amount in millilitres?

12 A chocolate has a mass of 200 g. Alma ate 60 g of the chocolate. What mass remains?

13 A pyramid has five triangular faces. How many sides has the shape on the base of the pyramid?

14 A parallelogram has been divided into two equal triangles.

If the area of each triangle is 12 cm², what was the area of the parallelogram?

15 The triangle is rotated a quarter turn clockwise about *X*.

Draw the image.

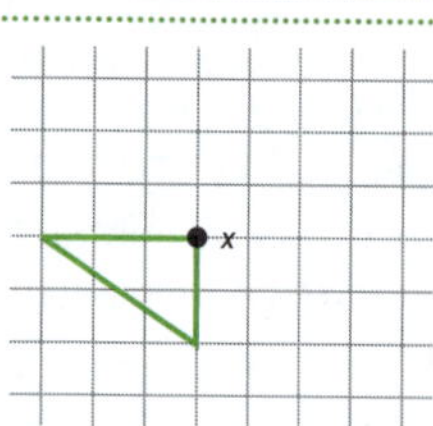

16 The clocks show the start and finish times for a dental appointment.

Complete the statement.

The minute hand moved through a ______ turn.

STATISTICS AND PROBABILITY

17 There are 100 tickets sold in a raffle. Nolan buys 10 tickets, Theo buys five tickets and Nathaniel buys one ticket. Circle the words that best describe the chance that Nathaniel's ticket is drawn to win the raffle prize.

unlikely even chance impossible

18 Lilian has a bag of jelly beans. A jelly bean is selected without looking, the colour recorded and eaten.

What was the total number of red, pink and black jelly beans eaten?

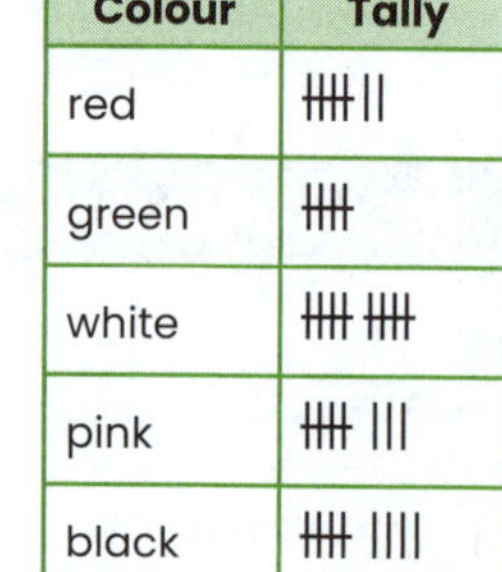

Colour	Tally
red	𝍸 II
green	𝍸
white	𝍸 𝍸
pink	𝍸 III
black	𝍸 IIII

NUMBER AND ALGEBRA

1 Here is a five-digit number with two identical missing digits. The sum of the five digits is 25.

2 ? 0 ? 9

What is the five-digit number, written in words?

2 The average of three numbers is found by adding the numbers and dividing the total by 3. In three games Theo scored 12, 15 and 6. What is his average score?

3 In April a pizza shop sold 3548 pizzas. In May 4652 pizzas were sold and in June another 3895. What was the total number of pizzas sold in the three months?

4 Tahlia is four times the age of her daughter Chloe. If Chloe is 9 years old, how old was Tahlia when Chloe was born?

5 Magaly collects stuffed toys. She has 43 toys in her collection. Her cousin gives her all her stuffed toys. If Magaly now has 81 toys, how many toys was she given by her cousin?

6 Jacqueline wrote a list of fractions.

$\frac{2}{3}$ $\frac{7}{8}$ $\frac{3}{4}$ $\frac{4}{5}$

Circle the smallest fraction.

7 A regular pentagon is cut into identical triangles. Cian shades three of the triangles. What part of this pentagon has been shaded, written as a decimal?

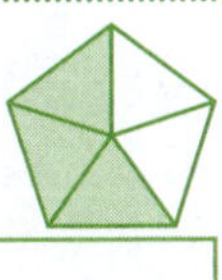

8 Brothers Jean and Remy are saving to buy their father a birthday present worth $200. Jean has saved $60 and Remy has saved $30 more than his brother. How much more do they need to save?

9 A sequence of numbers starts with 8 and increases by 6. What is the tenth number in the sequence?

MEASUREMENT AND SPACE

10 A wall has dimensions 12 m by 3 m. The wall is to be painted at a cost of $10 per m^2. What will be the cost to paint the wall?

11 A litre of water has a mass of 1 kg. An empty bucket has a mass of 1 kg. What is the total mass of a bucket containing 9 L?

12 At the airport Fiona checked in two suitcases. One bag had a mass of 16 kg and the other 12 kg. The airline allowed a total baggage mass of 30 kg. Is Fiona's total mass under or over the baggage allowance?

13 William draws a cube. The sum of the lengths of all the edges is 36 cm. What is the area of each face of the cube?

14 A square has been divided into four equal triangles.

If the area of the square was 36 cm^2, what is the area of each triangle?

15 The triangle is rotated a half turn about X.

Draw the image.

16 The clocks show the start and finish times for a journey.

Complete the statement.

The hour hand moved through a ______ turn.

STATISTICS AND PROBABILITY

17 There are 100 tickets sold in a raffle. Nolan buys 10 tickets, Theo buys five tickets and Nathaniel buys one ticket. Circle the words that best describe the chance that one of Nolan's tickets is drawn out to win the raffle prize.

unlikely even chance impossible

18 There are 50 jelly beans in a bag. One by one, jelly beans are selected without looking, the colour recorded and eaten.

How many jelly beans remain in the bag?

Colour	Tally
red	卌 II
green	卌
white	卌 卌
pink	卌 III
black	卌 IIII

NUMBER AND ALGEBRA

1 Jack wrote the statement 'Three odd numbers plus an even number gives an odd number'. Is the statement true or false?

2 In a shop there are six tricycles and eight bicycles for sale. What is the total number of wheels?

3 Evelyn baked some cupcakes. She arranged the cupcakes into five rows of eight cupcakes. Her mother placed the cupcakes into four containers. How many cupcakes were in each container?

4 Bo counts her sheep on her property. After a muster she decides to sell 120 sheep and keep 430 sheep. How many sheep did Bo originally have on the property?

5 Here are three numbered cards.

4 6 2

Logan and Owen use the cards to make three-digit numbers. Logan makes the largest possible number. Owen makes the smallest possible number. What is the difference between their two numbers?

6 Here are 10 oranges.

If half of the oranges are used to make juice, how many remain?

7 Aastha added a decimal to 0.7 to give 1. What decimal did she add?

8 Ivy charges $10 for every hour of babysitting. In a month she has babysat for 16 hours. How much money has she earned?

9 Violet multiplied 5 and 6. Her answer is 10 more than her age. How old is Violet?

MEASUREMENT AND SPACE

10 Lydia draws a rectangle on a centimetre grid. The width of the rectangle is 3 cm. The distance around the rectangle is 16 cm. What is the length of the rectangle?

11 Ella's drink bottle contains 900 mL of water. She drinks 300 mL. What amount remains?

12 A plane is scheduled to depart Sydney airport at 6:10 pm. If it was 27 minutes late, what was the time of departure?

13 How many rectangular faces does a hexagonal prism have?

14 Ella used six of these triangles to form a regular hexagon. Draw Ella's hexagon.

15 The shape is translated 5 units to the right and then 2 units to the left.

Draw the image.

16 How many quarter turns does the minute hand make between the times of 4 o'clock and 5 o'clock?

STATISTICS AND PROBABILITY

17 A bag contains three red balls and two white balls. A ball is chosen from the bag without looking. Circle the words that describe the chance a red ball is chosen.

less likely even chance more likely

18 The results of a survey of students' favourite Saturday activity are displayed in the graph.

How many more girls liked the movies than boys?

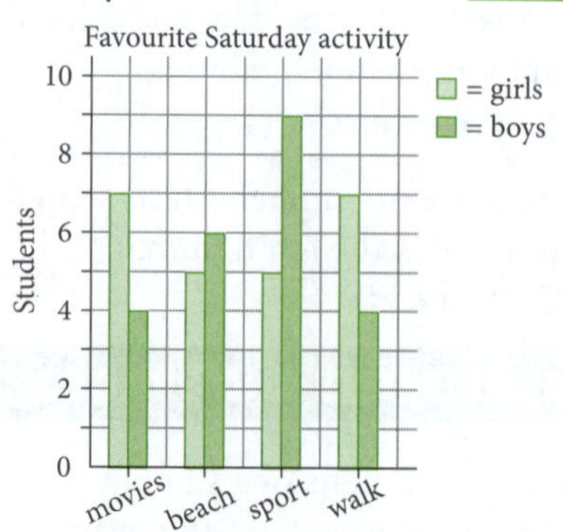

NUMBER AND ALGEBRA

1 True or false?
An odd number of odd numbers is added to an even number of even numbers.
The result is always odd.

2 A teacher gives each student in the class four plastic shapes. There are 23 students enrolled in the class but two students are absent. How many shapes are handed out by the teacher?

3 Luisa thinks of a number. She multiplies her number by 6 and the result is 48. What would have been the answer if she had divided her number by 2?

4 A fruit-shop owner has 80 green apples. He has 240 more red apples than green apples. What is the total number of red and green apples?

5 Here are four numbered cards.

4 5 7 2

Ella and Frida use the cards to make four-digit numbers. Ella makes the largest possible number. Frida makes the smallest possible number. What is the difference between their two numbers?

6 It is Lydia's 12th birthday. Her father places 12 candles on her cake. He places half the candles in one row and a third of the candles in a second row. The rest of the candles are in a third row. How many candles are in the third row?

7 How many 0.5s are in a whole?

8 Colette paid $50 for 2 kg of prawns and received $4 change. What was the cost of a kilogram of prawns?

9 Asher is 9 years old. In 6 years, he will be three times as old as his brother Silas is now. How old is Silas?

MEASUREMENT AND SPACE

10 A rectangle has a perimeter of 24 cm. Find the area if the length of the rectangle is 8 cm.

11 A 2-L bottle of soft drink is opened. Six glasses, each with a capacity of 200 mL, are filled with soft drink. What amount remains in the bottle?

12 Lillian left her home at 6:53 am. She walked for 1 h 16 min. What time did she arrive back home?

13 A prism has 18 edges. How many faces has the prism?

14 Freya used one square and four of these triangles to form a large square. Draw Freya's square.

15 The shape is translated 2 units down and then 3 units to the right.
Draw the image.

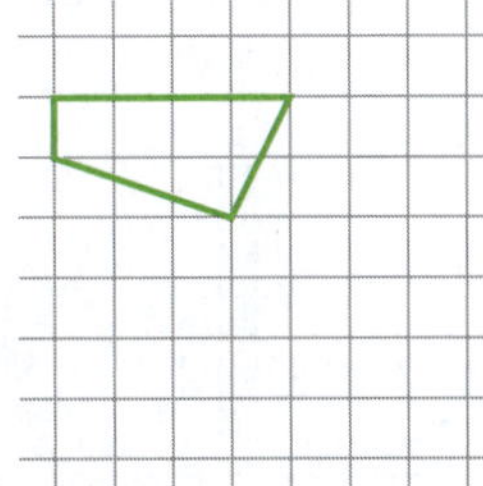

16 How many quarter turns does the minute hand make between the times of quarter to 5 and half past 7?

STATISTICS AND PROBABILITY

17 A bag contains three red balls and two white balls. A red ball is removed from the bag. Another ball is chosen without looking. Circle the words that describe the chance another red ball is chosen.

less likely even chance more likely

18 The results of a survey of students' favourite Saturday activity are displayed in the graph.
How many more girls than boys were surveyed?

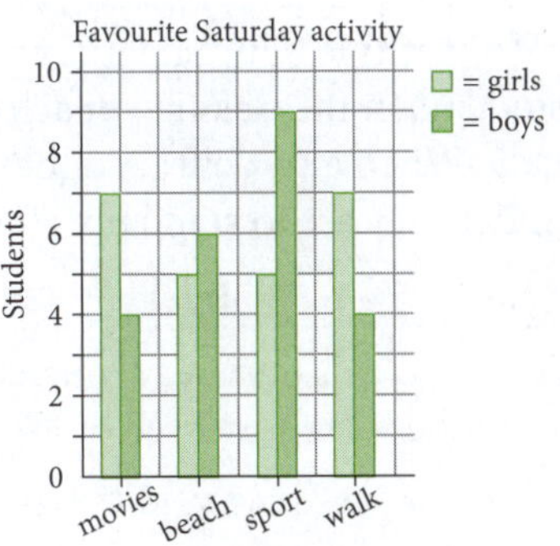

NAPLAN-STYLE TEST 2

1 Naomi wrote this number sentence.

$5 \times 3 \times 6 \times 2 \times 7 = \boxed{?} \times 14 \times 5$ What is the missing number?

2 Corey has drawn a number line and located the numbers 2 and 3.

Which of these is the missing number?

2 3 ?

A $3\frac{3}{4}$ **B** $3\frac{4}{5}$ **C** $4\frac{1}{4}$ **D** $4\frac{1}{3}$

3 Dane buys these vegetables at a supermarket.
Which of these is closest to the total cost of the vegetables?

Carrots	$2.90
Potatoes	$4.20
Lettuce	$3.80
Onions	$3.10
Celery	$2.90

A $15 **B** $17
C $19 **D** $22

4 Shapes are drawn on grid paper.
Which shape has a perimeter of 16 units and an area of 15 square units?

A **B** **C** **D**

5 Marcus has these five numbered cards. 4 6 2 7 3

Marcus wrote the largest possible three-digit odd number using the cards.
This number was then subtracted from 1000. What is the result?

6 How many of these flags have **more** than one line of symmetry?

Flag *P* Flag *Q* Flag *R* Flag *S*

A 0 **B** 1 **C** 2 **D** 3 **E** 4

7 This year Sally's birthday is on the second Sunday in July.
Her friend Agnes has her birthday exactly three weeks before Sally.
What is the date of Agnes's birthday?

July						
Sunday	Monday	Tuesday	Wednesday	Thursday	Friday	Saturday
						1
2	3	4	5	6	7	8
9	10	11	12	13	14	15
16	17	18	19	20	21	22
23	24	25	26	27	28	29
30	31					

A 18 June **B** 19 June **C** 26 June **D** 6 August

8 During a maths lesson, Mr Abrams calls out all the numbers from 1 to 100.
The students in the class have each been given a different number. Liam is given the number 2, Jack 3 and Sophia 5. When a student's number divides into Mr Abrams's number without a remainder they are to stand up. How many times will Liam, Jack and Sophia stand together?

A 1 **B** 2 **C** 3 **D** 4 **E** 5

9 Each shape in this number sentence stands for a different number. ● + ● = 12 ■ − ● = 8
What number is represented by ■?

A 4 **B** 10 **C** 12 **D** 14

10 Three friends live on a straight road. Rowan and Sammi live 160 m apart. Sammi and Theo live 70 m apart. Which of these could be the distance that Rowan and Theo live apart? Select **all** possible answers.

A 90 m **B** 110 m **C** 220 m **D** 230 m

11 Daniel arranges identical blocks into triangular shapes as shown in this pattern.

3 blocks 6 blocks 10 blocks

Daniel continues the pattern with more blocks.

How many blocks will be on the bottom row of the triangular shape containing 28 blocks?

A 5 **B** 6 **C** 7 **D** 8

12 Max is given a $100 gift card for her birthday. She uses the gift card to buy a book for $14 and a pair of jeans for $69. How much money value remains on the card? $

13 A bike shop recorded the number of bikes sold each month for the final five months of the year. How many more bikes were sold in August, September and October compared to November and December?

Month	Number of bikes
August	28
September	39
October	43
November	48
December	54

14 A drink dispenser contains 6 L 200 mL of water. Water is then poured into glasses each with a capacity of 200 mL. How many glasses can Jordan completely fill?

15 The pan balance shows identical cones and prisms, and a cylinder. The mass of a cone is 8 kg and a cylinder 12 kg. How much heavier is a cylinder than a prism?

A 4 kg **B** 6 kg **C** 8 kg **D** 10 kg

16 A farmer picked 760 oranges on Thursday, 1187 on Friday and 679 on Saturday. What was the total number of oranges picked in the three days?

17 A map is drawn on a grid. There is no compass drawn on the map but George knows that *Q* is east of *P*.

George placed a counter on *P*. He then moved the counter north 3 units and then west 2 units.

Which of these is the new location of the counter?

A H3 **B** B7 **C** B2 **D** B3

18 Oscar is riding 48 km to visit his cousin. In the first hour he rides half the distance. In the second hour he rides two-thirds of the remaining distance. What distance now remains? km

19 Troy has written all the numbers from 1 to 100. He crosses out the even numbers. He also crosses out the numbers that have digits that add to a number less than 15.

How many numbers remain?

20 A box contains 10 numbered balls. A ball is chosen from the box without looking. Which of these events are equally likely?

1 6 3 2 4
5 3 1 4 5

I selecting a number less than 4 II selecting an even number

III selecting an odd number IV selecting a number greater than 3

A I and II **B** I and III **C** II and III **D** I and IV **E** II and IV

WORKED SOLUTIONS & ANSWERS

Section 1

Unit 1A PAGE 10

1. 35 008
2. 87 320
3. 19 600
4. 10 000
5. 2081
6. 2004
7. 1545
8. 2
9. true
10. 3 thousands
11. 4000
12. 10 000
13. 20 000
14. 25 028
15. 31 000
16. thirty-two thousand and ninety
17. thirty-eight thousand (38 000)
18. 7538
19. 6890
20. 1797, 1837
21. 48 999, 49 888, 65 489, 65 498
22. 3000
23. 14 000
24. 1000
25. 5
26. 9

Unit 1B PAGE 11

1. **5316**
   The number is even so 6 must be the digit in the ones place. As the number is between 4000 and 7000, there is a 5 in the thousands place. As 3 × 1 = 3, there is a 3 in the hundreds place and a 1 in the ones place. The number is 5316.
2. **59 000**
   Look at the digit in the hundreds place. As 4 is less than 5, the distance is rounded down to 59 000 km, to the nearest thousand km.
3. **Shirley**
   In order the numbers are 1939, 1942, 1943 and 1948. The highest number is 1948. Shirley is the youngest person.
4. **77 777**
   Look for 5 identical numbers that add to 35. As 35 ÷ 5 = 7, the number is 77 777.
5. **361**
   The number needs to end in an odd digit. This can only be 1 as any other odd digit cannot satisfy the other two conditions. The digit in the hundreds place is 3 × 1 = 3. The digit in the tens place is 2 × 3 = 6. The number is 361.
6. **635**
   The largest number is 653. The second largest is 635.
7. **74 000**
   There is a 6 in the hundreds place. As 6 > 5, the number rounds up to 74 000.
8. **9841**
   As the number is odd, the digit in the ones place is odd. It must be 1 as the digit in the hundreds place is 8. The digit in the tens place is 4. As 9 > 8, the 9 is in the thousands place. The number is 9841.
9. **3996**
   The two 4s are 4000 and 4. As 1000 − 4 = 996, then 4000 − 4 = 3996. The difference is 3996.
10. **even**
    Any number rounded to the nearest hundred will be even as any number ending in 0 is even.
11. **56 800**
    Look at the digit in the tens place. As 4 < 5, the number rounds down to 56 800.
12. **35 679**
    To form the smallest number, use the digits arranged in ascending order. The number is 35 679.
13. **3036**
    The number should end in an even number. The only even number between 3000 and 3100 is 3036.
14. **654**
    The largest possible number is 653. One more than this number is 654.
15. **Olivia**
    40 ÷ 4 = 10. When the number 40 is called out, each girl has counted 10 numbers each. This means Olivia will call out the number 41.
16. **75**
    The number 7541 is 7 thousands, 5 hundreds, 4 tens and 9 ones. 7 thousand is 70 hundreds. As 70 + 5 = 75, there are 75 hundreds.
17. **10**
    3186 is 3200 to the nearest hundred. It is also 3190 to the nearest 10. The two numbers are 3200 and 3190. As 200 − 190 is 10, then 3200 − 3190 = 10.
18. **21 817**
    Look at the last 3 digits in each number. Compare 871, 781 and 817. The order is 871, 817 and 781. This means the middle number will be 21 817.
19. **4600**
    40 hundreds is 40 × 100 = 4000. 60 tens is 60 × 10 = 600. As 4000 + 600 = 4600, the total is 4600.
20. **2154**
    Suppose the digit in the ones place is 4. This means the digit in the hundreds place is a quarter of 4 which is 1. The digit in the thousands place is twice 1 which is 2. As 12 − 4 − 1 − 2 = 5, the digit in the tens place is 5. The number is 2154.
21. **25 000**
    Round Noah's numbers to the nearest thousand. His numbers are 9000, 5000 and 11 000. As 11 + 9 + 5 is 25, the total would be about 25 000.

Unit 2A PAGE 12

1. 40
2. 166
3. 120
4. 536
5. 2450
6. 95
7. 129
8. 500
9. 129
10. 1949
11. 4658
12. 28 100
13. 950
14. 61 962
15. 36

16. 620

17. 37

18. 79

19. 297

20. 1300

21. 213

22. 77

23. 19

24. 611

25. 2917

Unit 2B PAGE 13

1. **66**

The total is 22 + 23 + 21 = 45 + 21. As this is 66, there is a total of 66 students.

2. **379**

$$\begin{array}{rrrr} & 1 & 6 & 8 \\ + & 2 & 1 & 1 \\ \hline & 3 & 7 & 9 \\ \hline \end{array}$$

There is a total of 379 cards.

3. **173**

$$\begin{array}{rrrr} & & {}^{1}9 & 7 \\ + & & 7 & 6 \\ \hline & 1 & 7 & 3 \\ \hline \end{array}$$

The book has 173 pages.

4. **139**

As 59 + 21 = 80, Pow picked 80 oranges. As 80 + 59 = 139, a total of 139 oranges were picked.

5. **685 km**

$$\begin{array}{rrrr} & {}^{1}3 & {}^{1}8 & 7 \\ + & 2 & 9 & 8 \\ \hline & 6 & 8 & 5 \\ \hline \end{array}$$

Mila drove a total of 685 km.

6. **102**

$$\begin{array}{rrrr} & & {}^{1}6 & 4 \\ + & & 3 & 8 \\ \hline & 1 & 0 & 2 \\ \hline \end{array}$$

There are 102 chairs in the library.

7. **70**

18 + 18 = 36. There are 36 red counters.

$$\begin{array}{rrr} & {}^{2}3 & 6 \\ & 1 & 6 \\ + & 1 & 8 \\ \hline & 7 & 0 \\ \hline \end{array}$$

There is a total of 70 counters.

8. **177**

78 + 21 = 99. Mitchell has 99 cars. You need to find 99 + 78. This is 100 + 78 – 1 = 177. There is a total of 177 cars.

9. **50**

20 + 18 + 12 = 20 + 30. This is 50. Grace bought 50 balloons for the party.

10. **120**

$$\begin{array}{rrrr} & & {}^{1}6 & 9 \\ + & & 5 & 5 \\ \hline & 1 & 2 & 4 \\ \hline \end{array}$$

There is a 4 in the ones place in 124. As 4 < 5, the number rounds to 120.

11. **9301**

$$\begin{array}{rrrrr} & {}^{1}8 & {}^{1}6 & {}^{1}5 & 2 \\ + & & 6 & 4 & 9 \\ \hline & 9 & 3 & 0 & 1 \\ \hline \end{array}$$

Wendi received 9301 votes.

12. **274 km**

$$\begin{array}{rrrr} & & {}^{1}7 & 6 \\ & {}^{1}1 & 1 & 1 \\ + & & 8 & 7 \\ \hline & 2 & 7 & 4 \\ \hline \end{array}$$

Hunter rode 274 km.

13. **119**

As 28 + 10 = 38, Theo's father is 38 years old. As 38 + 33 = 71, Theo's grandfather is 71 years old.

$$\begin{array}{rrrr} & & 7 & 1 \\ & & 3 & 8 \\ + & & 1 & 0 \\ \hline & 1 & 1 & 9 \\ \hline \end{array}$$

The total of the ages is 119 years.

14. **38**

As the difference between 16 and 11 is 5, there will be 5 fewer passengers on the bus. As 43 – 5 is 38, there are now 38 passengers.

15. **45**

87 – 23 = 64.
64 – 19 = 64 – 20 + 1. This is 45.
Stathis keeps 45 balls.

16. **130**

$$\begin{array}{rrrr} & {}^{2}\cancel{3} & {}^{1}1 & 8 \\ - & 1 & 8 & 8 \\ \hline & 1 & 3 & 0 \\ \hline \end{array}$$

There are 130 vacant seats.

17. **188**

$$\begin{array}{rrrr} & {}^{1}\cancel{2} & {}^{11}\cancel{2} & {}^{1}5 \\ - & & 3 & 7 \\ \hline & 1 & 8 & 8 \\ \hline \end{array}$$

188 lobsters had been sold.

18. **28**

$$\begin{array}{rrrr} & {}^{1}\cancel{2} & {}^{10}\cancel{1} & {}^{1}5 \\ - & 1 & 8 & 7 \\ \hline & & 2 & 8 \\ \hline \end{array}$$

There were 28 more orders on Saturday than Friday.

19. **10**

As 22 + 15 = 37, then 220 + 150 = 370. As 370 – 360 = 10, there were 10 cookies not sold.

20. **495**

Maeve's number is 752. Olive's number is 257.

$$\begin{array}{rrrr} & {}^{6}\cancel{7} & {}^{14}\cancel{5} & {}^{1}2 \\ - & 2 & 5 & 7 \\ \hline & 4 & 9 & 5 \\ \hline \end{array}$$

The difference is 495.

21. **182**

$$\begin{array}{rrrr} & {}^{2}\cancel{3} & {}^{16}\cancel{7} & {}^{1}1 \\ - & 1 & 8 & 9 \\ \hline & 1 & 8 & 2 \\ \hline \end{array}$$

Beatrix's video had 182 more views.

22. **25 119 km**

The difference between the distances is 25 119 km.

$$\begin{array}{rrrrrr} & {}^{8}\cancel{9} & {}^{1}0 & 5 & {}^{2}\cancel{3} & {}^{1}2 \\ - & 6 & 5 & 4 & 1 & 3 \\ \hline & 2 & 5 & 1 & 1 & 9 \\ \hline \end{array}$$

Cory's car travelled 25 119 km further.

Unit 3A PAGE 14

1. 18

2. 27

3. 150

4. 160

5. 24

6. 45, 20, 395

7. 108, 5551

8. 8

9. 150

10. 180

11. 120

12. 6, 4, 1

13. 170

14. 3

15. 0

16. 56

17. 4

18. 4

19. 9

20. 9

21. 10

22. 12

23. 1

24. 3

25. 3

26. 30

Unit 3B — PAGE 15

1. **40**
$8 \times 5 = 40$. There are 40 coloured pencils.

2. **280**
$4 \times 7 = 28$. This means $40 \times 7 = 280$. There are 280 apples.

3. **30**
$6 \times 5 = 30$. The carriages can take up to 30 passengers.

4. **84**
You need to work out 6×14. This is the same as $6 \times 7 \times 2 = 42 \times 2 = 84$. Abbie swims a total of 84 laps.

5. **80**
$4 \times 20 = 80$. Sergio has 80 marbles.

6. **120**
A dozen is 12. As $12 \times 10 = 120$, there are 120 eggs.

7. **1500**
$5 \times 3 = 15$. This means $500 \times 3 = 1500$. There are 1500 sheets of paper.

8 **2400**
$6 \times 4 = 24$. This means $600 \times 4 = 2400$. Sully ran 2400 metres.

9. **144**
$16 \times 9 = 10 \times 9 + 6 \times 9$. This is $90 + 54 = 144$. There was a total of 144 players.

10 **800**
$2 \times 4 = 8$. In the question 20×40, there are two 0s. This means 20×40 will have two 0s. This means $20 \times 40 = 800$. There are 800 seats in the theatre.

11. **24**
As a dozen is 12, then half a dozen is 6. As $6 \times 4 = 24$, Lawrie will have 24 pieces of orange.

12. **6**
As $8 \times 3 = 24$ and $8 \times 4 = 32$, the farmer will fill 3 boxes and the fourth box will only be partially filled. As $30 - 24 = 6$, the fourth box will have 6 mangoes.

13. **>**
As $4 \times 12 = 48$, then $48 \div 4 = 12$.
As $6 \times 11 = 66$, then $66 \div 6 = 11$. As $12 > 11$, then $48 \div 4$ is greater than $66 \div 6$. The 'greater than' symbol is >.

14. **6**
As $2 \times 6 = 12$, then $20 \times 6 = 120$. This means $120 \div 20 = 6$. Bryce sold 6 books of raffle tickets.

15. **4**
As $6 \times 8 = 48$, there was a total of 48 crayons. As $12 \times 4 = 48$, then $48 \div 12 = 4$. Each student received 4 crayons each.

16. **7**
As $7 \times 7 = 49$, then $50 \div 7 = 7$, with remainder 1. There are 7 teams possible.

17. **4 minutes**
You need to work out $320 \div 80$, which has the same answer as $32 \div 8$.
As $8 \times 4 = 32$, then $32 \div 8 = 4$ and $320 \div 80$ is also 4. It will take 4 minutes.

18. **9**
$$\begin{array}{r} 9 \\ 5\overline{)45} \end{array}$$
There will be 9 books on each shelf.
The middle shelf will have 9 books.

19. **8**
As $24 + 24 = 48$, there are 24 chocolates in each layer.
As $3 \times 8 = 24$, then $24 \div 3 = 8$.
There are 8 chocolates in each row.

20. **4**
$8 \times 3 = 24$. There is a total of 24 coins. The number of new rows is $24 \div 6$. As $6 \times 4 = 24$, there are now 4 rows.

21. **5**
$$\begin{array}{r} 4\text{ r }1 \\ 3\overline{)13} \end{array}$$
$13 \div 3$ is 4 with a remainder of 1.
This means there will be 5 cars.

22. **8**
To find the number of stickers given to each student, divide 36 by 9.
As $36 \div 9 = 4$, each student receives 4 stickers. As $4 \times 2 = 8$, the two students were given a total of 8 stickers.

23. **24**
Look for the numbers that are 4 more than the multiples of 5. These are 9, 14, 19, 24, 29 … Also the numbers are divisible by 2 and 3 which means they are multiples of 6. The smallest number is 24.

24. 6
$7 \times 6 = 42$. Andrea baked 42 cupcakes. 3 dozen is $3 \times 12 = 36$.
As $42 - 36 = 6$, Andrea has 6 cupcakes remaining.

Unit 4A — PAGE 16

1. 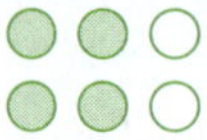

2. 3

3. $\frac{9}{10}$

4. true

5. 

6. $1\frac{5}{8}$

7. 5

8. $\frac{9}{4}$

9 2

10. 39

11. >

12. 0.06

13. 0.73

14. 9 hundredths

15. 20.34

16. 1.2

17. 45.37

18. 8

19. 25.37

20. $\frac{3}{100}$

21. 0.36, 0.83, 3.18, 3.7

22. 3.1

Unit 4B — PAGE 17

1. 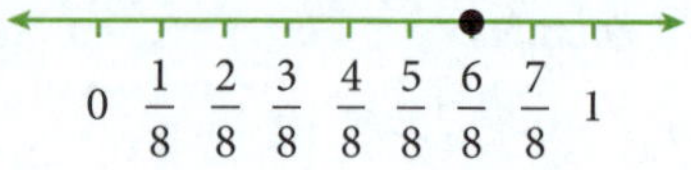

$\frac{3}{4}$ is equivalent to $\frac{6}{8}$. The number line could be labelled this way:

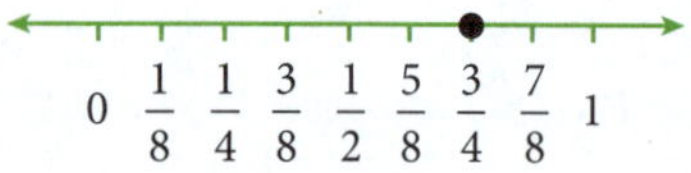

2. **3**

As $4 \times 3 = 12$, imagine the cards are arranged as 3 cards in each of 4 rows. One row of cards is one-quarter of the cards. If a row is turned over, Tayla has turned over 3 cards.

3. **4**

Imagine the buns arranged in 3 rows of 2 buns. 2 out of the 3 rows are removed to be eaten. As $2 \times 2 = 4$, Royce's family ate 4 buns.

4. **9**

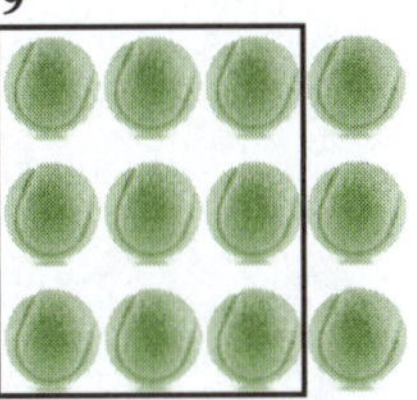

Jack drew a box around 3 out of 4 columns. As $3 \times 3 = 9$, there are 9 balls in the box.

5. **6**

Here is a shape made of 10 squares.

✓	✓	✓		
✓	✓	✓		

There are 5 columns of 2 squares. $\frac{3}{5}$ of the shape is 3 columns out of 5. There are 6 squares out of 10 squares. This means $\frac{3}{5} = \frac{6}{10}$. There are 6 tenths in $\frac{3}{5}$.

6. **12**

There are 4 quarters in each pizza. As $3 \times 4 = 12$, there is a total of 12 quarters.

7. **6**

To find a half you divide by 2. As $12 \div 2 = 6$, then 6 friends support the Tigers. As $12 - 6 = 6$, then 6 friends do not support the Tigers.

8. **4**

Matt shades $\frac{1}{2}$ of the shape which is 10 squares. Kurt shades $\frac{3}{5}$ of the remaining 10 squares which is 6 squares. This leaves 4 squares unshaded.

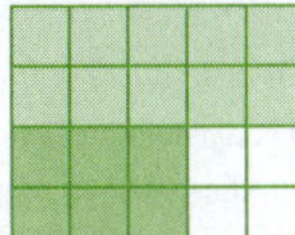

9. **3**

There are 6 squares. $\frac{1}{3}$ of the squares is $6 \div 3 = 2$. When $\frac{5}{6}$ of the shape is shaded there will be 5 shaded squares. As $5 - 2 = 3$, Reuben needs to shade another 3 squares.

10. **2**

As $\frac{1}{4}$ is less than $\frac{1}{2}$, then $2\frac{1}{4}$ rounds to 2.

11. **8**

To find one-third you can divide by 3. As $24 \div 3 = 8$, there are 8 red balloons.

12. $\mathbf{\frac{2}{6}, \frac{1}{3}, \frac{4}{12}}$

4 out of 12 squares are shaded. This is $\frac{4}{12}$ of the shape. Also 2 columns out of 6 are shaded. This is $\frac{2}{6}$ of the shape. Finally one-third of the shape is shaded. This is $\frac{1}{3}$ of the shape.

13. **20 m**

Look at the digit in the tenths place. As $4 < 5$, the height is rounded to 20 m.

14. **100**

There are 100 hundredths in one whole. This means 2 ones is 100 times larger than the 2 hundredths.

15. **1.8 m**

Look at the 6 in the hundredths place. As $6 > 5$, the height is rounded to 1.8 m.

16. **1.5**

As $1\frac{1}{2} + 1\frac{1}{2} = 3$, then half of 3 is $1\frac{1}{2}$. This is also written as 1.5.

17. **23.9**

To the nearest tenth means the number will round to either 23.8 or 23.9. 23.86 has 2 decimal places (or numbers after the decimal point). Look at the 6. As $6 > 5$, the 8 in the tenths place rounds up to 9. The number is 23.9.

18. **0.35**

0.3 is 0.30, 0.4 is 0.40. The missing number is halfway between 0.30 and 0.40. As the middle of 30 and 40 is 35, the missing decimal is 0.35.

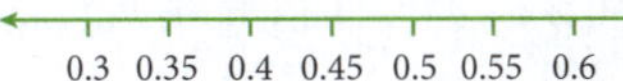

19. **Matilda**

Think of 1.4 as 1.40. All the girls are over 1 m, so you need to compare the two digits that are after the decimal point. In order these are 32, 35, 40 and 41. The second largest is 40. This means the second tallest has a height of 1.40 m. This is the height of Matilda.

20 $\mathbf{0.08, \frac{9}{100}, 0.6, \frac{7}{10}}$

Write the fractions as decimals with 2 decimal places. $\frac{7}{10} = 0.70$ and $\frac{9}{100} = 0.09$. The four numbers are 0.70, 0.08, 0.09, 0.60. Now compare 70, 8, 9 and 60. The order is 8, 9, 60, 70, which is 0.08, $\frac{9}{100}$, 0.6 and $\frac{7}{10}$.

21.

0.5 is $\frac{5}{10}$, which is the same as $\frac{1}{2}$. This means half of the shape should be shaded.

22. **2.2**

There are 7 units between 1.6 and 3. This means each unit is 0.2.

Labelling the number line shows that $A = 1.8$ and $B = 2.6$. The middle is 2.2.

Unit 5A PAGE 18

1. 389c
2. $19
3. 90c
4. $12
5. $3.40
6. $19 000
7. $1.40
8. $11.45
9. 1000
10. $25
11. 78c, 82c
12. 70c
13. $306.40
14. 4
15. $11.35
16. $20.50
17. $5.05
18. $110
19. $68

20. 90c
21. $30
22. $65
23. $160
24. $13
25. $30
26. $112

Unit 5B PAGE 19

1. **$5.85**
   First work out the number of cents to make $5. As 100 – 15 = 85, there will be 85 cents. Also, as 10 – 5 = 5, there will be $5. The total change is $5.85.
2. **$12.60**
   You need to work out $4.20 × 3. As 4 × 3 = 12 and 20 × 3 = 60, the total price will be $12.60.
3. **$11**
   100 – 89 = 100 – 90 + 1. This is 10 + 1 = 11. Tegan has $11 remaining on her gift card.
4. **$110**
   55 + 55 = 50 + 50 + 5 + 5. This is 100 + 10 = 110. Maddy is paid $110.
5. **$723**
   $$\begin{array}{r} {}^{8}\not{9}\;{}^{1}3\;9\;8 \\ -\;\;8\;6\;7\;5 \\ \hline 7\;2\;3 \\ \hline \end{array}$$
   Euan has saved $723 more than Jesse.
6. **$520**
   As 8 × 5 = 40, then 8 × 50 = 400. As 6 × 2 = 12, then 6 × 20 = 120. Corey has $400 + $120. This is a total of $520.
7. **$490**
   $$\begin{array}{r} \not{1}\;{}^{1}{}^{2}\not{3}\;{}^{1}5\;0 \\ -\;\;8\;6\;0 \\ \hline 4\;9\;0 \\ \hline \end{array}$$
   Harry needs another $490.
8. **$60**
   As 18 ÷ 3 = 6, then 180 ÷ 3 = 60. Each person paid $60. This means Mia paid $60.
9. **$1390**
   $$\begin{array}{r} {}^{1}6\;{}^{1}9\;5 \\ +\;\;6\;9\;5 \\ \hline 1\;3\;9\;0 \\ \hline \end{array}$$
   The cost is $1390.
10. **$15.20**
    From $4.80 to $5 is 20c. From $5 to $20 is $15. This means the total change is $15.20.
11. **$2060**
    $$\begin{array}{r} {}^{1}1\;{}^{1}1\;9\;0 \\ +\;\;8\;7\;0 \\ \hline 2\;0\;6\;0 \\ \hline \end{array}$$
    The total cost is $2060.
12. **$5.60**
    28 + 28 = 28 + 20 + 8. This is 48 + 8 = 56. This means $2.80 + $2.80 = $5.60.
13. **$15**
    Change each amount to cents.
    $$\begin{array}{r} {}^{1}7\;0\;0 \\ 3\;5\;0 \\ +\;\;4\;5\;0 \\ \hline 1\;5\;0\;0 \\ \hline \end{array}$$
    The total is 1500c or $15.
14. **$1600**
    As 3 × 4 = 12, then 3 × 400 = 1200. Harry has earned $1200.
    As 1200 + 400 = 1600, the boys have earned a total of $1600.
15. **$1.50**
    As 8 × 2 = 16, Cooper has $16. To work out the change, from $14.50, add 50c to make $15 and another $1 gives $16. Cooper will be given $1.50 change.
16. **$1.70**
    55 × 6 = 50 × 6 + 5 × 6. This is 300 + 30 which is 330. The apples cost $3.30. The change is 70 cents to make $4 and then $1 to make $5. The change is $1.70.
17. **20c**
    The $1.82 rounds down to $1.80. The change from $2 is 20c.
18. **$63**
    As 18 ÷ 2 = 9, the cost of a child ticket is $9. 18 × 2 = 36 and 3 × 9 = 27. Adding 36 and 27 is 63. The cost is $63.
19. **$15**
    As 20 ÷ 4 = 5, the cost of one pen is $5. As 5 × 3 = 15, the cost of 3 pens is $15.
20. **$240**
    As 23 – 19 = 4, each chair is $4 cheaper when bought from the second company. As 6 × 4 = 24, then 60 × 4 = 240. The school will save $240.
21. **$2**
    As 6 × 3 = 18, then 20 ÷ 6 = 3 with remainder 2. This means Gretel can buy 3 pies and she will be given $2 in change.
22. **$900**
    As 53 – 31 = 22, then $5300 – $3100 = $2200. Allie saved $2200. You need to find the difference between $3100 and $2200. As 31 – 22 = 9, then the difference is $900.

Unit 6A PAGE 20

1. 22
2. 45
3. 27 and 33
4. 4
5. 123
6. 32 and 64
7. 104
8. 2461 and 12 329
9. 998
10. 20
11. 98 and 90
12. 2100
13. 81
14. 16, 19, 22, 25
15. 2
16. 6
17. 4
18. 72
19. 3 000 000
20. 50
21. 15 and 4
22. 215 and 247
23. 95
24. 32, 16, 4
25. even

Unit 6B PAGE 21

1. **16**
   The list of numbers is 38, 31, 24, 17, 10. The number not on Talitah's list is 16.
2. **32**
   The number sentence is [?] – 12 = 20. The missing number is 20 + 12 which is 32.
3. **25**
   The pattern is 4, 7, 10, 13 … The pattern is adding 3. Continuing the pattern, 16, 19, 22, 25 … There will be 25 students in Group 8.
4. **23**
   The number sentence is 25 + [?] = 48. The missing number is 48 – 25 which is 23.

5. 6

As 6 × 7 = 42, the value of ● is 6.

6. 26

To find the number, you subtract 30 from 56. The number is 56 – 30 = 26.

7. 32

This means the missing number is 8 × 4 = 32.

8. 7

As 42 ÷ 7 = 6, the missing number is 7.

9. 29

5 × 9 = 45. You need to work out the missing number if ■ + 16 = 45. The missing number is the answer to 45 – 16. As 45 – 15 – 1 = 30 – 1 = 29, the missing number is 29.

10. 4

40 – 12 = 30 – 2 = 28. This means a number multiplied by 7 is 28. As 28 ÷ 7 = 4, Xavier's favourite number is 4.

11. 3

The smallest 5-digit odd number is 10 001. The largest 4-digit even number is 9998. By counting, the difference between these numbers is 3.

12. >

You are comparing 12 + 18 and 48 – 20. First 12 + 18 = 12 + 10 + 8. This is 22 + 8 = 30.
Also 48 – 20 = 28. As 30 > 28, the missing symbol is >.

13. 9

20 – 5 = 15. The question is 15 – ⬡ = 6. This means the missing number is 15 – 6 = 9.

14. 24

Eugenie's number pattern is 12, 20, 28, 36, 44. The second number is 20 and the fifth number is 44.
As 44 – 20 = 24, the difference is 24.

15. 11

You can write a number sentence to help work out the answer.
24 + [?] = 60 – 25.
As 60 – 25 = 40 – 5 = 35, work out 24 + [?] = 35. This means the missing number is 35 – 24 = 11.

16. 51

Here are Elise's numbers: 3, 15, 27, 39, 51. This means 51 is her fifth number.

17. 10

The sequence is ___, ___, 22, 28, 34 … The pattern rule is to add 6. You need to use subtracting 6 to find the first two numbers. As 22 – 6 = 16 and 16 – 6 = 10, the sequence is 10, 16, 22, 28, 34. The first number is 10.

18. 2

Here is the sequence: 128, 64, 32, 16, 8, 4, 2 … The seventh number is 2.

19. 25

The pattern is subtracting 15.
As 2 × 15 = 30, the sixth number will be 55 – 30 = 25.

20. 8

As 26 – 9 – 9 = 17 – 9 = 8, the sequence is 8, 17, 26 … The first number is 8.

21. 5

If ● + 8 = 12, then ● = 4. Now, if ▲ × 4 = 20, the value of ▲ is 5.

22 odd

If the result is odd when two numbers are multiplied, both numbers must be odd. This means Ellie's number is odd.

Unit 7A PAGE 22

1. 3000
2. 12
3. 1500
4. 8
5. 5 cm
6. 8 cm
7. 250
8. 14 cm
9. 12
10. 8 km 890 m, or 8.89 km
11. 5 cm
12. 15
13. 6.8 m
14. 6.25
15. 300 cm
16. 47
17. 15 cm^2
18. 600 cm^2
19. 12 cm^2
20. 18 cm^2
21. m^2
22. A

Unit 7B PAGE 23

1 177 cm

As 1 m is 100 cm, then 1 m 41 cm is 141 cm. As 141 + 36 = 177, Lavinia's mother is 177 cm tall.

2. 44 cm

A square has 4 equal sides.
11 × 4 = 44. The perimeter is 44 cm.

3. 1330 m or 1.33 km

$$\begin{array}{r} {}^{1}6\,{}^{1}6\,5 \\ +\ \ 6\,6\,5 \\ \hline 1\,3\,3\,0 \end{array}$$

The distance is 1330 m, or 1.33 km

4. 72 cm

24 × 3 = 20 × 3 plus 4 × 3. This is 60 + 12 = 72. The rectangle has a length of 72 cm.

5. 7.2 km

Twice 3 km is 6 km. Twice 600 m is 1200 m, which is 1 km 200 m. The total distance is 7 km 200 m, which can be written as 7.2 km.

6. 11 cm

55 × 2 is 55 + 55 = 110. Kaitlyn's line is 110 mm long. As 10 mm is 1 cm, the line is 11 cm.

7. 2336 mm

As there are 10 mm in 1 cm, then 32 cm = 320 mm. As there are 1000 mm in 1 m, then 2 m = 2000 mm.

$$\begin{array}{r} 1\,6 \\ 3\,2\,0 \\ +\ 2\,0\,0\,0 \\ \hline 2\,3\,3\,6 \end{array}$$

The total distance is 2336 mm.

8. 4 m

28 – 11 – 13 = 17 – 13. This is 4.
There is 4 m of fence not painted.

9. 727 m

$$\begin{array}{r} 9\,{}^{5}\not{6}\,{}^{1}5 \\ -\ \ 2\,3\,8 \\ \hline 7\,2\,7 \end{array}$$

The paddock has a width of 727 m.

10. 60 cm

As 100 cm is 1 m, the original length is 200 cm long. 200 – 95 – 45 = 105 – 45. This is 105 – 5 – 40 = 100 – 40 = 60. The length of the third piece is 60 cm.

11. 50 cm

As 1 m = 100 cm, then 5 m = 500 cm.
You need to divide 500 by 10.
As 50 ÷ 10 = 5, then 500 ÷ 10 = 50.
Each small piece is 50 cm long.

12. **178 cm**
$89 + 89 = 90 + 90 - 1 - 1$. This is $180 - 2$ which is 178. Owen will eventually be 178 cm tall.

13. **90 cm**
A regular octagon has 8 equal sides. As $8 \times 9 = 72$, then $72 \div 8 = 9$. This means $720 \div 8 = 90$. The length of each side is 90 cm.

14. **4600 m or 4.6 km**
$85 + 55 = 85 + 5 + 50 = 140$. This means $850 + 550 = 1400$. Also 6 km is 6000 m.

$$\begin{array}{r} {}^{5}6\;{}^{1}0\;0\;0 \\ -\;\;1\;4\;0\;0 \\ \hline 4\;6\;0\;0 \end{array}$$

The bus travelled 4600 m, or 4.6 km.

15. **10 m**
The perimeter of a rectangle is twice the total of the length and width. As $32 + 18 = 50$, then $3200 + 1800 = 5000$. As 2×5000 is 10 000, the perimeter is 10 000 mm, or 10 m.

16. **430 km**
You need to add 120, 120 and 190. As $12 + 12 + 19 = 24 + 19 = 43$, then $120 + 120 + 190 = 430$. This means Ruth drove 430 km.

17. **225 cm or 2.25 cm**
1.6 m is 1 m 60 cm. This can be written as 160 cm. As $160 + 65 = 225$, the string is 225 cm, or 2.25 m long.

18. **23 cm^2**
10 half-squares is the same as 5 squares. As $18 + 5 = 23$, the shape covers 23 cm^2.

19. **16 cm^2**
The shape is formed by joining a rectangle and a triangle.

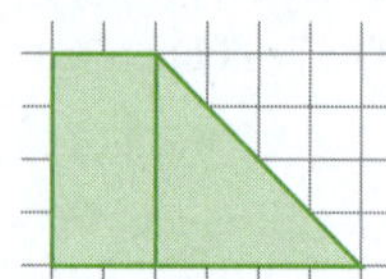

As $4 \times 2 = 8$, the rectangle covers 8 cm^2. The triangle covers 6 squares and 4 half-squares. This is a total of 8 cm^2. As $8 + 8 = 16$, the shape has an area of 16 cm^2.

20. **6 cm^2**
The rectangle is 4 cm long and 3 cm wide. As $4 \times 3 = 12$, the area of the rectangle is 12 cm^2. The triangle is half the size of the rectangle.
As $12 \div 2 = 6$, the area of the triangle is 6 cm^2.

21. **25 cm^2**
The square has 4 equal sides.
As $20 \div 4 = 5$, the side length is 5 cm.
As $5 \times 5 = 25$, the area is 25 cm^2.

22. **22 cm**
$30 \div 6 = 5$, so the width is 5 cm. The dimensions of the rectangle are 6 cm by 5 cm. As $6 + 5 = 11$, and $2 \times 11 = 22$, the perimeter is 22 cm.

Unit 8A PAGE 24

1. 7
2. 500
3. 2400 mL
4. spoon
5. 650 mL
6. 2 L
7. 9 and 60
8. 5
9. 1500 mL or 1.5 L
10. 6 and 450
11. 15 000
12. 60 kg
13. 2500 g
14. 3250
15. 4 kg
16. 10:15
17. 300
18. 50
19. 72
20. 2 pm
21. 5:45
22. 43
23. 14
24.

Unit 8B PAGE 25

1.

2. **240 L**
As $12 \times 10 = 120$, the jug has 120 L of water when half-full. As $120 \times 2 = 240$, the jug has a total capacity of 240 L.

3. **8300 mL or 8.3 L**
As 1 L is 1000 mL, then $\frac{1}{2}$ L is 500 mL and $2\frac{1}{2}$ L is 2500 mL.

$$\begin{array}{r} {}^{1}2\;5\;0\;0 \\ 8\;0\;0 \\ +\;\;5\;0\;0\;0 \\ \hline 8\;3\;0\;0 \end{array}$$

The total capacity is 8300 mL, or 8.3 L.

4. **14 L**
Half of 48 is $48 \div 2 = 24$.
As $24 - 10 = 14$, there is 14 L of petrol left in the tank.

5. **1260 mL**

$$\begin{array}{r} 4\;2\;0 \\ 4\;2\;0 \\ +\;\;\;4\;2\;0 \\ \hline 1\;2\;6\;0 \end{array}$$

The saucepan contains 1260 mL of soup.

6. **1480 mL or 1.48 L**
2 L = 2000 mL

$$\begin{array}{r} {}^{1}\not{2}\;{}^{1\,9}\not{0}\;{}^{1}0\;0 \\ -\;\;\;5\;2\;0 \\ \hline 1\;4\;8\;0 \end{array}$$

There is 1480 mL, or 1.48 L, of juice remaining.

7. **650 mL**
As each marking in Jug A is 200 mL, there is 400 mL in A. As each marking in Jug B is 250 mL, there is 250 mL in B.
As $400 + 250 = 650$, there is now 650 mL of water in Jug A.

8. **200 mL**
There is 2000 mL of soft drink in the bottle. As $6 \times 3 = 18$, then $6 \times 300 = 1800$. As $2000 - 1800$ is 200, there is 200 mL remaining in the bottle.

9. **8.3 kg, or 8300 g**
The water has a mass of 7500 g.

$$\begin{array}{r} {}^{1}7\;5\;0\;0 \\ -\;\;\;8\;0\;0 \\ \hline 8\;3\;0\;0 \end{array}$$

The total mass is 8300 g, or 8.3 kg.

10. **4530 g**
As 1 kg is 1000 g, then half a kilogram is 500 g.

$$\begin{array}{r} {}^{1}5\,0\,0 \\ 2\,8\,0 \\ 7\,5\,0 \\ +\ {}^{1}3\,0\,0\,0 \\ \hline 4\,5\,3\,0 \end{array}$$

The total mass is 4530 g.

11. **60 kg**
There are 12 cubes in the shape. As 12 × 5 = 60, the mass of Buddy's solid is 60 kg.

12. **26 kg**
37 + 37 = 30 + 30 + 7 + 7. This is 60 + 14 = 74. As 100 – 74 = 100 – 70 – 4 = 26, the mass of the other box is 26 kg.

13. **60 kg**
As 12 + 4 = 16, the mass of the cube is 16 kg. As 16 + 16 = 32, the mass of the sphere is 32 kg.
As 32 + 16 + 12 = 48 + 12 = 60, the total mass is 60 kg.

14. **13.1 kg**
3100 g is 3 kg 100 g. Adding another 10 kg is 13 kg 100 g. This can be written as 13.1 kg.

15. **36 kg**
Ignore the 2 cylinders and 2 spheres on both sides of the balance. This leaves 2 spheres and a cylinder in balance. As 2 × 18 = 36, the mass of a cylinder is 36 kg.

16. **300 kg**
25 × 12 = 25 × 4 × 3. This is 100 × 3 = 300. The total mass is 300 kg.

17. **10:03**
The clock shows the time of 17 minutes to 10. As 20 – 17 = 3, the bus arrived at 10:03.

18. **2:40 pm**
8:40 am to 12:40 pm is 4 hours. Another 2 hours is 2:40 pm.

19. **1 hour 45 minutes**
From 11:45 am to midday is 15 minutes. To 1:00 pm is 1 hour and 1:30 pm is another 30 minutes. This is a total of 1 hour 45 minutes.

20. **3:15 pm**
There are 60 minutes in one hour. As 60 – 45 = 15, the lesson started at 3:15 pm.

21. **11:55 pm**
There are 60 seconds in a minute. You need to work out the number of minutes in 300 seconds. The answer for 300 ÷ 60 is the same as the answer for 30 ÷ 6. This means 300 seconds equals 5 minutes. The time is 11:55 pm.

22. **4:58:30**
90 seconds is 1 minute 30 seconds. From 5 hours, subtracting 1 minute gives 4 h 59 min. Subtracting 30 seconds gives 4 h 58 min 30 s. This is shown as 4:58:30.

Unit 9A — PAGE 26

1. 2
2. 1
3. 5
4. cube
5. 18
6. 1
7. circle
8. 10
9. 8
10. View C
11. triangular prism
12. 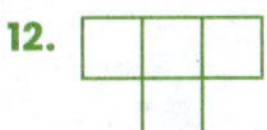
13. hexagonal pyramid
14. triangular prism
15. 
16. 2, 8
17. 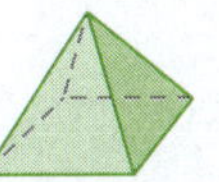

Unit 9B — PAGE 27

1. **sphere**
Cones, spheres and cylinders have curved surfaces. Only a sphere has no flat surfaces.

2. **rectangular prism**
The shape must be a rectangular prism.

3. **6**
A hexagonal prism has 18 edges. A rectangular prism has 12 edges. As 18 – 12 = 6, the difference is 6.

4. 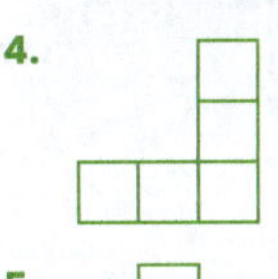

5. 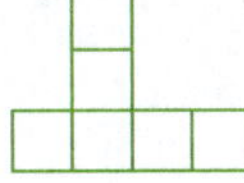

6. 

7. 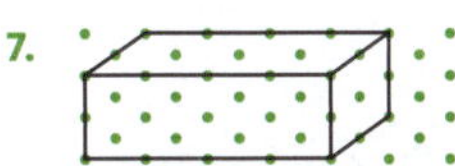

8. **square pyramid**
A square pyramid has a square face and four triangular faces.

9. **18**
A hexagonal pyramid has 12 edges. As 12 + 12 – 6 = 18, the new shape will have 18 edges.

10. **5 cm**
The dimensions of a rectangular prism are called length, width and height. As there are 12 edges, there are 4 lengths, 4 widths and 4 heights. As 40 ÷ 4 = 10, then length + width + height = 10 cm. As 10 – 3 – 2 = 5, the longest edge is 5 cm.

11. **1**
A square prism has 6 faces and a square pyramid has 5 faces.
As 6 – 5 = 1, there is 1 more face.

12. **156 cm²**
There are 4 identical triangles.
As 30 × 4 = 120, the total area of the triangles is 120 cm².
As 120 + 36 = 156, the area of all the faces is 156 cm².

Unit 10A — PAGE 28

1. **Suggested answer:**

2. parallelogram, triangle

3. 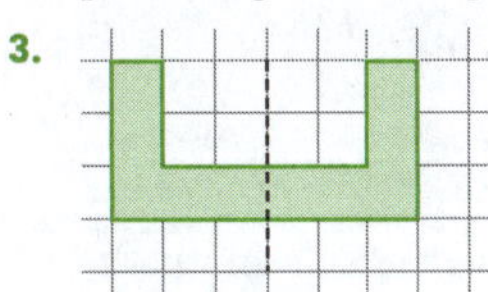

4. 

5. 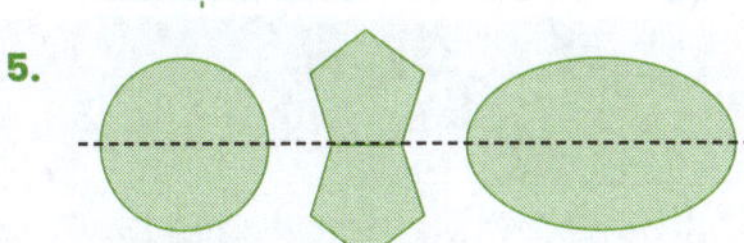

6. 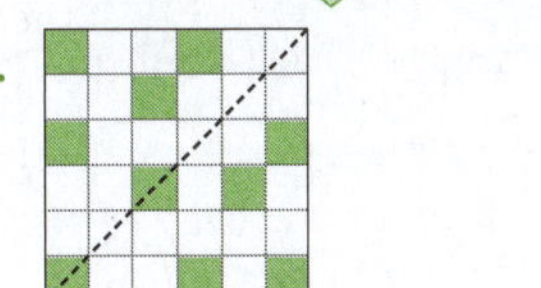

7.

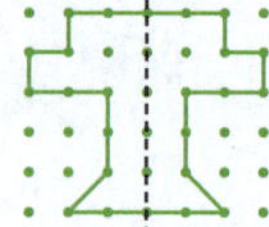

8.

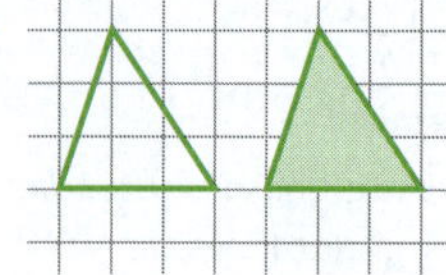

9.

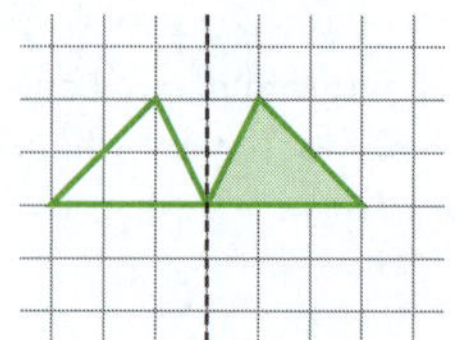

10.

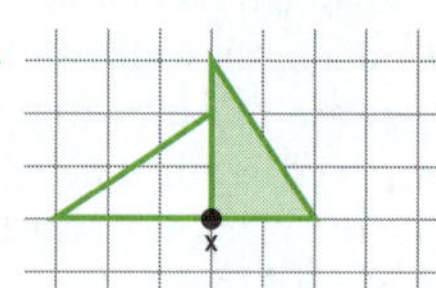

11. 5, left
12. a three-quarter turn

Unit 10B PAGE 29

1. **hexagon**

2. **Suggested answer:**

3. **Suggested answer:**

4. **4**

Simone needs to shade another 4 squares.

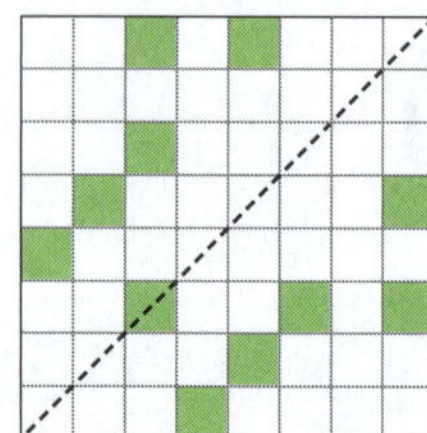

5. **9**

Francis needs to shade another 9 squares.

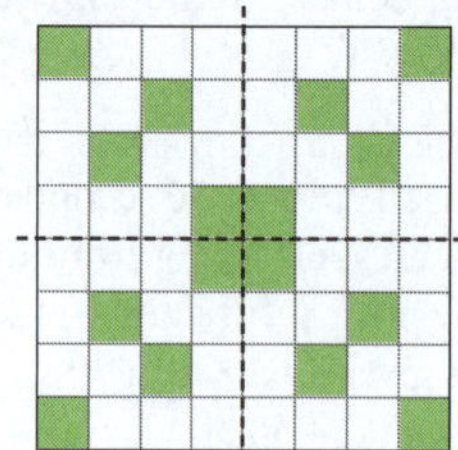

6.

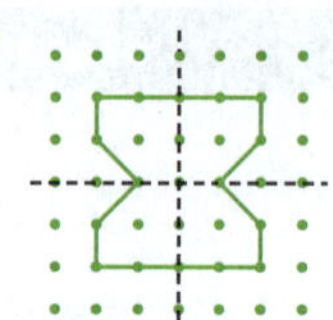

7.

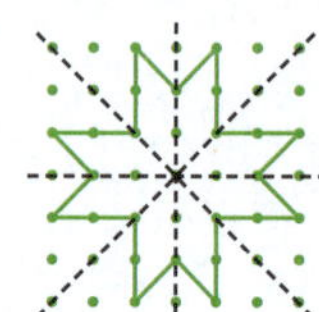

8.

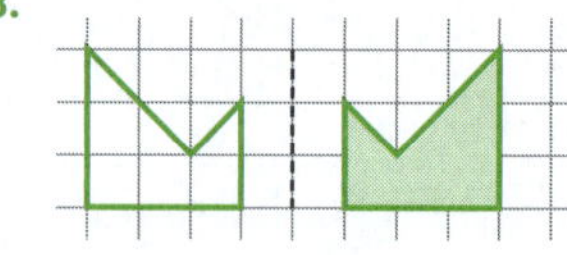

9.

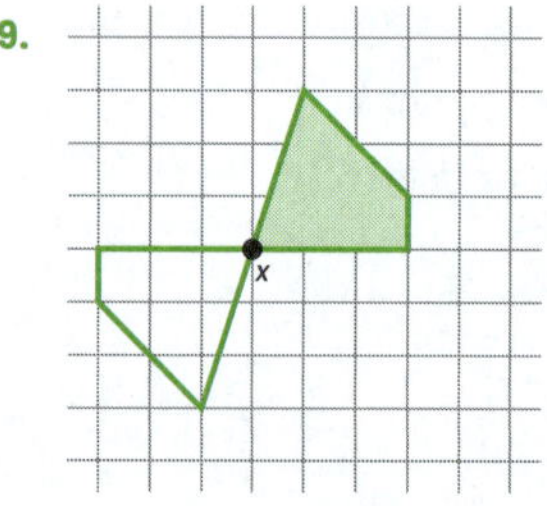

10.

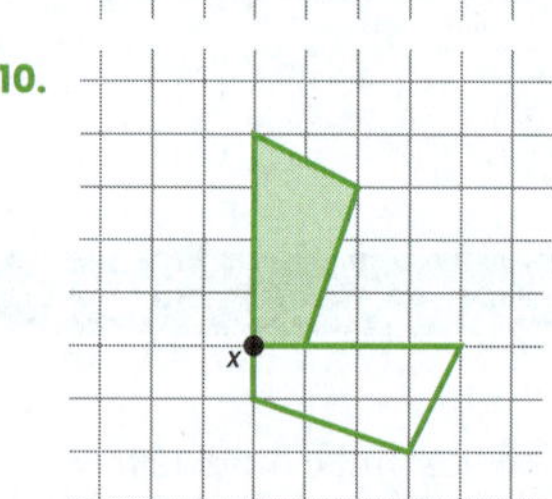

11. **5, 3, down**

The transformation is translate 5 units right, then translate 3 units down.

12.

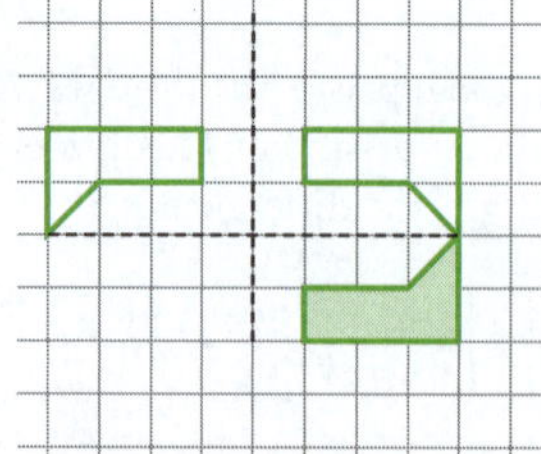

13.

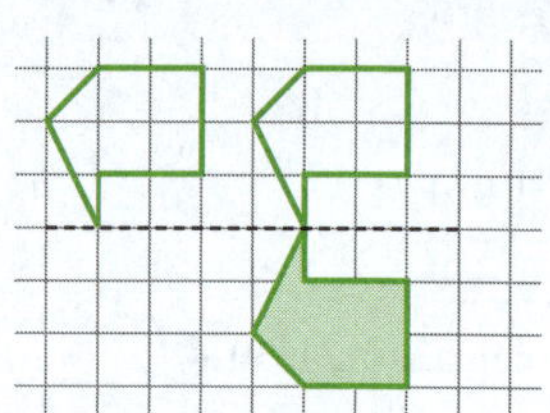

Unit 11A PAGE 30

1. C
2. 2, 4
3. *d*, *f*
4. 180°
5. *a*
6. C
7. *A* and *E*
8. east
9. north-east
10. south-west
11. 5 cm
12. 16 km
13. 12 km

Unit 11B PAGE 31

1. **9:55**

A quarter turn of the minute hand is 15 minutes. As 40 + 15 = 55, the time is 9:55.

2. **obtuse**

The angle is more than a right angle but less than two right angles (straight angle).

3. **8**

A complete revolution is 4 right angles. As 2 × 4 = 8, Emily has rotated through 8 right angles.

4.

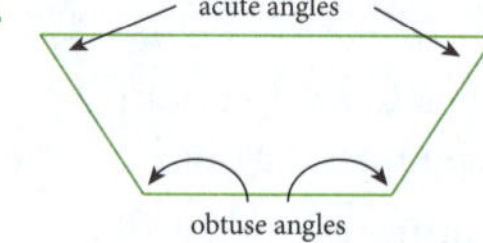

5. **acute**

The other angle must be an acute angle.

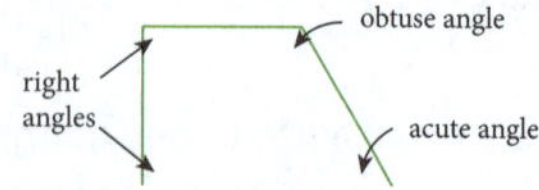

6. **true**

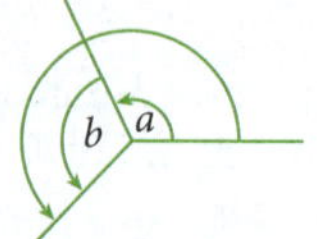

In the diagram, angles a and b are obtuse angles. Together they form a reflex angle.

7. **false**

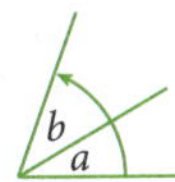

Here is a diagram that shows the new angle could be acute.

8. **10:05**

A three-quarter turn is 3 right angles. This is 45 minutes. As 20 + 45 = 65, the time is 5 minutes past 10 o'clock. This is written as 10:05.

9. **north-east**

On a compass, the direction north-east is opposite the direction south-west.

10. **south**

A three-quarter turn is 3 right angles. Tamir is now looking south.

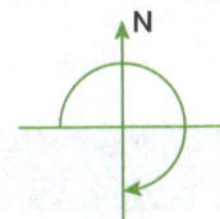

11. **12:27**

The clock shows 11:42. Three right angles is three quarters of an hour, or 45 minutes. As 60 – 42 = 18, and 45 – 18 = 27, Pedro's train arrives at 12:27.

12. **20 km**

The two points are 4 units apart on the map. The scale is 1 unit = 5 km. As 4 × 5 = 20, the distance is 20 km.

13.

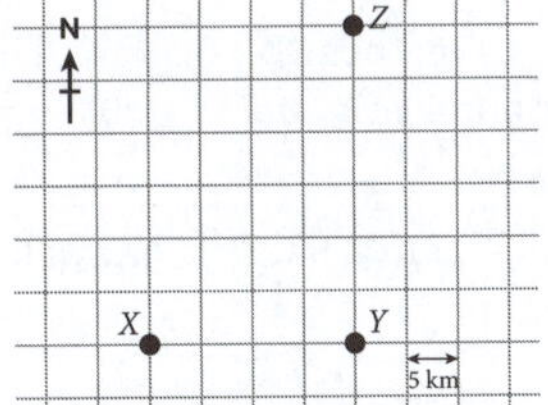

As 30 ÷ 5 = 6, Z is 6 units from Y in a northerly direction.

14. **south-east**

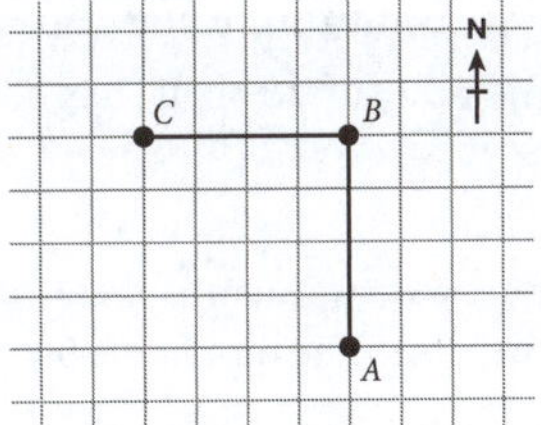

15. **4 km**

C and D are 6 units apart. You have been told they are 24 km apart. As 24 ÷ 6 = 4, the scale is 1 unit = 4 km.

16. **town *E***

E is in the middle of a line drawn from A to D.

17. **48 km**

Count the number of units. A to B is 2 units, B to C is 4 units and C to D is 6 units. As 2 + 4 + 6 = 12, the total distance on the map is 12 units. As 12 × 4 = 48, the total distance is 48 km.

Unit 12A PAGE 32

1. yellow
2. impossible
3. equally likely
4. very unlikely
5. 4
6. 6
7. 1, 3
8. possible
9. true
10. 5
11. purple
12. 7
13. 2
14. Friday
15. 5
16. 6

Unit 12B PAGE 33

1. **unlikely**

There are 4 even numbers and 2 odd numbers. This means it is unlikely that an odd number is rolled.

2. **soccer**

The graph shows 6 students said soccer was their favourite sport.

3. **2**

4 – 2 = 2. Two more students liked cricket than hockey.

4. **21**

3 + 2 + 4 + 6 + 3 + 3 = 21. There were 21 students surveyed.

5. **5**

Students are aged from 8 to 12. There were 5 students who were 8 years old.

6. **30**

5 + 7 + 6 + 8 + 4 = 30. There were 30 students.

7. **3**

As one symbol represents 2 cars, half a symbol represents 1 car. This means 3 cars were sold on Wednesday.

8. **6**

Friday has 4 symbols and Monday has 1 symbol. The difference is 3 symbols, which represents 6 cars.

9. **10**

Counting the symbols for Wednesday and Saturday is 4 whole symbols and 2 half symbols. This is a total of 5 symbols, which represents 10 cars.

10. **4**

Three cars are represented by one and a half symbols. You need to count the days that have 2 or more symbols. This occurred on Tuesday, Thursday, Friday and Saturday, which is 4 days.

11. **Wednesday**

The graph shows no dogs were groomed on Wednesday.

12. **5**

There were 9 dogs groomed on Friday and 4 on Tuesday. As 9 – 4 = 5, the difference is 5.

13. **4**

Monday 6, Thursday 8, Friday 9 and Saturday 5. This means at least 5 dogs were washed on 4 days.

14 **$600**

Thursday 8, Friday 9 and Sunday 3. As 8 + 9 + 3 = 20, there were 20 dogs groomed. As 2 × 3 = 6, then 20 × 30 = 600. The business made $600.

Section 2

Unit 1A PAGE 34

1 **four thousand and three**

There are 4 thousands, 0 hundreds, 0 tens and 3 ones. The number is four thousand and three.

2. **3287**

There are 3 thousands, 2 hundreds, 8 tens and 7 ones. This means the total is 3287.

3. **25 years**

60 – 35 = 60 – 30 – 5. This is 30 – 5 which is 25. The difference is 25 years.

4. 30

As 5 × 6 is 30, Ariana had a total of 30 cakes.

5. 9

As 5 × 9 = 45, then 45 ÷ 5 = 9. There are 9 marbles in each row.

6. $\frac{3}{4}$

There are four quarters in one whole. As 4 – 1 = 3, there are three quarters to complete.

7. 0.3

Label each marking on the number line. The decimal is 0.3.

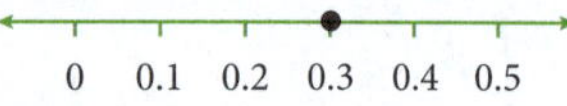

8. $1.20

2 lots of 50 is 100. As 100 + 20 = 120, Charlotte has 120 cents, which is $1.20.

9. 45

The pattern is adding 6. As 39 + 6 = 45, the next number is 45.

10. 123

There are 100 cm in 1 m. Adding 23 gives 123. There are 123 cm.

11. 45 L

As 9 × 5 = 45, there is 45 L in 5 buckets.

12. 90 kg

As 9 × 10 = 90, the total mass is 90 kg.

13.

14. 2

A rectangle has 2 lines of symmetry.

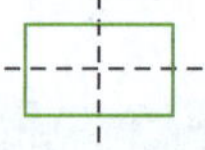

15

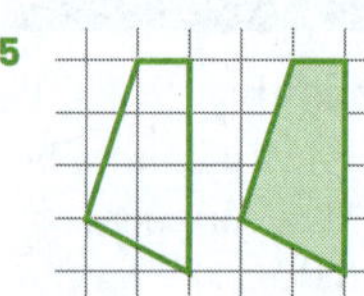

16. 56°

A right angle measures 90°. As 56 < 90, the angle smaller than a right angle measures 56°.

17. red

There are 2 red sections.

18. swimming

As 5 + 3 = 8, the highest number is 8. This means swimming was the most popular sport.

Unit 1B PAGE 35

1. 209 005

There are 2 hundred-thousands, 0 ten-thousands, 9 thousands, 0 hundreds, 0 tens and 5 ones. The number is 209 005.

2. 6070

Add the thousands first, then add the tens. As 4 + 2 = 6, then 4000 + 2000 = 6000. Also 30 + 40 = 70. The total is 6070.

3. 54

112 – 58 = 112 – 50 – 8. This is 62 – 8, which is 54. The difference is 54 points.

4. 35

There are five 7s. As 5 × 7 = 35, the total is 35.

5. true

Dividing 36 by 3 gives 12 and then dividing by 2 is 6. This means 12 ÷ 3 ÷ 2 = 6. Also 36 ÷ 6 = 6. As both answers are 6, the statement is true.

6. $\frac{1}{3}$

There are three-thirds in one whole. As 3 – 2 = 1, there is one-third to complete.

7. 0.15

Label each marking on the number line. The decimal is 0.15.

8. $1.45

As 7 × 2 = 14, then 7 × 20 = 140. As 140 + 5 = 145, Theodore has 145 cents, which is $1.45.

9. 10

The pattern is adding 9. The first number will be 9 less than 19. As 19 – 9 = 10, the missing number is 10.

10. 7036

There are 1000 mm in 1 m. 7 × 1000 = 7000. Adding 36 gives 7036. There are 7036 mm.

11. 180 L

As 9 × 2 = 18, then 9 × 20 = 180. Andrew uses 180 L.

12. 12 kg 800 g

As 3 × 4 = 12 and 200 × 4 = 800, the total mass is 12 kg 800 g.

13.

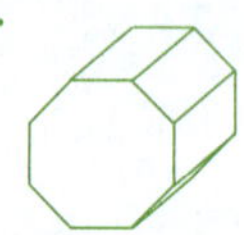

14. 0

A parallelogram has no lines of symmetry.

15.

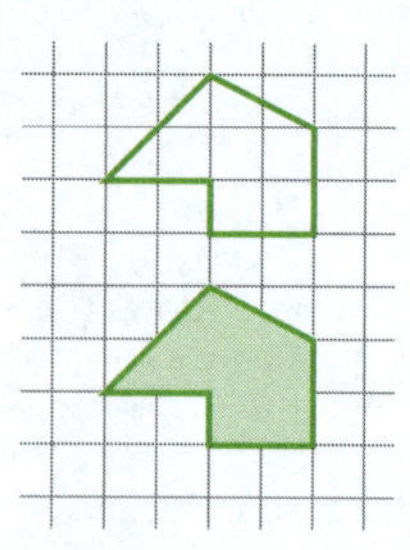

16.

17. 2

There are 3 sections with the number 2.

18. 30

Count the tallies of 5 and then add the remaining lines. 4 × 5 + 1 + 4 + 2 + 3 = 20 + 10, which is 30. This means 30 students were surveyed.

Unit 2A PAGE 36

1. 9380

Each number is larger than 9000. Look at the other three digits: 830, 380 and 308. These numbers in order are 308, 380 and 830. This means Christine's middle number will be 9380.

2. 98

50 + 40 + 8 is 90 + 8 = 98. The total is 98.

3. 60

As 9 – 3 = 6, then 90 – 30 = 60. The larger number is 60.

4. 21 km

As 7 × 3 = 21, Mary-Kate has walked 21 km.

5. 5

As 4 × 5 = 20, then 20 ÷ 4 = 5. There are 5 horses in each paddock.

6. $\frac{3}{5}$

There are five-fifths in one whole. As 5 – 2 = 3, $\frac{3}{5}$ of the shape has not been shaded.

7. 0.43

There are 0 ones, 4 tenths and 3 hundredths. The number is 0.43.

8. $3.75

375 = 300 + 75. As 300 cents is $3.00, another 75 cents is $3.75.

9. 15

The pattern is subtracting 5. 20 – 5 = 15. The next number is 15.

10. 12 m

30 – 18 = 30 – 10 – 8. This is 20 – 8, which is 12. Levi has 12 m to paint.

11. 600 mL

As 3 × 2 = 6, then 3 × 200 = 600. The total capacity is 600 mL.

12. 5 h

From 9:00 to midday is 3 h. Another 2 h is 2:00. As 3 + 2 = 5, the time difference is 5 hours.

13. 2

A cylinder has a curved surface and 2 flat surfaces.

14. Suggested answer:

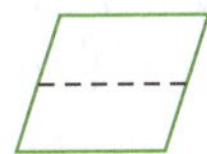

15. 4

The triangle has been translated 4 units to the right.

16. west

A quarter turn from south is west.

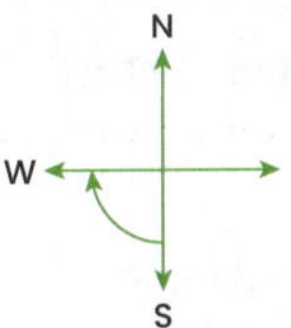

17. It will rain tomorrow.

The sun will certainly rise but it may, or may not, rain tomorrow.

18. 12

As 6 + 3 + 3 = 12, there were 12 vans not white in colour.

Unit 2B PAGE 37

1. 40 720

Three of the numbers are more than 40 000. The number 40 720 has 7 hundreds and 2 tens. It is the largest number.

2. 40

24 + 16 is 24 + 6 + 10. This is 30 + 10 = 40. Theo has 40 cards.

3. 443

$$\begin{array}{r} 764 \\ -\ 321 \\ \hline 443 \end{array}$$

The larger number is 443.

4. 54

6 × 9 = 54. Cam gives 54 balls to his friends.

5. 12

As 4 × 12 = 48, then 48 ÷ 4 = 12. Each student receives 12 counters.

6. $\frac{5}{12}$

There are 12-twelfths in one whole.

As 12 – 7 = 5, $\frac{5}{12}$ of the shape has not been shaded.

7. 8.09

There are 8 ones, 0 tenths and 9 hundredths. The number is 8.09.

8. $26.43

The number is 26 hundred and 43. This means 2643 cents is $26.43.

9. 92

The pattern is subtracting 6. The first number is 6 more than 86. As 86 + 6 = 92, the missing number is 92.

10. 57 cm

There are 100 cm in 1 m. 100 – 43 = 100 – 40 – 3. This is 60 – 3, which is 57. There is 57 cm of wire remaining on the roll.

11. 250 mL

As 50 ÷ 2 = 25, then 500 ÷ 2 = 250. There is 250 mL of oil in the can.

12. 3 h 30 min

From 8:30 to 9:00 is 30 min. Another 3 h is midnight. The time difference is 3 h 30 min.

13. 1

A cone has a curved surface and a flat surface.

14. Suggested answer:

15

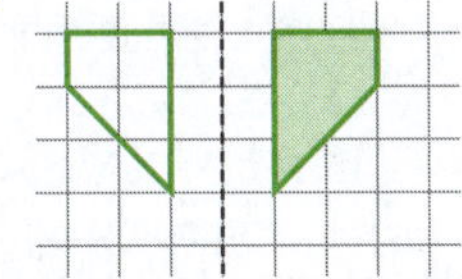

16. east

A half turn from east is west. This means that behind Scarlett is east.

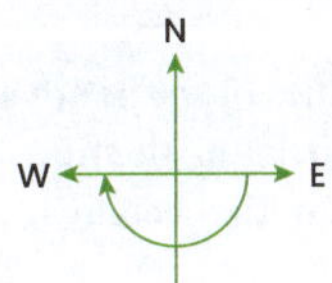

17. Tossing a head using a fair coin

There are 2 equally likely outcomes when tossing a fair coin.

18. 40

As 28 + 6 + 3 + 3 = 40, there were 40 vans that passed the school.

Unit 3A PAGE 38

1. 9

The number is forty-nine thousand, three hundred and seventy-eight. The 9 digit is in the thousands place.

2. 26

12 + 8 + 6 = 20 + 6, which is 26. Casey has 26 balloons.

3. 30

The number + 70 = 100. This means Barnaby's number is 100 – 70. As 10 – 7 = 3, then 100 – 70 = 30.

4. 48 m

6 × 8 = 48. Jean-Luc swam 48 m.

5. 8

As 7 × 8 = 56, then 56 ÷ 7 = 8. Liam can make 8 groups.

6.

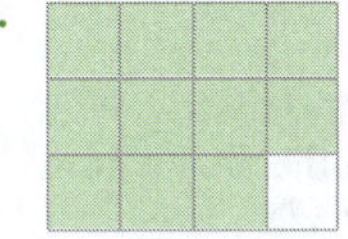

7.

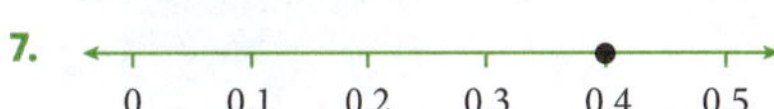

8. 538 cents

$5.38 is $5 + 38c. As 5 × 100 = 500, there are 500 cents in $5. As 500 + 38 = 538, there are 538 cents in $5.38.

9. 32

The pattern is multiplying by 2. As 16 × 2 = 32, the next number is 32.

10. 57 km

33 + 24 = 57. Lance rode a total of 57 km.

11. 400 mL

As 6 – 2 = 4, then 600 – 200 = 400. There is 400 mL remaining in the bottle.

12. 7000

There is 1000 g in 1 kg. This means there is 7000 g in 7 kg.

13. 12

The front face is a square with 4 edges. The back face is also a square with 4 edges. There are 4 more edges joining the front and back faces. As 4 × 3 = 12, there are 12 edges on the cube.

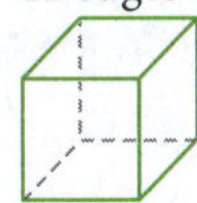

14. 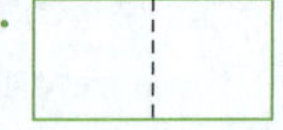

15. 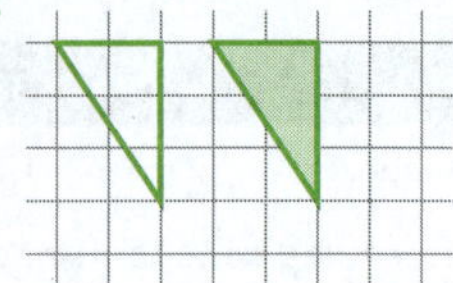

16. rectangle

A rectangle has 4 right angles.

17. 5

There are 3 balls numbered 5 but only one numbered 7.

18. 10

Each symbol represents 4 houses. This means a half-symbol represents 2 houses. As $2 \times 4 + 2 = 10$, there were 10 houses built in August.

Unit 3B PAGE 39

1. 58 382

The number will be of the form xx xxx. Write 3, 5 and 2 in their correct places. This is 3x5x2. Now place an 8 in the other two places. The number is 58 382.

2. 99

40 + 30 + 20 is 90. Also 1 + 2 + 6 = 9. The total is 99.

3. 611

The number plus 389 = 1000. This means Whitney's number is 1000 – 389.

$$\begin{array}{r} \not{1}\ {}^{9}\not{0}\ {}^{9}\not{0}\ {}^{1}0 \\ -\quad 3\ 8\ 9 \\ \hline 6\ 1\ 1 \end{array}$$

Whitney's number is 611.

4. 80

As $4 \times 2 = 8$, then $4 \times 20 = 80$. There are 80 legs on the desks.

5. 7

You need to work out $140 \div 20$. As $2 \times 7 = 14$, then $20 \times 7 = 14$. This means $140 \div 20 = 7$. Jason takes 7 lots of 20 away.

6. 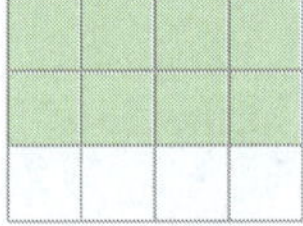

7. 0 0.01 0.02 0.03 0.04 0.05 0.06

8. 9040 cents

\$90.40 is \$90 + 40c.
As $90 \times 100 = 9000$, there are 9000 cents in \$90.

As 9000 + 40 = 9040, there are 9040 cents in \$90.40.

9. 160

The pattern is multiplying by 2.
As $8 \times 2 = 16$, then $80 \times 2 = 160$. The next number is 160.

10. 82 mm

1 cm is 10 mm. As $7 \times 10 = 70$, there is 70 mm in 7 cm. As 70 + 12 = 82, the total is 82 mm.

11. 1200 mL or 1.2 L

There is 2000 mL in 2 L. As 20 – 8 = 12, then 2000 – 800 = 1200. There is 1200 mL, or 1.2 L, remaining in the bottle.

12. 5250

There is 1000 g in 1 kg. This means there is 5000 g in 5 kg.
As 5000 + 250 = 5250, there is 5250 g in 5 kg 250 g.

13. 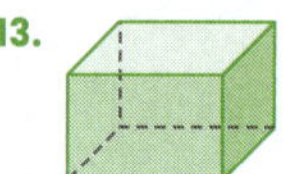

14. Suggested answer:

15. 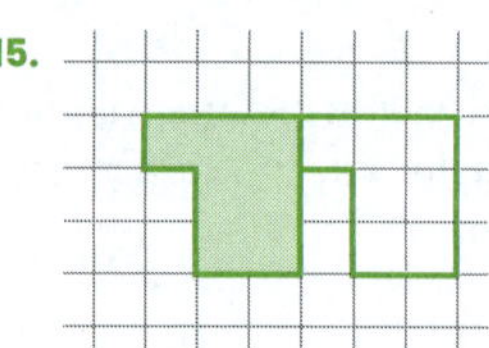

16. 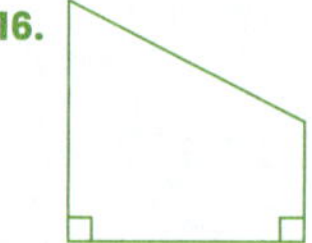

17. yes

There are no even numbers so it is impossible to select an even number.

18. 36

As 2 + 3 + 4 = 9, there are 9 house symbols for May, June and July. As $9 \times 4 = 36$, there were 36 houses built.

Unit 4A PAGE 40

1. 10

The two place values of the 4s are 400 and 40. As $40 \times 10 = 400$, the first 4 is 10 times larger than the second 4.

2. 45

37 + 8 is 37 + 3 + 5 = 45. There are 45 cows in the herd.

3. 55

100 – 45 = 100 – 40 – 5. This is 60 – 5 = 55. David keeps 55 marbles.

4. 120

As $6 \times 2 = 12$, then $60 \times 2 = 120$.

5. 2, 4

As $12 \div 2 = 6$ and $12 \div 4 = 3$, the numbers are 2 and 4.

6. 

7. 2 tenths

The number is fifty-eight point two nine. The place after the decimal is tenths. The place value is 2 tenths.

8. \$0.35

There are 100 cents in \$1.
As 100 – 65 = 100 – 60 – 5 = 35, there is change of 35 cents, or \$0.35.

9. even

Try some even numbers. 4 and 6 are even numbers. 4 + 6 = 10 and 10 is another even number. The result is always even.

10. 16 cm

One end of the pen is at 2 cm and the other end is at 18 cm. As 18 – 2 = 16, the length is 16 cm.

11. 5 L

500 + 500 = 1000 and 1000 mL = 1 L.
As 4 + 1 = 5, Andy buys 5 L of paint.

12. 25

From 3:25 to 3:30 is 5 minutes. There are another 20 minutes to 3:50. As 20 + 5 = 25, the time difference is 25 minutes.

13. 1

A sphere has 1 surface which is curved.

14. Suggested answer:

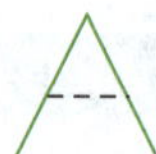

15. 4

As there are 4 quarters in a whole, there are 4 quarter turns in a full turn.

16. *R*

Village *R* is directly south of *X*.

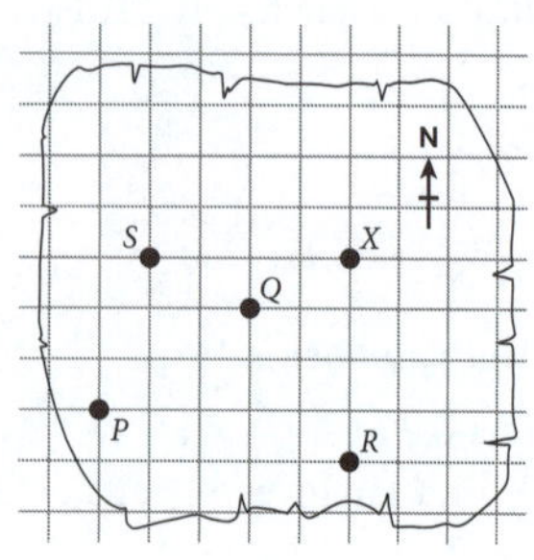

17. **3**
There are two 3s on the spinner. This means it is most likely to land on 3 than on any other number.

18. **12**
As 3 + 9 = 12, there are 12 members.

Unit 4B PAGE 41

1. **1000**
The two place values of the 4s are 40 000 and 40.
As 40 × 1000 = 40 000, the first 4 is 1000 times larger than the second 4.

2. **80**
44 + 30 + 6 = 74 + 6 which is 80.
Garry counted a total of 80 kangaroos.

3. **420**
1000 – 580 = 1000 – 500 – 80. This is 500 – 80, which is 420. There are 420 sheep waiting to be shorn.

4. **100 km**
As 5 × 2 = 10, then 5 × 20 = 100. Ross cycled a total distance of 100 km.

5. **6, 12, 18**
36 ÷ 6 = 6 and 36 ÷ 12 = 3. Also as 18 + 18 = 36, then 36 ÷ 18 = 2. The numbers are 6, 12 and 18.

6. **6**
Matthew will shade 6 circles.

7. **5 hundredths**
The number is ten point four five two. The second place after the decimal point is hundredths. The place value is 5 hundredths.

8. **$1.80**
From $3.20, adding 80 cents gives $4. Another $1 is $5. This means Declan received $1.80.

9. **odd**
It does not matter the size of the numbers. Adding an odd number to an even number always gives an odd answer.

10. **7 cm**
As 12 – 3 = 9, the crayon is 9 cm long. As 17 – 1 = 16, the pencil is 16 cm long. As 16 – 9 = 7, the pencil is 7 cm longer than the crayon.

11. **4500 mL**
There are 1000 mL in 1 L and 500 mL in $\frac{1}{2}$ L.
As 5000 – 500 = 4500, there is 4500 mL of water in the jug.

12. **1 h 50 min**
From 8:30 to 9:30 is 1 h. From 9:30 to 10:20 is 50 min. The total time is 1 h 50 min.

13. **1**
A hemisphere has 2 surfaces. It has 1 flat surface and 1 curved surface.

14. **Suggested answer:**
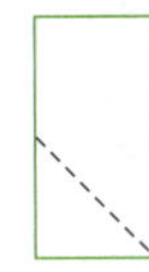

15. **quarter**
There are 4 quarters in a whole turn. As 4 – 3 = 1, a three-quarter turn in a clockwise direction is the same as a quarter turn in an anticlockwise direction.

16. **west**
Village *A* is west of *D*.
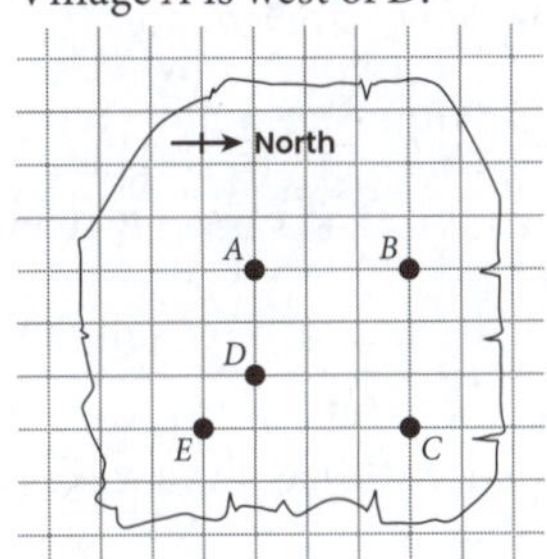

17. **no**
There are 4 sectors with odd numbers and only 2 with even numbers. This means it is not equally likely.

18. **19**
The numbers 14 and 15 are **between** 13 and 16. As 11 + 8 = 19, there are 19 members.

Unit 5A PAGE 42

1 **31 870**
6 hundred and 2 hundred is 8 hundred. The new number is 31 870.

2. **32**
17 + 15 = 17 + 10 + 5. This is 27 + 5 = 32. There is a total of 32 cards.

3. **500**
900 – 400 = 500

4. **32**
8 × 4 = 32. Alyson's answer is 32.

5. **2**
As 6 × 3 = 18, then 18 ÷ 6 = 3.
As 20 – 18 = 2, then 20 ÷ 6 = 3, with remainder 2.

6.

7 **4.300**
Zeros on the right-hand end of a decimal do not change the decimal. This means 4.300 is 4.3.

8. **$4.50**
Work out $10.00 – $5.50. From $5.50, adding 50c gives $6 and then another $4 is $10. The amount remaining is $4.50.

9. **8**
The missing number is 20 – 12 = 8. The missing number is 8.

10. **120 mm**
There are 10 mm in 1 cm.
As 12 × 10 = 120, the line is 120 mm long.

11. **700 mL**
The jug is marked in 100 mL units. There is 700 mL in the container.

12. **8 March**
As 20 – 12 = 8, Esme was born on 8 March.

13.

14.
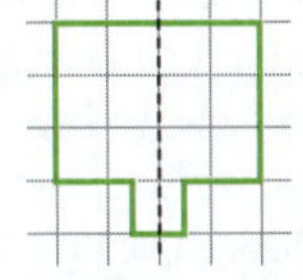

15.
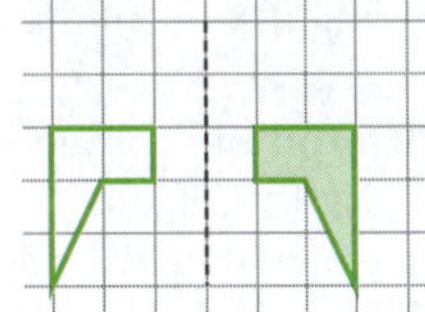

16. **6**
There are 6 angles in the regular hexagon and each angle is larger than a right angle.

17. **green**
There are more green balls than red balls. This means a green ball is more likely to be chosen.

18. **Friday**
Eight students said Friday was their favourite day.

Unit 5B PAGE 43

1. **148 739**

   3 thousand and 5 thousand is 8 thousand. The new number is 148 739.

2. **60**

   18 + 12 + 16 + 14 = 30 + 30 = 60. There were 60 books.

3. **6670**

   20 hundreds is 20 lots of 100 = 2000. This means 8670 – 2000 = 6670.

4. **36**

   12 × 3 = 36. There are 36 cans in the boxes.

5. **43**

   The number is 8 × 5 + 3. As 40 + 3 = 43, Soren's number is 43.

6. 

   $\frac{2}{3}$ is the same as .

7. **3.7**

   3.60 = 3.6. This means the largest decimal is 3.7.

8. **$10.50**

   Work out $40.00 – $29.50. From $29.50, adding 50c gives $30 and then another $10 is $40. The amount remaining is $10.50.

9. **36**

   The missing number is 110 – 74. This is 110 – 10 – 64 = 100 – 64, which is 36.

10. **27 cm**

    There is 10 mm in 1 cm. As 27 × 10 = 270, then 270 ÷ 10 = 27. The line is 27 cm long.

11. **300 mL**

    There is 1000 mL in 1 L. The jug shows a water level of 700 mL. As 10 – 7 = 3, then 1000 – 700 = 300. Another 300 mL is needed.

12. **8 April**

    As 31 – 28 = 3, there are 3 more days in March. As 11 – 3 = 8, Ben was born on 8 April.

13. 

14. 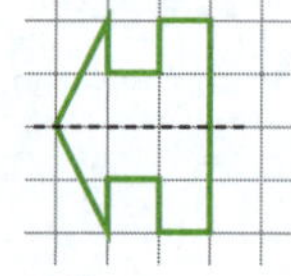

15. 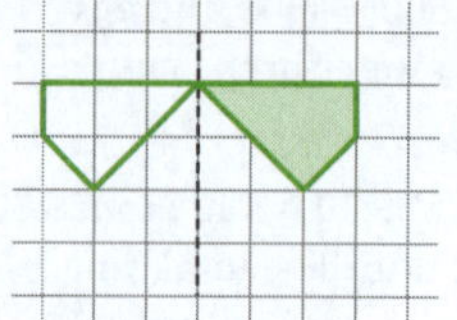

16. **Suggested answer:**

    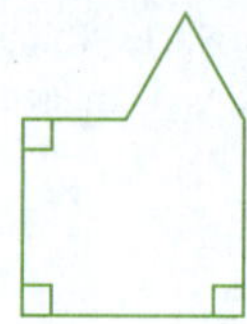

17. **no**

    A head or tail is equally likely.

18. **21**

    8 + 4 + 5 + 3 + 1 = 21. This means 21 students were surveyed.

Unit 6A PAGE 44

1. **5**

   The number is 26 240. There are 5 digits in the number.

2. **157**

   86 + 71 is 80 + 70 + 6 + 1. This is 150 + 7 = 157. There was a total of 157 koalas.

3. **42**

   96 – 54 = 96 – 50 – 4. This is 46 – 4 = 42. Mia has 42 cupcakes remaining.

4. **42**

   6 × 7 = 42. Breda bought 42 buns.

5. **8**

   As 3 × 8 = 24, then 24 ÷ 3 = 8. Dave has given mandarins to 8 friends.

6. $\frac{3}{8}$

   Three out of 8 rectangles have been shaded. This is written as $\frac{3}{8}$.

7. **3**

   There are 3 digits after the decimal point. This means there are 3 decimal places in the number.

8. **$11**

   Twice $5.50 is $5 + $5 + 50c + 50c. This is $10 + $1 = $11.

9. **22**

   Use the result of 42 – 20 = 22. The missing number is 22.

10. **14 cm**

    The rectangle has a length of 4 cm and a width of 3 cm. As 4 + 3 + 4 + 3 = 14, the perimeter is 14 cm.

11. **24**

    As 4 × 4 = 16, there are 16 cubes on the bottom layer. As 4 × 2 = 8, there are 8 cubes on the top layer. As 16 + 8 = 24, there is a total of 24 cubes.

12.

13. 

14. **Suggested answer:**

    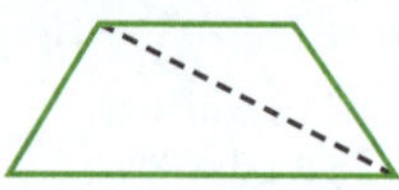

15. **5**

    The triangle has been translated 5 units to the left.

16. ***C***

    Town *C* is east of *B*.

17. 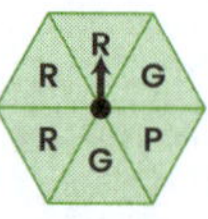

    Another 2 red and a green section need to be labelled.

18. **3**

    There are 3 dots in the column. This means 3 meat-free pies were sold.

Unit 6B PAGE 45

1. **6**

   The number is 108 041. There are 6 digits in the number.

2. **58**

   16 + 14 is 30. As 28 + 30 = 58, Hayley counted 58 birds.

3. **185**

   260 – 75 = 260 – 60 – 15. This is 200 – 15 = 185. Greg has 185 oranges remaining to be sold.

4. **160**

   As 8 × 2 = 16, then 8 × 20 = 160. Mila needs 160 baubles.

5. **5**

   As 9 × 5 = 45 and 48 – 45 = 3, Milo has 5 cards in each group.

6. $\frac{3}{4}$

   There are 6 out of 8 rectangles shaded. This is $\frac{6}{8}$, which can be rewritten as $\frac{3}{4}$.

7. **536.9**

   The number 536.9 has 1 decimal place.

8. **\$25.50**
You need to work out $3 \times \$8.50$.
As $3 \times \$8 = \$24$ and $3 \times 50c = \$1.50$, the total cost was \$25.50.

9. **15**
The missing number is $73 - 58$. This is $73 - 50 - 8 = 23 - 8$, which is 15. The missing number is 15.

10. **10 cm**
As $2 + 3 + 2 + 3 = 10$, the perimeter is 10 cm.

11. **13**
There are 8 cubes on the bottom layer, 3 on the middle layer and 2 on the top layer. As $8 + 3 + 2 = 13$, there is a total of 13 cubes.

12.

10:45 is 15 minutes to 11. This means the time will be 5 minutes after 11.

13.

14. **Suggested answer:**

15. **5, right**
The triangle has been translated 5 units to the right.

16. ***E* and *F***
Towns *E* and *F* are directly west of *D*.

17.
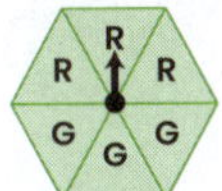

18. **14**
As $6 + 3 + 2 + 3 = 14$, there was a total of 14 pies sold.

Unit 7A PAGE 46

1. **4500**
Look at the digit in the tens place. As $2 < 5$, the number is 4500. The property is about 4500 ha.

2. **100**
$55 + 45 = 55 + 40 + 5$. This is $95 + 5$, which is 100. Sarina's total is 100.

3. **248**
$260 - 12 = 260 - 10 - 2$. This is $250 - 2 = 248$. There are 248 students seated.

4. **27**
$9 \times 3 = 27$. Dakota is 27 years old.

5. **4**
As $7 \times 5 = 35$ and $39 - 35 = 4$, Ophelia will have 4 plums left over.

6.
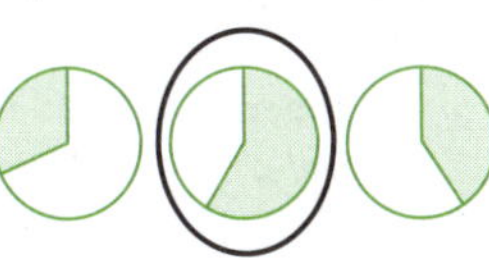

7. **9**
As 0.9 is 9 tenths, the missing digit is 9.

8. **\$13**
$40 - 27 = 40 - 20 - 7$. This is $20 - 7 = 13$. Willa is given \$13 change.

9. **32**
The pattern is dividing by 2. The first number is $2 \times 16 = 32$.

10. **9 cm²**
There are 9 small squares inside the shape. This means the area is 9 cm^2.

11. **6**
As $12 \div 2 = 6$, the jug can be filled 6 times.

12. **22 kg**
$15 + 7 = 15 + 5 + 2$. This is $20 + 2 = 22$. Sally has a mass of 22 kg.

13. **square**
A cube has 6 faces that are square in shape.

14.
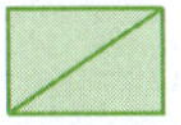

15.
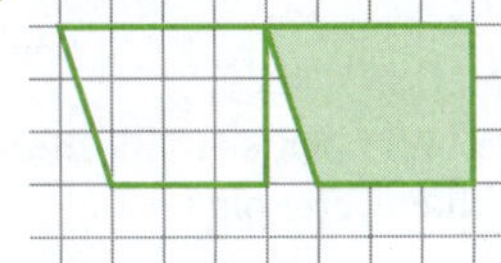

16. **2**
There are 2 halves in a whole. Two half turns is the same as a full turn.

17. **8**
As $5 + 3 = 8$, Emery recorded 8 heads.

18. **Abe**
The shortest column is \$20. Abe saved \$20.

Unit 7B PAGE 47

1. **127 409**
In the number 127 409, look at the 4 in the hundreds place. As $4 < 5$, the number rounds to 127 000. This means there could have been 127 409 visitors, which rounds to 127 000. None of the other numbers rounds to 127 000.

2. **1428**
$$\begin{array}{r} {}^{1}8\,5\,0 \\ +\ \ 5\,7\,8 \\ \hline 1\,4\,2\,8 \end{array}$$
The number is 1428.

3. **2110**
You need to work out $5720 - 3610$. $5000 - 3000 = 2000$. Also $700 - 600 = 100$ and $20 - 10 = 10$. This means $5720 - 3610 = 2110$.

4. **48**
$12 \times 4 = 48$. There are 48 kangaroos in the park.

5. **10**
$6 \times 10 = 60$ and $64 - 60 = 4$. Ivy can fill 10 boxes and will have 4 cakes left over.

6. **Shape A**
In shape B, 3 out of 6 rectangles are shaded. This is $\frac{1}{2}$ of the shape. In shape A, 3 shapes are shaded and 2 unshaded. This means more than half the shape is shaded.

7. **4**
The place value of the 4 is 4 tenths. This means the missing number is 4.

8. **\$11.60**
$\$5 + \$5 = \$10$ and $80c + 80c = \$1.60$. This means the total cost was \$11.60.

9. **10 000**
The pattern is dividing by 10. The first number is $10 \times 1000 = 10\,000$.

10. **18 cm**
$5 + 3 + 2 + 2 + 1 + 1 + 2 + 2 = 18$. The perimeter is 18 cm.

11. **18**
There are 12 cubes on the bottom layer and 6 on the top layer. As $12 + 6 = 18$, there is a total of 18 cubes.

12. **4 kg 540 g**
You need to double 2 kg and double 270 g. As $27 + 27 = 54$, then $270 + 270 = 540$. The total mass will be 4 kg 540 g.

13. **6**
A hexagonal prism has 2 faces that are hexagons and 6 rectangular faces.

14. **Suggested answer:**

15. 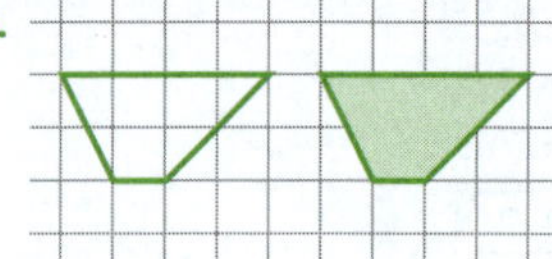

16. **2**

There are 2 quarters in a half. Two quarter turns is the same as a half turn.

17. **2**

As 5 × 2 + 4 = 14, there were 14 heads. As 5 × 3 + 1 = 16, there were 16 tails. As 16 – 14 = 2, Henry recorded 2 more tails than heads.

18. **$20**

Cam saved $40 and Abe saved $20. As 40 – 20 = 20, Cam saved $20 more than Abe.

Unit 8A PAGE 48

1. **9732**

The digits are arranged in descending order. The number is 9732.

2. **3**

Look at the ones first. 4 + 3 = 7. Now look at the tens. 6 + **?** = 9. The missing digit is 3.

3. **17**

45 – 28 = 45 – 25 – 3. This is 20 – 3 = 17. Marco has 17 watermelons remaining.

4. **66**

11 × 6 = 66. There are 66 children in the pool.

5. **8**

As 3 × 8 = 24, then 24 ÷ 3 = 8. The oranges will last 8 days.

6. $\frac{3}{4}$

The number line is marked in quarters. The fraction $\frac{3}{4}$ has been plotted.

7. **0.7**

7 tenths is written as 0.7.

8. **$20**

As 6 ÷ 3 = 2, then 60 ÷ 3= 20. Each child receives $20.

9. **47**

The missing number is 30 + 17 = 47.

10. **176 cm**

As 146 + 30 = 176, Simon's father is 176 cm tall.

11. **85 mL**

100 – 15 = 100 – 10 – 5. This is 90 – 5 = 85. There is 85 mL of cough syrup in the bottle.

12. 

As 15 + 2 = 17, the minute hand is 2 minutes after quarter past 9.

13. 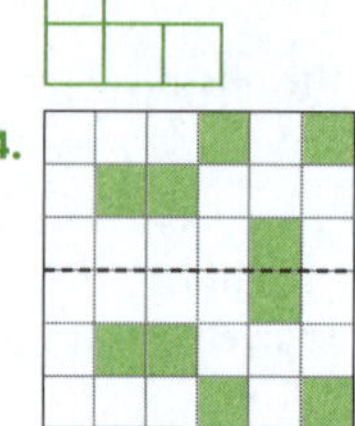

14. Three more squares need to be shaded.

15. **C4**

C4 is covered by the image.

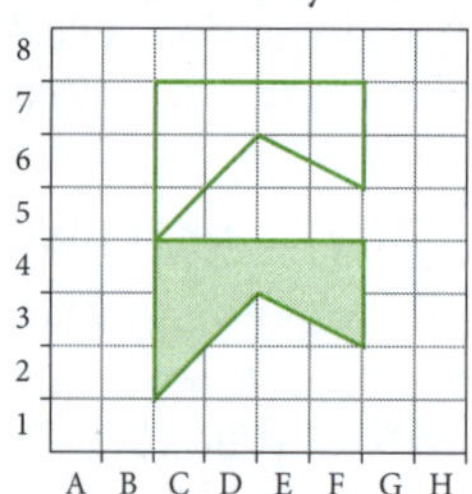

16. ***S***

Town *S* is south and west of *T*. This means *S* is south-west of *T*.

17. **possible**

There may be a student having a birthday tomorrow. This means it is possible.

18. **Saturday**

The highest number is 6. This means the most bikes were sold on Saturday.

Unit 8B PAGE 49

1. **3562**

Even numbers end in an even digit. The smallest 4-digit number is 3572. Subtracting 10 from 3572 gives 3562.

2. **4**

Look at the ones first. 8 + 5 = 3. Now the tens. 1 + 7 + [?] = 12. As 8 + 4 = 12, the missing digit is 4.

3. **338**

436 – 98 = 436 – 100 + 2. This is 336 + 2, which is 338. This means 338 cows have been milked.

4. **160**

16 × 10 = 160. There are 160 netball players.

5. **4**

6 × 11 = 66 and 70 – 66 = 4. This means 70 ÷ 6 = 11 and remainder 4.

6. $1\frac{1}{2}$

The number line is marked in halves. The number is halfway between 1 and 2. This means the number plotted is $1\frac{1}{2}$.

7 **8.3**

$8\frac{3}{10}$ is 8 ones and 3 tenths. This is written as 8.3.

8. **$59.95**

You need to look at the dollars. As 69 – 10 = 59, the new price is $59.95.

9. **73**

The missing number is 45 + 28. This is 45 + 20 + 8 = 65 + 8 = 73. The missing number is 73.

10. **206 km**

Both 13710 and 13916 start with 13. You need to work out the difference between 916 and 710. As 916 – 710 = 206, Naomi travelled 206 km.

11. **820 mL**

There are 1000 mL in 1 L. 1000 – 180 = 1000 – 100 – 80. This is 900 – 80 = 820. There is 820 mL of milk in the container.

12. 

As 60 – 48 = 12, the time is 12 minutes to 4.

13. 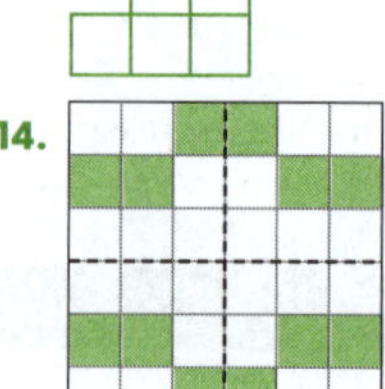

14. Four more squares need to be shaded.

15. **E3**

E3 is covered by the image.

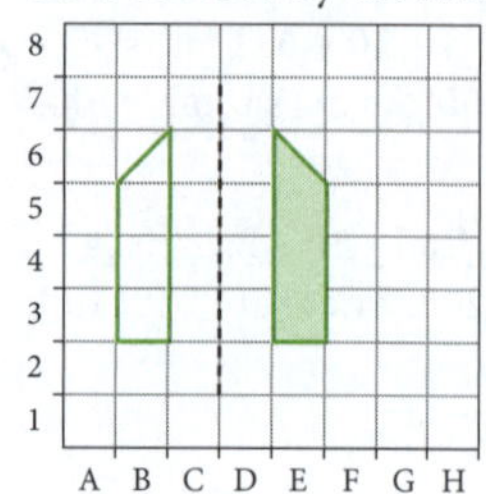

16. south-east

Town *T* is south and east of *P*. This means Olivia travelled south-east to *T*.

17. possible

The faces on the dice are numbered 1 to 6. This means there are 2 numbers out of 6 which are greater than 4. This is a possible chance.

18. 16

As 2 + 3 + 5 + 6 = 16, there was a total of 16 bikes sold.

Unit 9A PAGE 50

1. 1002

The numbers are 996, 998, 1000, 1002 … The fourth number is 1002.

2. 49

Add the larger numbers first. 26 + 14 is 40. As 40 + 9 = 49, Laila scored a total of 49 points.

3. 140

400 – 260 = 400 – 200 – 60. This is 200 – 60 = 140. This means 140 people visited after midday.

4. 48

$6 \times 8 = 48$. The 6 spiders have a total of 48 legs.

5. 4

As $6 \times 4 = 24$, then $24 \div 6 = 4$. Each necklace contains 4 shells.

6.

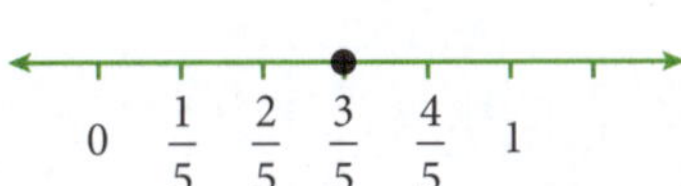

The number line is marked in fifths.

7. 0.27

27 hundredths is written as 0.27.

8. $6.60

As 6 × $1 is $6 and 6 × 10c is 60c, the total cost is $6.60.

9. 20

The numbers are increasing by 4. The missing number is 16 + 4 = 20.

10. 9 cm²

By counting, the area is 9 cm².

11. 9

There are 7 cubes on the bottom layer and 2 on the top layer. As 7 + 2 = 9, there is a total of 9 cubes.

12. 1 kg

As 5 + 5 = 10, then 500 + 500 = 1000. There is a total mass of 1000 g, or 1 kg.

13. 12

There are 4 edges on the rectangular base, 4 on the rectangular top and 4 more vertical edges. As $4 \times 3 = 12$, there is a total of 12 edges.

14. 2

A rectangle has 2 diagonals.

15.

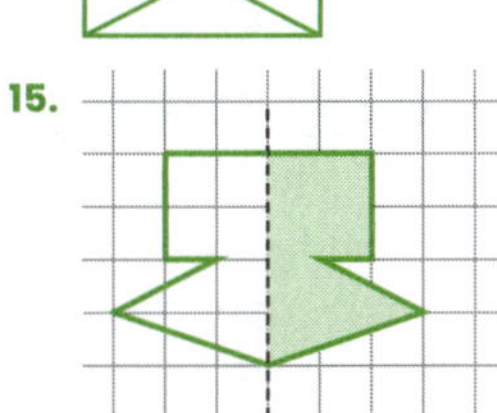

16. 10:15

A quarter turn takes a quarter of an hour. The time will be 10:15.

17. The number is less than 6.

All the numbers are less than 6 but not all are even. This means it is certain that the number is less than 6.

18. Dana

Dana was involved in only one activity.

Unit 9B PAGE 51

1. 2

The largest even 4-digit number is 9998 and the smallest odd 5-digit number is 10 001. The whole numbers between 9998 and 10 001 are 9999 and 10 000. This means there are 2 numbers.

2. 107

59 + 48 = 59 + 40 + 8. This is 99 + 8 which is 107. There were 107 points scored in the match.

3. 1900

56 – 37 = 56 – 36 – 1 = 19. This means 5600 – 3700 = 1900. There were 1900 Tigers supporters.

4. 56

$8 \times 7 = 56$. Jessica planted 56 bean plants.

5. 20

As $3 \times 2 = 6$, then $3 \times 20 = 60$. This means $60 \div 3 = 20$. There will be 20 birds in each enclosure.

6.

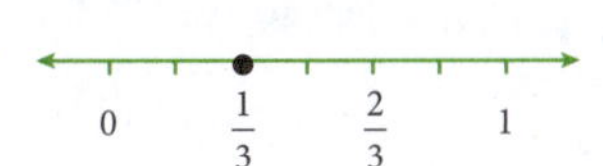

The number line is marked in sixths. $\frac{2}{6}$ is the same as $\frac{1}{3}$.

7. 3.09

$3\frac{9}{100}$ is 3 ones, 0 tenths and 9 hundredths. This is written as 3.09.

8. $430

380 + 50 = 380 + 20 + 30. This is 400 + 30 = 430. The usual price is $430.

9. 15

The numbers are decreasing by 4. The missing number is 19 – 4 = 15.

10. 10 cm²

There are 7 squares and 6 part-squares. The best estimate would be 10 cm².

11. 28 L

$8 \times 2 = 16$. An extra 16 L of water will be poured into the drum. As 12 + 16 = 28, the drum will now contain 28 L.

12. 770 g

110 = 100 + 10. Now, $100 \times 7 = 700$ and $10 \times 7 = 70$. As 700 + 70 = 770, Cassie uses 770 g of dog food each week.

13. 7

A pentagon has 5 sides. This means the prism has 2 faces in the shape of a pentagon and 5 rectangular faces as well. As 5 + 2 = 7, there is a total of 7 faces.

14.

15.

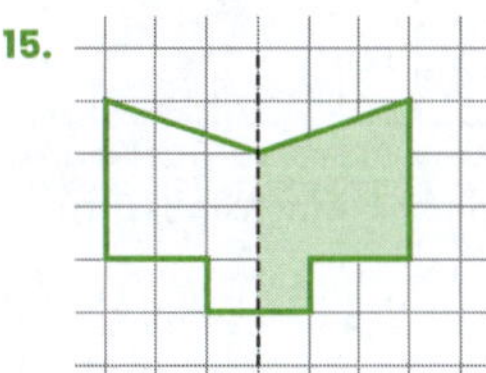

16. 2:15

17. The ball is even.

1, 3 and 5 are odd and 2 and 4 are even. There are more odd numbers than even. This means it is less likely that the number will be even.

18. 2

Ella (3) and Jack (5) were involved in more than 2 activities.

Unit 10A PAGE 52

1. **0**
   Joel's number is 8029. This means the number 0 is missing.
2. **51**
   $38 + 13 = 38 + 10 + 3$. This is $48 + 3 = 51$. There are now 51 passengers.
3. **27**
   $80 - 53 = 80 - 50 - 3$. This is $30 - 3 = 27$. Jamie needs 27 cards.
4. **18**
   $6 \times 3 = 18$. There are 18 slices of pizza.
5. **5**
   As $10 \times 5 = 50$, then $50 \div 10 = 5$. There are 5 shelves.
6. **3**
   4 divided into 7 is 1 with remainder 3. This means $\frac{7}{4} = 1\frac{3}{4}$. The missing number is 3.
7. **0.26**
   Less than 1 means there is a 0 in the ones place. After the decimal point there is a 2 followed by a 6. The number is 0.26.
8. **$18.60**
   $16 + 2 = 18$ and $50 + 10 = 60$. This means $16.50 + $2.10 = $18.60. Magnus paid a total of $18.60.
9. **25**
   Jay counts 10, 15, 20, 25. The fourth number is 25.
10. 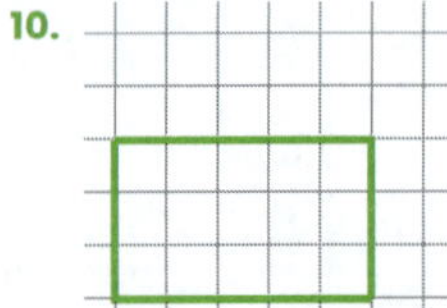
    The rectangle has dimensions 5 cm and 3 cm.
11. **30 cm³**
    As $10 \times 3 = 30$, the volume is 30 cm³.
12. **10:23**
    As $15 + 8 = 23$, the bus arrives at 10:23.
13. 
14. **1**
    The trapezium has 1 pair of parallel sides.
15. **D5**
    D5 is covered by the image.

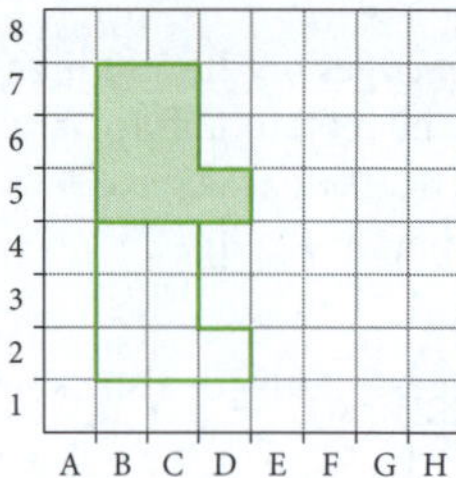

16. ***F***
    Town *F* is west of *E*.
17. **black**
    There are 12 red and 16 black jelly beans. This means it is more likely that the jelly bean was black.
18.

Season of birth	
Season	**Numbers**
Summer	6
Autumn	8
Winter	7
Spring	11

Unit 10B PAGE 53

1 **6**
   The 4-digit numbers start with 5. The numbers are 5128, 5182, 5218, 5281, 5812 and 5821. There are 6 numbers.
2. **183**
   $118 + 65 = 110 + 60 + 8 + 5$. This is $170 + 13 = 183$. This means 183 tickets have now been sold.
3. **32**
   A dozen is 12.
   As $5 \times 12 = 5 \times 10 + 5 \times 2 = 60$, Emily bought 60 eggs.
   $60 - 28 = 60 - 20 - 8$. This is $40 - 8$ which is 32. Emily has 32 eggs remaining.
4. **40**
   There are 4 quarters in each apple. As $10 \times 4 = 40$, there are 40 quarters.
5. **12**
   As $4 \times 12 = 48$, then $48 \div 4 = 12$. There are 12 tables in the restaurant.
6. **7**
   As there are 3 thirds in 1, there are 6 thirds in 2. As $6 + 1 = 7$, then $2\frac{1}{3} = \frac{7}{3}$. The missing number is 7.
7. **12.25**
   The number 12.25 is between 12 and 13. It has 2 tenths and 5 hundredths.
8. **$7.88**
   $3 + $4 = $7. Also, 68c + 20c = 88c. The total cost is $7.88.
9. **37**
   Roman counts all the numbers that are 2 more than multiples of 5. As 35 is a multiple of 5, then Roman will count 2 more than 35 which is 37.
10. If the perimeter is 18 cm, the length plus width will be 9 cm. As the length is 5 cm, the width is 4 cm.
11. **48 cm³**
    $12 \times 4 = 10 \times 4 + 2 \times 4$. This is $40 + 2 = 48$. The volume is 48 cm³.
12. **2:58**
    10 minutes before 3:10 is 3:00. Another 2 minutes before 3:00 is 2 minutes to 3:00 which is 2:58.
13. 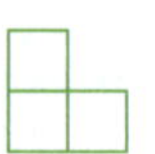
14 **17 cm**
    As $8 + 8 = 16$, the length of the third side must be less than 16 cm. This means it is impossible for the length to be 17 cm.
15. **C6**
    C6 is covered by the image.

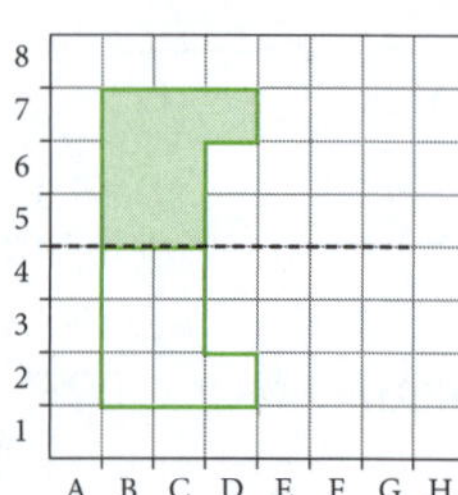

16. ***D***
    Town *D* is south-east of *B*.
17. **red**
    As $24 - 14 = 10$, there are 10 black jelly beans. There are more red jelly beans than black. This means it is more likely that the jelly bean was red.
18. **5**
    $6 + 9 + 10 = 25$. As $30 - 25 = 5$, there were 5 students born in summer.

Season of birth	
Season	Numbers
Summer	5
Autumn	6
Winter	9
Spring	10

Unit 11A PAGE 54

1. **70**
The number is three thousand, six hundred and seventy-two. The missing number is 70.

2. **64**
36 + 28 = 36 + 20 + 8. This is 56 + 8 which is 64. There are 64 passengers on the ferry.

3. **11**
The answer is the same as if you are working out 20 – 9, which is 11. You can check by writing 20 – 11 = 9.

4. **45**
9 × 5 = 45. There are 45 cards in the packets.

5. **4**
As 9 × 3 = 27, then 27 ÷ 9 = 3.
As 31 – 27 = 4, then 31 ÷ 9 = 3, with remainder 4.

6. **3**
As 4 – 1 = 3, Jayce needs to shade 3 more squares.

7. **4.39**
The number has 4 ones, 3 tenths and 9 hundredths. This is written as 4.39.

8. **$82**
43 + 39 = 43 + 40 – 1. This is 83 – 1 which is 82. The total is $82.

9. **50, 54**
The numbers follow the rule of adding 4. As 46 + 4 = 50 and 50 + 4 = 54, the two numbers are 50 and 54.

10. **815 cm**
There are 100 cm in 1 m.
As 8 × 100 = 800, there are 800 cm in 8 m. As 800 + 15 = 815, Callum threw 815 cm.

11. **1220 mL**
There are 1000 mL in 1 L.
As 1000 + 220 = 1220, there is 1220 mL of water in the jug.

12. **34 kg**
28 + 6 = 28 + 2 + 4. This is 30 + 4, which is 34. Loki has a mass of 34 kg.

13. **rectangular pyramid**
A rectangular pyramid has 4 triangular faces and a rectangular face as its base.

14. **0**
There are no lines of symmetry.

15.
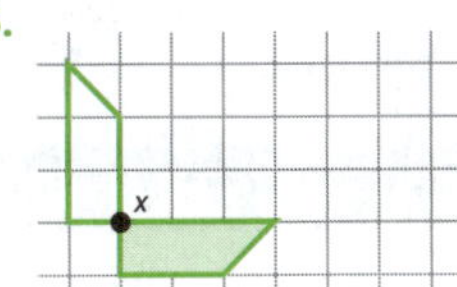

16. **smaller**
The angle between the 9 and 10 is smaller than a right angle.

17. **likely**
Two out of three shapes have 4 sides. This means it is likely.

18. **9**
Halfway between 8 and 10 is 9. Ava attended 9 times.

Unit 11B PAGE 55

1. **50 082**
There are 5 ten-thousands, 0 thousands, 0 hundreds, 8 tens and 2 ones. The number is 50 082.

2. **150 km**
30 + 30 + 45 + 45 = 60 + 90.
As 6 + 9 = 15, then 60 + 90 = 150.
Bethany cycled 150 km.

3. **26**
The answer is the same as if you are working out 60 – 34.
As 60 – 30 – 4 = 30 – 4 = 26, the number is 26.

4. **54**
A hexagon has 6 sides. As 9 × 6 = 54, there are 54 sides on the hexagons.

5. **69**
Dividing by 7 to give 9 with a remainder of 6. This means the number is 9 × 7 + 6. As 63 + 6 = 69, Silas's number is 69.

6. **3**
Two-thirds of the shape is 4 squares out of 6. As 4 – 1 = 3, Nicole needs to shade 3 more squares.

7. **604.05**
The number has 6 hundreds, 0 tens, 4 ones, 0 tenths and 5 hundredths. This is written as 604.05.

8. **$88**
40 + 32 = 72. As 72 + 16 = 88, the total is $88.

9. **66, 59**
The numbers follow the rule of subtracting 7. As 73 – 7 = 66 and 66 – 7 = 59, the two numbers are 66 and 59.

10. **18 m**
As 9 × 2 = 18, then 90 × 20 = 1800. This is 1800 cm, which is 18 m.

11. **5 L 410 mL**
8 – 3 = 5 and 670 – 260 = 410. There is 5 L 410 mL of water in the watering can.

12. **4300 g or 4.3 kg**
Multiplying by 10 places a 0 on the end of the number. This means 430 × 10 = 4300. The mass is 4300 g, which can be rewritten as 4.3 kg.

13. **hexagon**
The base will be a shape with 6 sides. This means the base is a hexagon.

14. **2**
There are 2 lines of symmetry.

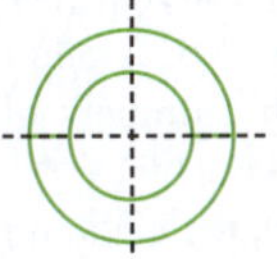

15.
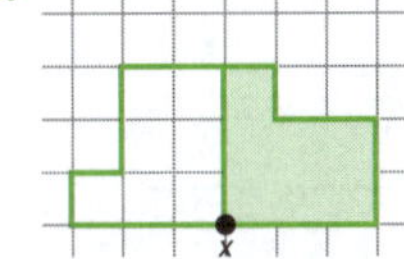

16. **larger**
The angle is a right angle when the minute hand is between the 2 and 3. At 11:20, the angle between the two hands is larger than a right angle.

17. **unlikely**
Only 1 in 5 shoppers receive a voucher. This means it is unlikely that Eva will receive a voucher.

18. **Cas**
Dee attended 3 nights. As 2 × 3 = 6, the person who attended on 6 nights was Cas.

Unit 12A PAGE 56

1. **3000**
In 2949 there is a 9 in the hundreds place. This means the number rounds up to 3000.

2. **34**
First 12 + 9 = 12 + 8 + 1. This is 21. 21 + 13 is 34. Deni has 34 marbles.

3. **28**
100 – 72 = 100 – 70 – 2. This is 30 – 2 which is 28. Carey needs 28 more sponsors.

4. **30**
6 × 5 = 30. There are 30 calculators.

5. **8**
As 4 × 8 = 32, then 32 ÷ 4 = 8. There are 8 apples in each layer.

6. 
As 3 × 2 = 6, one-third is 2 avocados.

7. **892.4**
A decimal point appears between the 2 and the 4. The number is 892.4.

8. **$4.75**
3c, 4c, 5c, 6c and 7c rounds to 5c. This means $4.77 rounds down to $4.75.

9. **2000**
Look at the number of zeros after 2 in the numbers in the sequence. The next number will be 2 followed by three 0s. Also the numbers follow the rule of multiplying by 10.
As 200 × 10 = 2000, the next number is 2000.

10. **5**
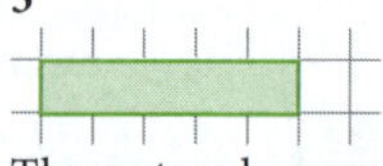
The rectangle covers 5 cm^2.

11. **360 L**
As 9 × 4 = 36, then 90 × 4 = 360. The people use a total of 360 L of water.

12. **quarter to 6**
As 10 + 5 = 15, the time is 15 minutes to 6. This is quarter to 6.

13. 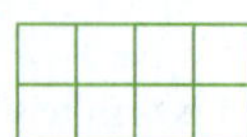

14. 
A square has 4 equal sides.

15. 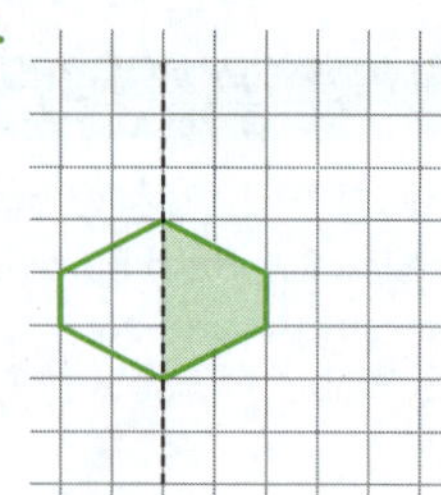

16. **west**
Xi walked west between *B* and *C*.

17. **impossible**
All the cards have odd numbers. This means it is impossible that an even number is chosen.

18. **1**
Olivia read 18 pages on Thursday, which was the only day she read more than 14 pages.

Unit 12B PAGE 57

1. **900 000**
Look at the 5 in the thousands place. This means the 9 in the ten-thousands place increases by 1, which then means the 8 in the hundred-thousands place increases to 9. The number rounds to 900 000.

2. **76**
First 36 + 24 = 36 + 20 + 4. This is 56 + 4 = 60. Now add 16. This is 60 + 16 which is 76. The students baked a total of 76 cupcakes.

3. **23**
110 – 87 = 110 – 80 – 7. This is 30 – 7 which is 23. The store has 23 books remaining.

4. **200**
As 5 × 4 = 20, then 5 × 40 = 200. There are 200 peaches.

5. **20**
$4\overline{)80}$ = 20
The missing number is 20.

6. **5**
There are 4 lots of 5 goals. This means Cali scored 5 goals.

7. **307.06**
The number is 3 hundreds, 0 tens, 7 ones, 0 tenths and 6 hundredths. The number is 307.06.

8. **$5.70**
$3 + $2 is $5. 50c + 21c is 71c, which rounds down to 70c. The total cost is $5.70.

9. **87**
The numbers follow the rule of adding 21.
66 + 21 = 66 + 20 + 1. This is 86 + 1 = 87. The next number is 87.

10. **20**
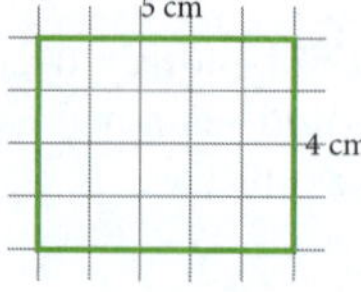

The rectangle covers 20 cm^2.

11. **1500 L**
39 000 – 37 500 = 39 000 – 37 000 – 500. This is 2000 – 500 = 1500. James added 1500 L of water.

12. 
It takes 10 minutes from 10 to 7 to 7:00. Another 15 minutes is 7:15, or quarter past 7.

13. 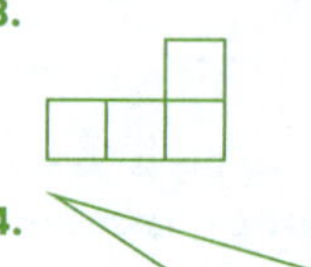

14. The triangle will have 3 sides of different lengths. An example is shown here.

15. 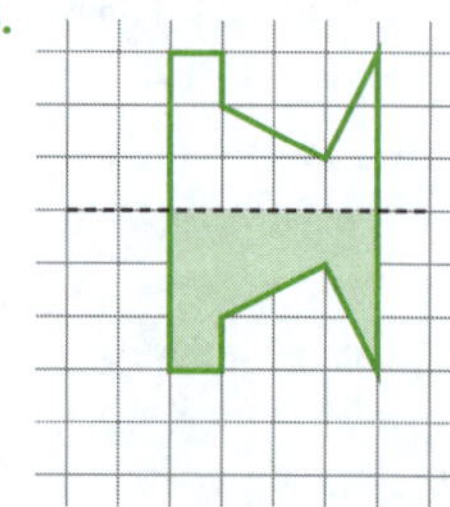

16. **east**
Here is the map with the compass. It might help to rotate your book a quarter turn. *C* is east of *D*.
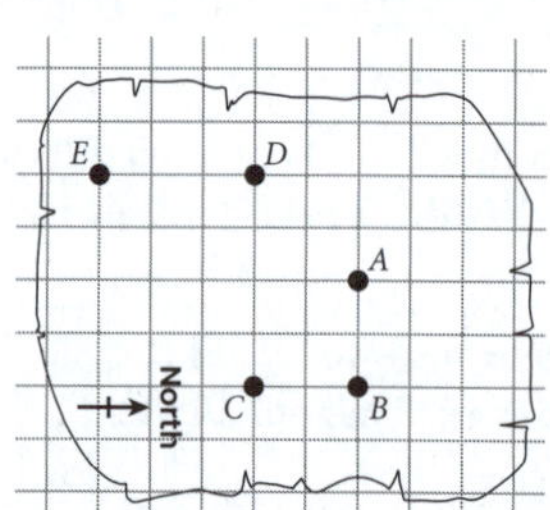

17. **likely**
Three cards out of 5 are numbered less than 6. This means it is likely a number less than 6 is chosen.

18. **50**
As 6 + 12 + 10 + 18 + 4 = 50, a total of 50 pages were read.

Unit 13A PAGE 58

1. **2367**
Writing the digits in ascending order will give the smallest possible number. The number is 2367.

2. **20**
First 3 × 6 = 18 and 2 × 1 = 1.
As 18 + 2 = 20, the total is 20.

3. **35**
98 – 63 = 98 – 60 – 3. This is 38 – 3 which is 35. There were 35 car spaces available.

4. **32**
As 8 × 4 = 32, Hiro will need 32 oranges.

5. **5**
As 8 × 5 = 40, then 40 ÷ 8 = 5. There are 5 paperclips in each group.

6. 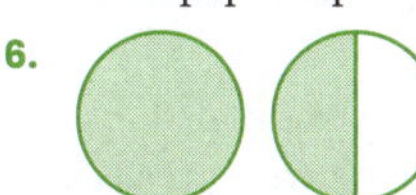

7. **19**
As 6 in the tenths place is more than 5, the number is rounded up to 19.

8. **$13**
50 – 37 = 50 – 30 – 7. This is 20 – 7 which is 13. Pallavi received change of $13.

9. **5100**
The pattern is adding 10. The missing number is 5100.

10. **21 km**
77 – 56 = 77 – 50 – 6. This is 27 – 6, which is 21. Esme has 21 km to drive.

11. **3 L**
As 5 – 2 = 3, Nicole uses 3 L when she uses a half-flush.

12. **150 g**
As 20 – 5 = 15, then 200 – 50 = 150. There is 150 g of peanuts remaining.

13. **hemisphere**
A cylinder has 2 flat surfaces. A cone has an apex. The shape is a hemisphere.

14. 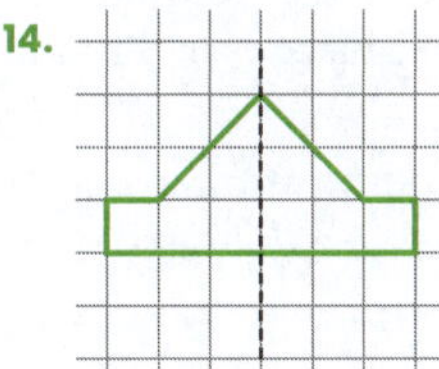

15. 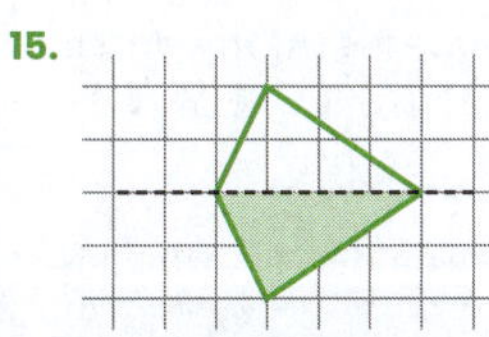

16. 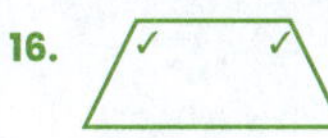

17. **unlikely**
Only 1 cup out of 3 has the small ball. This means it is unlikely Dylan is correct.

18. **15**
Sean scored 5 goals and Cam 10 goals. As 10 + 5 = 15, a total of 15 goals were scored by Sean and Cam.

Unit 13B PAGE 59

1. **498 321**
Writing the digits in descending order will give the greatest possible number. The digits 8 and 9 cannot be used as the first digit. The number is 498 321.

2. **50 years**
32 + 9 = 32 + 8 + 1.
This is 40 + 1 = 41. Scotty's father is 41 years old. As 41 + 9 = 50, the total is 50 years.

3. **420**
Look at 76 – 34.
As 76 – 30 – 4 = 46 – 4 = 42, this means 760 – 340 = 420. 420 more people voted for Tarek than James.

4. **3**
As 23 = 20 + [?], the missing number is 3.

5. **12**
As 10 × 12 = 120, then 120 ÷ 10 = 12. Each team is given 12 balls.

6. 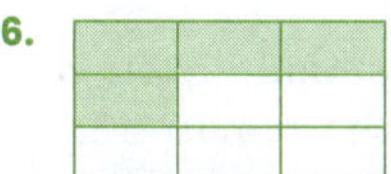

7. **13.84**
The number 13.84 rounds down to 13.8.

8. **$4.10**
$20 – $15 = $5. Subtracting another 90c is $4.10. Elena received change of $4.10.

9. **5678**
Each digit is increasing by 1. This means 4 + 1 = 5, 5 + 1 = 6, 6 + 1 = 7 and 7 + 1 = 8. The missing number is 5678.

10. **96 cm**
12 × 8 = 10 × 8 + 2 × 8. This is 80 + 16, which is 96. The total length is 96 cm.

11. **105 L**
15 × 7 = 10 × 7 + 5 × 7. This is 70 + 35 = 105. Liam uses 105 L of water.

12. **320 g**
As 4 × 8 = 32, then 4 × 80 = 320. The prism has a mass of 320 g.

13. **square prism (or rectangular prism)**
The new shape is a prism with a square base. It is a square prism or can be named a rectangular prism.

14. 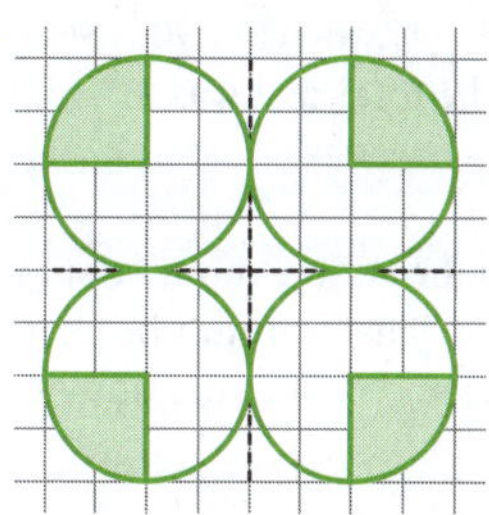

15.

16.

17. **unlikely**
As 1 + 1 + 1 = 3, Ariana must have rolled three ones. This is unlikely.

18. **4**
Jo (6), Gabby (9), Sean (5) and Cam (10), or 4 players, scored more than 3 goals.

Unit 14A PAGE 60

1. **60 mm**
As 32 is close to 30 and 19 is close to 20, you find 30 + 10 + 20. This is 60, which means the best estimate is 60 mm.

2. **52**
28 + 24 = 28 + 20 + 4. This is 48 + 4 = 52. Jayden sold a total of 52 cups.

3. **31**
47 – 16 = 47 – 10 – 6. This is 37 – 6 which is 31. Beth has uploaded 31 videos.

4. **14**
The man has 2 legs and each dog has 4 legs. As 3 × 4 = 12, and 12 + 2 = 14, Anna counted 14 legs.

5. **7**
As 6 × 7 = 42, then 42 ÷ 6 = 7. The cakes fill 7 boxes.

6 $\mathbf{\frac{3}{10}}$
The number line is marked in tenths. As 3 is between 2 and 4, *A* represents $\frac{3}{10}$.

7. **0.998**
Look at the digit in the ones place. As 0 is the smallest, then 0.998 is the smallest decimal.

8. **$17.90**
As 11 + 6 = 17, then $11.90 + $6 is $17.90. The total cost was $17.90.

9. $\frac{9}{10}$
The sequence of the numerators is 1, 3, 5, 7 ... The next number is 9, which means the missing number is $\frac{9}{10}$.

10. **160 cm**
As 2 is less than 5, the length rounds down to 160.

11. **11**
There are 8 cubes on the bottom layer and 3 on the top layer. As 8 + 3 = 11, there is a total of 11 cubes.

12. **10**
There are 60 minutes in 1 hour. As 70 − 60 = 10, then 70 minutes = 1 h 10 min. The missing number is 10.

13.

14. **5 cm**
A rhombus has 4 equal sides. You need to find 20 ÷ 4, which is 5. The length of each side is 5 cm.

15.
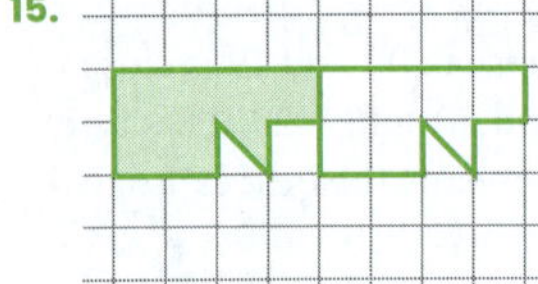

16. **20 km**
By counting, there are 4 units between *B* and *C*. As 5 × 4 = 20, the distance is 20 km.

17. **false**
The only colours are green and blue. There is a small chance that the arrow lands on blue.

18. **2**
The column above 0 hours shows that 2 students did not watch any television.

Unit 14B PAGE 61

1. **45 000**
23 890 is close to 24 000 and 19 711 is close to 20 000. 24 + 20 is 44, which is close to 45. The best estimate would be 45 000.

2. **44**
You need to find 9 + 15 + 10 + 10. This is 24 + 20 = 44. Mona scored 44 goals.

3. **10**
As 45 − 15 = 30, Xavier is 30 years old. As 30 − 20 = 10, Huan is 10 years old.

4. **1500**
500 × 3 = 500 + 500 + 500. This is 1000 + 500 which is 1500. There are 1500 sheets of paper.

5. **100**
As 15 × 100 = 1500, then 1500 ÷ 15 = 100. There are one hundred 15s in 1500.

6. **20**
There was the same number of white cars as not white. This means there were 20 cars that were not white.

7. **3.1**
As 3 is larger than 2, the answer is 3.09 or 3.1. As 3.1 = 3.10, you need to compare 3.09 and 3.10. As 10 > 9, the largest decimal is 3.1.

8. **$54**
80 − 26 = 80 − 20 − 6. This is 60 − 6, which is 54. The gift cost $54.

9. $\frac{9}{8}$ **or** $1\frac{1}{8}$
The sequence of the numerators is 1, 3, 5, 7 ... The next number is 9, which means the missing number is $\frac{9}{8}$. This can be rewritten as $1\frac{1}{8}$.

10. **48 cm**
24 + 24 = 24 + 20 + 4. This is 44 + 4 = 48. The combined length is 48 cm.

11. **12**
There are 8 cubes on the bottom layer, 2 on the second layer and 2 on the top layer. As 8 + 2 + 2 = 12, there is a total of 12 cubes.

12. **2 and 30**
There are 60 minutes in 1 hour. This means there are 120 minutes in 2 h. As 50 − 20 = 30, then 150 − 120 = 30. In 150 min there are 2 h 30 min. The missing numbers are 2 and 30.

13.

14. **32 cm**
10 − 4 = 6. The sides of the kite are 10 cm, 10 cm, 6 cm and 6 cm. As 10 + 10 + 6 + 6 = 32, the total is 32 cm.

15.
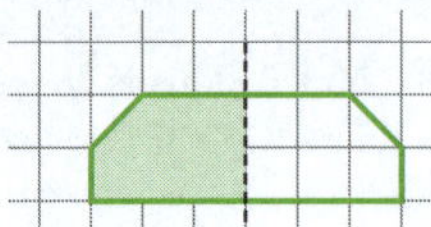

16. **400 m**
The map shows Ava and Vic live 3 units apart. As 3 units represents 300 m, then 1 unit represents 100 m. Meg and Vic live 4 units apart. This means Meg lives 400 m from Vic.

17. **true**
The spinner has been divided into 3 equal areas. There are 2 greens and 1 blue. It is more likely the arrow will point to green. The statement is true.

18. **10**
At least 3 hours means the total number of students who watched 3 or 4 hours. As 7 + 3 = 10, there were 10 students who watched at least 3 hours of television.

Unit 15A PAGE 62

1. **79**
The number cannot start with a 6 in the tens place because 6 + 10 = 16. As 7 + 9 = 16, the number is 79.

2. **29°**
You need to find 8 + 16 + 5 = 8 + 21. This is 29. The temperature was 29°.

3. **22**
48 − 26 = 48 − 20 − 6. This is 28 − 6 = 22. The other players scored 22 points.

4. **36**
6 × 4 = 24. As 24 + 12 = 36, Tom originally had 36 marbles in the bag.

5. **2**
As 8 × 2 = 16, and 20 − 16 = 4, the most each child can be given is 2 toys.

6. **4**
There are 2 half-dozens in a dozen. As 2 × 2 = 4, the eggs will last 4 days.

7. **6.5**
The number would be $6\frac{1}{2}$, which is rewritten as 6.5.

8. **$16.90**
8c and 9c round up. This means $16.88 rounds up to $16.90.

9. **0.48**
The numbers are increasing by 3 hundredths, or 0.03.
As 45 + 3 = 48, the missing number is 0.48.

10. 4 mm or 0.4 cm

There are 10 mm in 1 cm. This means there are 30 mm in 3 cm. As 30 – 26 = 4, one eraser is 4 mm, or 0.4 cm, longer than the other.

11. 400 mL

As half of the shampoo has been used, another half remains in the bottle. As 8 ÷ 2 = 4, then 800 ÷ 2 = 400. There is 400 mL remaining in the bottle.

12. 8 kg

As 24 ÷ 3 = 8, the mass of each block is 8 kg.

13. square pyramid

A square pyramid has 4 triangular faces and a square base. There are 8 edges.

14.

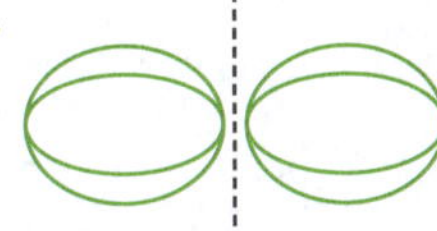

15.

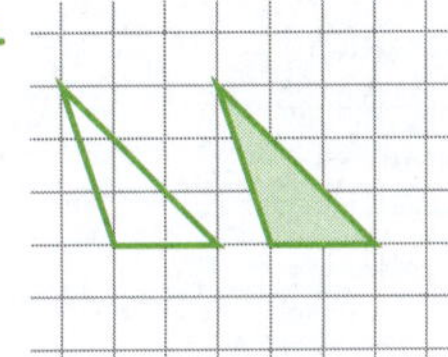

16.

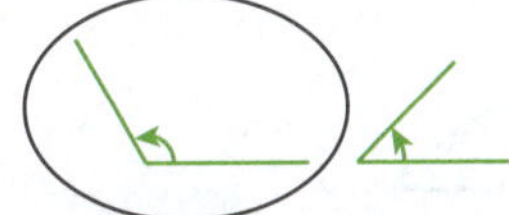

17. red, black

The other pair is when Naomi selects a red ball and a black ball. The missing pair is red, black.

18. 9

Look for the number which is in the rainy column and in the cool row. This means there were 9 cool and rainy days.

Unit 15B — PAGE 63

1. 259

The number starts with a 2 so the other two digits add to 14. As 5 + 9 = 14, the number is 259.

2. 400

285 + 115 = 200 + 100 + 85 + 15. This is 300 + 100 which is 400. There are now 400 balls in the pit.

3. 8

As 20 + 20 = 40, Andrew ate 40 blueberries. As 48 – 40 = 8, there are 8 blueberries remaining.

4. 75

25 × 3 = 25 + 25 + 25. This is 50 + 25 which is 75. There is a total of 75 sweets.

5. 6

As 60 ÷ 10 = 6, there are 6 squares in each row.

6 $\frac{1}{3}$

One row out of 3 rows is $\frac{1}{3}$. Roman has turned $\frac{1}{3}$ of the cards over.

7. 6.82

You can rewrite 6.8 as 6.80. Now look for the number in the middle of 80 and 84. This is 82. The decimal is 6.82.

8. $9.95

$6 + $3 = $9. Also, 80c + 15c = 95c. The total cost was $9.95.

9. 1.03

The numbers are increasing by 4 hundredths, or 0.04. As 99 + 4 = 103, the missing number is 103 hundredths, which is 1.03.

10. 42 cm or 0.42 m

There are 100 cm in 1 m. This means 1.4 m is 140 cm. 140 – 98 = 140 – 100 + 2. This is 40 + 2 = 42. Stella needs to grow 42 cm, or 0.42 m.

11. 2 L

500 + 500 + 500 + 500 = 1000 + 1000 = 2000. The bottles will hold 2000 mL, which is 2 L.

12. 6 kg

As 18 ÷ 6 = 3, the mass of each bag of rice is 3 kg. As 3 × 2 = 6, the total mass of 2 bags is 6 kg.

13. hexagonal pyramid, cube

A hexagonal pyramid has 12 edges, a pentagonal prism has 15 edges and a cube has 12 edges.

14.

15.

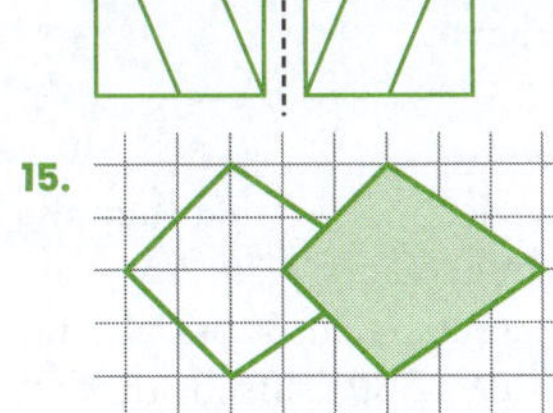

16. 2

There are 2 angles that are larger than a right angle but smaller than a straight angle.

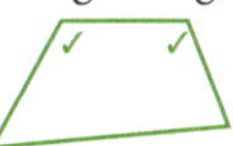

17. 8

Each of the 4 T-shirts can be worn with each of the 2 pairs of shorts. This means you multiply the numbers. As 4 × 2 = 8, there are 8 outfits.

18. 8

2 + 9 = 11 and 6 + 13 = 19. As 19 – 11 = 8, there were 8 more dry days than rainy days.

NAPLAN-style Test 1 — PAGES 64–65

1. C

There are 12 cupcakes. One-third of 12 is 12 ÷ 3 = 4. As 12 – 4 = 8, there are 8 cupcakes remaining.

2. D

Erin uses a $20 note to buy the dog toy. From $12.35, adding 65c gives $13. Another $7 gives $20. This means Erin received $7.65 in change.

3. D

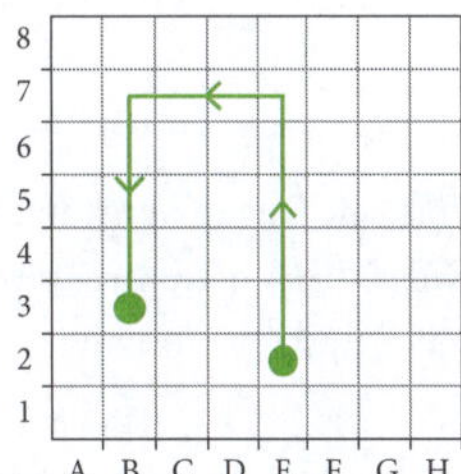

The counter moves to E7, then left to B7 and then down to B3.

4. C

The smallest odd 3-digit number is 101. The largest even 2-digit number is 98. As 101 – 98 = 3, the difference is 3.

5. B

Figure 1 has an area of 7 small squares, Figure 2 (10), Figure 3 (8) and Figure 4 (9). This means Figure 2 has the greatest area, then Figure 4, Figure 3 and then Figure 1. The order is 2, 4, 3, 1.

6. 24

The first light flashes after 8, 16, 24 … seconds. The second light flashes after 12, 24 … seconds. This means both lights flash after 24 seconds.

7. **B**

As 50 – 34 = 16, it will be 16 years until Bianca's mother is 50. As 16 + 6 = 22, Bianca will be 22 years old.

8. **D**

As $\frac{1}{2}+\frac{1}{2}=1$, Donna walks 1 km each day. There are 5 days from Monday to Friday. As 5 × 1 = 5, Donna walks 5 km.

9. **E**

Look at the numbers in the sequence. The rule is adding 8. As 17 – 8 = 9, the first number is 9.

10. **A**

There is a quarter of the circle shaded. As each rectangle has dimensions 4 units by 3 units, the rectangle has 12 small squares. As 12 ÷ 4 = 3, look for the rectangle with 3 small squares that are shaded. The rectangle is option A.

11. **C**

Halfway between 500 and 1000 is 750. The water level is between 500 and 750. From the options, the best estimate is 675 mL.

12. **C**

This sign has one line of symmetry. Option A has 0 lines of symmetry, option B has 2 and option D has 3.

13. **1, 3 and 6**

The spinner has the numbers 1 to 6. The possible results are 1, 3 and 6.

14. **3264**

$$\begin{array}{r} {}^{1}2\,{}^{1}3\;9\;0 \\ +\quad 8\;7\;4 \\ \hline 3\;2\;6\;4 \\ \hline \end{array}$$

This means 3264 spectators attended this year's game.

15. **B**

As 60 ÷ 4 = 30 ÷ 2 = 15, for every ticket sold, $15 is donated. As 15 × 2 = 30, then 15 × 200 = 3000. A total of $3000 was raised from the entry tickets.

16. **A**

Remove a cylinder from both sides of the balance. This means 2 cylinders have a mass of 10 kg, and so 4 cylinders have a mass of 20 kg.

17. **B**

Owen went to bed at 8:30 pm and got out of bed the next morning at 6:50 am. From 8:30 to 8:50 is 20 minutes. From 8:50 pm to 6:50 am is 10 hours. The total time is 10 hours 20 minutes.

18. **C**

As 60 – 40 = 20, Heidi has 20 more pages to read. She still needs to read $\frac{20}{60}$ of the book, which is $\frac{1}{3}$.

19. **C, F**

The number must end in either 0 or 5. As 4 + 5 = 9 and 7 + 0 = 7, the numbers are 45 and 70.

20. **55**

There are 15 minutes in a quarter of an hour. 19 + 17 + 13 + 6 = 19 + 30 + 6 which is 55. There are 55 shoppers who drive for longer than quarter of an hour.

Unit 16A PAGE 66

1. **85**

7 + 6 = 13, but 76 is an even number. As 8 + 5 = 13, the number is 85.

2. **56**

As 8 × 7 = 56, Penelope needs 56 eggs.

3. **160**

You can first work out the difference between 34 and 18. 34 – 18 = 34 – 10 – 8. This is 24 – 8 = 16. This means 340 – 180 = 160. The smaller number is 160.

4. **203**

110 + 93 = 110 + 90 + 3. This is 200 + 3 = 203. There was a total of 203 customers.

5. **6**

5 × 6 = 30 and 32 – 30 = 2. Natasha can form 6 groups and there will be 2 hats left over.

6. $\mathbf{\frac{3}{10}}$

As 10 – 7 = 3, there are 3 squares not shaded. This means $\frac{3}{10}$ is unshaded.

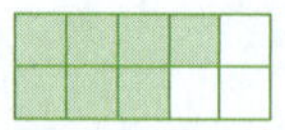

7. **3.04, 3.2, 3.3**

Rewrite the decimals so that they all have 2 decimal places: 3.20, 3.30, 3.04. Now compare 20, 30 and 4. The order is 4, 20 and 30. This means the decimals in ascending order are 3.04, 3.2, 3.3.

8. **$2.80**

Change both amounts to cents. 195 + 85 = 195 + 5 + 80. This is 200 + 80, which is 280. The total is $2.80.

9. **11**

As 12 + 8 = 20, the number sentence is 20 + ? = 31. As 31 – 20 = 11, the missing number is 11.

10. **50 cm**

There is 100 cm in 1 m. Half of 100 is 50. Each piece is 50 cm.

11. **8 L**

As 16 ÷ 2 = 8, the urn contains 8 L of water.

12. **120**

There are 60 seconds in a minute. As 6 + 6 = 12, then 60 + 60 = 120. There are 120 seconds.

13. **1**

William drew a cone. It has 1 curved surface.

14.

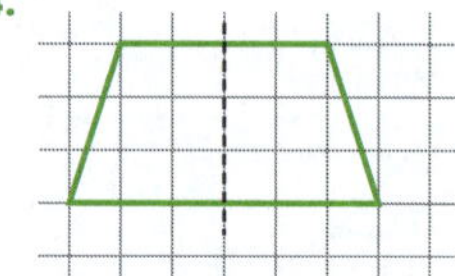

15.

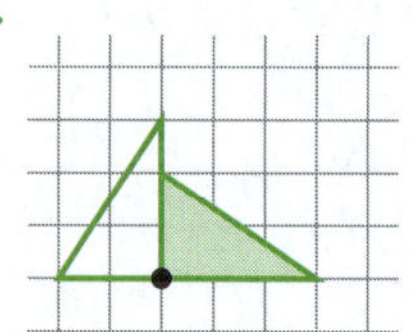

16.

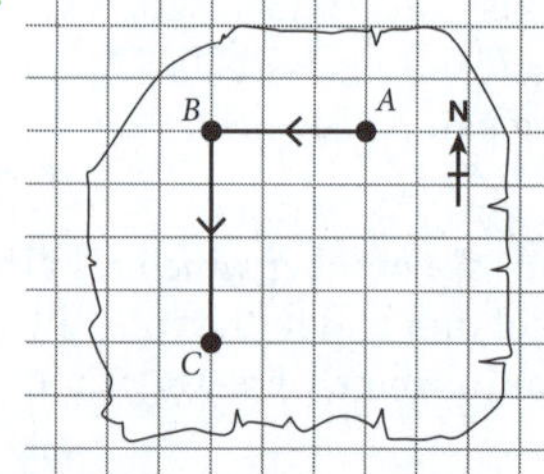

17. **red**

There are 3 red balls, 2 blue balls and 2 yellow balls. The most likely colour is red.

18. **5**

Looking at the column for mango, there were 5 students.

Unit 16B PAGE 67

1. **842**

The number in the ones place is 2. The number in the tens place is 4 and the number in the hundreds place is 8. The number is 842.

2. **39**

There are 5 school days in each week. As $8 \times 5 = 40$, and $40 - 1 = 39$, there are 39 remaining school days.

3. **8709**

$$\begin{array}{r} {}^{0}\not{1}\,{}^{13}\not{4}\,{}^{1}3\;8\;9 \\ -\quad 5\;6\;8\;0 \\ \hline 8\;7\;0\;9 \\ \hline \end{array}$$

The larger number is 8709.

4. **574**

$$\begin{array}{r} {}^{1}2\,{}^{1}7\;6 \\ +\;\;2\;9\;8 \\ \hline 5\;7\;4 \\ \hline \end{array}$$

There was a total of 574 passengers.

5. **15**

As $150 \div 10 = 15$, then $154 \div 10 = 15$, with remainder 4. This means 15 bags can be filled.

6. $\frac{1}{5}$

Layla shaded 3 out of the 5 columns, which means she shaded 6 squares. After Tess shades, there are only 2 squares not shaded. This is $\frac{1}{5}$ of the shape.

7. **5.24**

You can rewrite 5 as 5.00. Now look for the number in the middle of 0 and 48 This is 24. The decimal is 5.24.

8. **$42.90**

Change the money into cents and then add.

$$\begin{array}{r} {}^{1}2\,{}^{1}1\;5\;0 \\ 7\;9\;0 \\ +\;\;1\;3\;5\;0 \\ \hline 4\;2\;9\;0 \\ \hline \end{array}$$

The total amount received was 4290 cents, which is $42.90.

9. **8**

$25 + 15 + 12$ is $40 + 12 = 52$. The number sentence is $52 + \boxed{?} = 60$. As $60 - 52 = 8$, the missing number is 8.

10. **3250 mm**

There are 1000 m in 1 m. This means $\frac{1}{2}$ m is $1000 \div 2 = 500$ and $\frac{1}{4}$ m is $500 \div 2 = 250$. The length is 3250 mm.

11. **850 mL**

1700 is in the middle of 1600 and 1800. As half of 1600 is 800 and half of 1800 is 900, then half of 1700 is 850. The jug contains 850 mL.

12. **270**

There are 60 seconds in a minute. As $4 \times 6 = 24$, then $4 \times 60 = 240$. Also there are 30 seconds in half a minute. Adding 240 and 30 is 270. There are 270 seconds.

13. **4**

The shape is a rectangular pyramid. There are 4 triangular faces.

14. **1**

The kite has 1 line of symmetry.

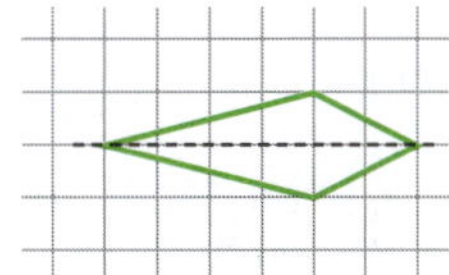

15.

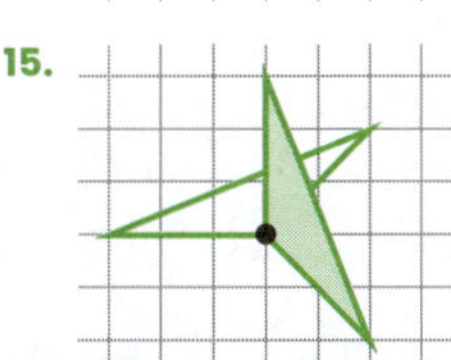

16. **north-east**

After walking the same distance south as west, Anna will now walk north-east towards *A*.

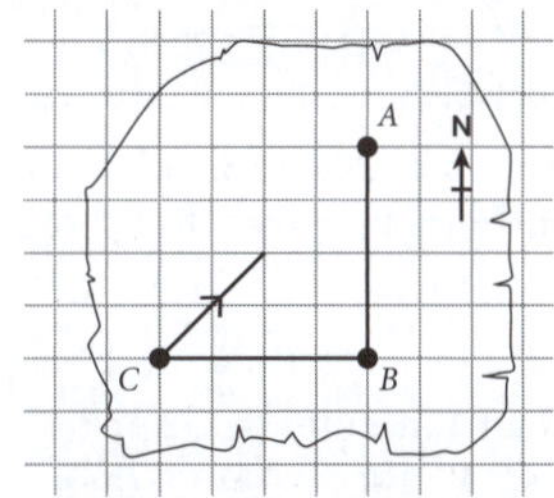

17. **1**

Counting the tally marks: $3 + 2 + 4 + 5 + 3 = 17$. As $18 - 17 = 1$, the number 5 was rolled only once.

18. **17**

As $4 + 6 + 5 + 2 = 17$, there were 17 students surveyed.

Unit 17A PAGE 68

1 **83 m**

68 and 74 round to 70. For 83, there is a 3 in the ones place. As $3 < 5$, then 83 rounds to 80. The tree could be 83 m high.

2. **4**

As $7 \times 4 + 2$ is $28 + 2 = 30$, the missing number is 4.

3. **476**

$316 + 160 = 300 + 100 + 16 + 60$. This is $400 + 76$ which is 476.

4. **311**

$335 - 24 = 335 - 20 - 4$. This is $315 - 4$, which is 311. There are 311 students present.

5. **9**

As $19 = 10 + 9$, the missing number is 9.

6. $\frac{3}{8}$

As $8 - 5 = 3$, there are 3 slices not eaten. This is 3 out of 8, which is written as $\frac{3}{8}$.

7. **37**

As 0.37 is 37 hundredths, the missing number is 37.

8. **$0.60**

As $7 \times 2 = 14$, then $70 \times 2 = 140$. The oranges cost $1.40. As $100 - 40 = 60$, she will receive $0.60.

9. **25**

5 squared is $5 \times 5 = 25$. The missing number is 25.

10. **12 cm**

The other two sides are 3 cm and 4 cm. As $3 + 4 + 5 = 12$, the perimeter is 12 cm.

11. **100 mL**

The jug is half full.
As $200 \div 2 = 100$, there is 100 mL of water.

12. **400 g**

Look at the digit in the tens place. As $3 < 5$, the mass rounds down to 400 g.

13.

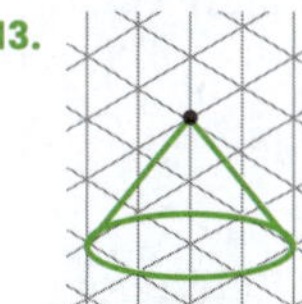

14.

15. **quarter to 4 or 3:45**

A quarter turn is 15 minutes. The time will be 15 minutes after 3:30. This time is quarter to 4, or 3:45.

16. **1**

A triangle can have 0 or 1 right angle.

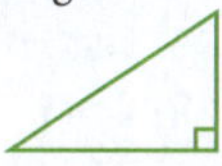

17. **even chance**

There are 2 As and 2 Ns. This makes it equally likely to choose an A.

18. **3**

There were 3 students who showered for 6 minutes.

Unit 17B PAGE 69

1. **23 499**

2301 is rounded to 2000. 22 499 rounds to 22 000 and 23 501 rounds to 24 000. The population could be 23 499, which rounds to 23 000.

2. **9 and 5**

$9 \times 7 = 63$ and $63 + 5 = 68$. The missing numbers are $A = 9$ and $B = 5$.

3. **859**

$$\begin{array}{r} {}^{1}4\ 7\ 6 \\ +\ \ 3\ 8\ 3 \\ \hline 8\ 5\ 9 \\ \hline \end{array}$$

Andrew scored a total of 859 runs.

4. **1550**

$$\begin{array}{r} {}^{2}\not{3}\,{}^{1}{}^{3}\not{4}\,{}^{1}0\ 0 \\ -\ \ 1\ 8\ 5\ 0 \\ \hline 1\ 5\ 5\ 0 \\ \hline \end{array}$$

There are 1550 blue seats in the grandstand.

5. **60**

$4 \times 15 = 2$ lots of 15×2. This is 2 lots of 30, which is 60. There are 60 mangoes.

6. **36**

If Maverick is a quarter of Tom's age, then Tom must be 4 times Maverick's age. As $4 \times 9 = 36$, Tom is 36 years old.

7. **40**

As $0.4 = 0.40$, the decimal is 40 hundredths. This means the missing number is 40.

8. **$1**

As $20 + 80 = 100$, $3.20 plus 80 cents is $4. As $5 - 4 = 1$, Harvey will be given $1 change.

9. **9**

Think of a number multiplied by itself that equals 81. As $9 \times 9 = 81$, the missing number is 9.

10. **16 cm**

$2 + 2 + 2 + 2 + 4 + 4 = 16$. The perimeter is 16 cm.

11. **750 mL**

There are 1000 mL in 1 L. The jug is three-quarters full. Half full is 500 mL. Halfway between 500 and 1000 is 750. There is 750 mL of water in the jug.

12. **9 kg**

As there are 1000 g in 1 kg, round the mass to the nearest 1000. The 6 in the hundreds place is more than 5, so the mass rounds to 9000 g. This is 9 kg.

13.

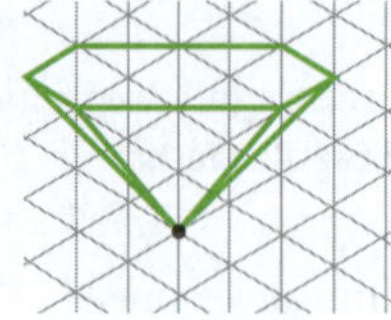

14.

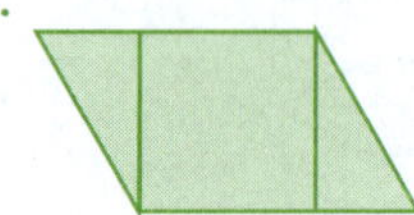

15. **5 to 7, or 6:55**

A three-quarter turn is 45 minutes. From 6:10, add 45 minutes is 6:55. This time is 5 to 7, or 6:55.

16. **yes**

It is possible to have 3 angles that are larger than a right angle.

17. **less likely**

There are 2 Bs and 3 other letters. This makes it less likely to choose a B.

18. **13**

Less than 4 minutes is 1, 2 or 3 minutes. As $2 + 4 + 7 = 13$, there were 13 students who showered for less than 4 minutes.

Unit 18A PAGE 70

1. **56 789**

The digits are written in ascending order. The number is 56 789.

2. **28**

$46 - 18 = 46 - 20 + 2$. This is $26 + 2 = 28$. There were 28 adult passengers.

3. **6, 2**

$24 \div 6 = 4$ with no remainder. $24 \div 2 = 12$ with no remainder. The two numbers are 6 and 2.

4. **118**

$39 + 36 + 43 = 30 + 30 + 40 + 9 + 6 + 3$. This is $100 + 18$, which is 118. There is a total of 118 students.

5. **45**

$15 \times 3 = 15 + 15 + 15$. This is $30 + 15$ which is 45. This means 45 people can ride the roller-coaster.

6. $\mathbf{\frac{2}{5}}$

There are 5 columns of circles. 2 out of 5 columns are shaded. This means $\frac{2}{5}$ of the circles are shaded.

7. **0.4**

Dividing by 10 is like making a fraction with a denominator of 10. This means $4 \div 10 = 0.4$.

8. **$53.10**

5308 cents is $53.08. This is rounded to $53.10.

9. **13**

As $25 - 12 = 13$, the rule is start with 12 and add 13.

10. **16 cm²**

There are 4 rows of 4 squares. As $4 \times 4 = 16$, the area is 16 cm².

11. **1.5 L**

There are 1000 mL in 1 L and 500 mL in half a litre. This means 1500 mL is one and a half litres, which is written as 1.5 L.

12. **4 kg**

As $2 \times 3 = 6$, Rebecca bought 6 kg of dog food. As $6 - 2 = 4$, there is 4 kg remaining.

13. **10**

The number of sides on the base tells you the number of rectangular faces. There are 8 rectangular faces plus the top and bottom. This means there are 10 faces.

14.

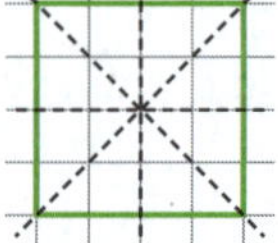

The shape is a square which has 4 lines of symmetry.

15. **G6**

E4 and E5 are covered by the image. G6 is not covered.

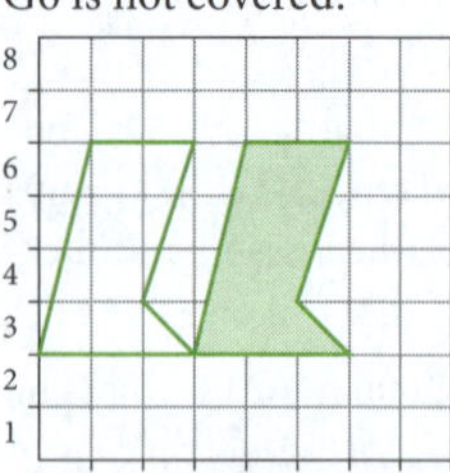

16. **west**

As S is west of R, Emilia was walking towards the west.

17.

Equal areas of red and yellow mean there is an equal chance of landing on red or yellow.

18. 10

Half a symbol represents 2 books. As $4 + 4 + 2 = 10$, the group read 10 books.

Unit 18B PAGE 71

1. 31 579

The smallest 5-digit number larger than 25 000 will start with a 3. Courtney's number will be 31 579.

2. 1178

$$\begin{array}{r} 2\ {}^{8}\cancel{9}\ {}^{1}{}^{5}\cancel{6}\ {}^{1}4 \\ -\ \ 1\ \ 7\ \ 8\ \ 6 \\ \hline 1\ \ 1\ \ 7\ \ 8 \end{array}$$

There were 1178 children on the cruise.

3. 8, 3, 2

As $25 - 1 = 24$, look for the numbers that can divide into 24 with no remainder. The numbers are 8, 3 and 2.

4. 1268

$$\begin{array}{r} {}^{1}6\ \ 7\ \ 5 \\ +\ \ 5\ \ 9\ \ 3 \\ \hline 1\ \ 2\ \ 6\ \ 8 \end{array}$$

A total of 1268 eggs were produced.

5. 92

$10 \times 6 = 60$ and $8 \times 4 = 32$. As $60 + 32 = 92$, Kellan has stacked 92 coins.

6. 4

$\frac{3}{4}$ of the shapes is 6 out of 8. As $6 - 2 = 4$, Rylee still needs to shade 4 shapes.

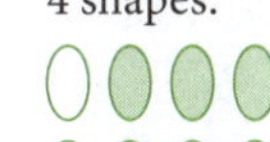

7. 0.09

Dividing by 100 is like making a fraction with a denominator of 100. This means $9 \div 100 = 0.09$.

8. $12

$12 + 6 = 18$. As $30 - 18 = 20 - 8 = 12$, Florence has $12 remaining on the card.

9. 4

Use 16 and 4. As $16 \div 4 = 4$, the rule is start with 256 and divide by 4.

10. 64 cm²

As $8 \times 8 = 64$, the area is 64 cm^2.

11. 0.75 L

There are 1000 mL in 1 L. This means 750 mL is 0.75 L.

12. 910 g

As $60 + 50 = 110$, then $860 + 50 = 910$. The mass of Horatio's fish was 910 g.

13. pentagon

As $15 \div 3 = 5$, the base has 5 sides. This means the shape is a pentagonal prism. It has 5 rectangular faces and 2 pentagonal faces.

14.

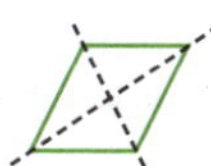

15. B3

B3 is covered by the original shape.

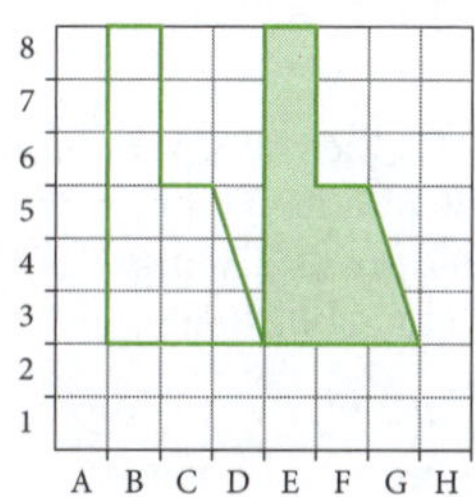

16. south

As *Q* is south of *R*, Emilia will be walking towards the south.

17. 4

1 out of the 2 possible outcomes is heads. This means you would expect 4 heads out of the 8 tosses.

18. 32

There are 7 full symbols and 2 half symbols.
As $7 \times 4 + 2 + 2 = 28 + 4 = 32$, a total of 32 books were read.

Unit 19A PAGE 72

1. 68 000

There is a 5 in the hundreds place. This means the number rounds up to 68 000.

2. 398

$$\begin{array}{r} 2\ \ 7\ \ 6 \\ +\ \ 1\ \ 2\ \ 2 \\ \hline 3\ \ 9\ \ 8 \end{array}$$

There are 398 students enrolled in the school.

3. 2

As $9 \times 5 = 45$ and $47 - 45 = 2$, there will be 2 left over.

4. 75

$$\begin{array}{r} {}^{0}\cancel{1}\ {}^{1}{}^{1}\cancel{2}\ {}^{1}0 \\ -\ \ 4\ \ 5 \\ \hline 7\ \ 5 \end{array}$$

Anna has read 75 pages.

5. 120

There are 6 items in half a dozen. As $6 \times 2 = 12$, then $6 \times 20 = 120$. Carrick bought 120 rolls.

6. $2\frac{3}{4}$

$2 + \frac{3}{4}$ is written as $2\frac{3}{4}$.

7. 5.9

The number 5.87 has 2 decimal places. As there is a 7 in the second decimal place, the 8 in the first decimal place increases by 1. The new number is 5.9.

8. 4

$2 + 20c + 10c + 5c = $2.35. There are 4 coins.

9. 2.8

The pattern is increasing by 0.3. As $2.5 + 0.3 = 2.8$, the missing number is 2.8.

10. 24 cm

A square has 4 equal sides. As $4 \times 6 = 24$, the perimeter is 24 cm.

11. 2

There are 8 cubes on the bottom layer and 2 on the top layer.
As $8 + 2 = 10$, there is a total of 10 cubes. As $12 - 10 = 2$, the shape needs another 2 cubes.

12. 9

From 8 am to midday is 4 hours. From midday to 5 pm is 5 hours. As $4 + 5 = 9$, the shop is open for 9 hours.

13.

14. 3

As $6 \div 2 = 3$, there are 3 rectangles needed.

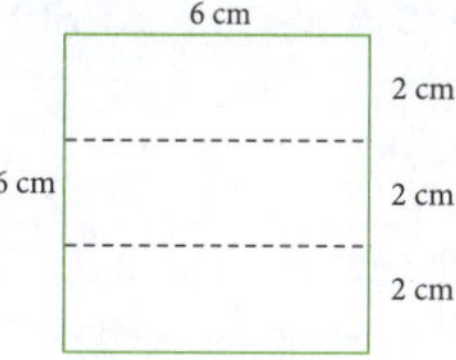

15. 4, right

Look at a vertex on the image on the left. Count the units to the corresponding vertex on the image. The shape has been translated 4 units to the right.

16. **4**

There are 4 angles that are smaller than a right angle.

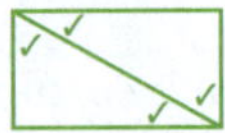

17. **3**

Paolo can choose strawberry and chocolate, or strawberry and caramel, or chocolate and caramel. This means there are 3 different combinations.

18. **17**

There were 8 votes for a bird and 9 for a dog. As 8 + 9 = 17, there was a total of 17 votes.

Unit 19B PAGE 73

1. **130 000**

There is a 7 in the tens place. This means the number rounds up to 129 500. Eliza's new number is 129 500. As there is a 5 in the hundreds place, this number rounds up to 130 000. Nicola's new number is 130 000.

2. **300**

$$\begin{array}{r} {}^{1}1\,{}^{1}7\,6 \\ +\ 1\,2\,4 \\ \hline 3\,0\,0 \end{array}$$

The cinema has a total of 300 seats.

3. **6**

9 × 9 = 81 and 87 – 81 = 6. There are 9 groups and 6 left over.

4. **220**

Look at 50 – 28.
As 50 – 20 – 8 = 30 – 8 = 22, there are 220 tickets yet to be sold.

5. **90**

5 × 8 = 40 and 5 × 10 = 50.
As 40 + 50 = 90, there are 90 seats in the first 10 rows.

6. $\mathbf{\frac{10}{3}}$

As there are 3 thirds in one whole, there are 9 thirds in 3. As 9 + 1 = 10, there are 10 thirds. This is written as $\frac{10}{3}$.

7. **14.5**

Look at the number 14.462. As there is a 6 in the hundredths place, the 4 in the tenths place increases by 1. The new number is 14.5.

8. **5**

$5 – $2 is $3. Also, $3 – 15c is $2.85. As $2.85 = $2 + 50c + 20c + 10c + 5c, there are 5 coins.

9. **12.3**

As 12.9 – 12.6 = 0.3, the pattern is increasing by 0.3.
As 12.6 – 0.3 = 12.3, the fourth number is 12.3.

10. **2 cm by 4 cm, 5 cm by 1 cm**

If the perimeter of the rectangle is 12 cm, the sum of the length and width is 6 cm. As 2 + 4 = 6 and 5 + 1 = 6, the rectangles with a perimeter of 12 cm have dimensions 2 cm by 4 cm and 5 cm by 1 cm.

11. **1250 mL or 1.25 L**

750 + 500 = 700 + 50 + 500. This is 1200 + 50 = 1250. Dustin bought 1250 mL, or 1.25 L, of oil.

12. **2**

As 4 × 3 = 12, then 40 × 3 = 120. As there are 60 minutes in 1 hour, then 120 minutes equals 2 hours. Tamir trains for a total of 2 hours.

13.

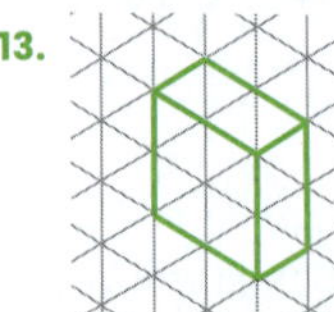

14. **4**

There are 4 squares needed.

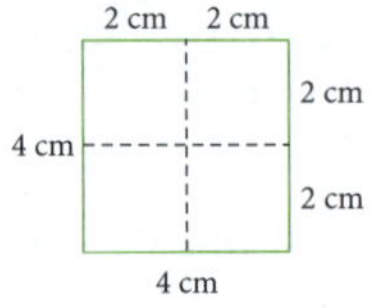

15.

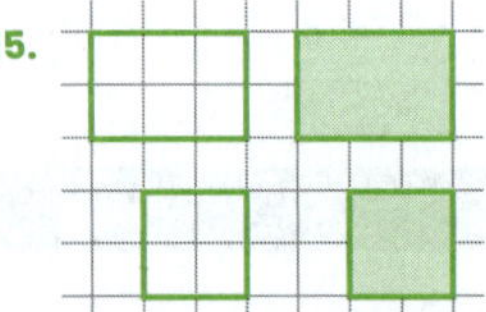

16. **6**

There are 6 angles that are smaller than a right angle.

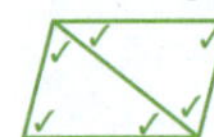

17. **red**

It does not matter where the arrow landed on the first 2 spins. There are more red sections than blue so it is likely the arrow stops on red.

18. **4**

Fish (4), bird (8), dog (9) and cat (4). This means there were 4 pets that received at least 3 votes.

Unit 20A PAGE 74

1. **1296**

The number 1296 has a 1 in the thousands and 9 in the tens place. It also has a 2 in the hundreds place and a 6 in the ones place.

2. **160**

As 2 × 8 = 16, then 20 × 8 = 160. Matt bought 160 screws.

3. **63**

$$\begin{array}{r} {}^{1}2\,4 \\ 1\,8 \\ +\ 2\,1 \\ \hline 6\,3 \end{array}$$

There is a total of 63 pencils.

4. **28**

103 – 75 = 103 – 70 – 5. This is 33 – 5, which is 28. There are 28 apartments not sold.

5. **8**

45 + 3 = 48. The number is 48 ÷ 6, which is 8.

6 $\mathbf{\frac{7}{10}}$

As 10 – 3 = 7, Perveen has $\frac{7}{10}$ of her pocket money remaining.

7. **0.3**

3 out of 10 squares have been shaded. This is written as $\frac{3}{10}$, which is 0.3.

8. **$3.05**

$20 – $16 = $4. Also, $4 – 95c is $3.05. Elias will be given $3.05 change.

9. **<**

8 × 5 = 40 and 6 × 7 = 42. As 40 is less than 42, the symbol is <.

10. **2.5**

There are 100 cm in 1 m. 50 cm is $\frac{1}{2}$ m, or 0.5 m. This means 2 m 50 cm = 2.5 m.

11. **800 mL**

As half of 16 is 8, then half of 1600 is 800. The jug contains 800 mL when half full.

12. **58 g**

64 – 6 = 64 – 4 – 2. This is 60 – 2 = 58. The chicken egg had a mass of 58 g.

13.

14. **5**

Another 5 squares need to be shaded.

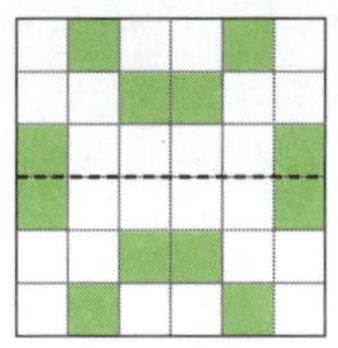

15.

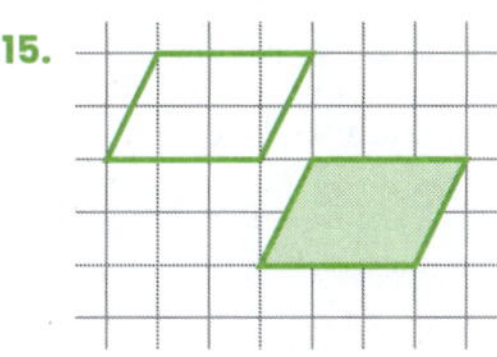

16. **south**

Both *C* and *E* are south of *B*.

17. **purple**

There are now 2 purple cards and 1 green card. This means it is more likely Ivy will select a purple card.

18. **7**

There were 7 dogs in the park.

Unit 20B PAGE 75

1. **3033**

3 + 3 + 3 + 3 = 12. You need to find the number 300 less than 3333. This means the number is 3033.

2. **36**

You need to find 3 × 6 × 2. This is 18 × 2. 18 + 18 = 18 + 10 + 8 = 36. There are 36 shoes in Emma's wardrobe.

3. **40**

As 9 + 4 = 13, Sophia read 13 books. As 13 + 5 = 18, Ava read 18 books. You need to add 9, 13 and 18. As 18 + 13 = 31 and 31 + 9 = 40, the total is 40 books.

4. **18 452**

As 23 – 5 = 18, then 23 452 – 5000 = 18 452.

5. **20**

Think of the multiples of 5: 5, 10, 15, 20 … Also, think of the numbers that are 2 more than the multiples of 6: 6 + 2 = 8, 12 + 2 = 14, 18 + 2 = 20 … The first number common to both lists is 20.

6. $\frac{1}{4}$

Imagine the first square is shaded. There are four quarters in the second square. As 3 quarters are shaded, there is 1 quarter not shaded.

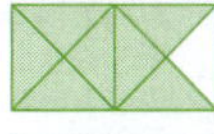

7.

0.7 is $\frac{7}{10}$. This means 7 out of the 10 squares need to be shaded.

8. **$0.50**

$5 + $4 = $9. Also, 30c + 20c = 50c. Stathis has spent a total of $9.50. As $10 – $9 = $1, and $1 – 50c = 50c, Stathis will have 50c left.

9. =

$$\begin{array}{r} {}^{6}\not{7}\,{}^{1}{}^{5}\not{6}\,{}^{1}3 \\ -\;\;5\;\;6\;\;8 \\ \hline 1\;\;9\;\;5 \\ \hline \end{array}$$

Also 120 + 75 = 120 + 70 + 5, which is 190 + 5 = 195. As both expressions equal 195, the symbol is =.

10. **5.08**

There are 1000 mm in 1 m. 80 mm is $\frac{80}{1000}$ m. This can be written as $\frac{8}{100}$, or 0.08 m. This means 5 m 80 mm = 5.08 m.

11. **750 mL**

375 + 375 = 375 + 300 + 70 + 5. This is 675 + 70 + 5 = 745 + 5 = 750. Two cans contain a total of 750 mL.

12. **840 g**

You need to find 12 × 70. 12 × 7 is 10 × 7 + 2 × 7. This is 70 + 14 = 84. This means 12 × 70 = 840. The total mass of eggs is 840 g.

13.

14. **14**

Another 14 squares need to be shaded.

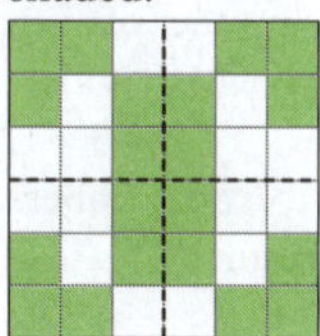

15.

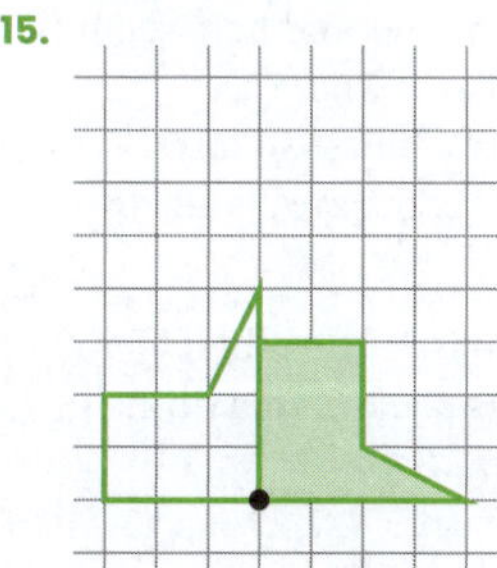

This is the same as a quarter turn in a clockwise direction.

16. **north-west**

C is north-west of *D*.

17. **blue**

There are 2 blue discs and 3 purple discs. This means it is less likely Ezekiel will select a blue disc.

18. **9 am**

The most popular time is when the most dogs are at the park. This occurred at 9 am.

Unit 21A PAGE 76

1. **6758**

6 + 5 + 8 = 19. As 26 – 19 = 7, the missing digit is 7. The number is 6758.

2. **150**

15 × 10 = 150. There was a total of 150 students.

3. **92**

67 + 25 = 67 + 20 + 5. This is 87 + 5 = 92. His grandmother will be 92.

4. **20**

As 8 ÷ 4 = 2, then 80 ÷ 4 = 20. There are 20 rubber bands in each group.

5. **27**

46 – 19 = 46 – 20 + 1. This is 26 + 1 = 27. Selena received 27 more text messages than she sent.

6. **6**

Lexie has shaded 6 squares. As 12 – 6 = 6, there are 6 squares not shaded.

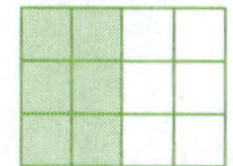

7. **true**

$\frac{1}{2}$ = 0.5. As 0.4 is less than 0.5, the statement is true.

8. **$11.50**

6 + 5 = 11 so $6.50 + $5 is $11.50.

9. **odd**

Ming's numbers could be 1, 3 and 5. As 1 × 3 × 5 = 15, the answer is odd. The answer is always odd no matter which three odd numbers are used.

10. **8 cm²**

Count the squares and half-squares inside the triangle. There are 6 squares and 4 half-squares. As 6 + 2 = 8, the area is 8 cm².

11. **160 mL**

You need to work out 200 – 40. As 20 – 4 = 16, then 200 – 40 = 160. Tim drank 160 mL of milk.

12. **25**
Quarter past 10 is 10:15 and 20 to 11 is 10:40. You need to work out the difference between 40 and 15.
As 40 – 15 = 40 – 10 – 5 = 25, there are 25 minutes between the two times.

13. 

14. There is only 1 line of symmetry.

15. **E5**
E5 will be covered by the image.

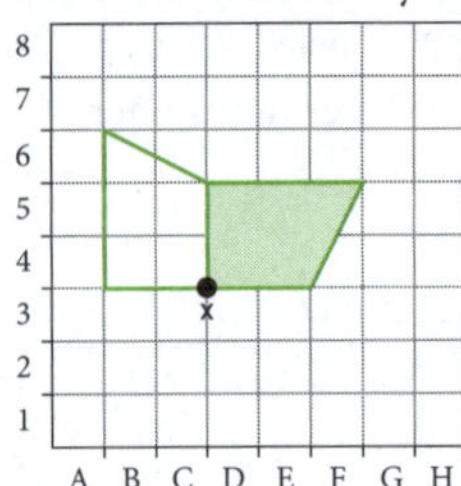

16. ***b*, c and *e***
An obtuse angle is larger than a right angle but smaller than a straight angle. Angles *b*, *c* and *e* are obtuse.

17. **orange**
As 5 is the largest number, the most likely fruit is an orange.

18. **100**
Using the column for Red, the house earned halfway between 80 and 120 points. This means the Red house earned 100 points.

Unit 21B PAGE 77

1. **7915**
As 9 – 4 = 5, there is a 5 in the ones place. As 9 – 2 = 7, there is a 7 in the thousands place. As 9 + 5 + 7 = 21, and 22 – 21 = 1, there is a 1 in the tens place. The number is 7915.

2. **84**
There are 7 days in a week. To work out 12 × 7, you can add 10 × 7 and 2 × 7. This is 70 + 14 which is 84. Ryan reads 84 pages.

3. **134**
You need to work out 32 + 32 + 35 + 35. As 32 + 32 = 64 and 35 + 35 = 70, find the total of 70 and 64.
70 + 60 + 4 = 130 + 4, which is 134. He completed 134 push-ups.

4. **3**
There are 60 minutes in one hour and 120 minutes in 2 hours. You need to find 120 ÷ 40. As 12 ÷ 4 = 3, then 120 ÷ 40 is also 3. This means 3 games can be played in 2 hours.

5. **4**
34 – 19 = 34 – 20 + 1. This is 14 + 1 = 15. There are 19 birds in one tree and 15 birds in the other.
As 19 – 15 = 4, there were 4 more birds.

6 $\mathbf{\frac{1}{4}}$
Ellie shades 1 column and Josie shades 2 columns. There is 1 out of 4 columns not shaded. This is $\frac{1}{4}$ of the shape.

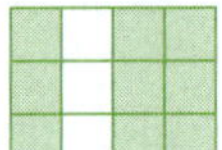

7. **2.5 km**
$\frac{1}{2}+\frac{1}{2}+\frac{1}{2}+\frac{1}{2}+\frac{1}{2}=1+1+\frac{1}{2}$. This is $2\frac{1}{2}$ km, which can be written as 2.5 km.

8. **$11.30**
$5 + $3 = $8 and 50c + 20c = 70c. Eliana spent $8.70. 30c makes $9, and $20 – $9 = $11. This means Eliana has $11.30 remaining.

9. **even**
An even number of odd numbers has a total which is even. An example is 3 + 5 = 8. An odd number of even numbers has a total which is also even. An example is 2 + 4 + 6 = 12. Finally adding two even numbers will give an even result.

10. **12 cm²**
Count the squares and half-squares inside the shape. There are 10 squares and 4 half-squares.
As 10 + 2 = 12, the area is 12 cm².

11. **250 mL**
As half of 50 is 25, then half of 500 is 250. There is 250 mL remaining in the bottle.

12. **4:40**
Suppose Helena started work at 9:00. Adding 3 hours is midday and then another 5 hours is 5:00. As she started at 20 to 9, she finishes at 20 to 5. This is written as 4:40.

13. 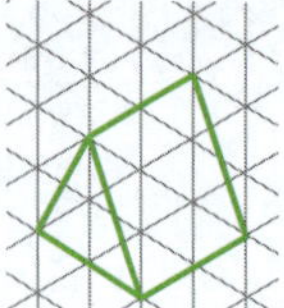

14. **4**
The shape is a square. A square has 4 lines of symmetry.

15. **F6**
F6 will be covered by the image.

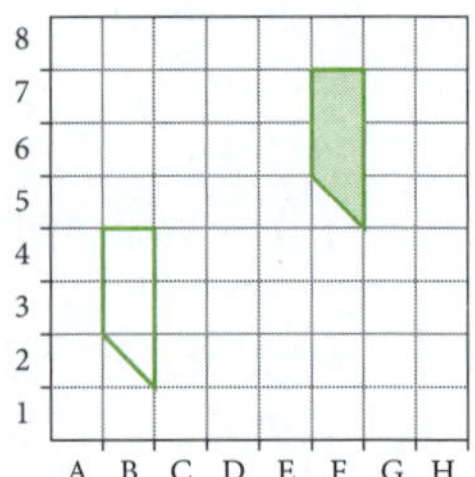

16. **2**
The diagram shows two right angles forming a straight angle.

17. **4**
There are more 4s on the dice than any other number. This means the most likely number will be 4.

18. **340**
Blue (180 points) and Green (160 points) were the two top houses. As 18 + 16 = 34, then 180 + 160 = 340. The two houses earned a total of 340 points.

Unit 22A PAGE 78

1. **Poppy**
Compare the three numbers 1946, 1968 and 1959. The highest number is 1968. As Poppy was born last, she is the youngest.

2. **900**

	3	8	7
+	5	1	0
	8	9	7

The exact total is 897. This is rounded to 900, to the nearest hundred.

3. **64**
As 4 + 4 = 8, there are 8 rows of 8 squares. As 8 × 8 = 64, there is a total of 64 squares.

4. **12**
As 36 ÷ 3 = 12, Benjamin will take the tablets for 12 days.

5. 135

$$\begin{array}{r} 2\ 8\ 9 \\ -\ 1\ 5\ 4 \\ \hline 1\ 3\ 5 \end{array}$$

There are 135 seats available.

6.

7. 3

$\frac{30}{100}$ is 0.30. This can also be written 0.3, which is $\frac{3}{10}$. The missing number is 3.

8. $7.30

$4 + $2 is $6. 60c + 70c = 130c, which is $1.30. $6 + $1.30 is $7.30.

9. 80

The pattern is dividing by 2. You need to work out 160 ÷ 2.
As 16 ÷ 2 = 8, then 160 ÷ 2 = 80. The missing number is 80.

10. 42 m

70 – 28 = 70 – 20 – 8. This is 50 – 8, which is 42. There is 42 m of fencing still to be built.

11. 1.234 L

There are 1000 mL in 1 L. This means 1234 mL can be written as 1.234 L.

12. 45 kg

15 + 15 + 15 = 30 + 15, which is 45. The total mass of the sand was 45 kg.

13. 4

Each of the cubes will have 4 faces painted and 2 faces not painted. There are 4 cubes.

14.

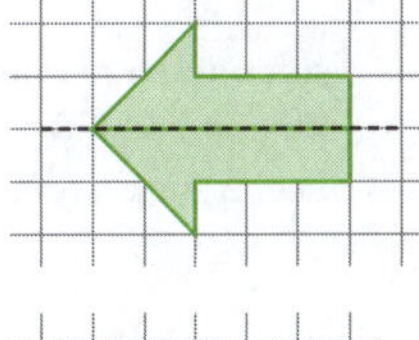

15.

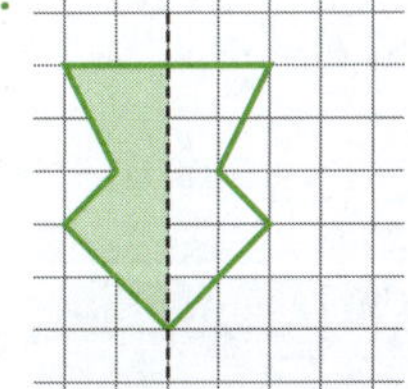

16. west

Isabella drove north from *R* to *Q* and then west towards *P*.

17.

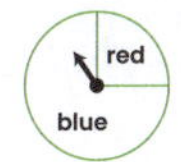

Look for the spinner with the smaller red area.

18. 80

As 10 – 2 = 8, then 100 – 20 = 80. There were 80 more child tickets than senior tickets sold.

Unit 22B PAGE 79

1. 7685

Compare the digits in the hundreds place, then the digits in the tens place. The order is 586, 658, 685, 856, 865. The middle of these numbers is 685. This means the middle of the original numbers is 7685.

2. 133 000

$$\begin{array}{r} ^{1}4\ ^{1}6\ \ ^{1}3\ ^{1}9\ 1 \\ +\ \ 8\ 6\ \ 8\ 3\ 9 \\ \hline 1\ 3\ 3\ \ 2\ 3\ 0 \end{array}$$

The exact total is 133 230. There is a 2 in the hundreds place. This means the total rounds to 133 000, to the nearest thousand.

3. 24

As 6 – 3 = 3, there are 3 more red balls than blue balls in each bag. As 8 × 3 = 24, there are 24 more red balls than blue balls.

4. 21

There are 4 different balloon colours. You need to find 84 ÷ 4.

$$4\overline{)84}\ \ 21$$

There are 21 pink balloons.

5. 1372

$$\begin{array}{r} ^{2}3\ ^{9}0\ ^{9}0\ ^{1}0 \\ -\ 1\ 6\ 2\ 8 \\ \hline 1\ 3\ 7\ 2 \end{array}$$

There are 1372 empty seats.

6.

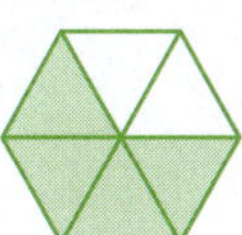

7. 8

$\frac{48}{10}$ is an improper fraction. It can be rewritten as $4\frac{8}{10}$. This means the missing number is 8.

8. $63.15

Change each amount to cents.

$$\begin{array}{r} ^{1}1\ ^{2}1\ 8\ 0 \\ 2\ 9\ 5\ 0 \\ +\ 2\ 1\ 8\ 5 \\ \hline 6\ 3\ 1\ 5 \end{array}$$

The total is $63.15.

9. 16

Look at the sequence from last number to first. The sequence can be expressed as 1, 4, ?, 64, 256. The rule for the new sequence of numbers is multiplying by 4.
As 4 × 4 = 16, the missing number is 16.

10. 132 cm

40 + 26 + 40 + 26 = 80 + 52. This is 132. The painting will need 132 cm of frame.

11. 24

As 4 × 3 = 12, Evelyn can fill 12 cups using the water in the container. As 12 × 2 = 24, she can fill 24 cups with two containers.

12. 80 kg

As 4 × 10 = 40, the people generate 40 kg of waste each week.
As 40 + 40 = 80, the people generate 80 kg in a fortnight.

13. 8

Each of the cubes will have 3 faces painted and 3 faces not painted. There are 8 cubes.

14.

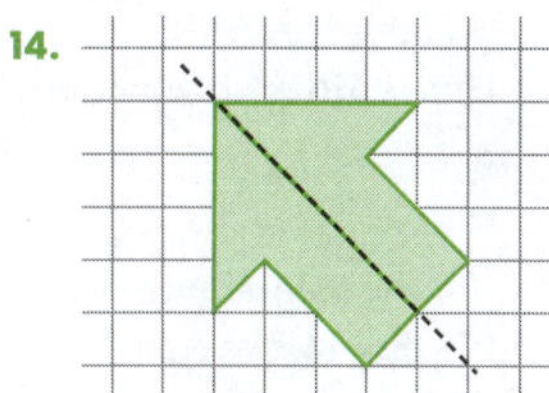

15.

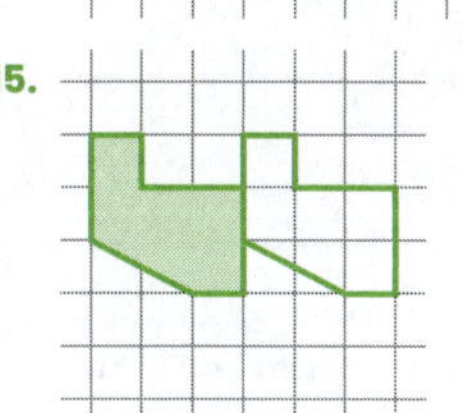

16. north-east

Town *Q* is north-east of *T*.

17.

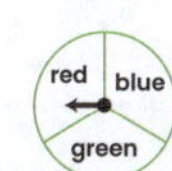

Look for the spinner with the smallest blue area.

18. 10

As 100 + 70 + 20 = 190, and 200 – 190 = 10, there were still 10 seats available for sale.

Unit 23A PAGE 80

1. **38 927**
   The swap means the number changes from 32 687 to 38 627. There is currently a 6 in the hundreds place. As 6 + 3 = 9, the final number is 38 927.
2. **13**
   39 is 30 + 9. As 30 ÷ 3 = 10 and 9 ÷ 3 = 3, there are 13 balls in each group.
3. **45**
   110 – 65 = 110 – 60 – 5. This is 50 – 5 = 45. Michael rode 45 km on the second day.
4. **44**
   18 + 15 + 11 = 33 + 11 = 44. A total of 44 laps were completed.
5. **40**
   As 4 × 8 = 32, Janami is 32 years old. As 32 + 8 = 40, the sum of their ages is 40.
6. **10**
   There are 5 fifths, or $\frac{5}{5}$, in 1.
   As 2 × 5 = 10, there are 10 fifths in 2.
7. **0.5**
   Half of the circle is shaded. This is written as $\frac{1}{2}$, or 0.5.
8. **$17**
   Two lots of $8.50 is $8 + $8 + 50c + 50c. This is $16 + $1, which is $17.
9. **14**
   As 24 – 5 = 19, the second number was 19. As 19 – 5 = 14, the first number was 14.
10. **8 cm**
    As 24 ÷ 3 = 8, each side is 8 cm long.
11. **12 cm³**
    As 6 × 2 = 12, there are 12 cubes. This means the volume is 12 cm³.
12. **18 km**
    As 6 × 3 = 18, Tony can cycle 18 km.
13. 
14. **octagon**
    Levi drew an octagon.

15. **D4**
    D4 is covered by the image.
    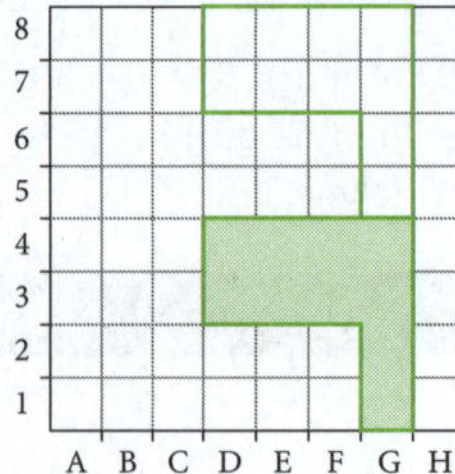

16. **six o'clock**
    The clock could be showing six o'clock.

17. **orange**
    The largest number is 7. This is the number of orange balls. This means the colour which is most likely to be chosen is orange.
18. **4**
    The graph shows 2 symbols on Monday. This means each symbol represents 4 dogs.

Unit 23B PAGE 81

1. **95 967**
   5 less than 100 000 is 99 995. The new number is 95 967.
2. **6**
   As 12 × 2 = 24, there was a total of 24 strawberries. 3 + 1 = 4. The strawberries were shared between 4 children. As 24 ÷ 4 = 6, Willow ate 6 strawberries.
3. **8285**

	⁰~~1~~	¹7	⁸9	¹3	8
–		9	6	5	3
		8	2	8	5

   Jen walked 8285 steps.
4. **11 506**

		¹4	¹9	¹6	7
+		6	5	3	9
	1	1	5	0	6

   There was a total of 11 506 cars.
5. **62**
   4 × 3 = 12. This means 12 students travelled by car. As 50 + 12 = 62, a total of 62 students went to the zoo.
6. **$\frac{5}{8}, \frac{7}{12}, \frac{26}{50}$**
   Look for a fraction where the denominator is more than twice the numerator. This means the fractions are $\frac{5}{8}$, $\frac{7}{12}$ and $\frac{26}{50}$.
7. **2.5**
   There are $2\frac{1}{2}$ shaded circles. This can be written as 2.5.
8. **$20.05**
   $79.95 is 5c less than $80. You can work out $100 – $80 + 5c. This is $20 + 5c which is $20.05.
9. **90**
   As 4 × 7 = 28, the first number was 28 more than 62. As 62 + 28 = 90, the first number was 90.
10. **9 cm²**
    As 24 ÷ 2 = 12, the perimeter of the square is 12 cm. As 12 ÷ 4 = 3, the square has a side length of 3 cm. As 3 × 3 = 9, the area of the square is 9 cm².
11. **18 cm³**
    There are 10 cubes in the bottom layer and 8 cubes in the top layer. As 10 + 8 = 18, the volume is 18 cm³.
12. **120 km**
    As there are 60 min in 1 h, then 90 min = $1\frac{1}{2}$ h. 80 km in 1 h means 40 km in $\frac{1}{2}$ h.
    As 80 + 40 = 120, Angus will drive 120 km in 90 minutes.
13. 
14. **4**
    A triangle has 3 sides and a pentagon 5 sides. As 3 + 5 = 8, and 32 ÷ 8 = 4, Aurora drew 4 of each shape. She drew 4 pentagons.
15. **F6**
    F6 is covered by the image.
    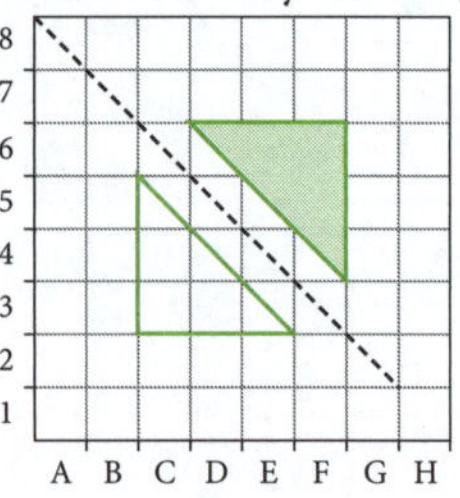

16. **4**
    The diagram shows four right angles forming a revolution.

17. **purple**
There are now 3 pink balls and 4 purple balls in the bag. This means a purple ball is more likely to be chosen.

18. **19**
The graph shows $3\frac{1}{2}$ symbols on Friday. This means each symbol represents 2 dogs.
As $4 + 5 + 7 + 3 = 19$, there were 19 dogs washed.

Unit 24A PAGE 82

1. **100**
3862 rounded to the nearest thousand is 4000 and to the nearest hundred is 3900.
As $4000 - 3900 = 100$, the difference is 100.

2. **37**
You need to find $48 - 27 + 16$. First $48 - 27 = 21$. Now $21 + 16 = 37$. There are now 37 passengers.

3. **8**
Look at the ones first. $5 + 7 = 12$. Now the tens. $1 + 4 + \boxed{?} = 13$. The missing digit is 8.

4. **5**
$22 + 23 = 45$. There are 45 students to be organised into 9 equal groups. As $45 \div 9 = 5$, there will be 5 students in each group.

5. **12 000 L**
As $3 \times 4 = 12$, then $3 \times 4000 = 12000$. Andy has a total of 12 000 L of water.

6. **3**
There are 2 halves in a whole.
As $2 + 1 = 3$, there are 3 halves in $1\frac{1}{2}$.

7. **27.39**
As $20 + 7 = 27$, the decimal is 27.39.

8. **$2.70**
$5 – $2 is $3. Now $3 – 30c is $2.70. The ice cream cost $2.70.

9. **8**
As $4 \times 5 = 20$, the number sentence is $20 = 28 - \boxed{?}$. This means the missing number is $28 - 20 = 8$.

10. **2 cm**
As $2 \times 3 = 6$, then the width is 2 cm.

11. **500 mL**
The level of water is halfway between 400 and 600. As 5 is in the middle of 4 and 6, the middle of 400 and 600 is 500. There is 500 mL of water in the jug.

12. **75 g**
$50 + 25 = 50 + 20 + 5$. This is $70 + 5$, which is 75. Jason consumed 75 g of sugar.

13. **2**
There are 2 hemispheres in a sphere.

14. **8**
A square has 4 lines of symmetry and a rectangle has 2 lines of symmetry. As $4 \times 2 = 8$, Minh's answer is 8.

15. 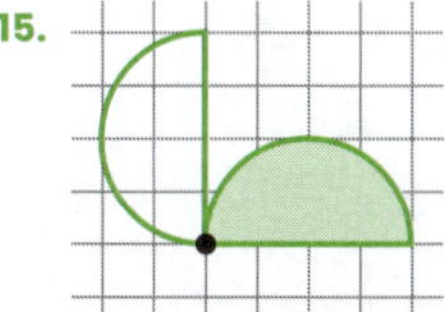

16. **Suggested answer:**

17. 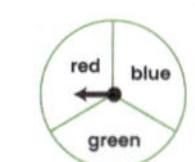

It is impossible to spin yellow on a spinner that does not have a yellow section.

18. **18**
As $6 + 12 = 18$, there were 18 students in bed by 9:00.

Unit 24B PAGE 83

1. **Jenna**
126 479 rounded to the nearest thousand is 126 000 and to the nearest hundred is 126 500. This means Jenna's rounding gives a higher number.

2. **62**
As $35 - 8 = 27$, Henry is 27 years old. $35 + 27 = 35 + 20 + 7$, which is $55 + 7 = 62$. The sum of their ages is 62.

3. **4**
Look at the tens first. $1 + 3 + 5 = 9$. Now the hundreds. $2 + \boxed{?} = 6$. The missing digit is 4.

4. **30**
You need to find $150 \div 5$.
As $15 \div 5 = 3$, then $150 \div 5 = 30$.
There are 30 children on the ferry.

5. **56**
As $10 - 3 = 7$, there have been 7 buckets sold. As $7 \times 8 = 56$, there have been 56 apples sold.

6. **12**
There are 10 tenths in a whole. Also $\frac{1}{5} = \frac{2}{10}$. As $10 + 2 = 12$, there are 12 tenths in $1\frac{1}{5}$.

7. **0.2**
0.2 can be written as 0.20, which is $\frac{20}{100}$. Comparing $\frac{3}{100}$ and $\frac{20}{100}$, the larger number is $\frac{20}{100}$, which is 0.2.

8. **$7.55**
3 × $4 = $12 and 3 × 15c = 45c. The total cost was $12.45. Adding 55c gives $13 and another $7 gives $20. Fiona received $7.55 change.

9. **3**
As $48 \div 6 = 8$ and $11 - 6 = 5$, the number sentence is $8 = 5 + \boxed{?}$. This means the missing number is $8 - 5 = 3$.

10. **32 cm²**
As $2 \times 4 = 8$, the width of the rectangle is 4 cm. As $8 \times 4 = 32$, the area is 32 cm^2.

11. **700 mL**
There is 500 mL in Jug A and 200 mL in Jug B. As $500 + 200 = 700$, there is now 700 mL in Jug B.

12. **760 g**
There is 1000 g in 1 kg.
$1000 - 240 = 1000 - 200 - 40$. This is $800 - 40 = 760$. There is 760 g of flour remaining in the bag.

13. **4**
The pyramid has a triangular base and three other triangular faces. This means there is a total of 4 triangular faces.

14. **60°**
Opposite angles of a parallelogram are equal. This means the angle measures 60° also.

15. 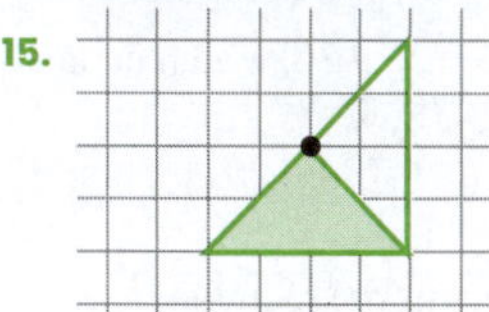

16. **Suggested answer:**

17.

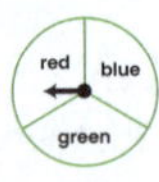

Red is more likely to be spun on the spinner that has a larger red area.

18. **23**

As 12 + 9 + 2 = 23, there were 23 students who went to bed after 9:00.

Unit 25A PAGE 84

1. **87 534**

The digit in the ones place must be even. The rest of the numbers are written in descending order. This means the number is 87 534.

2. **11**

As 88 ÷ 8 = 11, Sofia has drawn 11 octagons.

3. **4**

As 24 = 20 + 4, the missing number is 4.

4. **810**

To find 430 + 380 you can add the hundreds and then add the tens. 400 + 300 = 700 and 30 + 80 = 110. 700 + 110 = 810. The girls collected a total of 810 coins.

5. **41**

116 – 75 = 116 – 70 – 5. This is 46 – 5 = 41. There are 41 bikes remaining.

6. **2**

There are three columns of squares. Kinsley can shade one column. This means she shades 2 squares.

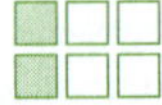

7. 0 0.1 0.2 0.3 0.4 0.5 0.6 0.7 0.8 0.9 1

The number line has been marked in tenths, or 0.1s. As $\frac{7}{10}$ is written as 0.7, it is between 0.6 and 0.8.

8. **$65**

35 + 15 + 15 = 35 + 30, which equals 65. The cost is $65.

9. $4\frac{1}{5}$

The numbers in the sequence are increasing by $\frac{1}{5}$. The missing number is $4\frac{1}{5}$.

10. **55 cm**

There are 100 cm in 1 m. 100 – 45 = 100 – 40 – 5. This is 60 – 5 = 55. The shorter piece is 55 cm.

11. **840 mL**

420 + 420 = 400 + 400 + 20 + 20. This is 800 + 40 = 840. The cans hold a total of 840 mL of soup.

12. **14 minutes**

As 10 + 4 = 14, the journey took 14 minutes.

13. **pyramid**

A pyramid has triangular faces.

14. **Suggested answer:**

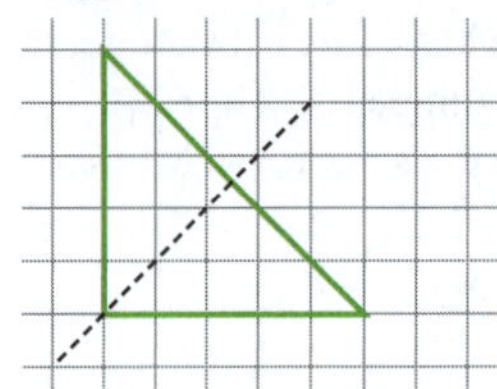

15.

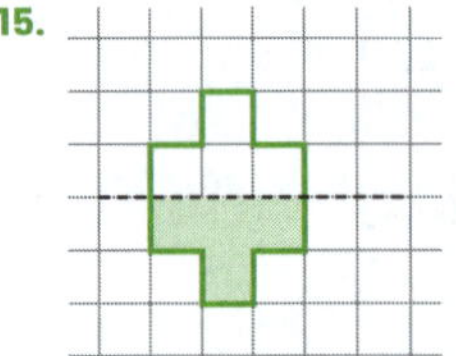

16.

17. **red**

As the smallest section is red, it is least likely to land on red.

18. **11**

Look at the Year 4 row and the Charlotte column. This means there were 11 votes by Year 4 students for Charlotte.

Unit 25B PAGE 85

1. **62 387**

The digit in the ones place must be odd. For the smallest number larger than 5000, the thousands digit is a 6. Use the 7 in the ones place and the other digits in ascending order. The number is 62 387.

2. **2**

As 10 × 4 = 40, there is a total of 40 biscuits. 40 ÷ 20 has the same answer as 4 ÷ 2. This means 40 ÷ 20 = 2. Each person eats 2 biscuits.

3. **20**

As 19 = 20 – 1, then 30 × 19 = 30 × 20 – 30 × 1. The missing number is 20.

4. **606**

The numbers are 200, 202 and 204. As 200 + 200 + 200 + 2 + 4 = 606, the total is 606.

5. **35**

You need to find 96 – 23 – 38. First 96 – 23 = 73. 73 – 38 = 73 – 40 + 2. This is 33 + 2 = 35. Abbie has 35 candles remaining.

6. **6**

Imagine the squares in 4 rows of 2. The squares in 3 out of the 4 rows are shaded. As 3 × 2 = 6, there are 6 shaded squares.

Suggested answer:

7.

$\frac{36}{100}$ can be written as 0.36. The number line is marked in 0.02s. As 0.3 = 0.30 and 0.4 = 0.40, then 0.36 is the third marking between 0.30 and 0.40.

8. **$140**

As 4 ÷ 2 = 2, then 40 ÷ 2 = 20. The price of a child ticket is $20. As 4 × 20 = 80 and 3 × 20 = 60, you need to add 80 and 60. As 8 + 6 = 14, then $80 + $60 = $140. The total cost is $140.

9. $\frac{4}{5}$

Rewrite the sequence as $\frac{12}{5}$, $\frac{10}{5}$, $\frac{8}{5}$, $\frac{6}{5}$, ?. The numerators are decreasing by 2. The missing number is $\frac{4}{5}$.

10. **180 cm²**

As 2 × 9 = 18, then 20 × 9 = 180. The area is 180 cm^2.

11. **6 L**

One-third of 9 is 9 ÷ 3 = 3. There is 3 L remaining in the tank. As 9 – 3 = 6, Jack needs 6 L to fill the tank.

12. **8**

There are 60 seconds in 1 minute. You need to work out how many 60s there are in 480, which is 480 ÷ 60. As 48 ÷ 6 = 8, then 480 ÷ 60 = 8. Shae practised for 8 minutes.

13. **25 cm²**

A cube has 6 identical faces.
As $5 \times 5 = 25$, the area of each square face is 25 cm².

14.

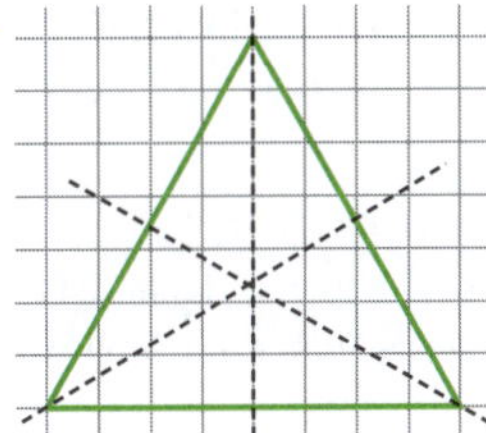

15.

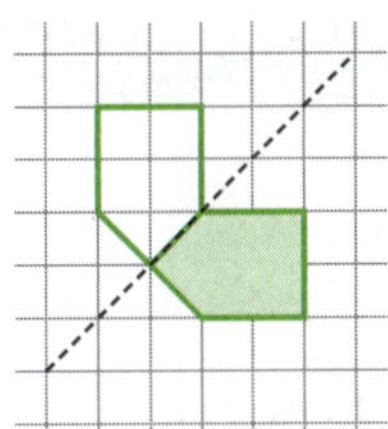

16.

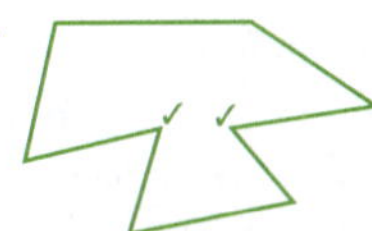

17. **yellow**

As the largest section is yellow, it is most likely to land on yellow.

18. **12**

As $6 + 4 + 8 = 18$, Olivia received 18 votes. As $13 + 12 + 5 = 30$, Olivia received 30 votes. As $30 - 18 = 12$, there were 12 more votes for Harper than Olivia.

Unit 26A PAGE 86

1. **5432**

The digits are 5, 4, 3 and 2. Fatima's PIN is 5432.

2. **664**

$$\begin{array}{r} {}^{1}3\ {}^{1}7\ 6 \\ +\ \ 2\ \ 8\ \ 8 \\ \hline 6\ \ 6\ \ 4 \end{array}$$

There are 664 pages in the book.

3. **80**

As $25 - 5 = 20$, Harper answered 20 questions correctly. As $4 \times 2 = 8$, then $4 \times 20 = 80$. Harper scored 80 marks.

4. **157**

$$\begin{array}{r} {}^{1}\cancel{2}\ {}^{1}{}^{0}\cancel{1}\ {}^{1}0 \\ -\ \ \ \ 5\ \ 3 \\ \hline 1\ \ 5\ \ 7 \\ \hline \end{array}$$

Igor has 157 stickers remaining.

5. **4**

As $3 \times 8 = 24$, there is a total of 24 students. As $24 \div 6 = 4$, there are 4 students in each group.

6. **7**

To find one-third of a number you can divide by 3. As $21 \div 3 = 7$, there are 7 children who do not have a sibling.

7. **1.3**

13 tenths can be written as $\frac{13}{10}$. This is an improper fraction and can be written as the mixed numeral $1\frac{3}{10}$. As $\frac{3}{10}$ is 0.3, the answer is 1.3.

8. **$188**

$112 + 76 = 112 + 70 + 6$. This is $182 + 6$ which is 188. The boys raised a total of $188.

9. **56**

$28 + 28 = 28 + 20 + 8$. This is $48 + 8 = 56$.

10. **5 cm**

There are 6 equal sides on a regular hexagon. As $30 \div 6 = 5$, each side has a length of 5 cm.

11. **700 L**

As $1000 - 300 = 700$, then $9000 - 8300 = 700$. Ava needs 700 L of water to fill the pond.

12. **185 g**

$120 + 65 = 120 + 60 + 5$. This is $180 + 5$, which equals 185. The mass is now 185 g.

13. **8**

A rectangular prism has 6 faces. There are 2 more faces on this shape. As $6 + 2 = 8$, there are 8 faces.

14. **Suggested answer:**

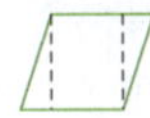

15.

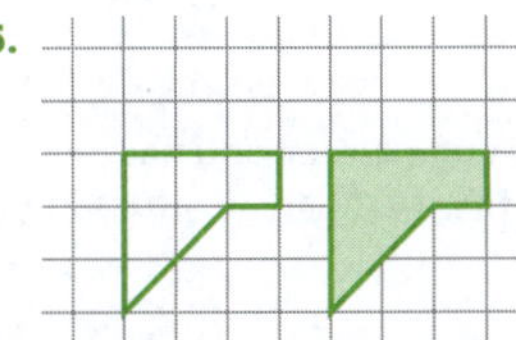

16.

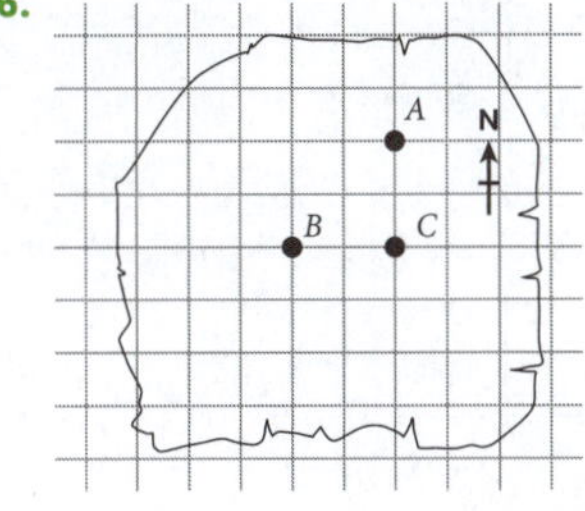

17. **3**

There are 6 faces and half of them are green and half are purple. There are 3 green faces.

18. **5**

Looking at the column for 1 sibling, there were 5 students.

Unit 26B PAGE 87

1. **2431**

Benji's original PIN was 4653. Subtracting 2 from each of the digits means his new PIN is 2431.

2. **6455**

$$\begin{array}{r} {}^{1}3\ {}^{1}5\ 6\ 3 \\ +\ \ 2\ \ 8\ \ 9\ \ 2 \\ \hline 6\ \ 4\ \ 5\ \ 5 \end{array}$$

There was a total of 6455 votes for the two candidates.

3. **5000**

50 lots of 100 is 5000. There are 5000 chairs.

4. **26**

$$\begin{array}{r} 1\ {}^{0}\cancel{1}\ {}^{1}{}^{1}\cancel{2}\ {}^{1}3 \\ -\ \ 1\ \ 0\ \ 9\ \ 7 \\ \hline 2\ \ 6 \\ \hline \end{array}$$

There are 26 students absent.

5. **2**

As $4 \times 6 = 24$, Eleanor has 24 dolls. As $24 \div 12 = 2$, there are 2 rows of dolls.

6. **9**

As $1 - \frac{3}{4}$ is $\frac{1}{4}$, Isaac still needs to collect $\frac{1}{4}$ of the set. As $36 \div 4 = 9$, Isaac needs to collect another 9 cards.

7. **2.54**

254 is $200 + 54$. 254 hundredths is 200 hundredths = 2, plus 54 hundredths = 0.54. This means 254 hundredths = 2.54.

8. **$204**

$$\begin{array}{r} {}^{1}7\ 8 \\ +\ \ 6\ \ 3 \\ \hline 1\ \ 4\ \ 1 \end{array}$$

Freya has saved $141.

$$\begin{array}{r} {}^{1}1\ 4\ 1 \\ +\ \ \ \ 6\ \ 3 \\ \hline 2\ \ 0\ \ 4 \end{array}$$

A total of $204 has been saved.

9. **32 km**

$8 + 8 = 16$. Now double 16 is 32. Lauren walked 32 km.

10. **4 cm²**

As $4 \times 2 = 8$, the area of the rectangle is 8 cm². As $8 \div 2 = 4$, the area of the triangle is 4 cm².

11. **1.25 L**

There are 1000 mL in 1 L. This means 1250 mL = 1.25 L.

12. **3050 g**

There are 2000 g in 2 kg.
$2000 + 500 + 500 + 50 =$
$2000 + 1000 + 50$, which is 3050. The mass was 3050 g.

13. **18**

There are 6 edges seen at the front of the shape. There are 6 edges at the back of the shape and 6 other edges. As $6 \times 3 = 18$, there is a total of 18 edges.

14.

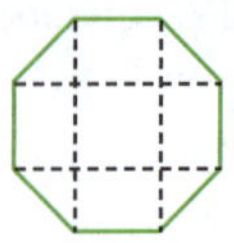

15.

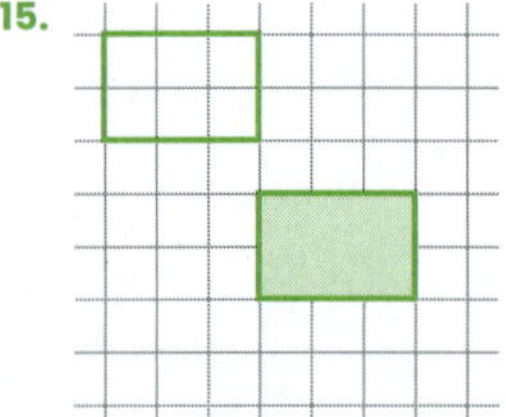

16.

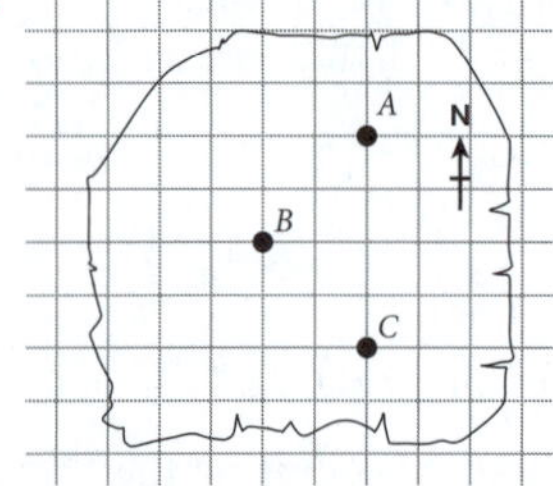

17. **impossible**

As there are no purple faces, it is impossible.

18. **13**

$5 + 7 + 1 = 13$. There were 13 students with at least one sibling.

Unit 27A — PAGE 88

1. **85 000**

Ben's number written in digits is 85 273. There is a 2 in the hundreds place, which is less than 5. His number rounds down to 85 000.

2. **6**

Look at the tens column. $7 - 6 = 1$. The missing digit is 6.

$$\begin{array}{r} 878 \\ -\ 365 \\ \hline 513 \end{array}$$

3. **24**

$4 - 1 = 3$. There are now 3 chocolates in each bag. As $8 \times 3 = 24$, there is a total of 24 chocolates in the bags.

4. **664**

$$\begin{array}{r} {}^{1}3\,{}^{1}7\,6 \\ +\ 2\,8\,8 \\ \hline 6\,6\,4 \end{array}$$

The total enrolment is 664 students.

5. **8**

Each person has 2 legs.
As $32 \div 2 = 16$, there are 16 people competing. As $16 \div 2 = 8$, there are 8 people on each team.

6. **6**

To find one-quarter of a number you can divide by 4. As $24 \div 4 = 6$, there were 6 cakes not sold.

7. **0.7**

As $3 + 4 = 7$, then $\frac{3}{10} + \frac{4}{10} = \frac{7}{10}$. This is written as 0.7.

8. **$10**

As $30 \times 2 = 60$, Delphi has $60.
As $30 + 20 = 50$, Maeve has $50.
As $60 - 50 = 10$, Delphi has $10 more than Maeve.

9. **80**

As $4 \times 2 = 8$, then $40 \times 2 = 80$. The fortieth number was 80.

10. **32 cm**

$10 + 6 + 10 + 6 = 16 + 16$. This is 32. The perimeter is 32 cm.

11. **10 kg**

$10 \times 1 = 10$, the mass is 10 kg.

12. **6 g**

As $6 \times 2 = 12$, then $6 \times 20 = 120$. This means $120 \div 20 = 6$. Each marble has a mass of 6 g.

13. **1**

Only the cube on the end has 5 painted faces. There is only 1 cube.

14. **9**

The hexagon has 9 diagonals.

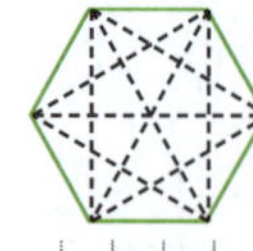

15.

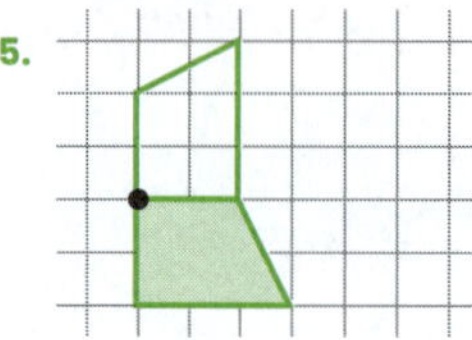

16. ***f***

The four angles in a square are all right angles. Angle *f* is a right angle.

17. **red**

There are more red jelly beans than black. It is more likely a red jelly bean is chosen.

18. **7**

Halfway between 6 and 8 is 7. This means 7 people voted for Japanese food.

Unit 27B — PAGE 89

1. **7900**

Indiah originally wrote the number 7868. There is a 6 in the tens place. This means the number rounds up to 7900, to the nearest 100.

2. **8**

Look at the tens column. 5 – [?] = 7 cannot be done. 15 – [?] = 7 means the missing number is 8. Checking the hundreds column,
$3 - 2 = 1$. The missing digit is 8.

$$\begin{array}{r} 2\,{}^{3}4\,{}^{1}5\,7 \\ -\ \ 2\,8\,4 \\ \hline 2\,1\,7\,3 \end{array}$$

3. **120**

A dozen is 12. You need to work out $12 \times 5 \times 2$. First $5 \times 2 = 10$.
As $12 \times 10 = 120$, there are 120 eggs laid.

4. **16 638**

$$\begin{array}{r} 9\,2\,0\,7 \\ +\ 7\,4\,3\,1 \\ \hline 1\,6\,6\,3\,8 \end{array}$$

The total attendance was 16 638.

5. **3**

You need to work out $66 \div 22$. This can be found using 22 × [?] = 66.
As $2 \times 3 = 6$, then $22 \times 3 = 66$. Each student receives 3 blocks.

6. **12**

As $25 - 1 = 24$, there are 24 other students in Cameron's class.
As $24 \div 2 = 12$, Cameron will invite 12 classmates.

7. **10**

The first 6 has a value of 0.6. The second 6 has a value of 0.06. The first 6 has 10 times the value of the second.

8. **4**

You need to work out how many 20s are in 120. As $12 \div 2 = 6$, then $120 \div 20 = 6$. This means she sold

6 scarfs. As 10 – 6 = 4, there were 4 scarfs not sold.

9. even

Every pair of odd numbers adds to an even number. This means Quinn's total is even.

10. 84 mm

As there are 10 m in 1 cm, there are 30 mm in 3 cm. 30 + 12 + 30 + 12 = 60 + 24. This is 84. The perimeter is 84 mm.

11. 250 g or 0.25 kg

As 1000 mL has a mass of 1000 g, then 250 mL has a mass of 250 g, or 0.25 kg.

12. 700 g

As 34 + 26 = 60, then 340 + 260 = 600. Also 600 + 100 = 700 so the total mass is 700 g.

13. 1

Look at the bottom row of 6 cubes. The second of these cubes has 2 painted faces. There is only 1 cube.

14. 20

Look at the pattern in the table. The number of diagonals is increasing by 2, then 3, then 4, then 5. As 14 + 6 = 20, an octagon has 20 diagonals.

15.

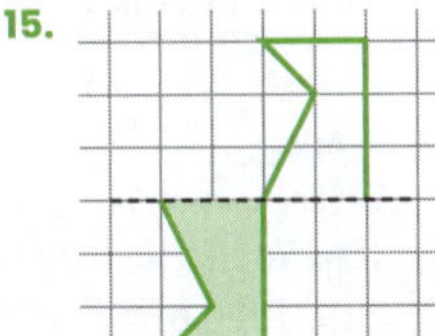

16. 5

Angle *f* is a right angle. The other 5 angles are acute.

17. red

When there are 3 red and 2 blue sections it will be less likely to spin blue. The missing colour is red.

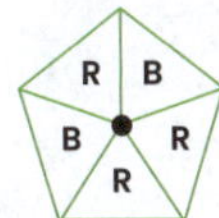

18. 8

If 12 voted for Indian, then 8 voted for Greek and 16 for Thai. As 16 – 8 = 8, there were 8 more votes for Thai than Greek.

Unit 28A PAGE 90

1. 2984

In 4982 there is a 4 in the thousands place and a 2 in the ones place. Swapping these two digits gives the number 2984.

2. 142

$$\begin{array}{r} 2\ 7\ 8 \\ -\ 1\ 3\ 6 \\ \hline 1\ 4\ 2 \end{array}$$

The difference is 142.

3. 2150

$$\begin{array}{r} {}^{1}1\ 7\ 5\ 0 \\ +\ \ \ 4\ 0\ 0 \\ \hline 2\ 1\ 5\ 0 \end{array}$$

There is a total of 2150 passengers.

4. 28

8 × 3 = 24. The team earned 24 points from the wins. As 4 × 1 = 4, the team earned 4 points from the draws. As 24 + 4 = 28, the team has a total of 28 points.

5. 32 ÷ 4 = 8, 32 ÷ 8 = 4

The two correct mathematical sentences are 32 ÷ 4 = 8 and 32 ÷ 8 = 4.

6. 7

To find one-third of a number you can divide by 3. As 21 ÷ 3 = 7, Bella has already read 7 of the books on the list.

7. 2.4

The number line has been marked in tenths, or 0.1s. This means the missing number is 2.4.

8. $97.50

9750 can be read as 97 hundred and 50. As 100 cents is one dollar, then this amount can be written as $97.50.

9. 22

As 9 × 2 = 18 and 18 + 4 = 22, the missing number is 22.

10. 4 cm

8 + 8 = 16. As 20 – 16 = 4, the length of the third side is 4 cm.

11. 21 L

50 – 29 = 50 – 30 + 1. This is 20 + 1 = 21. There is 21 L remaining.

12. 9:53

35 + 18 = 35 + 10 + 8. This is 45 + 8, which is 53. The bus arrived at 9:53.

13. 12

There are 6 faces on both dice. As 2 × 6 = 12, there is a total of 12 faces.

14. 3

Another 3 squares need to be shaded.

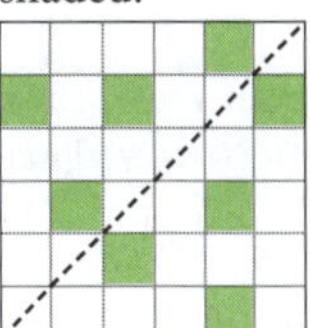

15.

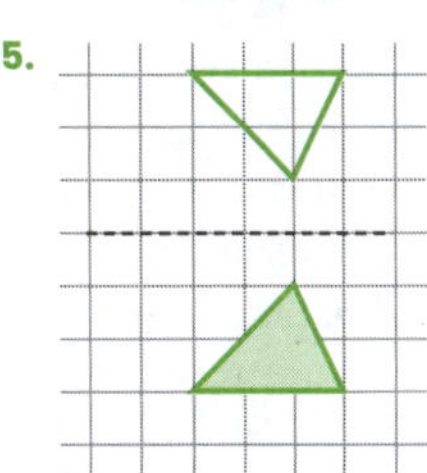

16. north-west

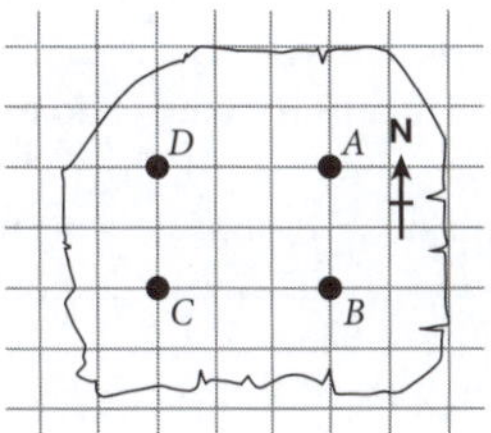

Here is the map showing the compass. *D* is north-west of *B*.

17.

R B
R

There will be 2 red balls and a blue ball.

18. 4

As 6 – 2 = 4, there are 4 more blonde students than red-haired students.

Unit 28B PAGE 91

1. 9867

The digits are 6, 7, 8 and 9. The last digit must be the smaller odd digit. Use the remaining digits in descending order. The number is 9867.

2. 9100

$$\begin{array}{r} {}^{0}\not{1}\ 3\ 8\ 9\ 6 \\ -\ \ \ 4\ 7\ 5\ 3 \\ \hline 9\ 1\ 4\ 3 \end{array}$$

The difference between the two numbers is 9143. As there is a 4 in the tens place, the number rounds to 9100.

3 **16949**

$$\begin{array}{r} {}^{1}7\ {}^{1}5\ 6\ 0 \\ 3\ 7\ 8\ 6 \\ +\ \ 5\ 6\ 0\ 3 \\ \hline 1\ 6\ 9\ 4\ 9 \end{array}$$

The factory processed 16 949 bottles.

4. **72**

You need to work out $4 \times 9 \times 2$. $4 \times 9 = 36$ and $36 + 36$ is 72. This means there are 72 bedrooms in the building.

5. ■ ÷ ● = ▲ **and** ■ ÷ ▲ = ●

You could replace the shapes with numbers. For example, if ▲ = 2, ● = 5 and ■ = 10, then $2 \times 5 = 10$.

Here are two correct mathematical sentences: $10 \div 5 = 2$ and $10 \div 2 = 5$. This means the two correct sentences are ■ ÷ ● = ▲ and ■ ÷ ▲ = ●.

6. **3**

Half the students do not catch a bus. $12 \div 2 = 6$ means 6 students do not catch a bus. As $6 \div 2 = 3$, then 3 students do not walk. This means there were 3 students who do not catch a bus or walk.

7. **4.6**

Each mark on the number line is 2 tenths, or 0.2. As $3 \times 2 = 6$, the missing number is 4.6.

8. **$239.60**

Change each amount to cents.

$$\begin{array}{r} {}^{1}9\ \ 6\ {}^{1}2\ 8 \\ 5\ 6\ 3\ 0 \\ +\ \ 8\ 7\ 0\ 2 \\ \hline 2\ 3\ 9\ 6\ 0 \end{array}$$

Jordie spent 23 960 cents, which is $239.60.

9. ***A* = 14, *B* = 12**

As $3 \times 7 = 21$ and $21 - 7 = 14$, the value of *A* is 14. To 29, add 7 to get 36. Now dividing 36 by 3 gives 12. The value of *B* is 12.

10. **100 cm²**

There are 4 equal sides in a square. As $40 \div 4 = 10$, the length of each side is 10 cm. As $10 \times 10 = 100$, the area is 100 cm^2.

11. **50 L**

$32 + 28 = 60$. Also, $60 - 10 = 50$. This means 50 L of petrol was used during the trip.

12. **25 min**

There are 60 minutes in 1 hour. $60 - 35 = 60 - 30 - 5$. This is $30 - 5 = 25$. The difference in the times is 25 minutes.

13. As $6 = 2 \times 3$, $8 = 2 \times 4$, $12 = 4 \times 3$, the prism has dimensions 4 cm, 3 cm and 2 cm. Here is a prism with a rectangular base of 4 cm by 3 cm. The prism has a depth of 2 cm.

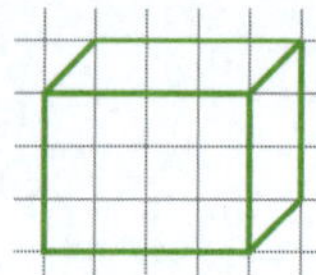

There are other correct answers.

14. **6**

Another 6 squares need to be shaded.

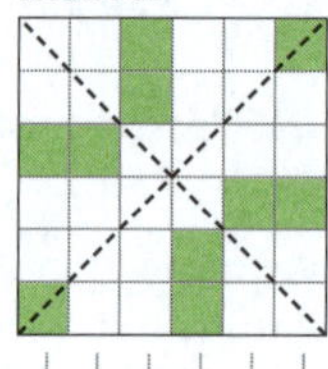

15.

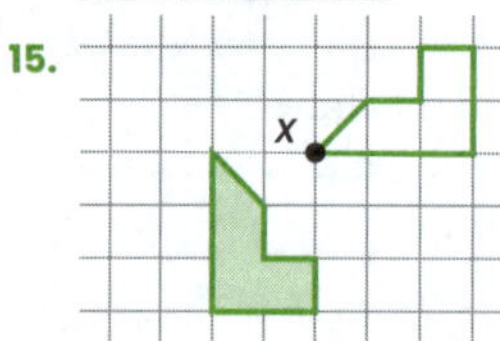

16. **west**

Here is the map showing the compass. *B* is west of *A*.

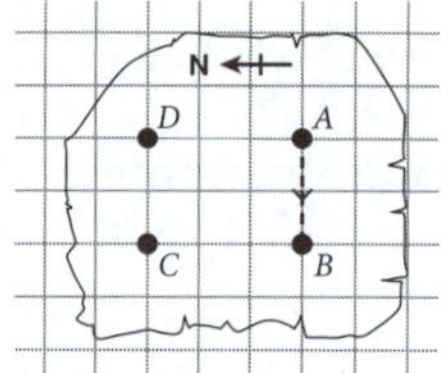

17.

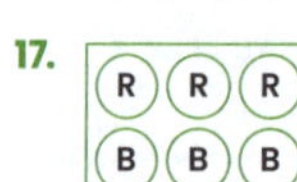

There will be 3 red balls and 3 blue balls.

18. **8**

As $5 + 2 + 6 + 8 = 21$, there were 21 students surveyed. As $29 - 21 = 8$, there were 8 students not surveyed.

Unit 29A PAGE 92

1. **6357**

$7 + 6 + 3$ is 16. As $21 - 16 = 5$, the missing digit is 5. The number is 6357.

2. **22**

$4 \times 5 + 2$ is $20 + 2 = 22$. Boris is 22 years old.

3. **895**

$790 + 105 = 790 + 100 + 5$. This is $890 + 5$ which is 895. Hunter house had scored 895 points.

4. **72**

6×12 is $6 \times 10 + 6 \times 2$. This is $60 + 12$ which is 72. There is a total of 72 carrots.

5. **26**

$48 - 13 - 9 = 35 - 9$. This is 26. Harlow keeps 26 golf balls.

6. $\mathbf{\frac{1}{8}}$

Each of the fractions has a 1 in the numerator. Comparing the denominators, the largest number is 8. This means $\frac{1}{8}$ is the smallest fraction.

7. **0.4**

The shape is made of 10 rectangles. As 4 of the 10 rectangles are shaded, there is $\frac{4}{10}$ of the shape shaded. This is written as 0.4.

8. **$22**

$50 - 28 = 50 - 20 - 8$. This is $30 - 8$ which is 22. Hazel has spent $22.

9. **47**

The numbers in the sequence are increasing by 7. As $33 + 7 = 40$ and $40 + 7 = 47$, the sixth number is 47.

10. **102 cm**

Use 1 cm = 10 mm and 1 m = 1000 mm. Change each length to mm. As $102 \times 10 = 1020$, the three lengths are 1001 mm, 1000 mm and 1020 mm. As 1020 is the highest number, the greatest length is 102 cm.

11. **4500 mL**

4.5 is $4\frac{1}{2}$. There is 4000 mL in 4 L and 500 mL in $\frac{1}{2}$ L.

As $4000 + 500 = 4500$, there is 4500 L in 4.5 L.

12. **140 g**

As $20 - 6 = 14$, then $200 - 60 = 140$. There is 140 g remaining.

13. **5**

The shape on the base has sides that match the number of triangular faces. The shape will have 5 sides.

14. **24 cm²**

As $12 \times 2 = 24$, the area of the parallelogram was 24 cm^2.

15. 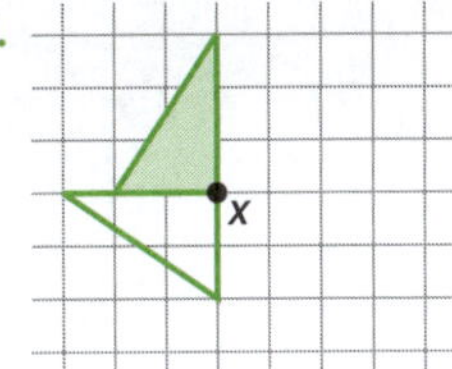

16. **half**
From 4:30 to 5:00 is half an hour. This means the minute hand moved through a half turn.

17. **unlikely**
There is a small chance that Nathaniel's ticket will be drawn out. There is an unlikely chance.

18. **24**
As $7 + 8 + 9 = 24$, there was a total of 24 red, pink and black jelly beans eaten.

Unit 29B PAGE 93

1 **twenty-seven thousand and seventy-nine**
$2 + 0 + 9$ is 11. As $25 - 11 = 14$, the missing digits add to 14.
As $14 \div 2 = 7$, each missing digit is 7. The number is 27 079, which is written as twenty-seven thousand and seventy-nine.

2. **11**
$12 + 15 + 6 = 33$. As $33 \div 3 = 11$, the average score is 11.

3. **12 095**

$$\begin{array}{r} {}^{2}3\ {}^{1}5\ {}^{1}4\ 8 \\ 4\ 6\ 5\ 2 \\ +\quad 3\ 8\ 9\ 5 \\ \hline 1\ 2\ 0\ 9\ 5 \end{array}$$

There were 12 095 pizzas sold in the three months.

4. **27**
$4 \times 9 = 36$. Tahlia is 36 years old. As $36 - 9 = 27$, Tahlia was 27 when Chloe was born.

5. **38**
$81 - 43 = 81 - 40 - 3$. This is $41 - 3$ which is 38. She was given 38 stuffed toys.

6. $\frac{2}{3}$
Look for the largest amount needed to be added to each fraction to give 1. $\frac{2}{3}$ needs $\frac{1}{3}$, $\frac{7}{8}$ needs $\frac{1}{8}$, $\frac{3}{4}$ needs $\frac{1}{4}$ and $\frac{4}{5}$ needs $\frac{1}{5}$. As $\frac{1}{3}$ is the largest fraction needed, then $\frac{2}{3}$ is the smallest fraction on the list.

7. **0.6**
As 3 of the 5 triangles are shaded, there is $\frac{3}{5}$ of the shape shaded.
$\frac{3}{5} = \frac{6}{10}$. This is written as 0.6.

8. **$50**
As $60 + 30 = 90$, Remy has saved $90. As $90 + 60 = 150$, the brothers have saved $150. As $200 - 150 = 50$, they need to save another $50.

9. **62**
The tenth number is 9 lots of 6 added on to 8. As $9 \times 6 = 54$ and $54 + 8 = 62$, the tenth number is 62.

10. **$360**
As $12 \times 3 = 36$, the area of the wall is $36\ m^2$. As $36 \times 10 = 360$, the cost is $360.

11. **10 kg**
The water will have a mass of 9 kg. As $9 + 1 = 10$, the total mass is 10 kg.

12. **under**
$16 + 12 = 28$. Fiona's total mass is 28 kg, which is under the baggage allowance.

13. **9 cm²**
There are 12 edges on a cube. As $36 \div 12 = 3$, each edge is 3 cm long. As $3 \times 3 = 9$, the area of each face is $9\ cm^2$.

14. **9 cm²**
As $36 \div 4 = 9$, the area of each triangle is $9\ cm^2$.

15. 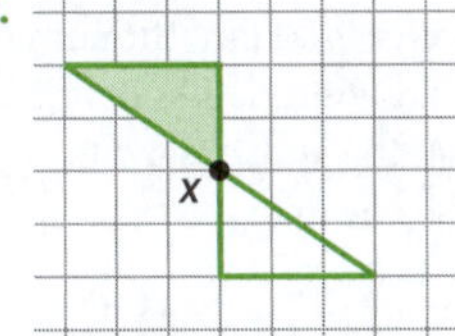

16. **quarter**
From 2:30 to 5:30 is 3 hours. This means the hour hand moved through a quarter turn.

17. **unlikely**
Nolan has 10 tickets but there are 90 other tickets. The chance that one of his tickets will be drawn is still unlikely to occur.

18. **11**
Count the jelly beans already eaten. As $6 \times 5 + 2 + 3 + 4 = 39$, there are 39 jelly beans eaten. As $50 - 39 = 11$, there are still 11 jelly beans remaining in the bag.

Unit 30A PAGE 94

1. **true**
When three odd numbers are added the answer is still odd. Adding an even number will give an odd answer. Try $1 + 3 + 5$. This total is 9. Adding 2 gives $9 + 2 = 11$ which is odd. The statement is true.

2. **34**
As $6 \times 3 = 18$, there are 18 wheels on the tricycles. As $8 \times 2 = 16$, there are 16 wheels on the bicycles.
As $18 + 16 = 18 + 10 + 6 = 34$, there is a total of 34 wheels.

3. **10**
As $5 \times 8 = 40$, Evelyn baked a total of 40 cupcakes. To find the number of cupcakes in each container you need to find $40 \div 4$. This means there were 10 cupcakes in each container.

4. **550**
As $43 + 12 = 55$, then $430 + 120 = 550$. Bo had 550 sheep on the property.

5. **396**
Logan's number is 642 and Owen's number is 246. You need to subtract the numbers to find the difference.

$$\begin{array}{r} {}^{5}6\ {}^{13}4\ {}^{1}2 \\ -\quad 2\ 4\ 6 \\ \hline 3\ 9\ 6 \end{array}$$

The difference between their numbers is 396.

6. **5**
If one row is removed, one row remains. This means 5 oranges remain.

7. **0.3**
0.7 = 7 tenths and 1 whole = 10 tenths. As $7 + 3 = 10$, Aastha added 3 tenths, or 0.3.

8. **$160**
As $16 \times 10 = 160$, Ivy has earned $160.

9. **20**
$5 \times 6 = 30$. As $30 - 10 = 20$, Violet is 20 years old.

10. **5 cm**
The rectangle has 2 lengths and 2 widths which add to 16 cm. This means that 1 length and 1 width add to 8 cm. As $8 - 3 = 5$, the length is 5 cm.

11. **600 mL**
As $9 - 3 = 6$, then $900 - 300 = 600$. There is 600 mL of water remaining.

12. 6:37 pm

10 + 27 = 37. The plane departed at 6:37 pm.

13. 6

A hexagon has 6 sides. A hexagonal prism has 2 faces that are hexagons and 6 rectangular faces.

14.

15.

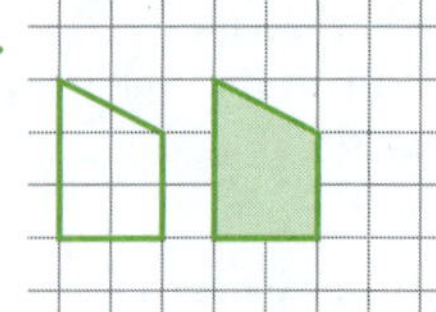

Five to the right and then 2 to the left means a single translation of 3 units to the right.

16. 4

The minute hand makes one revolution. As there are 4 quarters in a whole, there are 4 quarter turns.

17. more likely

There are 3 red balls and 2 white balls. This makes it more likely to choose a red ball.

18. 3

The graph shows 7 girls and 4 boys said movies was their favourite activity. As 7 – 4 = 3, the difference is 3 students.

Unit 30B PAGE 95

1. true

An odd number of odd numbers will add to an odd number. An even number of even numbers will add to an even number. Adding an odd number and an even number always gives an odd answer. Try 1 + 3 + 5 which is 9. Now 2 + 4 = 6.
As 9 + 6 = 15, the answer is odd. The statement is true.

2. 84

23 – 2 = 21. There are 21 students present. 4 × 21 = 4 × 20 + 4 × 1. This is 80 + 4, which is 84. The teacher hands out 84 shapes.

3. 4

As 48 ÷ 6 = 8, Luisa's number is 8.
As 8 ÷ 2 = 4, the answer would have been 4.

4. 400

240 + 80 = 300 + 20 which is 320. There are 80 green apples and 320 red apples. As 32 + 8 = 40, then 320 + 80 = 400. There is a total of 400 apples.

5. 5085

Ella's number is 7542 and Frida's number is 2457. You need to subtract the numbers to find the difference.

```
  7 ⁴5 ¹³4 ¹2
–  2  4  5  7
  5  0  8  5
```

The difference between their numbers is 5085.

6. 2

As 12 ÷ 2 = 6, there are 6 candles in the first row. As 12 ÷ 3 = 4, there are 4 candles in the first second row. As 12 – 6 – 4 = 2, there are 2 candles in the third row.

7. 2

$0.5 = \frac{5}{10} = \frac{1}{2}$. This means the question is how many halves are in a whole. As there as 2 halves in a whole, there are two 0.5s in a whole.

8. $23

As 50 – 4 = 46, the prawns cost $46.
As 46 ÷ 2 = 23, the cost of each kg of prawns was $23.

9. 5

The answer is the missing number in the number sentence 9 + 6 = 3 × [?].
This means 15 = 3 × [?].
As 15 ÷ 3 = 5, Silas is 5 years old.

10. 32 cm²

If the perimeter is 24 cm, the sum of the length and width is 12 cm.
As 12 – 8 = 4, the width is 4 cm.
As 8 × 4 = 32, the area of the rectangle is 32 cm².

11. 800 mL

As 6 × 2 = 12, then 6 × 200 = 1200.
There is 2000 mL in 2 L.
As 2000 – 1200 = 800, there is 800 mL of soft drink remaining in the bottle.

12. 8:09 am

One hour past 6:53 is 7:53. Now, 7 more minutes is 8 o'clock and then another 9 minutes is 8:09.

13. 8

As 18 ÷ 3 = 6, the base of the prism has 6 sides. The 3D shape is a hexagonal prism. It has 6 rectangular faces and 2 hexagonal faces. As 6 + 2 = 8, there are 8 faces.

14.

15.

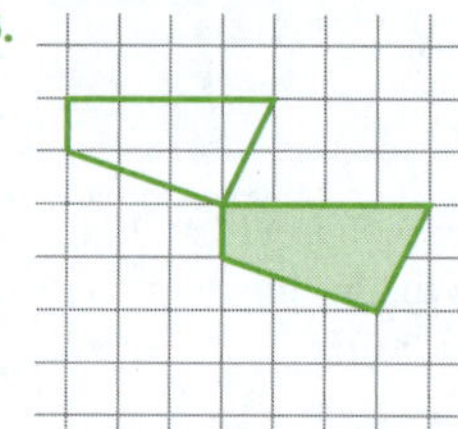

16. 11

From quarter to 5 to half past 5 is 45 minutes, which is 3 quarter turns.
From half past 5 to half past 7 is 2 hours. As 2 × 4 = 8, there are 8 quarter turns in 2 hours.
As 3 + 8 = 11, there are 11 quarter turns.

17. even chance

There are now 2 red balls and 2 white balls. This makes it an even chance to choose a red ball.

18. 1

As 7 + 5 + 5 + 7 = 24, there were 24 girls surveyed.
As 4 + 6 + 9 + 4 = 23, there were 23 boys surveyed. As 24 – 23 = 1, there was 1 more girl than boy surveyed.

NAPLAN-style Test 2 PAGES 96–97

1. 18

As 7 × 2 = 14, the number sentence can be rewritten as 5 × 3 × 6 × 2 × 7 = 5 × [?] × 14. As 3 × 6 = 18, the missing number is 18.

2. D

The number line is marked in thirds. The missing number is $4\frac{1}{3}$.

$4\frac{1}{3}$

2 $2\frac{1}{3}$ $2\frac{2}{3}$ 3 $3\frac{1}{3}$ $3\frac{2}{3}$ 4 [?] $4\frac{2}{3}$

3. B

Work out the approximate costs of each: carrots $3, potatoes $4, lettuce $4, onions $3 and celery $3.
As 3 + 4 + 4 + 3 + 3 = 17, the closest amount is $17.

4. C

Each shape has a perimeter of 16 units. As 5 × 3 = 15, shape C has an area of 15 square units.

5. **237**

The number must have an odd digit in the ones place. Use the largest digit in the hundreds place and the next largest in the tens place. This number is 763.
1000 – 763 = 1000 – 700 – 63. This is 300 – 63 which is 237.

6. **B**

Flag *Q* has no line of symmetry. Flags *P* and *S* have 1 line of symmetry. Flag *R* has 2 lines of symmetry. This means there is only 1 flag with at least 2 lines of symmetry.

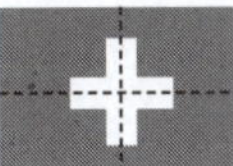

7. **A**

Sally's birthday is 9 July. There are 30 days in June. Two weeks before 9 July is 25 June. As 25 – 7 = 18, Agnes has her birthday on 18 June.

8. **C**

Look for a number that can be divided by 2, 3 and 5. These numbers are 30, 60 and 90. The 3 students will stand together for 3 numbers.

9. **D**

If 2 ●s = 12, then ● = 6. Replacing the circle means ■ – 6 = 8, which means that ■ = 14.

10. **A, D**

There are two possible answers. If Theo lives between Rowan and Sammi, then 160 – 70 = 90 means the distance is 90 m. If Sammi lives between Rowan and Theo, then 160 + 70 = 230 means the distance is 230 m. They can live either 90 m or 230 m apart.

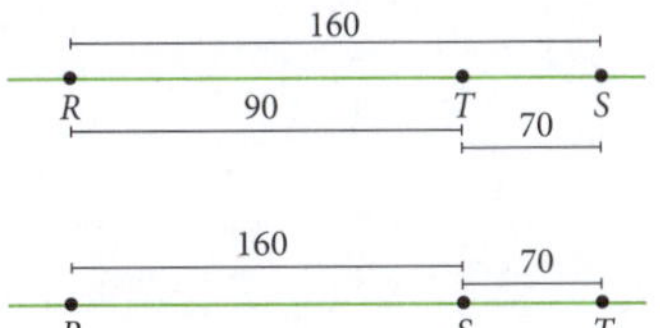

11. **C**

The number of blocks in each triangle is 3, 6, 10. The next numbers are 10 + 5 = 15, then 15 + 6 = 21, then 21 + 7 = 28. This means there will be 7 blocks on the bottom row.

12. **17**

69 + 14 = 69 + 10 + 4, which is 83. Max has spent $83. As 100 – 83 = 17, Max has $17 value on the gift card.

13. **8**

28 + 39 + 43 = 67 + 43 which is 110. Also, 48 + 54 = 102. As 110 – 102 = 8, there were 8 more bikes sold.

14. **31**

There are 1000 mL in 1 litre.
As 1000 ÷ 200 = 5, each litre can fill 5 glasses. As 6 × 5 = 30 and 30 + 1 = 31, Jordan can fill 31 glasses.

15. **C**

Remove a cone and a prism from both sides of the balance. This means a cylinder has the same mass as a cone and a prism. As 12 = 8 + prism, the prism has a mass of 4 kg. As 12 – 4 = 8, a cylinder is 8 kg heavier than a prism.

16. **2626**

$$
\begin{array}{r}
{}^{2}7\,{}^{1}6\,0 \\
{}^{1}1\,1\,8\,7 \\
+\quad 6\,7\,9 \\
\hline
2\,6\,2\,6
\end{array}
$$

The farmer picked a total of 2626 oranges.

17. **D**

The counter starts at E5, then moves to B5 and finishes at B3.

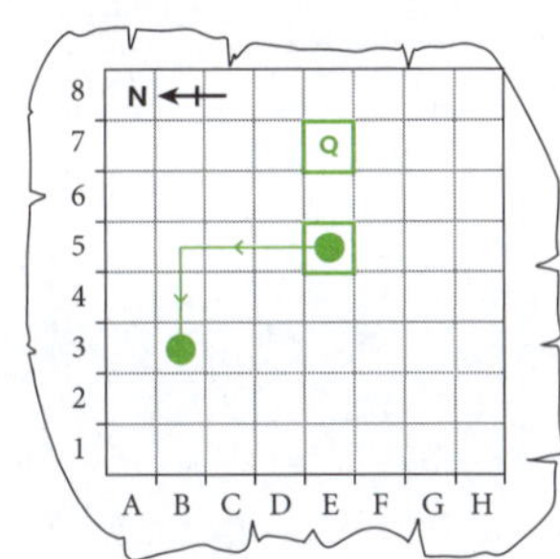

18. **8**

As 48 ÷ 2 = 24, Oscar has 24 km remaining after the first hour. As 24 ÷ 3 = 8, he has 8 km remaining after the second hour.

19. **6**

The digits must add to 15, 16, 17 or 18. These numbers are **69**, 78, **79**, **87**, 88, **89**, 96, **97**, 98 and **99**. There are 6 numbers not crossed out.

20. **D**

There are 5 numbers less than 4. There are 4 even numbers and 6 odd numbers. There are 5 numbers greater than 3. Events I and IV are equally likely.

NOTES